About This Book

This book teaches you all about the Java language and how to use it to create applets and applications. By the time you get through with this book, you'll know enough about Java to do just about anything, inside an applet or out.

Who Should Read This Book

This book is intended for people with at least some basic programming background, which includes people with years of programming experience or people with only a small amount of experience. If you understand what variables, loops, and functions are, you'll be just fine for this book. The sorts of people who might want to read this book include you, if

☐ You're a real whiz at HTML, understand CGI programming (in perl, AppleScript, Visual Basic, or some other popular CGI language) pretty well, and want to move on to the next level in Web page design.

☐ You had some Basic or Pascal in school and you have a basic grasp of what programming is, but you've heard Java is easy to learn, really powerful, and very cool.

☐ You've programmed C and C++ for many years, you've heard this Java thing is becoming really popular and you're wondering what all the fuss is all about.

☐ You've heard that Java is really good for Web-based applets, and you're curious about how good it is for creating more general applications.

What if you know programming, but you don't know object-oriented programming? Fear not. This book assumes no background in object-oriented design. If you know object-oriented programming, in fact, the first couple of days will be easy for you.

How This Book Is Structured

This book is intended to be read and absorbed over the course of three weeks. During each week, you'll read seven chapters that present concepts related to the Java language and the creation of applets and applications.

Conventions

 Note: A Note box presents interesting pieces of information related to the surrounding discussion.

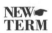 **Technical Note:** A Technical Note presents specific technical information related to the surrounding discussion.

Tip: A Tip box offers advice or teaches an easier way to do something.

 Caution: A Caution box alerts you to a possible problem and gives you advice to avoid it.

 Warning: A Warning box advises you about potential problems and helps you steer clear of disaster.

 New terms are introduced in New Term boxes, with the term in italics.

A type icon identifies some new HTML code that you can type in yourself.

An Output icon highlights what the same HTML code looks like when viewed by either Netscape or Mosaic.

An analysis icon alerts you to the author's line-by-line analysis.

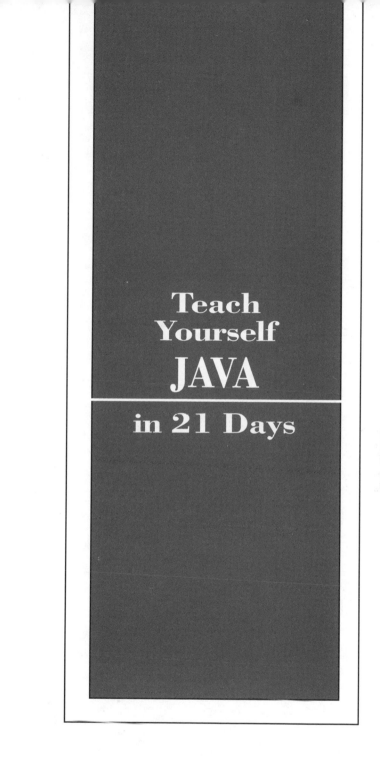

Teach Yourself JAVA
in 21 Days

Teach Yourself
JAVA
in 21 Days

Laura Lemay
Charles L. Perkins

sams
.net

201 West 103rd Street
Indianapolis, Indiana 46290

To Eric, for all the usual reasons
(moral support, stupid questions, comfort in dark times).
LL

For RKJP, ARL, and NMH
the three most important people in my life.
CLP

Copyright ©1996 by Sams.net Publishing and its licensors

FIRST EDITION

International Standard Book Number: 1-57521-030-4

Library of Congress Catalog Card Number: 95-78866

99 98 97 96   4 3 2 1

Interpretation of the printing code: the rightmost double-digit number is the year of the book's printing; the rightmost single-digit, the number of the book's printing. For example, a printing code of 96-1 shows that the first printing of the book occurred in 1996.

Composed in AGaramond and MCPdigital by Macmillan Computer Publishing

Printed in the United States of America

President, Sams Publishing:	*Richard K. Swadley*
Publisher, Sams.net Publishing:	*George Bond*
Publishing Manager:	*Mark Taber*
Managing Editor:	*Cindy Morrow*
Marketing Manager:	*John Pierce*

Acquisitions Editor
Mark Taber

Development Editor
Fran Hatton

Software Development Specialist
Merle Newlon

Production Editor
Nancy Albright

Technical Reviewer
Patrick Chan

Editorial Coordinator
Bill Whitmer

Technical Edit Coordinator
Lynette Quinn

Formatter
Frank Sinclair

Editorial Assistant
Carol Ackerman

Cover Designer
Tim Amrhein

Book Designer
Alyssa Yesh

Production Team Supervisor
Brad Chinn

Production
Michael Brumitt
Jason Hand
Cheryl Moore
Ayanna Lacey
Nancy Price
Bobbi Satterfield
Tim Taylor
Susan Van Ness
Mark Walchle
Todd Wente

Indexer
Tim Griffin

Overview

Contents

Acknowledgments

From Laura Lemay:

To Sun's Java team, for all their hard work on Java the language and on the browser, and particularly to Jim Graham, who demonstrated Java and HotJava to me on very short notice in May and planted the idea for this book.

To everyone who bought my previous books, and liked them. Buy this one too.

From Charles L. Perkins:

To Patrick Naughton, who first showed me the power and the promise of OAK (Java) in early 1993.

To Mark Taber, who shepherded this lost sheep through his first book.

About the Authors

Laura Lemay is a technical writer and a nerd. After spending six years writing software documentation for various computer companies in Silicon Valley, she decided writing books would be much more fun (but has still not yet made up her mind). In her spare time she collects computers, e-mail addresses, interesting hair colors, and nonrunning motorcycles. She is also the perpetrator of *Teach Yourself Web Publishing with HTML in 14 Days*.

You can reach her by e-mail at lemay@lne.com, or visit her home page at http://www.lne.com/lemay/.

Charles L. Perkins is the founder of Virtual Rendezvous, a company building what it spent two years designing: a software layer above Java that will foster socially focused, computer-mediated, real-time filtered interactions between people's personas in the virtual environments of the near future. In previous lives, he has evangelized NeXTSTEP, Smalltalk, and UNIX, and has degrees in both physics and computer science. Before attempting this book, he was an amateur columnist and author. He's done research in speech recognition, neural nets, gestural user interfaces, computer graphics, and language theory, but had the most fun working at Thinking Machines and Xerox PARC's Smalltalk group. In his spare time, he reads textbooks for fun.

You can reach him via e-mail at virtual@rendezvous.com, or visit his Java page at http://rendezvous.com/java.

Introduction

The World Wide Web, for much of its existence, has been a method for distributing passive information to a widely distributed number of people. The Web has, indeed, been exceptionally good for that purpose. With the addition of forms and image maps, Web pages began to become interactive—but the interaction was often simply a new way to get at the same information. The limitations of Web distribution were all too apparent once designers began to try to stretch the boundaries of what the Web can do. Even other innovations, such as Netscape's server push to create dynamic animations, were merely clever tricks layered on top of a framework that wasn't built to support much other than static documents with images and text.

Enter Java, and the capability for Web pages of containing Java applets. Applets are small programs that create animations, multimedia presentations, real-time (video) games, multi-user networked games, and real interactivity—in fact, most anything a small program can do, Java applets can. Downloaded over the net and executed inside a Web page by a browser that supports Java, applets are an enormous step beyond standard Web design.

The disadvantage of Java is that to create Java applets right now, you need to write them in the Java language. Java is a programming language, and as such, creating Java applets is more difficult than creating a Web page or a form using HTML. Soon there will be tools and programs that will make creating Java applets easier—they may be available by the time you read this. For now, however, the only way to delve into Java is to learn the language and start playing with the raw Java code. Even when the tools come out, you may want to do more with Java than the tools can provide, and you're back to learning the language.

That's where *Teach Yourself Java in 21 Days* comes in. This book teaches you all about the Java language and how to use it to create not only applets, but also applications, which are more general Java programs that don't need to run inside a Web browser. By the time you get through with this book, you'll know enough about Java to do just about anything, inside an applet or out.

Who Should Read This Book

Teach Yourself Java in 21 Days is intended for people with at least some basic programming background—which includes people with years of programming experience and people with only a small amount of experience. If you understand what variables, loops, and functions are, you'll be just fine for this book. The sorts of people who might want to read this book include you, if one or more of the following is true:

☐ You're a real whiz at HTML, understand CGI programming (in perl, AppleScript, Visual Basic, or some other popular CGI language) pretty well, and want to move onto the next level in Web page design.

☐ You had some Basic or Pascal in school, you've got a basic grasp of what programming is, but you've heard Java is easy to learn, really powerful, and very cool.

☐ You've programmed C and C++ for many years, you've heard this Java thing is becoming really popular, and you're wondering what all the fuss is all about.

☐ You've heard that Java is really good for Web-based applets, and you're curious about how good it is for creating more general applications.

What if you know programming, but you don't know object-oriented programming? Fear not. *Teach Yourself Java in 21 Days* assumes no background in object-oriented design. If you know object-oriented programming, the first couple of days will be easy for you.

What if you're a rank beginner? This book might move a little fast for you. Java is a good language to start with, though, and if you take it slow and work through all the examples, you may still be able to pick up Java and start creating your own applets.

How This Book Is Organized

Teach Yourself Java in 21 Days describes Java primarily in its current state—what's known as the beta API (Application Programming Interface). This is the version of Java that Netscape and other browsers, such as Spyglass's Mosaic, support. A previous version of Java, the alpha API, was significantly different from the version described in this book, and the two versions are not compatible with each other. There are other books that describe only the alpha API, and there may still be programs and browsers out there that can only run using alpha Java programs.

Teach Yourself Java in 21 Days uses primarily Java beta because that is the version that is most current and is the version that will continue to be used in the future. The alpha API is obsolete and will eventually die out. If you learn Java using beta API, you'll be much better prepared for any future changes (which will be minor) than if you have to worry about both APIs at once.

Java is still in development. "Beta" means that Java is not complete and that things may change between the time this book is being written and the time you read this. Keep this in mind as you work with Java and with the software you'll use to create and compile programs. If things aren't behaving the way you expect, check the Web sites mentioned at the end of this introduction for more information.

Teach Yourself Java in 21 Days covers the Java language and its class libraries in 21 days, organized as three separate weeks. Each week covers a different broad area of developing Java applets and applications.

In the first week, you'll learn about the Java language itself:

☐ Day 1 is the basic introduction: what Java is, why it's cool, and how to get the software. You'll also create your first Java applications and applets.

☐ On Day 2, you'll explore basic object-oriented programming concepts as they apply to Java.

☐ On Day 3, you start getting down to details with the basic Java building blocks: data types, variables, and expressions such as arithmetic and comparisons.

☐ Day 4 goes into detail about how to deal with objects in Java: how to create them, how to access their variables and call their methods, and how to compare and copy them. You'll also get your first glance at the Java class libraries.

☐ On Day 5, you'll learn more about Java with arrays, conditional statements. and loops.

☐ Day 6 is the best one yet. You'll learn how to create classes, the basic building blocks of any Java program, as well as how to put together a Java application (an application being a Java program that can run on its own without a Web browser).

☐ Day 7 builds on what you learned on Day 6. On Day 7, you'll learn more about how to create and use methods, including overriding and overloading methods and creating constructors.

Week 2 is dedicated to applets and the Java class libraries:

☐ Day 8 provides the basics of applets—how they're different from applications, how to create them, and the most important parts of an applet's life cycle. You'll also learn how to create HTML pages that contain Java applets.

☐ On Day 9, you'll learn about the Java classes for drawing shapes and characters to the screen—in black, white, or any other color.

☐ On Day 10, you'll start animating those shapes you learned about on Day 9, including learning what threads and their uses are.

☐ Day 11 covers more detail about animation, adding bitmap images and audio to the soup.

☐ Day 12 delves into interactivity—handling mouse and keyboard clicks from the user in your Java applets.

☐ Day 13 is ambitious; on that day you'll learn about using Java's Abstract Windowing Toolkit to create a user interface in your applet including menus, buttons, checkboxes, and other elements.

☐ On Day 14, you explore the last of the main Java class libraries for creating applets: windows and dialogs, networking, and a few other tidbits.

Week 3 finishes up with advanced topics, for when you start doing larger and more complex Java programs, or when you want to learn more:

☐ On Day 15, you'll learn more about the Java language's modifiers—for abstract and final methods and classes as well as for protecting a class's private information from the prying eyes of other classes.

- ☐ Day 16 covers interfaces and packages, useful for abstracting protocols of methods to aid reuse and for the grouping and categorization of classes.

- ☐ Day 17 covers exceptions: errors and warnings and other abnormal conditions, generated either by the system or by you in your programs.

- ☐ Day 18 builds on the thread basics you learned on Day 10 to give a broad overview of multithreading and how to use it to allow different parts of your Java programs to run in parallel.

- ☐ On Day 19, you'll learn all about the input and output streams in Java's I/O library.

- ☐ Day 20 teaches you about native code—how to link C code into your Java programs to provide missing functionality or to gain performance.

- ☐ Finally, on Day 21, you'll get an overview of some of the "behind-the-scenes" technical details of how Java works: the bytecode compiler and interpreter, the techniques Java uses to ensure the integrity and security of your programs, and the Java garbage collector.

Conventions Used in This Book

Text that you type and text that should appear on your screen is presented in `monospace` type:

```
It will look like this.
```

to mimic the way text looks on your screen. Variables and placeholders will appear in `monospace italic`.

The end of each chapter offers common questions asked about that day's subject matter with answers from the authors.

Web Sites for Further Information

Before, while, and after you read this book, there are two Web sites that may be of interest to you as a Java developer.

The official Java web site is at `http://java.sun.com/`. At this site, you'll find the Java development software, the HotJava web browser, and online documentation for all aspects of the Java language. It has several mirror sites that it lists online, and you should probably use the site "closest" to you on the Internet for your downloading and Java Web browsing. There is also a site for developer resources, called Gamelan, at `http://www.gamelan.com/`.

This book also has a companion Web site at `http://www.lne.com/Web/Java/`. Information at that site includes examples, more information and background for this book, corrections to this book, and other tidbits that were not included here.

WEEK

AT A GLANCE

1

2

3

4

5

6

7

☐ Creating Classes and Applications in Java

Defining constants, instance and class variables, and methods

☐ More About Methods

Overloading methods

Constructor methods

Overriding methods

An Introduction to Java Programming

by Laura Lemay

Hello and welcome to *Teach Yourself Java in 21 Days!* Starting today and for the next three weeks you'll learn all about the Java language and how to use it to create applets, as well as how to create stand-alone Java applications that you can use for just about anything.

 NEW **TERM** An *applet* is a dynamic and interactive program that can run inside a Web page displayed by a Java-capable browser such as HotJava or Netscape 2.0.

The *HotJava browser* is a World Wide Web browser used to view Web pages, follow links, and submit forms. It can also download and play applets on the reader's system.

That's the overall goal for the next three weeks. Today, the goals are somewhat more modest, and you'll learn about the following:

☐ What exactly Java and HotJava are, and their current status

☐ Why you should learn Java—its various features and advantages over other programming languages

☐ Getting started programming in Java—what you'll need in terms of software and background, as well as some basic terminology

☐ How to create your first Java programs—to close this day, you'll create both a simple Java application and a simple Java applet!

What Is Java?

Java is an object-oriented programming language developed by Sun Microsystems, a company best known for its high-end Unix workstations. Modeled after C++, the Java language was designed to be small, simple, and portable across platforms and operating systems, both at the source and at the binary level (more about this later).

Java is often mentioned in the same breath as HotJava, a World Wide Web browser from Sun like Netscape or Mosaic (see Figure 1.1). What makes HotJava different from most other browsers is that, in addition to all its basic Web features, it can also download and play applets on the reader's system. Applets appear in a Web page much in the same way as images do, but unlike images, applets are dynamic and interactive. Applets can be used to create animations, figures, or areas that can respond to input from the reader, games, or other interactive effects on the same Web pages among the text and graphics.

Although HotJava was the first World Wide Web browser to be able to play Java applets, Java support is rapidly becoming available in other browsers. Netscape 2.0 provides support for Java applets, and other browser developers have also announced support for Java in forthcoming products.

Figure 1.1.

The HotJava browser.

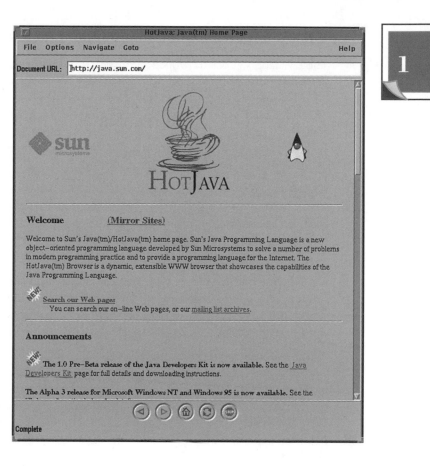

To create an applet, you write it in the Java language, compile it using a Java compiler, and refer to that applet in your HTML Web pages. You put the resulting HTML and Java files on a Web site much in the same way that you make ordinary HTML and image files available. Then, when someone using the HotJava browser (or other Java-aware browser) views your page with the embedded applet, that browser downloads the applet to the local system and executes it, and then the reader can view and interact with your applet in all its glory (readers using other browsers won't see anything). You'll learn more about how applets, browsers, and the World Wide Web work together further on in this book.

The important thing to understand about Java is that you can do so much more with it besides create applets. Java was written as a full-fledged programming language in which you can accomplish the same sorts of tasks and solve the same sorts of problems that you can in other programming languages, such as C or C++. HotJava itself, including all the networking, display, and user interface elements, is written in Java.

Java's Past, Present, and Future

The Java language was developed at Sun Microsystems in 1991 as part of a research project to develop software for consumer electronics devices—television sets, VCRs, toasters, and the other sorts of machines you can buy at any department store. Java's goals at that time were to be small, fast, efficient, and easily portable to a wide range of hardware devices. It is those same goals that made Java an ideal language for distributing executable programs via the World Wide Web, and also a general-purpose programming language for developing programs that are easily usable and portable across different platforms.

The Java language was used in several projects within Sun, but did not get very much commercial attention until it was paired with HotJava. HotJava was written in 1994 in a matter of months, both as a vehicle for downloading and running applets and also as an example of the sort of complex application that can be written in Java.

At the time this book is being written, Sun has released the beta version of the Java Developer's Kit (JDK), which includes tools for developing Java applets and applications on Sun systems running Solaris 2.3 or higher for Windows NT and for Windows 95. By the time you read this, support for Java development may have appeared on other platforms, either from Sun or from third-party companies.

Note that because the JDK is currently in beta, it is still subject to change between now and when it is officially released. Applets and applications you write using the JDK and using the examples in this book may require some changes to work with future versions of the JDK. However, because the Java language has been around for several years and has been used for several projects, the language itself is quite stable and robust and most likely will not change excessively. Keep this beta status in mind as you read through this book and as you develop your own Java programs.

Support for playing Java programs is a little more confusing at the moment. Sun's HotJava is not currently included with the Beta JDK; the only available version of HotJava is an older alpha version, and, tragically, applets written for the alpha version of Java do not work with the beta JDK, and vice versa. By the time you read this, Sun may have released a newer version of HotJava which will enable you to view applets.

The JDK does include an application called appletviewer that allows you to test your Java applets as you write them. If an applet works in the appletviewer, it should work with any Java-capable browser. You'll learn more about applet viewer later today.

What's in store for the future? In addition to the final Java release from Sun, other companies have announced support for Java in their own World Wide Web browsers. Netscape Communications Corporation has already incorporated Java capabilities into the 2.0 version of their very popular Netscape Navigator Web browser—pages with embedded Java applets can be viewed and played with Netscape. With support for Java available in as popular a browser as Netscape, tools to help develop Java applications (debuggers, development environments, and so on) most likely will be rapidly available as well.

Why Learn Java?

At the moment, probably the most compelling reason to learn Java—and probably the reason you bought this book—is that HotJava applets are written in Java. Even if that were not the case, Java as a language has significant advantages over other languages and other programming environments that make it suitable for just about any programming task. This section describes some of those advantages.

Java Is Platform-Independent

Platform independence is one of the most significant advantages that Java has over other programming languages, particularly for systems that need to work on many different platforms. Java is platform-independent at both the source and the binary level.

NEW☛ *Platform-independence* is a program's capability of moving easily from one computer
TERM system to another.

At the source level, Java's primitive data types have consistent sizes across all development platforms. Java's foundation class libraries make it easy to write code that can be moved from platform to platform without the need to rewrite it to work with that platform.

Platform-independence doesn't stop at the source level, however. Java binary files are also platform-independent and can run on multiple problems without the need to recompile the source. How does this work? Java binary files are actually in a form called bytecodes.

NEW☛ *Bytecodes* are a set of instructions that looks a lot like some machine codes, but that is not
TERM specific to any one processor.

Normally, when you compile a program written in C or in most other languages, the compiler translates your program into machine codes or processor instructions. Those instructions are specific to the processor your computer is running—so, for example, if you compile your code on a Pentium system, the resulting program will run only on other Pentium systems. If you want to use the same program on another system, you have to go back to your original source, get a compiler for that system, and recompile your code. Figure 1.2 shows the result of this system: multiple executable programs for multiple systems.

Things are different when you write code in Java. The Java development environment has two parts: a Java compiler and a Java interpreter. The Java compiler takes your Java program and instead of generating machine codes from your source files, it generates bytecodes.

Figure 1.2.

Traditional compiled programs.

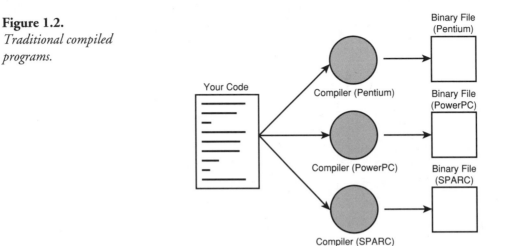

To run a Java program, you run a program called a bytecode interpreter, which in turn executes your Java program (see Figure 1.3). You can either run the interpreter by itself, or—for applets—there is a bytecode interpreter built into HotJava and other Java-capable browsers that runs the applet for you.

Figure 1.3.

Java programs.

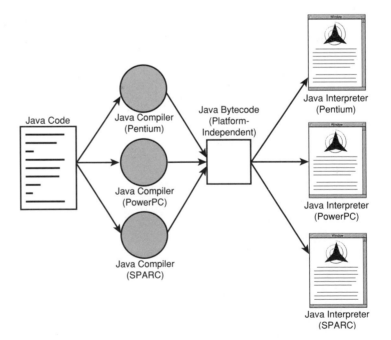

Why go through all the trouble of adding this extra layer of the bytecode interpreter? Having your Java programs in bytecode form means that instead of being specific to any one system, your programs can be run on any platform and any operating or window system as long as the Java interpreter is available. This capability of a single binary file to be executable across platforms is crucial to what enables applets to work, because the World Wide Web itself is also platform-independent. Just as HTML files can be read on any platform, so applets can be executed on any platform that is a Java-capable browser.

The disadvantage of using bytecodes is in execution speed. Because system-specific programs run directly on the hardware for which they are compiled, they run significantly faster than Java bytecodes, which must be processed by the interpreter. For many Java programs, the speed may not be an issue. If you write programs that require more execution speed than the Java interpreter can provide, you have several solutions available to you, including being able to link native code into your Java program or using tools to convert your Java bytecodes into native code. Note that by using any of these solutions, you lose the portability that Java bytecodes provide. You'll learn about each of these mechanisms on Day 20.

Java Is Object-Oriented

To some, object-oriented programming (OOP) technique is merely a way of organizing programs, and it can be accomplished using any language. Working with a real object-oriented language and programming environment, however, enables you to take full advantage of object-oriented methodology and its capabilities of creating flexible, modular programs and reusing code.

Many of Java's object-oriented concepts are inherited from C++, the language on which it is based, but it borrows many concepts from other object-oriented languages as well. Like most object-oriented programming languages, Java includes a set of class libraries that provide basic data types, system input and output capabilities, and other utility functions. These basic classes are part of the Java development kit, which also has classes to support networking, common Internet protocols, and user interface toolkit functions. Because these class libraries are written in Java, they are portable across platforms as all Java applications are.

You'll learn more about object-oriented programming and Java tomorrow.

Java Is Easy to Learn

In addition to its portability and object-orientation, one of Java's initial design goals was to be small and simple, and therefore easier to write, easier to compile, easier to debug, and, best of all, easy to learn. Keeping the language small also makes it more robust because there are fewer chances for programmers to make difficult-to-find mistakes. Despite its size and simple design, however, Java still has a great deal of power and flexibility.

Java is modeled after C and C++, and much of the syntax and object-oriented structure is borrowed from the latter. If you are familiar with C++, learning Java will be particularly easy for you, because you have most of the foundation already.

Although Java looks similar to C and C++, most of the more complex parts of those languages have been excluded from Java, making the language simpler without sacrificing much of its power. There are no pointers in Java, nor is there pointer arithmetic. Strings and arrays are real objects in Java. Memory management is automatic. To an experienced programmer, these omissions may be difficult to get used to, but to beginners or programmers who have worked in other languages, they make the Java language far easier to learn.

Getting Started with Programming in Java

Enough background! Let's finish off this day by creating two real Java programs: a stand-alone Java application and an applet that you can view in either in the appletviewer (part of the JDK) or in a Java-capable browser. Although both these programs are extremely simple, they will give you an idea of what a Java program looks like and how to compile and run it.

Getting the Software

In order to write Java programs, you will, of course, need a Java development environment. At the time this book is being written, Sun's Java Development Kit provides everything you need to start writing Java programs. The JDK is available for Sun SPARC systems running Solaris 2.2 or higher and for Windows NT and Windows 95. You can get the JDK from several places:

☐ The CD-ROM that came with this book contains the full JDK distribution. See the CD information for installation instructions.

☐ The JDK can be downloaded from Sun's Java FTP site at `ftp://java.sun.com/pub/` or from a mirror site (`ftp://www.blackdown.org/pub/Java/pub/is one`).

Note: The Java Development Kit is currently in beta release. By the time you read this, The JDK may be available for other platforms, or other organizations may be selling Java development tools as well.

Although Netscape and other Java-aware browsers provide an environment for playing Java applets, they do not provide a mechanism for developing Java applications. For that, you need separate tools—merely having a browser is not enough.

Applets and Applications

Java applications fall into two main groups: applets and applications.

Applets, as you have learned, are Java programs that are downloaded over the World Wide Web and executed by a Web browser on the reader's machine. Applets depend on a Java-capable browser in order to run (although they can also be viewed using a tool called the appletviewer, which you'll learn about later today).

Java applications are more general programs written in the Java language. Java applications don't require a browser to run, and in fact, Java can be used to create most other kinds of applications that you would normally use a more conventional programming language to create. HotJava itself is a Java application.

A single Java program can be an applet or an application or both, depending on how you write that program and the capabilities that program uses. Throughout this first week, you'll be writing mostly HotJava applications; then you'll apply what you've learned to write applets in Week 2. If you're eager to get started with applets, be patient. Everything that you learn while you're creating simple Java applications will apply to creating applets, and it's easier to start with the basics before moving onto the hard stuff. You'll be creating plenty of applets in Week 2.

Creating a Java Application

Let's start by creating a simple Java application: the classic Hello World example that all language books use to begin.

As with all programming languages, your Java source files are created in a plain text editor, or in an editor that can save files in plain ASCII without any formatting characters. On Unix, emacs, ped, or vi will work; on Windows, Notepad or DOS Edit are both text editors.

Fire up your editor of choice, and enter the Java program shown in Listing 1.1. Type this program, as shown, in your text editor. Be careful that all the parentheses, braces, and quotes are there.

Listing 1.1. Your first Java application.

```
1: class HelloWorld {
2:     public static void main (String args[]) {
3:         System.out.println("Hello World!");
4:     }
5: }
```

>
>
> **Warning:** The numbers before each line are part of the listing and not part of the program; they're there so I can refer to specific line numbers when I explain what's going on in the program. Do not include them in your own file.

This program has two main parts:

☐ All the program is enclosed in a class definition—here, a class called `HelloWorld`.

☐ The body of the program (here, just the one line) is contained in a routine called `main()`. In Java applications, as in a C or C++ program, `main()` is the first routine that is run when the program is executed.

You'll learn more about both these parts of a Java application as the book progresses.

Once you finish typing the program, save the file. Conventionally, Java source files are named the same name as the class they define, with an extension of `.java`. This file should therefore be called `HelloWorld.java`.

Now, let's compile the source file using the Java compiler. In Sun's JDK, the Java compiler is called `javac`.

To compile your Java program, Make sure the javac program is in your execution path and type `javac` followed by the name of your source file:

```
javac HelloWorld.java
```

> **Note:** In these examples, and in all the examples throughout this book, we'll be using Sun's Java compiler, part of the JDK. If you have a third-party development environment, check with the documentation for that program to see how to compile your Java programs.

The compiler should compile the file without any errors. If you get errors, go back and make sure that you've typed the program exactly as it appears in Listing 1.1.

When the program compiles without errors, you end up with a file called HelloWorld.class, in the same directory as your source file. This is your Java bytecode file. You can then run that bytecode file using the Java interpreter. In the JDK, the Java interpreter is called simply `java`. Make sure the java program is in your path and type `java` followed by the name of the file without the .class extension:

```
java HelloWorld
```

If your program was typed and compiled correctly, you should get the string `"Hello World!"` printed to your screen as a response.

> **Note:** Remember, the Java compiler and the Java interpreter are different things. You use the Java compiler (`javac`) for your Java source files to create .class files, and you use the Java interpreter (`java`)to actually run your class files.

Creating a Java Applet

Creating applets is different from creating a simple application, because Java applets run and are displayed inside a Web page with other page elements and as such have special rules for how they behave. Because of these special rules for applets in many cases (particularly the simple ones), creating an applet may be more complex than creating an application.

For example, to do a simple Hello World applet, instead of merely being able to print a message, you have to create an applet to make space for your message and then use graphics operations to paint the message to the screen.

> **Note:** Actually, if you run the Hello World application as an applet, the `Hello World` message prints to a special window or to a log file, depending on how the browser has screen messages set up. It will not appear on the screen unless you write your applet to put it there.

In the next example, you create that simple Hello World applet, place it inside a Web page, and view the result.

First, you set up an environment so that your Java-capable browser can find your HTML files and your applets. Much of the time, you'll keep your HTML files and your applet code in the same directory. Although this isn't required, it makes it easier to keep track of each element. In this example, you use a directory called HTML that contains all the files you'll need.

```
mkdir HTML
```

Now, open up that text editor and enter Listing 1.2.

Listing 1.2. The Hello World applet.

```
1: import java.awt.Graphics;
2:
3: class HelloWorldApplet extends java.applet.Applet {
4:
5:     public void paint(Graphics g) {
6:         g.drawString("Hello world!", 5, 25);
7:     }
8:}
```

Save that file inside your HTML directory. Just like with Java applications, give your file a name that has the same name as the class. In this case, the filename would be HelloWorldApplet.java.

Features to note about applets? There are a couple I'd like to point out:

☐ The import line at the top of the file is somewhat analogous to an #include statement in C; it enables this applet to interact with the JDK classes for creating applets and for drawing graphics on the screen.

☐ The paint() method displays the content of the applet onto the screen. Here, the string Hello World gets drawn. Applets use several standard methods to take the place of main(), which include init() to initialize the applet, start() to start it running, and paint() to display it to the screen. You'll learn about all of these in Week 2.

Now, compile the applet just as you did the application, using javac, the Java compiler.

```
javac HelloWorldApplet.java
```

Again, just as for applications, you should now have a file called HelloWorldApplet.class in your HTML directory.

To include an applet in a Web page, you refer to that applet in the HTML code for that Web page. Here, you create a very simple HTML file in the HTML directory (see Listing 1.3).

 Listing 1.3. The HTML with the applet in it.

```
1: <HTML>
2: <HEAD>
3: <TITLE>Hello to Everyone!</TITLE>
4: </HEAD><BODY>
5: <P>My Java applet says:
6: <APPLET CODE="HelloWorldApplet.class" WIDTH=150 HEIGHT=25>
7: </BODY>
8: </HTML>
```

You refer to an applet in your HTML files with the <APPLET> tag. You'll learn more about <APPLET> later on, but here are two things to note:

☐ Use the CODE attribute to indicate the name of the class that contains your applet.

☐ Use the WIDTH and HEIGHT attributes to indicate the size of the applet. The browser uses these values to know how big a chunk of space to leave for the applet on the page. Here, a box 150 pixels wide and 25 pixels high is created.

Save the HTML file in your HTML directory, with a descriptive name (for example, you might name your HTML file the same name as your applet—HellowWorldApplet.html).

And now, you're ready for the final test—actually viewing the result of your applet. To view the applet, you need one of the following:

☐ A browser that supports Java applets, such as Netscape 2.0.

☐ The appletviewer application, which is part of the JDK. The appletviewer is not a Web browser and won't enable you to see the entire Web page, but it's acceptable for testing to see how an applet will look and behave if there is nothing else available.

> **Note:** Do not use the alpha version of HotJava to view your applets; applets developed with the beta JDK and onward cannot be viewed by the alpha HotJava. If, by the time you read this, there is a more recent version of HotJava, you can use that one instead.

If you're using a Java-capable browser such as Netscape to view your applet files, you can use the Open Local... item under the File menu to navigate to the HTML file containing the applet (make sure you open the HTML file and not the class file). You don't need to install anything on a Web server yet; all this works on your local system.

If you don't have a Web browser with Java capabilities built into it, you can use the appletviewer program to view your Java applet. To run appletviewer, just indicate the path to the HTML file on the command line:

```
appletviewer HTML/HelloWorldApplet.html
```

> **Tip:** Although you can start appletviewer from the same directory as your HTML and class files, you may not be able to reload that applet without quitting appletviewer first. If you start appletviewer from some other directory (as in the previous command line), you can modify and recompile your Java applets and then just use the Reload menu item to view the newer version.

Now, if you use the browser to view the applet, you see something similar to the image shown in Figure 1.4. If you're using appletviewer, you won't see the text around the applet (My Java applet says...), but you will see the Hello World itself.

Figure 1.4.
The Hello World applet.

My Java Applet says: Hello world!

Summary

Today, you got a basic introduction to the Java language and its goals and features. Java is a programming language, similar to C or C++, in which you can develop a wide range of programs. The most common use of Java at the moment is in creating applets for HotJava, an advanced World Wide Web browser also written in Java. Applets are Java programs that are downloaded and run as part of a Web page. Applets can create animations, games, interactive programs, and other multimedia effects on Web pages.

Java's strengths lie in its portability—both at the source and at the binary level, in its object-oriented design—and in its simplicity. Each of these features help make applets possible, but they also make Java an excellent language for writing more general-purpose programs that do not require HotJava or other Java-capable browser to run. These general-purpose Java programs are called applications. HotJava itself is a Java application.

To end this day, you experimented with an example applet and an example application, getting a feel for the differences between the two and how to create, compile, and run Java programs—or, in the case of applets, how to include them in Web pages. From here, you now have the foundation to create more complex applications and applets.

Q&A

Q I'd like to use HotJava as my regular Web browser. You haven't mentioned much about HotJava today.

A The focus of this book is primarily on programming in Java and in the HotJava classes, rather than on using HotJava itself. Documentation for using the HotJava browser comes with the HotJava package.

Q I know a lot about HTML, but not much about computer programming. Can I still write Java programs?

A If you have no programming experience whatsoever, you most likely will find programming Java significantly more difficult. However, Java is an excellent language to learn programming with, and if you patiently work through the examples and the exercises in this book, you should be able to learn enough to get started with Java.

Q **According to today's lesson, Java applets are downloaded via HotJava and run on the reader's system. Isn't that an enormous security hole? What stops someone from writing an applet that compromises the security of my system—or worse, that damages my system?**

A Sun's Java team has thought a great deal about the security of applets within Java-capable browsers and has implemented several checks to make sure applets cannot do nasty things:

- ☐ Java applets cannot read or write to the disk on the local system.
- ☐ Java applets cannot execute any programs on the local system.
- ☐ Java applets cannot connect to any machines on the Web except for the server from which they are originally downloaded.

In addition, the Java compiler and interpreter check both the Java source code and the Java bytecodes to make sure that the Java programmer has not tried any sneaky tricks (for example, overrunning buffers or stack frames).

These checks obviously cannot stop every potential security hole, but they can significantly reduce the potential for hostile applets. You'll learn more about security issues later on in this book.

Q **I followed all the directions you gave for creating a Java applet. I loaded it into HotJava, but `Hello World` didn't show up. What did I do wrong?**

A I'll bet you're using the alpha version of HotJava to view the applet. Unfortunately, between alpha and beta, significant changes were made as to how applets are written. The result is that you can't view beta applets (as this one was) in the alpha version of HotJava, nor can you view alpha applets in browsers that expect beta applets. To view the applet, either use a different browser, or use the appletviewer application that comes with the JDK.

Object-Oriented Programming and Java

by Laura Lemay

Object-oriented programming (OOP) is one of the bigger programming buzzwords of recent years, and you can spend years learning all about object-oriented programming methodologies and how they can make your life easier than The Old Way of programming. It all comes down to organizing your programs in ways that echo how things are put together in the real world.

Today, you'll get an overview of object-oriented programming concepts in Java and how they relate to how you structure your own programs:

- [ ] What classes and objects are, and how they relate to each other
- [ ] The two main parts of a class or object: its behaviors and its attributes
- [ ] Class inheritance and how inheritance affects the way you design your programs
- [ ] Some information about packages and interfaces

If you're already familiar with object-oriented programming, much of today's lesson will be old hat to you. You may want to skim it and go to a movie today instead. Tomorrow, you'll get into more specific details.

Thinking in Objects: An Analogy

Consider, if you will, Legos. Legos, for those who do not spend much time with children, are small plastic building blocks in various colors and sizes. They have small round bits on one side that fit into small round holes on other Legos so that they fit together snugly to create larger shapes. With different Lego bits (Lego wheels, Lego engines, Lego hinges, Lego pulleys), you can put together castles, automobiles, giant robots that swallow cities, or just about anything else you can create. Each Lego bit is a small object that fits together with other small objects in predefined ways to create other larger objects.

Here's another example. You can walk into a computer store and, with a little background and often some help, assemble an entire PC computer system from various components: a motherboard, a CPU chip, a video card, a hard disk, a keyboard, and so on. Ideally, when you finish assembling all the various self-contained units, you have a system in which all the units work together to create a larger system with which you can solve the problems you bought the computer for in the first place.

Internally, each of those components may be vastly complicated and engineered by different companies with different methods of design. But you don't need to know how the component works, what every chip on the board does, or how, when you press the A key, an "A" gets sent to your computer. As the assembler of the overall system, each component you use is a self-contained unit, and all you are interested in is how the units interact with each other. Will this video card fit into the slots on the motherboard and will this monitor work with this video card? Will each particular component speak the right commands to the other components it interacts with so that each part of the computer is understood by every other part? Once you know what the interactions are between the components and can match the interactions, putting together the overall system is easy.

What does this have to do with programming? Everything. Object-oriented programming works in exactly this same way. Using object-oriented programming, your overall program is made up of lots of different self-contained components (objects), each of which has a specific role in the program and all of which can talk to each other in predefined ways.

Objects and Classes

Object-oriented programming is modeled on how, in the real world, objects are often made up of many kinds of smaller objects. This capability of combining objects, however, is only one very general aspect of object-oriented programming. Object-oriented programming provides several other concepts and features to make creating and using objects easier and more flexible, and the most important of these features is that of classes.

NEW☞ TERM A *class* is a template for multiple objects with similar features. Classes embody all the features of a particular set of objects.

When you write a program in an object-oriented language, you don't define actual objects. You define classes of objects.

For example, you might have a Tree class that describes the features of all trees (has leaves and roots, grows, creates chlorophyll). The Tree class serves as an abstract model for the concept of a tree—to reach out and grab, or interact with, or cut down a tree you have to have a concrete instance of that tree. Of course, once you have a tree class, you can create lots of different instances of that tree, and each different tree instance can have different features (short, tall, bushy, drops leaves in Autumn), while still behaving like and being immediately recognizable as a tree (see Figure 2.1).

NEW☞ TERM An *instance* of a class is another word for an actual object. If classes are an abstract representation of an object, an instance is its concrete representation.

So what, precisely, is the difference between an instance and an object? Nothing, really. Object is the more general term, but both instances and objects are the concrete representation of a class. In fact, the terms instance and object are often used interchangeably in OOP language. An instance of a tree and a tree object are both the same thing.

In an example closer to the sort of things you might want to do in Java programming, you might create a class for the user interface element called a button. The Button class defines the features of a button (its label, its size, its appearance) and how it behaves (does it need a single click or a double click to activate it, does it change color when it's clicked, what does it do when it's activated?). Once you define the Button class, you can then easily create instances of that button—that is, button objects—that all take on the basic features of the button as defined by the class, but may have different appearances and behavior based on what you want that particular button to do. By creating a Button class, you don't have to keep rewriting the code for each individual button you want to use in your program, and you can reuse the Button class to create different kinds of buttons as you need them in this program and in other programs.

Figure 2.1.
The tree class and tree instances.

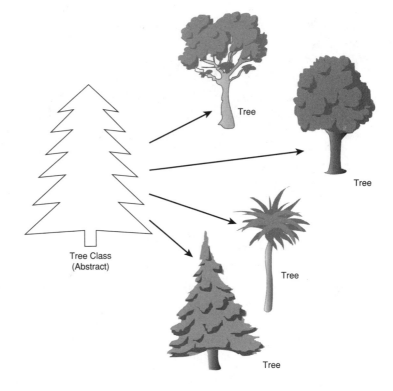

Tree

Tree

Tree

Tree Class
(Abstract)

Tree

> **Tip:** If you're used to programming in C, you can think of a class as sort of creating a new composite data type by using struct and typedef. Classes, however, can provide much more than just a collection of data, as you'll discover in the rest of today's lesson.

When you write a Java program, you design and construct a set of classes. Then, when your program runs, instances of those classes are created and discarded as needed. Your task, as a Java programmer, is to create the right set of classes to accomplish what your program needs to accomplish.

Fortunately, you don't have to start from the very beginning: the Java environment comes with a library of classes that implement a lot of the basic behavior you need—not only for basic programming tasks (classes to provide basic math functions, arrays, strings, and so on), but also for graphics and networking behavior. In many cases, the Java class libraries may be enough so that all you have to do in your Java program is create a single class that uses the standard class libraries. For complicated Java programs, you may have to create a whole set of classes with defined interactions between them.

NEW TERM   A *class library* is a set of classes.

Behavior and Attributes

Every class you write in Java is generally made up of two components: attributes and behavior. In this section, you'll learn about each one as it applies to a thoeretical class called `Motorcycle`. To finish up this section, you'll create the Java code to implement a representation of a motorcycle.

Attributes

Attributes are the individual things that differentiate one object from another and determine the appearance, state, or other qualities of that object. Let's create a theoretical class called `Motorcycle`. The attributes of a motorcycle might include the following:

- ☐ *Color:* red, green, silver, brown
- ☐ *Style:* cruiser, sport bike, standard
- ☐ *Make:* Honda, BMW, Bultaco

Attributes of an object can also include information about its state; for example, you could have features for engine condition (off or on) or current gear selected.

Attributes are defined by variables; in fact, you can consider them analogous to global variables for the entire object. Because each instance of a class can have different values for its variables, each variable is called an instance variable.

NEW TERM   *Instance variables* define the attributes of an object. The class defines the kind of attribute, and each instance stores its own value for that attribute.

Each attribute, as the term is used here, has a single corresponding instance variable; changing the value of a variable changes the attribute of that objcct. Instance variables may be set when an object is created and stay constant throughout the life of the object, or they may be able to change at will as the program runs.

In addition to instance variables, there are also class variables, which apply to the class itself and to all its instances. Unlike instance variables, whose values are stored in the instance, class variables' values are stored in the class itself. You'll learn about class variables later on this week; you'll learn more specifics about instance variables tomorrow.

Behavior

A class's behavior determines what instances of that class do when their internal state changes or when that instance is asked to do something by another class or object. Behavior is the way objects can do anything to themselves or have anything done to them. For example, to go back to the theoretical Motorcycle class, here are some behaviors that the Motorcycle class might have:

- ☐ Start the engine
- ☐ Stop the engine
- ☐ Speed up
- ☐ Change gear
- ☐ Stall

To define an object's behavior, you create methods, which look and behave just like functions in other languages, but are defined inside a class. Java does not have functions defined outside classes (as C++ does).

NEW☞ TERM   *Methods* are functions defined inside classes that operate on instances of those classes.

Methods don't always affect only a single object; objects communicate with each other using methods as well. A class or object can call methods in another class or object to communicate changes in the environment or to ask that object to change its state.

Just as there are instance and class variables, there are also instance and class methods. Instance methods (which are so common they're usually just called methods) apply and operate on an instance; class methods apply and operate on a class (or on other objects). You'll learn more about class methods later on this week.

Creating a Class

Up to this point, today's lesson has been pretty theoretical. In this section, you'll create a working example of the Motorcycle class so that you can see how instance variables and methods are defined in a class. You'll also create a Java application that creates a new instance of the Motorcycle class and shows its instance variables.

Note: I'm not going to go into a lot of detail about the actual syntax of this example here. Don't worry too much about it if you're not really sure what's going on; it will become clear to you later on this week. All you really need to worry about in this example is understanding the basic parts of this class definition.

Ready? Let's start with a basic class definition. Open up that editor and enter the following:

```
class Motorcycle {

}
```

Congratulations! You've now created a class. Of course, it doesn't do very much at the moment, but that's a Java class at its very simplest.

First, let's create some instance variables for this class—three of them, to be specific. Just below the first line, add the following three lines:

```
String make;
String color;
boolean engineState;
```

Here, you've created three instance variables: two, `make` and `color`, can contain `String` objects (`String` is part of that standard class library mentioned earlier). The third, `engineState`, is a boolean that refers to whether the engine is off or on.

Technical Note: `boolean` in Java is a real data type that can have the value `true` or `false`. Unlike C, booleans are not numbers. You'll hear about this again tomorrow so you won't forget.

Now let's add some behavior (methods) to the class. There are all kinds of things a motorcycle can do, but to keep things short, let's add just one method—a method that starts the engine. Add the following lines below the instance variables in your class definition:

```
void startEngine() {
    if (engineState == true)
        System.out.println("The engine is already on.");
    else {
        engineState = true;
        System.out.println("The engine is now on.");
    }
}
```

The startEngine method tests to see whether the engine is already running (in the line engineState == true) and, if it is, merely prints a message to that effect. If the engine isn't already running, it changes the state of the engine to true and then prints a message.

With your methods and variables in place, save the program to a file called Motorcycle.java (remember, you should always name your Java files the same names as the class they define). Here's what your program should look like so far:

```
class Motorcycle {

    String make;
    String color;
    boolean engineState;

    void startEngine() {
        if (engineState == true)
            System.out.println("The engine is already on.");
        else {
            engineState = true;
            System.out.println("The engine is now on.");
        }
    }
}
```

> **Tip:** The indentation of each part of the class isn't important to the Java compiler. Using some form of indentation, however, makes your class definition easier for you and for other people to read. The indentation used here, with instance variables and methods indented from the class definition, is the style used throughout this book. The Java class libraries use a similar indentation. You can choose any indentation style that you like.

Before you compile this class, let's add one more method. The showAtts method prints the current values of the instance variables in an instance of your Motorcycle class. Here's what it looks like:

```
void showAtts() {
    System.out.println("This motorcycle is a "
        + color + " " + make);
    if (engineState == true)
        System.out.println("The engine is on.");
    else System.out.println("The engine is off.");
}
```

The showAtts method prints two lines to the screen: the make and color of the motorcycle object, and whether or not the engine is on or off.

Save that file again and compile it using `javac`:

```
javac Motorcycle.java
```

Note: After this point, I'm going to assume you know how to compile and run Java programs. I won't repeat this information after this.

What happens if you now use the Java interpreter to run this compiled class? Try it. Java assumes that this class is an application and looks for a `main` method. This is just a class, however, so it doesn't have a `main` method. The Java interpreter (`java`) gives you an error like this one:

```
In class Motorcycle: void main(String argv[]) is not defined
```

To do something with the Motorcycle class—for example, to create instances of that class and play with them—you're going to need to create a Java application that uses this class or add a `main` method to this one. For simplicity's sake, let's do the latter. Listing 2.1 shows the `main()` method you'll add to the Motorcycle class (you'll go over what this does in a bit).

Listing 2.1. The `main()` method for `Motorcycle.java`.

```
 1: public static void main (String args[]) {
 2:     Motorcycle m = new Motorcycle();
 3:     m.make = "Yamaha RZ350";
 4:     m.color = "yellow";
 5:     System.out.println("Calling showAtts...");
 6:     m.showAtts();
 7:     System.out.println("--------");
 8:     System.out.println("Starting engine...");
 9:     m.startEngine();
10:     System.out.println("--------");
11:     System.out.println("Calling showAtts...");
12:     m.showAtts();
13:     System.out.println("--------");
14:     System.out.println("Starting engine...");
15:     m.startEngine();
16:}
```

With the `main()` method, the Motorcycle class is now an application, and you can compile it again and this time it'll run. Here's how the output should look:

```
Calling showAtts...
This motorcycle is a yellow Yamaha RZ350
The engine is off.
--------
```

```
Starting engine...
The engine is now on.
--------
Calling showAtts...
This motorcycle is a yellow Yamaha RZ350
The engine is on.
--------
Starting engine...
The engine is already on.
```

The contents of the main() method are all going to look very new to you, so let's go through it line by line so that you at least have a basic idea of what it does (you'll get details about the specifics of all of this tomorrow and the day after).

The first line declares the main() method. The main() method always looks like this; you'll learn the specifics of each part later this week.

Line 2, Motorcycle m = new Motorcycle(), creates a new instance of the Motorcycle class and stores a reference to it in the variable m. Remember, you don't usually operate directly on classes in your Java programs; instead, you create objects from those classes and then modify and call methods in those objects.

Lines 3 and 4 set the instance variables for this motorcycle object: the make is now a Yamaha RZ350 (a very pretty motorcycle from the mid-1980s), and the color is yellow.

Lines 5 and 6 call the showAtts() method, defined in your motorcycle object. (Actually, only 6 does; 5 just prints a message that you're about to call this method.) The new motorcycle object then prints out the values of its instance variables—the make and color as you set in the previous lines—and shows that the engine is off.

Line 7 prints a divider line to the screen; this is just for prettier output.

Line 9 calls the startEngine() method in the motorcycle object to start the engine. The engine should now be on.

Line 12 prints the values of the instance variables again. This time, the report should say the engine is now on.

Line 15 tries to start the engine again, just for fun. Because the engine is already on, this should print the error message.

Inheritance, Interfaces, and Packages

Now that you have a basic grasp of classes, objects, methods, variables, and how to put it all together in a Java program, it's time to confuse you again. Inheritance, interfaces, and packages are all mechanisms for organizing classes and class behaviors. The Java class libraries use all these concepts, and the best class libraries you write for your own programs will also use these concepts.

Inheritance

Inheritance is one of the most crucial concepts in object-oriented programming, and it has a very direct effect on how you design and write your Java classes. Inheritance is a powerful mechanism that means when you write a class you only have to specify how that class is different from some other class, while also giving you dynamic access to the information contained in those other classes.

NEW☞ With inheritance, all classes—those you write, those from other class libraries that you use,
TERM and those from the standard utility classes as well—are arranged in a strict hierarchy (see Figure 2.2).

Each class has a superclass (the class above it in the hierarchy), and each class can have one or more subclasses (classes below that class in the hierarchy). Classes further down in the hierarchy are said to inherit from classes further up in the hierarchy.

Figure 2.2.

A class hierarchy.

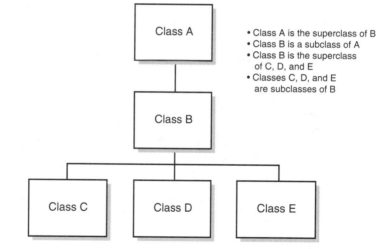

- Class A is the superclass of B
- Class B is a subclass of A
- Class B is the superclass of C, D, and E
- Classes C, D, and E are subclasses of B

Subclasses inherit all the methods and variables from their superclasses—that is, in any particular class, if the superclass defines behavior that your class needs, you don't have to redefine it or copy that code from some other class. Your class automatically gets that behavior from its superclass, that superclass gets behavior from its superclass, and so on all the way up the hierarchy. Your class becomes a combination of all the features of the classes above it in the hierarchy.

At the top of the Java class hierarchy is the class Object; all classes inherit from this one superclass. Object is the most general class in the hierarchy; it defines behavior specific to all objects in the Java class hierarchy. Each class farther down in the hierarchy adds more information and becomes more tailored to a specific purpose. In this way, you can think of a class hierarchy as defining very abstract concepts at the top of the hierarchy and those ideas becoming more concrete the farther down the chain of superclasses you go.

Most of the time when you write new Java classes, you'll want to create a class that has all the information some other class has, plus some extra information. For example, you may want a version of a Button with its own built-in label. To get all the Button information, all you have to do is define your class to inherit from Button. Your class will automatically get all the behavior defined in Button (and in Button's superclasses), so all you have to worry about are the things that make your class different from Button itself. This mechanism for defining new classes as the differences between them and their superclasses is called *subclassing*.

NEW 🖝 *Subclassing* involves creating a new class that inherits from some other class in the class
TERM hierarchy. Using subclassing, you only need to define the differences between your class and its parent; the additional behavior is all available to your class through inheritance.

What if your class defines entirely new behavior, and isn't really a subclass of another class? Your class can also inherit directly from Object, which still allows it to fit neatly into the Java class hierarchy. In fact, if you create a class definition that doesn't indicate its superclass in the first line, Java automatically assumes you're inheriting from Object. The Motorcycle class you created in the previous section inherited from Object.

Creating a Class Hierarchy

If you're creating a larger set of classes, it makes sense for your classes not only to inherit from the existing class hierarchy, but also to make up a hierarchy themselves. This may take some planning beforehand when you're trying to figure out how to organize your Java code, but the advantages are significant once it's done:

☐ When you develop your classes in a hierarchy, you can factor out information common to multiple classes in superclasses, and then reuse that superclass's information over and over again. Each subclass gets that common information from its superclass.

☐ Changing (or inserting) a class further up in the hierarchy automatically changes the behavior of the lower classes—no need to change or recompile any of the lower classes, because they get the new information through inheritance and not by copying any of the code.

For example, let's go back to that Motorcycle class, and pretend you created a Java program to implement all the features of a motorcycle. It's done, it works, and everything is fine. Now, your next task is to create a Java class called Car.

Car and Motorcycle have many similar features—both are vehicles driven by engines. Both have transmissions and headlamps and speedometers. So, your first impulse may be to open up your Motorcycle class file and copy over a lot of the information you already defined into the new class Car.

A far better plan is to factor out the common information for Car and Motorcycle into a more general class hierarchy. This may be a lot of work just for the classes Motorcycle and Car, but once you add Bicycle, Scooter, Truck, and so on, having common behavior in a reuseable superclass significantly reduces the amount of work you have to do overall.

Let's design a class hierarchy that might serve this purpose. Starting at the top is the class Object, which is the root of all Java classes. The most general class to which motorcycle and car both belong might be called Vehicle. A vehicle, generally, is defined as a thing that propels someone from one place to another. In the Vehicle class, you define only the behavior that enables someone to be propelled from point a to point b, and nothing more.

Below Vehicle? How about two classes: PersonPoweredVehicle and EnginePoweredVehicle? EnginePoweredVehicle is different from Vehicle because is has an engine, and the behaviors might include stopping and starting the engine, having certain amounts of gasoline and oil, and perhaps the speed or gear in which the engine is running. Person-powered vehicles have some kind of mechanism for translating people motion into vehicle motion—pedals, for example. Figure 2.3 shows what you have so far.

Figure 2.3.
The basic vehicle hierarchy.

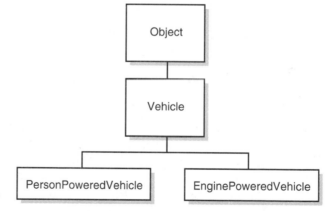

Now, let's become even more specific. With EnginePoweredVehicle, you might have several classes: Motorcycle, Car, Truck, and so on. Or you can factor out still more behavior and have intermediate classes for TwoWheeled and FourWheeled vehicles, with different behaviors for each (see Figure 2.4).

Finally, with a subclass for the two-wheeled engine-powered vehicles you can finally have a class for motorcycles. Alternatively, you could additionally define scooters and mopeds, both of which are two-wheeled engine-powered vehicles but have different qualities from motorcycles.

Where do qualities such as make or color come in? Wherever you want them to go—or, more usually, where they fit most naturally in the class hierarchy. You can define the make and color on Vehicle, and all the subclasses will have those variables as well. The point to remember is that you have to define a feature or a behavior only once in the hierarchy; it's automatically reused by each subclass.

Figure 2.4.
Two-wheeled and four-wheeled vehicles.

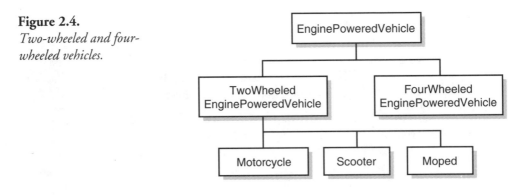

How Inheritance Works

How does inheritance work? How is it that instances of one class can automatically get variables and methods from the classes further up in the hierarchy?

For instance variables, when you create a new instance of a class, you get a "slot" for each variable defined in the current class and for each variable defined in all its superclasses. In this way, all the classes combine to form a template for the current object and then each object fills in the information appropriate to its situation.

Methods operate similarly: new objects have access to all the method names of its class and its superclasses, but method definitions are chosen dynamically when a method is called. That is, if you call a method on a particular object, Java first checks the object's class for the definition of that method. If it's not defined in the object's class, it looks in that class's superclass, and so on up the chain until the method definition is found (see Figure 2.5).

Things get complicated when a subclass defines a method that has the same signature (name and number and type of arguments) as a method defined in a superclass. In this case, the method definition that is found first (starting at the bottom and working upward toward the top of the hierarchy) is the one that is actually executed. Because of this, you can purposefully define a method in a subclass that has the same signature as a method in a superclass, which then "hides" the superclass's method. This is called *overriding* a method. You'll learn all about methods on Day 7.

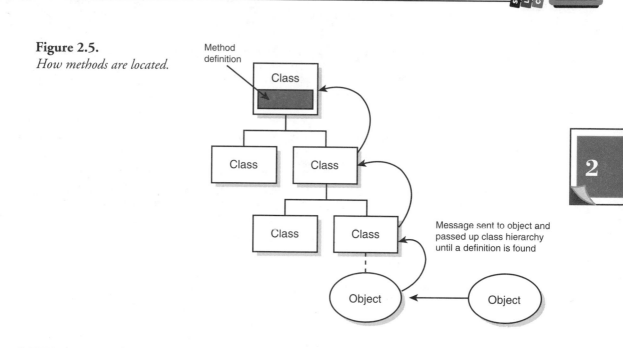

Figure 2.5.
How methods are located.

Method
definition

Class

Class   Class

Class   Class

Message sent to object and
passed up class hierarchy
until a definition is found

Object   Object

NEW☛   *Overriding* a method is creating a method in a subclass that has the same signature (name,
TERM   number and type of arguments) as a method in a superclass. That new method then hides
the superclass's method (see Figure 2.6).

Figure 2.6.
Overriding methods.

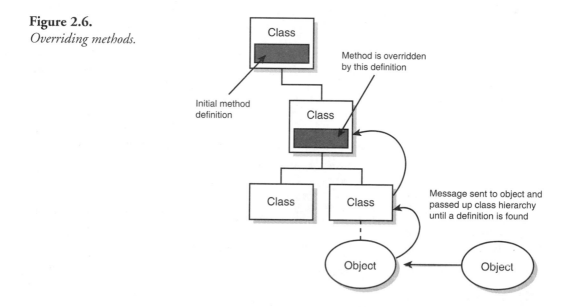

Class

Method is overridden
by this definition

Class

Initial method
definition

Class   Class

Message sent to object and
passed up class hierarchy
until a definition is found

Object   Object

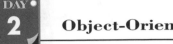

Single and Multiple Inheritance

Java's form of inheritance, as you learned in the previous sections, is called single inheritance. Single inheritance means that each Java class can have only one superclass (although any given superclass can have multiple subclasses).

In other object-oriented programming languages, such as C++ and Smalltalk, classes can have more than one superclass, and they inherit combined variables and methods from all those classes. This is called multiple inheritance. Multiple inheritance can provide enormous power in terms of being able to create classes that factor just about all imaginable behavior, but it can also significantly complicate class definitions and the code to produce them. Java makes inheritance simpler by being only singly inherited.

Interfaces and Packages

Java has two remaining concepts to discuss here: packages and interfaces. Both are advanced topics for implementing and designing groups of classes and class behavior. You'll learn about both interfaces and packages on Day 16, but they are worth at least introducing here.

Recall that Java classes have only a single superclass, and they inherit variables and methods from that superclass and all its superclasses. Although single inheritance makes the relationship between classes and the functionality those classes implement easy to understand and to design, it can also be somewhat restricting—in particular, when you have similar behavior that needs to be duplicated across different "branches" of the class hierarchy. Java solves this problem of shared behavior by using the concept of interfaces.

NEW☞
TERM An *interface* is a collection of method names, without actual definitions, that indicate that a class has a set of behaviors in addition to the behaviors the class gets from its superclasses.

Although a single Java class can have only one superclass (due to single inheritance), that class can also implement any number of interfaces. By implementing an interface, a class provides method implementations (definitions) for the method names defined by the interface. If two very disparate classes implement the same interface, they can both respond to the same method calls (as defined by that interface), although what each class actually does in response to those method calls may be very different.

You don't need to know very much about interfaces right now. You'll learn more as the book progresses, so if all this is very confusing, don't panic!

The final new Java concept for today is that of packages.

NEW☞
TERM *Packages* in Java are a way of grouping together related classes and interfaces. Packages enable modular groups of classes to be available only if they are needed and eliminate potential conflicts between class names in different groups of classes.

You'll learn all about packages, including how to create and use them, in Week 3. For now, there are only a few things you need to know:

☐ The class libraries in the Java Developer's Kit are contained in a package called java. The classes in the java package are guaranteed to be available in any Java implementation, and are the *only* classes guaranteed to be available across different implementations. The java package itself contains other packages for classes that define the language itself, the input and output classes, some basic networking, and the window toolkit functions. Classes in other packages (for example, classes in the sun or netscape packages) may be available only in specific implementations.

☐ By default, your Java classes have access to only the classes in java.lang (the base language package inside the java package). To use classes from any other package, you have to either refer to them explicitly by package name or import them in your source file.

☐ To refer to a class within a package, list all the packages that class is contained in and the class name, all separated by periods (.). For example, take the Color class, which is contained in the awt package (awt stands for Abstract Windowing Toolkit). The awt package, in turn, is inside the java package. To refer to the Color class in your program, you use the notation java.awt.Color.

Creating a Subclass

To finish up today, let's create a class that is a subclass of another class and override some methods. You'll also get a basic feel for how packages work in this example.

Probably the most typical instance of creating a subclass, at least when you first start programming in Java, is in creating an applet. All applets are subclasses of the class Applet (which is part of the java.applet package). By creating a subclass of Applet, you automatically get all the behavior from the window toolkit and the layout classes that enables your applet to be drawn in the right place on the page and to interact with system operations, such as keypresses and mouse clicks.

In this example, you'll create an applet similar to the Hello World applet from yesterday, but one that draws the Hello string in a larger font and a different color. To start this example, let's first construct the class definition itself. Remember the HTML and classes directories you created yesterday? Let's go back to those, go back to your text editor, and enter the following class definition:

```
public class HelloAgainApplet extends java.applet.Applet {
}
```

Here, you're creating a class called HelloAgainApplet. Note the part that says extends java.applet.Applet—that's the part that says your applet class is a subclass of the Applet class.

Note that because the `Applet` class is contained in the `java.applet` package, you don't have automatic access to that class, and you have to refer to it explicitly by package and class name.

The other part of this class definition is the `public` keyword. Public means that your class is available to the Java system at large once it is loaded. Most of the time you need to make a class `public` only if you want it to be visible to all the other classes in your Java program; but applets, in particular, must be declared to be public. (You'll learn more about `public` classes in Week 3.)

A class definition with nothing in it doesn't really have much of a point; without adding or overriding any of its superclasses' variables or methods, there's no point to creating a subclass at all. Let's add some information to this class to make it different from its superclass.

First, add an instance variable to contain a `Font` object:

```
Font f = new Font("TimesRoman",Font.BOLD,36);
```

The `f` instance variable now contains a new instance of the class `Font`, part of the `java.awt` package. This particular font object is a Times Roman font, boldface, 36 points high. In the previous Hello World applet, the font used for the text was the default font: 12 point Times Roman. Using a font object, you can change the font of the text you draw in your applet.

By creating an instance variable to hold this font object, you make it available to all the methods in your class. Now let's create a method that uses it.

When you write applets, there are several "standard" methods defined in the applet superclasses that you will commonly override in your applet class. These include methods to initialize the applet, to start it running, to handle operations such as mouse movements or mouse clicks, or to clean up when the applet stops running. One of those standard methods is the `paint()` method, which actually displays your applet on screen. The default definition of `paint()` doesn't do anything—it's an empty method. By overriding `paint()`, you tell the applet just what to draw on the screen. Here's a definition of `paint()`:

```
public void paint(Graphics g) {
    g.setFont(f);
    g.setColor(Color.red);
    g.drawString("Hello again!", 5, 25);
}
```

There are two things to know about the `paint()` method. First, note that this method is declared `public`, just as the applet itself was. The `paint()` method is actually `public` for a different reason—because the method it's overriding is also `public`. If you try to override a method in your own class that's `public` in a superclass, you get a compiler error, so the `public` is required.

Secondly, note that the `paint()` method takes a single argument: an instance of the `Graphics` class. The `Graphics` class provides platform-independent behavior for rendering fonts, colors, and basic drawing operations. You'll learn a lot more about the `Graphics` class in Week 2, when you create more extensive applets.

Inside your `paint()` method, you've done three things:

- ☐ You've told the graphics object that the default drawing font will be the one contained in the instance variable f.

- ☐ You've told the graphics object that the default color is an instance of the Color class for the color red.

- ☐ Finally, you've drawn your `"Hello Again!"` string onto the screen itself, at the x and y positions of 5 and 25. The string will be rendered in the default font and color.

For an applet this simple, this is all you need to do. Here's what the applet looks like so far:

```
public class HelloAgainApplet extends java.applet.Applet {

  Font f = new Font("TimesRoman",Font.BOLD,36);

  public void paint(Graphics g) {
    g.setFont(f);
    g.setColor(Color.red);
    g.drawString("Hello again!", 5, 50);
  }
}
```

If you've been paying attention, you'll notice something is wrong with this example up to this point. If you don't know what it is, try saving this file (remember, save it to the same name as the class: HelloAgainApplet.java) and compiling it using the Java compiler. You should get a bunch of errors similar to this one:

```
HelloAgainApplet.java:7: Class Graphics not found in type declaration.
```

Why are you getting these errors? Because the classes you're referring to are part of a package. Remember that the only package you have access to automatically is java.lang. You referred to the Applet class in the first line of the class definition by referring to its full package name (java.applet.Applet). Further on in the program, however, you referred to all kinds of other classes as if they were already available.

There are two ways to solve this problem: refer to all external classes by full package name or import the appropriate class or package at the beginning of your class file. Which one you choose to do is mostly a matter of choice, although if you find yourself referring to a class in another package lots of times, you may want to import it to cut down on the amount of typing.

In this example, you'll import the classes you need. There are three of them: Graphics, Font, and Color. All three are part of the java.awt package. Here are the lines to import these classes. These lines go at the top of your program, before the actual class definition:

```
import java.awt.Graphics;
import java.awt.Font;
import java.awt.Color;
```

> **Tip:** You also can import an entire package of (`public`) classes by using an asterisk (*) in place of a specific class name. For example, to import all the classes in the awt package, you can use this line:
>
> ```
> import java.awt.*;
> ```

Now, with the proper classes imported into your program, HelloAgainApplet should compile cleanly to a class file. To test it, create an HTML file with the <APPLET> tag as you did yesterday. Here's an HTML file to use:

```
<HTML>
<HEAD>
<TITLE>Another Applet</TITLE>
</HEAD>
<BODY>
<P>My second Java applet says:
<APPLET CODE="HelloAgainApplet.class" WIDTH=200 HEIGHT=50>
</APPLET>
</BODY>
</HTML>
```

For this HTML example, your Java class file is in the same directory as this HTML file. Save the file to HelloAgainApplet.html and fire up your Java-aware browser or the Java applet viewer. Figure 2.7 shows the result you should be getting (the Hello Again string is red).

Figure 2.7.
The Hello Again applet.

My second Java applet says:

Hello Again!

Summary

If this is your first encounter with object-oriented programming, a lot of the information in this chapter is going to seem really theoretical and overwhelming. Fear not—the further along in this book you get, and the more Java applications you create, the easier it is to understand.

One of the biggest hurdles of object-oriented programming is not necessarily the concepts, it's their names. OOP has lots of jargon surrounding it. To summarize today's material, here's a glossary of terms and concepts you learned today:

Class: A template for an object, which contains variables and methods representing behavior and attributes. Classes can inherit variables and methods from other classes.

Object: A concrete instance of some class. Multiple objects that are instances of the same class have access to the same methods, but often have different values for their instance variables.

Instance: The same thing as an object; each object is an instance of some class.

Superclass: A class further up in the inheritance hierarchy than its child, the subclass.

Subclass: A class lower in the inheritance hierarchy than its parent, the superclass. When you create a new class, that's often called *subclassing*.

Instance method: A method defined in a class, which operates on an instance of that class. Instance methods are usually called just *methods*.

Class method: A method defined in a class, which can operate on the class itself or on any object.

Instance variable: A variable that is owned by an individual instance and whose value is stored in the instance.

Class variable: A variable that is owned by the class and all its instances as a whole, and is stored in the class.

Interface: A collection of abstract behavior specifications that individual classes can then implement.

Package: A collection of classes and interfaces. Classes from packages other than java.lang must be explicitly imported or referred to by full package name.

Q&A

Q Methods are effectively functions that are defined inside classes. If they look like functions and act like functions, why aren't they called functions?

A Some object-oriented programming languages do call them functions (C++ calls them member functions). Other object-oriented languages differentiate between functions inside and outside a body of a class or object, where having separate terms is important to understanding how each works. Because the difference is relevant in other languages, and because the term method is now in such common use in object-oriented technology, Java uses the word as well.

Q I understand instance variables and methods, but not class variables and methods.

A Most everything you do in a Java program will be with objects. Some behaviors and attributes, however, make more sense if they are stored in the class itself rather than in the object. For example, to create a new instance of a class, you need a method that is defined for the class itself, not for an object. (Otherwise, how can you create an instance of class? You need an object to call the new method in, but you don't have an object yet.) Class variables, on the other hand, are often used when you have an attribute whose value you want to share with the instances of a class.

Most of the time, you'll use instance variables and methods. You'll learn more about class variables and methods later on this week.

Java Basics

by Laura Lemay

On Days 1 and 2, you learned about Java programming in very broad terms—what a Java program and an executable look like, and how to create simple classes. For the remainder of this week, you're going to get down to details and deal with the specifics of what the Java language looks like.

Today, you won't define any classes or objects or worry about how any of them communicate inside a Java program. Rather, you'll draw closer and examine simple Java statements—the basic things you can do in Java within a method definition such as main().

Today you'll learn about the following:

- [ ] Java statements and expressions
- [ ] Variables and data types
- [ ] Comments
- [ ] Literals
- [ ] Arithmetic
- [ ] Comparisons
- [ ] Logical operators

Technical Note: Java looks a lot like C++, and—by extension—like C. Much of the syntax will be very familiar to you if you are used to working in these languages. If you are an experienced C or C++ programmer, you may want to pay special attention to the Technical Notes (such as this one), because they will provide information about the specific differences between these and other traditional languages and Java.

Statements and Expressions

A statement is the simplest thing you can do in Java; a statement forms a single Java operation. All the following are simple Java statements:

```
int i = 1;
import java.awt.Font;
System.out.println("This motorcycle is a "
    + color + " " + make);
m.engineState = true;
```

Statements sometimes return values—for example, when you add two numbers together or test to see whether one value is equal to another. These kind of statements are called expressions. We'll discuss these later on today.

The most important thing to remember about Java statements is that each one ends with a semicolon. Forget the semicolon and your Java program won't compile.

Java also has compound statements, or blocks, which can be placed wherever a single statement can. Block statements are surrounded by braces ({}). You'll learn more about blocks in Chapter 5, "Arrays, Conditionals, and Loops."

Variables and Data Types

Variables are locations in memory in which values can be stored. They have a name, a type, and a value. Before you can use a variable, you have to declare it. After it is declared, you can then assign values to it.

Java actually has three kinds of variables: instance variables, class variables, and local variables.

Instance variables, as you learned yesterday, are used to define attributes or the state for a particular object. Class variables are similar to instance variables, except their values apply to all that class's instances (and to the class itself) rather than having different values for each object.

Local variables are declared and used inside method definitions, for example, for index counters in loops, as temporary variables, or to hold values that you need only inside the method definition itself. They can also be used inside blocks ({}), which you'll learn about later this week. Once the method (or block) finishes executing, the variable definition and its value cease to exist. Use local variables to store information needed by a single method and instance variables to store information needed by multiple methods in the object.

Although all three kinds of variables are declared in much the same ways, class and instance variables are accessed and assigned in slightly different ways from local variables. Today, you'll focus on variables as used within method definitions; tomorrow, you'll learn how to deal with instance and class variables.

> **Note:** Unlike other languages, Java does not have global variables—that is, variables that are global to all parts of a program. Instance and class variables can be used to communicate global information between and among objects. Remember, Java is an object-oriented language, so you should think in terms of objects and how they interact, rather than in terms of programs.

Declaring Variables

To use any variable in a Java program, you must first declare it. Variable declarations consist of a type and a variable name:

```
int myAge;
String myName;
boolean isTired;
```

Variable definitions can go anywhere in a method definition (that is, anywhere a regular Java statement can go), although they are most commonly declared at the beginning of the definition before they are used:

```
public static void main (String args÷]) {
    int count;
    String title;
    boolean isAsleep;
...
}
```

You can string together variable names with the same type:

```
int x, y, z;
String firstName, LastName;
```

You can also give each variable an initial value when you declare it:

```
int myAge, mySize, numShoes = 28;
String myName = "Laura";
boolean isTired = true;
int a = 4, b = 5, c = 6;
```

If there are multiple variables on the same line with only one initializer (as in the first of the previous examples), the initial value applies to only the last variable in a declaration. You can also group individual variables and initializers on the same line using commas, as with the last example, above.

Local variables must be given values before they can be used (your Java program will not compile if you try to use an unassigned local variable). For this reason, it's a good idea always to give local variables initial values. Instance and class variable definitions do not have this restriction (their initial value depends on the type of the variable: null for instances of classes, 0 for numeric variables, '\0' for characters, and false for booleans).

Notes on Variable Names

Variable names in Java can start with a letter, an underscore (_), or a dollar sign ($). They cannot start with a number. After the first character, your variable names can include any letter or number. Symbols, such as %, *, @, and so on, are often reserved for operators in Java, so be careful when using symbols in variable names.

In addition, the Java language uses the Unicode character set. Unicode is a character set definition that not only offers characters in the standard ASCII character set, but also several million other characters for representing most international alphabets. This means that you can use accented characters and other glyphs as legal characters in variable names, as long as they have a Unicode character number above 00C0.

> **Caution:** The Unicode specification is a two-volume set of lists of thousands of characters. If you don't understand Unicode, or don't think you have a use for it, it's safest just to use plain numbers and letters in your variable names. You'll learn a little more about Unicode later on.

Finally, note that the Java language is case-sensitive, which means that uppercase letters are different from lowercase letters. This means that the variable X is different from the variable x, and a rose is not a Rose is not a ROSE. Keep this in mind as you write your own Java programs and as you read Java code other people have written.

By convention, Java variables have meaningful names, often made up of several words combined. The first word is lowercase, but all following words have an initial uppercase letter:

```
Button theButton;
long reallyBigNumber;
boolean currentWeatherStateOfPlanetXShortVersion;
```

Variable Types

In addition to the variable name, each variable declaration must have a type, which defines what values that variable can hold. The variable type can be one of three things:

- [ ] One of the eight basic primitive data types
- [ ] The name of a class
- [ ] An array

You'll learn about how to declare and use array variables in Chapter 5.

The eight primitive data types handle common types for integers, floating-point numbers, characters, and boolean values (true or false). They're called primitive because they're built into the system and are not actual objects, which makes them more efficient to use. Note that these data types are machine-independent, which means that you can rely on their sizes and characteristics to be consistent across your Java programs.

There are four Java integer types, each with different ranges of values (as listed in Table 3.1). All are signed, which means they can hold either positive or negative numbers. Which type you choose for your variables depends on the range of values you expect that variable to hold; if a value becomes too big for the variable type, it is truncated.

Table 3.1. Integer types.

Type	Size	Range
byte	8 bits	−128 to 127
short	16 bits	−32,768 to 32,767
int	32 bits	−2,147,483,648 to 2,147,483,647
long	64 bits	−9223372036854775808 to 9223372036854775807

Floating-point numbers are used for numbers with a decimal part. Java floating-point numbers are compliant with IEEE 754 (an international standard for defining floating-point numbers and arithmetic). There are two floating-point types: float (32 bits, single-precision) and double (64 bits, double-precision).

The char type is used for individual characters. Because Java uses the Unicode character set, the char type has 16 bits of precision, unsigned.

Finally, the boolean type can have one of two values, true or false. Note that unlike in other C-like languages, boolean is not a number, nor can it be treated as one. All tests of boolean variables should test for true or false.

In addition to the eight basic data types, variables in Java can also be declared to hold an instance of a particular class:

```
String LastName;
Font basicFont;
OvalShape myOval;
```

Each of these variables can then hold only instances of the given class. As you create new classes, you can declare variables to hold instances of those classes (and their subclasses) as well.

Technical Note: Java does not have a typedef statement (as in C and C++). To declare new types in Java, you declare a new class; then variables can be declared to be of that class's type.

Assigning Values to Variables

Once a variable has been declared, you can assign a value to that variable by using the assignment operator =:

```
size = 14;
tooMuchCaffiene = true;
```

Comments

Java has three kinds of comments. /* and */ surround multiline comments, as in C or C++. All text between the two delimiters is ignored:

```
/* I don't know how I wrote this next part; I was working
   really late one night and it just sort of appeared. I
   suspect the code elves did it for me. It might be wise
   not to try and change it.
*/
```

Comments cannot be nested; that is, you cannot have a comment inside a comment.

Double-slashes (//) can be used for a single line of comment. All the text up to the end of the line is ignored:

```
int vices = 7; // are there really only 7 vices?
```

The final type of comment begins with /** and ends with */. These are special comments that are used for the javadoc system. Javadoc is used to generate API documentation from the code. You won't learn about javadoc in this book; you can find out more information from the documentation that came with Sun's Java Developer's Kit or from Sun's Java home page (http://java.sun.com).

Literals

Literals are used to indicate simple values in your Java programs.

NEW☞
TERM
Literal is a programming language term, which essentially means that what you type is what you get. For example, if you type 4 in a Java program, you automatically get an integer with the value 4. If you type 'a', you get a character with the value a.

Literals may seem intuitive most of the time, but there are some special cases of literals in Java for different kinds of numbers, characters, strings, and boolean values.

Number Literals

There are several integer literals. 4, for example, is a decimal integer literal of type int (although you can assign it to a variable of type byte or short because it's small enough to fit into those types). A decimal integer literal larger than an int is automatically of type long. You also can force a smaller number to a long by appending an L or l to that number (for example, 4L is a long integer of value 4). Negative integers are preceded by a minus sign—for example, -45.

Integers can also be expressed as octal or hexadecimal: a leading 0 indicates that a number is octal—for example, 0777 or 0004. A leading 0x (or 0X) means that it is in hex (0xFF, 0XAF45).

Hexadecimal numbers can contain regular digits (0–9) or upper- or lowercase hex digits (a–f or A–F).

Floating-point literals usually have two parts: the integer part and the decimal part—for example, 5.677777. Floating-point literals result in a floating-point number of type `double`, regardless of the precision of that number. You can force the number to the type `float` by appending the letter f (or F) to that number—for example, 2.56F.

You can use exponents in floating-point literals using the letter e or E followed by the exponent (which can be a negative number): 10e45 or .36E-2.

Boolean Literals

Boolean literals consist of the keywords `true` and `false`. These keywords can be used anywhere you need a test or as the only possible values for boolean variables.

Character Literals

Character literals are expressed by a single character surrounded by single quotes: 'a', '#', '3', and so on. Characters are stored as 16-bit Unicode characters. Table 3.2 lists the special codes that can represent nonprintable characters, as well as characters from the Unicode character set. The letter d in the octal, hex, and Unicode escapes represents a number or a hexadecimal digit (a–f or A–F).

Table 3.2. Character escape codes.

Escape	Meaning
\n	Newline
\t	Tab
\b	Backspace
\r	Carriage return
\f	Formfeed
\\	Backslash
\'	Single quote
\"	Double quote
\ddd	Octal
\xdd	Hexadecimal
\udddd	Unicode character

Technical Note: C and C++ programmers should note that Java does not include character codes for \a (bell) or \v (vertical tab).

String Literals

A combination of characters is a string. Strings in Java are instances of the class String. Strings are not simple arrays of characters as they are in C or C++, although they do have many array-like characteristics (for example, you can test their length and add and delete individual characters as if they were arrays). Because string objects are real objects in Java, they have methods that enable you to combine, test, and modify strings very easily.

String literals consist of a series of characters inside double quotes:

```
"Hi, I'm a string literal."
"" //an empty string
```

Strings can contain character constants such as newline, tab, and Unicode characters:

```
"A string with a \t tab in it"
"Nested strings are \"strings inside of\" other strings"
"This string brought to you by Java\u2122"
```

In the last example, the Unicode code sequence for \u2122 produces a trademark symbol (™).

Note: Just because you can represent a character using a Unicode escape does not mean your computer can display that character—the computer or operating system you are running may not support Unicode, or the font you're using may not have a glyph (picture) for that character. All that Unicode escapes in Java provide is a way to encode special characters for systems that support Unicode.

When you use a string literal in your Java program, Java automatically creates an instance of the class String for you with the value you give it. Strings are unusual in this respect; the other literals do not behave in this way (none of the primitive base types are actual objects), and usually creating a new object involves explicitly creating a new instance of a class. You'll learn more about strings, the String class, and the things you can do with strings later today and tomorrow.

Expressions and Operators

Expressions are the simplest form of statement in Java that actually accomplishes something.

NEW☞ *Expressions* are statements that return a value.
TERM
Operators are special symbols that are commonly used in expressions.

Arithmetic and tests for equality and magnitude are common examples of expressions. Because they return a value, you can assign that result to a variable or test that value in other Java statements.

Operators in Java include arithmetic, various forms of assignment, increment and decrement, and logical operations. This section describes all these things.

Arithmetic

Java has five operators for basic arithmetic (see Table 3.3).

Table 3.3. Arithmetic operators.

Operator	Meaning	Example
+	Addition	`3 + 4`
–	Subtraction	`5 – 7`
*	Multiplication	`5 * 5`
÷	Division	`14 ÷ 7`
%	Modulus	`20 % 7`

Each operator takes two operands, one on either side of the operator. The subtraction operator (-) can also be used to negate a single operand.

Integer division results in an integer. Because integers don't have decimal fractions, any remainder is ignored. The expression `31 ÷ 9`, for example, results in `3` (9 goes into 31 only 3 times).

Modulus (%) gives the remainder once the operands have been evenly divided. For example, `31 % 9` results in `4` because 9 goes into 31 three times, with 4 left over.

Note that, for integers, the result type of most operations is an `int` or a `long`, regardless of the original type of the operands. Large results are of type `long`; all others are `int`. Arithmetic wherein one operand is an integer and another is a floating point results in a floating-point result. (If you're interested in the details of how Java promotes and converts numeric types from one type to another, you may want to check out the Java Language Specification; that's more detail than I want to cover here.)

Listing 3.1 is an example of simple arithmetic.

Listing 3.1. Simple arithmetic.

```
1: class ArithmeticTest {
2: public static void main (String[] args) {
3:     short x = 6;
4:     int y = 4;
5:     float a = 12.5f;
6:     float b = 7f;
7:
8:     System.out.println("x is " + x + ", y is " + y);
9:     System.out.println("x + y = " + (x + y));
10:     System.out.println("x - y = " + (x - y));
11:     System.out.println("x / y = " + (x / y));
12:     System.out.println("x % y = " + (x % y));
13:
14:     System.out.println("a is " + a + ", b is " + b;
15:     System.out.println("a / b = " + (a / b));
16: }
17:
18: }
```

```
x is 6, y is 4
x + y = 10
x - y = 2
x / y = 1
x % y = 2
a is 12.5, b is 7
a / b = 1.78571
```

In this simple Java application (note the `main()` method), you initially define four variables in lines 3 through 6: x and y, which are integers (type `int`), and a and b, which are floating-point numbers (type `float`). Keep in mind that the default type for floating-point literals (such as 12.5) is `double`, so to make sure these are numbers of type `float`, you have to use an `f` after each one (lines 5 and 6).

The remainder of the program merely does some math with integers and floating point numbers and prints out the results.

There is one other thing to mention about this program: the method `System.out.println()`. You've seen this method on previous days, but you haven't really learned exactly what it does. The `System.out.println()` method merely prints a message to the standard output of your system—to the screen, to a special window, or maybe just to a special log file, depending on your system and the development environment you're running (Sun's JDK prints it to the screen). The `System.out.println()` method takes a single argument—a string—but you can use + to concatenate values into a string, as you'll learn later today.

More About Assignment

Variable assignment is a form of expression; in fact, because one assignment expression results in a value, you can string them together like this:

```
x = y = z = 0;
```

In this example, all three variables now have the value 0.

The right side of an assignment expression is always evaluated before the assignment takes place. This means that expressions such as x = x + 2 do the right thing; 2 is added to the value of x, and then that new value is reassigned to x. In fact, this sort of operation is so common that Java has several operators to do a shorthand version of this, borrowed from C and C++. Table 3.4 shows these shorthand assignment operators.

Table 3.4. Assignment operators.

Expression	Meaning
x += y	x = x + y
x -= y	x + x − y
x *= y	x = x * y
x ÷= y	x = x ÷ y

Technical Note: If you rely on complicated side effects of subexpressions on either side of these assignments, the shorthand expressions may not be entirely equivalent to their longhand equivalents. For more information about very complicated expressions, evaluation order, and side effects, you may want to consult the Java Language Specification.

Incrementing and Decrementing

As in C and C++, the ++ and -- operators are used to increment or decrement a value by 1. For example, x++ increments the value of x by 1 just as if you had used the expression x = x + 1. Similarly x-- decrements the value of x by 1.

These increment and decrement operators can be prefixed or postfixed; that is, the ++ or -- can appear before or after the value it increments or decrements. For simple increment or decrement expressions, which one you use isn't overly important. In complex assignments, where you are assigning the result of an increment or decrement expression, which one you use makes a difference.

Take, for example, the following two expressions:

```
y = x++;
y = ++x;
```

These two expressions give very different results because of the difference between prefix and postfix. When you use postfix operators (x++ or x--), y gets the value of x before before x is incremented; using prefix, the value of x is assigned to y after the increment has occurred. Listing 3.2 is a Java example of how all this works.

Type

Listing 3.2. Test of prefix and postfix increment operators.

```
 1: class PrePostFixTest {
 2:
 3: public static void main (String args[]) {
 4:     int x = 0;
 5:     int y = 0;
 6:
 7:     System.out.println("x and y are " + x + " and " + y );
 8:     x++;
 9:     System.out.println("x++ results in " + x);
10:     ++x;
11:     System.out.println("++x results in " + x);
12:     System.out.println("Resetting x back to 0.");
13:     x = 0;
14:     System.out.println("— — — — — —");
15:     y = x++;
16:     System.out.println("y = x++ (postfix) results in:");
17:     System.out.println("x is " + x);
18:     System.out.println("y is " + y);
19:     System.out.println("— — — — — —");
20:
21:     y = ++x;
22:     System.out.println("y = ++x (prefix) results in:");
23:     System.out.println("x is " + x);
24:     System.out.println("y is " + y);
25:     System.out.println("— — — — — —");
26:
27: }
28:
29: }
```

Output

```
x and y are 0 and 0
x++ results in 1
++x results in 2
Resetting x back to 0.
— — — — —
y = x++ (postfix) results in:
x is 1
y is 0
— — — — —
y = ++x (prefix) results in:
x is 2
y is 2
— — — — —
```

3

Analysis In the first part of this example, you increment x alone using both `prefix` and `postfix` increment operators. In each, x is incremented by 1 each time. In this simple form, using either `prefix` or `postfix` works the same way.

In the second part of this example, you use the expression y = x++, in which the `postfix` increment operator is used. In this result, the value of x is incremented *after* that value is assigned to y. Hence the result: y is assigned the original value of x (0), and then x is incremented by 1.

In the third part, you use the `prefix` expression y = ++x. Here, the reverse occurs: x is incremented before its value is assigned to y. Because x is 1 from the previous step, its value is incremented (to 2), and then that value is assigned to y. Both x and y end up being 2.

> **Technical Note:** Technically, this description is not entirely correct. In reality, Java *always* completely evaluates all expressions on the right of an expression before assigning that value to a variable, so the concept of "assigning x to y before x is incremented" isn't precisely right. Instead, Java takes the value of x and "remembers" it, evaluates (increments) x, and *then* assigns the original value of x to y. Although in most simple cases this distinction may not be important, for more complex expressions with side effects it may change the behavior of the expression overall. See the Language Specification for many more details about the details of expression evaluation in Java.

Comparisons

Java has several expressions for testing equality and magnitude. All of these expressions return a boolean value (that is, `true` or `false`). Table 3.5 shows the comparison operators:

Table 3.5. Comparison operators.

Operator	Meaning	Example
==	Equal	x == 3
!=	Not equal	x != 3
<	Less than	x < 3
>	Greater than	x > 3
	Less than or equal to	x 3
	Greater than or equal to	x 3

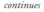

Logical Operators

Expressions that result in boolean values (for example, the comparison operators) can be combined by using logical operators that represent the logical combinations AND, OR, XOR, and logical NOT.

For AND combinations, use either the & or &&. The expression will be true only if both operands tests are also true; if either expression is false, the entire expression is false. The difference between the two operators is in expression evaluation. Using &, both sides of the expression are evaluated regardless of the outcome. Using &&, if the left side of the expression is false, the entire expression returns false, and the right side of the expression is never evaluated.

For OR expressions, use either ¦ or ¦¦. OR expressions result in true if either or both of the operands is also true; if both operands are false, the expression is false. As with & and &&, the single ¦ evaluates both sides of the expression regardless of the outcome; with ¦¦, if the left expression is true, the expression returns true and the right side is never evaluated.

In addition, there is the XOR operator ^, which returns true only if its operands are different (one true and one false, or vice versa) and false otherwise (even if both are true).

In general, only the && and ¦¦ are commonly used as actual logical combinations. &, ¦, and ^ are more commonly used for bitwise logical operations.

For NOT, use the ! operator with a single expression argument. The value of the NOT expression is the negation of the expression; if x is true, !x is false.

Bitwise Operators

Finally, here's a short summary of the bitwise operators in Java. These are all inherited from C and C++ and are used to perform operations on individual bits in integers. This book does not go into bitwise operations; it's an advanced topic covered better in books on C or C++. Table 3.6 summarizes the bitwise operators.

Table 3.6. Bitwise operators.

Operator	Meaning
&	Bitwise AND
¦	Bitwise OR
^	Bitwise XOR
<<	Left shift
>>	Right shift
>>>	Zero fill right shift

continues

Table 3.6. continued

Operator	Meaning
~	Bitwise complement
<<=	Left shift assignment (x = x << y)
>>=	Right shift assignment (x = x >> y)
>>>=	Zero fill right shift assignment (x = x >>> y)
x&=y	AND assignment (x = x & y)
x¦=y	OR assignment (x + x | y)
x^=y	NOT assignment (x = x ^ y)

Operator Precedence

Operator precedence determines the order in which expressions are evaluated. This, in some cases, can determine the overall value of the expression. For example, take the following expression:

```
y = 6 + 4 / 2
```

Depending on whether the 6 + 4 expression or the 4 ÷ 2 expression is evaluated first, the value of y can end up being 5 or 8. Operator precedence determines the order in which expressions are evaluated, so you can predict the outcome of an expression. In general, increment and decrement are evaluated before arithmetic, arithmetic expressions are evaluated before comparisons, and comparisons are evaluated before logical expressions. Assignment expressions are evaluated last.

Table 3.8 shows the specific precedence of the various operators in Java. Operators further up in the table are evaluated first; operators on the same line have the same precedence and are evaluated left to right based on how they appear in the expression itself. For example, give that same expression y = 6 + 4 ÷ 2, you now know, according to this table, that division is evaluated before addition, so the value of y will be 8.

Table 3.7. Operator precedence.

Operator	Notes
. [] ()	Parentheses () group expressions; dot (.) is used for access to methods and variables within objects and classes (discussed tomorrow); [] is used for arrays (discussed later on in the week)
++ -- ! ~ instanceof	Returns true or false based on whether the object is an instance of the named class or any of that class's superclasses (discussed tomorrow)

Operator	Notes
new (type)expression	The new operator is used for creating new instances of classes; () in this case is for casting a value to another type (you'll learn about both of these tomorrow)
* ÷ %	Multiplication, division, modulus
+ -	Addition, subtraction
<< >> >>>	Bitwise left and right shift
< >	Relational comparison tests
== !=	Equality
&	AND
^	XOR
¦	OR
&&	Logical AND
¦¦	Logical OR
? :	Shorthand for if...then...else (discussed on Day 5)
= += -= *= ÷= %= ^=	Various assignments
&= ¦= <<= >>= >>>=	

You can always change the order in which expressions are evaluated by using parentheses around the expressions you want to evaluate first. You can nest parentheses to make sure expressions evaluate in the order you want them to (the innermost parenthetical expression is evaluated first). The following expression results in a value of 5, because the 6 + 4 expression is evaluated first, and then the result of that expression (10) is divided by 2:

```
y = (6 + 4) / 2
```

Parentheses also can be useful in cases where the precedence of an expression isn't immediately clear—in other words, they can make your code easier to read. Adding parentheses doesn't hurt, so if they help you figure out how expressions are evaluated, go ahead and use them.

String Arithmetic

One special expression in Java is the use of the addition operator (+) to create and concatenate strings. In most of the previous examples shown today and in earlier lessons, you've seen lots of lines that looked something like this:

```
System.out.println(name + " is a " + color " beetle");
```

The output of that line (to the standard output) is a single string, with the values of the variables (here, name and color), inserted in the appropriate spots in the string. So what's going on here?

The + operator, when used with strings and other objects, creates a single string that contains the concatenation of all its operands. If any of the operands in string concatenation is not a string, it is automatically converted to a string, making it easy to create these sorts of output lines.

> **Technical Note:** An object or type can be converted to a string if you implement the method toString(). All objects have a default string representation (the name of the class followed by brackets), but most classes override toString() to provide a more meaningful printable representation.

String concatenation makes lines such as the previous one especially easy to construct. To create a string, just add all the parts together—the descriptions plus the variables—and output it to the standard output, to the screen, to an applet, or anywhere.

The += operator, which you learned about earlier, also works for strings. For example, take the following expression:

```
myName += " Jr.";
```

This expression is equivalent to this:

```
myName = myName + " Jr.";
```

just as it would be for numbers. In this case, it changes the value of myName (which might be something like John Smith to have a Jr. at the end (John Smith Jr.).

Summary

As you learned in the last two lessons, a Java program is made up primarily of classes and objects. Classes and objects, in turn, are made up of methods and variables, and methods are made up of statements and expressions. It is those last two things that you've learned about today; the basic building blocks that enable you to create classes and methods and build them up to a full-fledged Java program.

Today, you learned about variables, how to declare them and assign values to them; literals for easily creating numbers, characters, and strings; and operators for arithmetic, tests, and other simple operations. With this basic syntax, you can move on tomorrow to learning about working with objects and building simple useful Java programs.

To finish up this summary, Table 3.8 is a list of all the operators you learned about today so that you can refer back to them.

Table 3.8. Operator summary.

Operator	Meaning
+	Addition
–	Subtraction
*	Multiplication
÷	Division
%	Modulus
<	Less than
>	Greater than
	Less than or equal to
	Greater than or equal to
==	Equal
!=	Not equal
&&	Logical AND
¦¦	Logical OR
!	Logical NOT
&	AND
¦	OR
^	XOR
<<	Left shift
>>	Right shift
>>>	Zero fill right shift
~	Complement
=	Assignment
++	Increment
--	Decrement
+=	Add and assign
-=	Subtract and assign
*=	Multiply and assign
÷=	Divide and assign
%=	Modulus and assign
&=	AND and assign

continues

Table 3.8. continued

Operator	Meaning
¦=	OR and assign
<<=	Left shift and assign
>>=	Right shift and assign
>>>=	Zero fill right shift and assign

Q&A

Q I didn't see any way to define constants.

A You can't create local constants in Java; you can create only constant instance and class variables. You'll learn how to do this tomorrow.

Q What happens if you declare a variable to be some integer type and then give it a number outside the range of values that variable can hold?

A Logically, you would think that the variable is just converted to the next larger type, but this isn't what happens. What does happen is called *overflow*. This means that if a number becomes too big for its variable, that number wraps around to the smallest possible negative number for that type and starts counting upward toward zero again.

Because this can result in some very confusing (and wrong) results, make sure that you declare the right integer type for all your numbers. If there's a chance a number will overflow its type, use the next larger type instead.

Q How can you find out the type of a given variable?

A If you're using the base types (`int`, `float`, `boolean`), and so on, you can't. If you care about the type, you can convert the value to some other type by using casting (you'll learn about this tomorrow).

If you're using class types, you can use the `instanceof` operator, which you'll learn more about tomorrow.

Q Why does Java have all these shorthand operators for arithmetic and assignment? It's really hard to read that way.

A The syntax of Java is based on C++, and therefore on C. One of C's implicit goals is the capability of doing very powerful things with a minimum of typing. Because of this, shorthand operators, such as the wide array of assignments, are common.

There's no rule that says you have to use these operators in your own programs, however. If you find your code to be more readable using the long form, no one will come to your house and make you change it.

Working with Objects

by Laura Lemay

Let's start today's lesson with an obvious statement: because Java is an object-oriented language, you're going to be dealing with a lot of objects. You'll create them, modify them, move them around, change their variables, call their methods, combine them with other objects—and, of course, develop classes and use your own objects in the mix.

Today, therefore, you'll learn all about the Java object in its natural habitat. Today's topics include:

- ☐ Creating instances of classes
- ☐ Testing and modifying class and instance variables in your new instance
- ☐ Calling methods in that object
- ☐ Casting (converting) objects and other data types from one class to another
- ☐ Other odds and ends about working with objects
- ☐ An overview of the Java class libraries

Creating New Objects

When you write a Java program, you define a set of classes. As you learned on Day 2, classes are templates for objects; for the most part, you merely use the class to create instances and then work with those instances. In this section, therefore, you'll learn how to create a new object from any given class.

Remember strings from yesterday? You learned that using a string literal—a series of characters enclosed in double-quotes—creates a new instance of the class String with the value of that string.

The String class is unusual in that respect—although it's a class, there's an easy way to create instances of that class using a literal. The other classes don't have that shortcut; to create instances of those classes you have to do so explicitly by using the new operator.

Note: What about the literals for numbers and characters? Don't they create objects, too? Actually, they don't. The primitive data types for numbers and characters create numbers and characters, but for efficiency, they aren't actually objects. You can put object-wrappers around them if you need to treat them like objects (you'll learn how to do this later).

Using *new*

To create a new object, you use new with the name of the class you want to create an instance of, then parentheses after that:

```
String str = new String();

Random r = new Random();

Motorcycle m2 = new Motorcycle()
```

The parentheses are important; don't leave them off. The parentheses can be empty, in which case the most simple, basic object is created, or the parentheses can contain arguments that determine the initial values of instance variables or other initial qualities of that object. The number and type of arguments you can use with new are defined by the class itself by using a special method called a constructor; you'll learn about how to create constructors in your own classes later on this week.

Caution: Some classes may not enable you to create instances without any arguments. Check the class to make sure.

For example, take the Date class, which creates date objects. Listing 4.1 is a Java program that shows three different ways of creating a Date object using new:

Type

Listing 4.1. Laura's Date program.

```
 1: import java.util.Date;
 2:
 3: class CreateDates {
 4:
 5:     public static void main (String args[]) {
 6:         Date d1, d2, d3;
 7:
 8:         d1 = new Date();
 9:         System.out.println("Date 1: " + d1);
10:
11:         d2 = new Date(71, 7, 1, 7, 30);
12:         System.out.println("Date 2: " + d2);
13:
14:         d3 = new Date("April 3 1993 3:24 PM");
15:         System.out.println("Date 3: " + d3);
16:     }
17: }
```

```
Date 1: Sun Nov 26 19:10:56 PST 1995
Date 2: Sun Aug 01 07:30:00 PDT 1971
Date 3: Sat Apr 03 15:24:00 PST 1993
```

Analysis In this example, three different dates are created by using different arguments to new. The first instance (line 8) uses new with no arguments, which creates a Date object for today's date (as the first line of the output shows).

The second Date object you create in this example has five integer arguments. The arguments represent a date: year, month, day, hours, and seconds. And, as the output shows, this creates a Date object for that particular date: Sunday, August first, 1971, at 7:30 AM.

The third version of Date takes one argument, a string, representing the date as a text string. When the Date object is created, that string is parsed, and a Date object with that date and time is created (see the third line of output). The date string can take many different formats; see the API documentation for the Date class (part of the java.util package) for information about what strings you can use.

What *new* Does

What does new do? When you use the new operator, several things happen: first, the new instance of the given class is created, and memory is allocated for it. In addition (and most importantly), when the new object is created, a special method defined in the given class is called. This special method is called a constructor.

NEW☞ TERM *Constructors* are special methods for creating and initializing new instances of classes. Constructors initialize the new object and its variables, create any other objects that object needs, and generally perform any other operations the object needs to run.

Multiple constructor definitions in a class can each have a different number or type of arguments—then, when you use new, you can specify different arguments in the argument list, and the right constructor for those arguments will be called. That's how each of those different versions of new that were listed previously can create different things.

When you create your own classes, you can define as many constructors as you need to implement that class's behavior. You'll learn how to create constructors on Day 7.

A Note on Memory Management

Memory management in Java is dynamic and automatic. When you create a new object in Java, Java automatically allocates the right amount of memory for that object in the heap. You don't have to allocate any memory for any objects explicitly; Java does it for you.

What happens when you're finished with that object? How do you de-allocate the memory that object uses? The answer is again: memory management is automatic. Once you finish with an object, that object no longer has any live references to it (it won't be assigned to any variables you're still using or stored in any arrays). Java has a garbage collector that looks for unused objects and reclaims the memory that those objects are using. You don't have to do any explicit freeing of memory; you just have to make sure you're not still holding onto an object you want to get rid of. You'll learn more specific details about the Java garbage collector and how it works on Day 21.

Accessing and Setting Class and Instance Variables

Now you have your very own object, and that object may have class or instance variables defined in it. How do you work with those variables? Easy! Class and instance variables behave in exactly the same ways as the local variables you learned about yesterday; you just refer to them slightly differently than you do regular variables in your code.

Getting Values

To get at the value to an instance variable, you use dot notation.

NEW ☞ With *dot notation*, an instance or class variable name has two parts: the object on the left
TERM side of the dot, and the variable on the right side of the dot.

For example, if you have an object assigned to the variable myObject, and that object has a variable called var, you refer to that variable's value like this:

```
myObject.var;
```

This form for accessing variables is an expression (it returns a value), and both sides of the dot are also expressions. This means that you can nest instance variable access. If that var instance variable itself holds an object, and that object has its own instance variable called state, you can refer to it like this:

```
myObject.var.state;
```

Dot expressions are evaluated left to right, so you start with myObject's variable var, which points to another object with the variable state. You end up with the value of that state variable.

Changing Values

Assigning a value to that variable is equally easy—just tack an assignment operator on the right side of the expression:

```
myObject.var.state = true;
```

Listing 4.2 is an example of a program that tests and modifies the instance variables in a Point object. Point is part of the java.awt package and refers to a coordinate point with an x and a y value.

Type **Listing 4.2. The TestPoint Class.**

```
1: import java.awt.Point;
2:
3: class TestPoint {
4:
5:     public static void main (String args[]) {
6:         Point thePoint = new Point(10,10);
7:
8:         System.out.println("X is " + thePoint.x);
9:         System.out.println("Y is " + thePoint.y);
10:
11:         System.out.println("Setting X to 5.");
12:         thePoint.x = 5;
13:         System.out.println("Setting y to 15.");
14:         thePoint.y = 15;
15:
16:         System.out.println("X is " + thePoint.x);
17:         System.out.println("Y is " + thePoint.y);
18:
19:     }
20: }
```

```
X is 10
Y is 10
Setting X to 5.
Setting y to 15.
X is 5
Y is 15
```

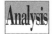 In this example, you first create an instance of Point where X and Y are both 10 (line 6). Lines 8 and 9 print out those individual values, and you can see dot notation at work there. Lines 11 through 14 change the values of those variables to 5 and 15, respectively. Finally, lines 16 and 17 print out the values of X and Y again to show how they've changed.

Class Variables

Class variables, as you learned before, are variables that are defined and stored in the class itself. Their values, therefore, apply to the class and to all its instances.

With instance variables, each new instance of the class gets a new copy of the instance variables that class defines. Each instance can then change the values of those instance variables without affecting any other instances. With class variables, there is only one copy of that variable. Every instance of the class has access to that variable, but there is only one value. Changing the value of that variable changes it for all the instances of that class.

You define class variables by including the `static` keyword before the variable itself. You'll learn more about this on Day 6. For example, take the following partial class definition:

```
class FamilyMember {
    static String surname = "Johnson";
    String name;
    int age;
    ...
}
```

Instances of the class `FamilyMember` each have their own values for name and age. But the class variable surname has only one value for all family members. Change surname, and all the instances of `FamilyMember` are affected.

To access class variables, you use the same dot notation as you do with instance variables. To get or change the value of the class variable, you can use either the instance or the name of the class on the left side of the dot. Both the lines of output in this example print the same value):

```
FamilyMember dad = new FamilyMember()
System.out.println("Family's surname is: " + dad.surname);
System.out.println("Family's surname is: " + FamilyMember.surname);
```

Because you can use an instance to change the value of a class variable, it's easy to become confused about class variables and where their values are coming from (remember, the value of a class variable affects all the instances). For this reason, it's a good idea to use the name of the class when you refer to a class variable—it makes your code easier to read and strange results easier to debug.

Calling Methods

Calling a method in objects is similar to referring to its instance variables: method calls also use dot notation. The object whose method you're calling is on the left side of the dot; the name of the method and its arguments is on the right side of the dot:

```
myObject.methodOne(arg1, arg2, arg3);
```

Note that all methods must have parentheses after them, even if that method takes no arguments:

```
myObject.methodNoArgs();
```

If the method you've called results in an object that itself has methods, you can nest methods as you would variables:

```
myObject.getClass().getName();
```

You can combine nested method calls and instance variable references as well:

```
myObject.var.methodTwo(arg1, arg2);
```

`System.out.println()`, the method you've been using all through the book this far, is a great example of nesting variables and methods. The `System` class (part of the `java.lang` package) describes system-specific behavior. `System.out` is a class variable that contains an instance of the class `PrintStream` that points to the standard output of the system. `PrintStream` instances have a `println()` method that prints a string to that output stream.

Listing 4.3 shows an example of calling some methods defined in the `String` class. Strings include methods for string tests and modification, similar to what you would expect in a string library in other languages.

Listing 4.3. Several Uses of `String` methods.

```
 1: class TestString {
 2:
 3:     public static void main (String args[]) {
 4:         String str = "Now is the winter of our discontent";
 5:
 6:         System.out.println("The string is: " + str);
 7:         System.out.println("Length of this string: "
 8:                 + str.length());
 9:         System.out.println("The character at position 5: "
10:                 + str.charAt(5));
11:         System.out.println("The substring from 11 to 18: "
12:                 + str.substring(11, 18));
13:         System.out.println("The index of the character d: "
14:                 + str.indexOf('d'));
15:         System.out.print("The index of the beginning of the ");
16:         System.out.println("substring \"winter\":"
17:                 + str.indexOf("winter"));
18:         System.out.println("The string in upper case: "
19:                 + str.toUpperCase());
20:     }
21: }
```

```
The string is: Now is the winter of our discontent
Length of this string: 35
The character at position 5: s
The substring from positions 11 to 18: winter
The index of the character d: 25
The index of the beginning of the substring "winter": 11
The string in upper case: NOW IS THE WINTER OF OUR DISCONTENT
```

Analysis In line 4, you create a new instance of `String` by using a string literal (it's easier that way than using `new` and then putting the characters in individually). The remainder of the program simply calls different string methods to do different operations on that string:

☐ Line 6 prints the value of the string we created in line 4: `"Now is the winter of our discontent"`.

- Line 7 calls the length() method in the new String object. This string has 35 characters.

- Line 9 calls the charAt() method, which returns the character at the given position in the string. Note that string positions start at 0, so the character at position 5 is s.

- Line 11 calls the substring() method, which takes two integers indicating a range and returns the substring at those starting and ending points. The substring() method can also be called with only one argument, which returns the substring from that position to the end of the string.

- Line 13 calls the indexOf() method, which returns the position of the first instance of the given character (here, 'd').

- Line 15 shows a different use of the indexOf() method, which takes a string argument and returns the index of the beginning of that string.

- Finally, line 18 uses the toUpperCase() method to return a copy of the string in all uppercase.

Class Methods

Class methods, like class variables, apply to the class as a whole and not to its instances. Class methods are commonly used for general utility methods that may not operate directly on an instance of that class, but fit with that class conceptually. For example, the String class contains a class method called valueOf(), which can take one of many different types of arguments (integers, booleans, other objects, and so on). The valueOf() method then returns a new instance of String containing the string value of the argument it was given. This method doesn't operate directly on an existing instance of String, but getting a string from another object or data type is definitely a String-like operation, and it makes sense to define it in the String class.

Class methods can also be useful for gathering general methods together in one place (the class). For example, the Math class, defined in the java.lang package, contains a large set of mathematical operations as class methods—there are no instances of the class Math, but you can still use its methods with numeric or boolean arguments.

To call a class method, use dot notation as you do with instance methods. As with class variables, you can use either an instance of the class or the class itself on the left site of the dot. However, for the same reasons noted in the discussion on class variables, using the name of the class for class variables makes your code easier to read. The last two lines in this example produce the same result:

```
String s, s2;
s = "foo";
s2 = s.valueOf(5);
s2 = String.valueOf(5);
```

References to Objects

As you work with objects, one important thing going on behind the scenes is the use of references to those objects. When you assign objects to variables, or pass objects as arguments to methods, you are passing references to those objects, not the objects themselves or copies of those objects.

An example should make this clearer. Examine the following snippet of code:

```java
import java.awt.Point;

class ReferencesTest {

    public static void main (String args[]) {
        Point pt1, pt2;
        pt1 = new Point(100, 100);
        pt2 = pt1;

        pt1.x = 200;
        pt1.y = 200;
        System.out.println("Point1: " + pt1.x + ", " + pt1.y);
        System.out.println("Point2: " + pt2.x + ", " + pt2.y);
    }
}
```

In this program, you declare two variables of type Point, and assign a new Point object to pt1. Then you assign the value of pt1 to pt2.

Now, here's the challenge. After changing pt1's x and y instance variables, what will pt2 look like?

Here's the output of that program:

```
Point1: 200, 200
Point2: 200, 200
```

As you can see, pt2 was also changed. When you assign the value of pt1 to pt2, you actually create a reference from p2 to the same object to which pt1 refers. Change the object that pt2 refers to, and you also change the object that pt1 points to, because both are references to the same object.

Figure 4.1.

References.

The fact that Java uses references becomes particularly important when you pass arguments to methods. You'll learn more about this later on today, but keep these references in mind.

> **Technical Note:** There are no explicit pointers or pointer arithmetic in Java—just references. However, because of Java references, you have most of the capabilities that you have with pointers without the confusion and lurking bugs that explicit pointers can create.

Casting and Converting Objects and Primitive Types

Sometimes in your Java programs you may have a value stored somewhere that is the wrong type. Maybe it's an instance of the wrong class, or perhaps it's a `float` and you want it to be an `int`, or it's an integer and you want it to be a string. To convert the value of one type to another, you use a mechanism called casting.

NEW☞
TERM *Casting* is a mechanism of converting the value of an object or primitive type into another type. The result of a cast is a new object or value; casting does not affect the original object or value.

Although the concept of casting is a simple one, the rules for what types in Java can be converted to what other types are complicated by the fact that Java has both primitive types (`int`, `float`, `boolean`), and object types (`String`, `Point`, `Window`, and so on). Because of these three types, there are three forms of casts and conversions to talk about in this section:

☐ Casting between primitive types: `int` to `float` to `boolean`

☐ Casting between object types: an instance of a class to an instance of another class

☐ Converting primitive types to objects and then extracting primitive values back out of those objects

Casting Primitive Types

Casting between primitive types enables you to "convert" the value of one type to another primitive type—for example, to assign a number of one type to a variable of another type. Casting between primitive types most commonly occurs with the numeric types; boolean values cannot be cast to any other primitive type. You can, however, cast 1 or 0 to boolean values.

Often, if the type you are casting to is "larger" than the type of the value you're converting, you may not have to use an explicit cast. You can often automatically treat a byte or a character as an `int`, for example, or an `int` as a `long`, an `int` as a `float`, or anything as a `double` automatically. In this case, because the larger type provides more precision than the smaller, no loss of information occurs when the value is cast.

To convert a large value to smaller type, you must use an explicit cast, because converting that value may result in a loss of precision. Explicit casts look like this:

```
(typename) value
```

In this form, *typename* is the name of the type you're converting to (for example: short, int, float, boolean), and *value* is an expression that results in the value you want to convert. This expression divides the values of x by the value of y and casts the result to an int:

```
(int) (x / y);
```

Note that because the precedence of casting is higher than that of arithmetic, you have to use parentheses so that the result of the division is what gets cast to an int.

Casting Objects

Instances of classes can also be cast to instances of other classes, with one restriction: the class of the object you're casting and the class you're casting it to must be related by inheritance; that is, you can cast an object only to an instance of its class's sub- or superclass—not to any random class.

Analogous to converting a primitive value to a larger type, some objects may not need to be cast explicitly. In particular, because instances' subclasses usually contain all the information that instances' superclasses do, you can use an instance of a subclass anywhere a superclass is expected. Suppose you have a method that takes two arguments: one of type Object, and one of type Number. You don't have to pass instances of those particular classes to that method. For the Object argument, you can pass any subclass of Object (any object, in other words), and for the Number argument you can pass in any instance of any subclass of Number (Integer, Boolean, Float, and so on).

Casting an object to an instance of one of that object's superclasses loses the information the original subclass provided and requires a specific cast. To cast an object to another class, you use the same casting operation that you used for base types:

```
(classname) object
```

In this case, *classname* is the name of the class you want to cast the object to, and *object* is a reference to the object you're casting. Note that casting creates a new instance of the new class with all the information that the old object contained; the old object still continues to exist as it did before.

Here's a (fictitious) example of a cast of an instance of the class GreenApple to an instance of the class Apple (where GreenApple is theoretically a subclass of Apple):

```
GreenApple a;
Apple a2;
```

```
a = new GreenApple();
a2 = (Apple) a;
```

In addition to casting objects to classes, you can also cast objects to interfaces—but only if that object's class or one of its superclasses actually implements that interface. Casting an object to an interface then enables you to call one of that interface's methods even if that object's class does not directly implement that interface. You'll learn more about interfaces in Week 3.

Converting Primitive Types to Objects and Vice Versa

Now you know how to cast a primitive type to another primitive type and how to cast between classes. How can you cast one to the other?

You can't! Primitive types and objects are very different things in Java and you can't automatically cast or convert between the two. However, the java.lang package includes several special classes that correspond to each primitive data type: Integer for ints, Float for floats, Boolean for booleans, and so on.

Using class methods defined in these classes, you can create an object-equivalent for all the primitive types using new. The following line of code creates an instance of the Integer class with the value 35:

```
Integer intObject = new Integer(35);
```

Once you have actual objects, you can treat those values as objects. Then, when you want the primitive values back again, there are methods for that as well—for example, the intValue() method extracts an int primitive value from an Integer object:

```
int theInt = intObject.intValue();  // returns 35
```

See the Java API documentation for these special classes for specifics on the methods for converting primitives to and from objects.

Odds and Ends

This section is a catchall for other information about working with objects, in particular:

- ☐ Comparing objects
- ☐ Copying objects
- ☐ Finding out the class of any given object
- ☐ Testing to see whether an object is an instance of a given class

Comparing Objects

Yesterday, you learned about operators for comparing values: equals, not equals, less than, and so on. Most of these operators work only on primitive types, not on objects. If you try to use other values as operands, the Java compiler produces errors.

The exception to this rule is with the operators for equality: == (equal) and != (not equal). These operators, when used with objects, tests whether the two operands refer to exactly the same object.

What should you do if you want to be able to compare instances of your class and have meaningful results? You have to implement special methods in your class, and you have to call those methods using those method names.

> **Technical Note:** Java does not have the concept of operator overloading—that is, the capability of defining the behavior of the built-in operators by defining methods in your own classes. The built-in operators remain defined only for numbers.

A good example of this is the String class. It is possible to have two strings, two independent objects in memory with the same values—that is, the same characters in the same order. According to the == operator, however, those two String objects will not be equal, because although their contents are the same, they are not the same object.

The String class, therefore, defines a method called equals() that tests each character in the string and returns true if the two strings have the same values. Listing 4.4 illustrates this.

Type

Listing 4.4. A Test of String Equality.

```
 1: class EqualsTest {
 2:
 3:     public static void main (String args[]) {
 4:         String str1, str2;
 5:         str1 = "she sells sea shells by the sea shore.";
 6:         str2 = str1;
 7:
 8:         System.out.println("String1: " + str1);
 9:         System.out.println("String2: " + str2);
10:         System.out.println("Same object? " + (str1 == str2));
11:
12:         str2 = new String(str1);
13:
14:         System.out.println("String1: " + str1);
15:         System.out.println("String2: " + str2);
16:         System.out.println("Same object? " + (str1 == str2));
17:         System.out.println("Same value? " + str1.equals(str2));
18:     }
19: }
```

```
String1: she sells sea shells by the sea shore.
String2: she sells sea shells by the sea shore.
Same object? true
String1: she sells sea shells by the sea shore.
String2: she sells sea shells by the sea shore.
Same object? false
Same value? true
```

The first part of this program (lines 4 through 6) declares two variables, str1 and str2, assigns the literal she sells sea shells by the sea shore. to str1, and then assigns that value to str2. As you know from object references, now str1 and str2 point to the same object, and the test at line 10 proves that.

In the second part, you create a new string object with the value of str1. Now you have two different string objects with the same value. Testing them to see whether they're the same object by using the == operator (line 16) returns the expected answer, as does testing them using the equals method (line 17) to compare their values.

> **Technical Note:** Why can't you just use another literal when you change str2, rather than using new? String literals are optimized in Java—if you create a string using a literal, and then use another literal with the same characters, Java knows enough merely to give you the first String object back. Both strings are the same objects—to create two separate objects you have to go out of your way.

4

Copying Objects

Recall from the section on object references that assigning variables and passing objects as arguments to methods affect only the object's reference and doesn't create copies of those objects. How do you create copies of objects? There are two ways: the copy() method and the clone() method.

The copy() method (defined in Object, and so available to all objects), takes a single argument—another instance of the same class—and copies the values of all the argument's instance variables into the instance variables of the current object (the one in which you're calling the method). Note that if those instance variables in turn hold references to objects, only the references are copied, not the objects.

```
Point pt1, pt2, pt3;
pt1 = new Point(0,0);
pt2 = new Point(100,100);

pt2.copy(pt1); // pt1's values are copied into pt2; both now are (0,0).
```

The clone() method is similar to copy(), except that clone() takes no arguments. The clone() method creates a new instance of the same class as the source object and then copies the values of the instance variables (either primitive types or references to other objects). clone() returns an instance of the class Object; to use it as an instance of the original class you have to cast it. Here's an example that clones the Point object in pt2 and stores the result in pt3:

```
pt3 = (Point) pt2.clone();
```

Determining the Class of an Object

Want to find out the class of an object? Here's the way to do it for an object assigned to the variable obj:

```
String name = obj.getClass().getName();
```

What does this do? The getClass() method is defined in the Object class, and as such is available for all objects. The result of that method is a Class object (where Class is itself a class), which has a method called getName(). getName() returns a string representing the name of the class.

Another test that might be useful to you is the instanceof operator. instanceof has two operands: an object on the left, and the name of a class on the right. The expression returns true or false based on whether the object is an instance of the named class or any of that class's superclasses:

```
"foo" instanceof String // true
Point pt = new Point(10,10);
pt instanceof String // false
```

The instanceof operator can also be used for interfaces; if an object implements an interface, the instanceof operator with an interface name on the right side returns true. You'll learn all about interfaces in Week 3.

The Java Class Libraries

To finish up today, let's look at the some of the Java class libraries. Actually, you've had some experience with them already, so they shouldn't seem that strange.

The Java class libraries provide the set of classes that are guaranteed to be available in any commercial Java environment (for example, in HotJava or in Netscape 2.0). Those classes are in the java package and include all the classes you've seen so far in this book, plus a whole lot more classes you'll learn about later on in this book (and more you may not learn about at all).

The Java Developer's Kit comes with documentation for all the Java class libraries, which includes descriptions of each class's instance variables, methods, constructors, interfaces, and so on. A shorter summary of the Java API is in Appendix B as well. Exploring the Java class libraries and their methods and instance variables is a great way to figure out what Java can and cannot do, as well as a starting point for your own development.

Here are the class packages that are part of the Java class libraries:

- [ ] `java.lang`: Classes that apply to the language itself, which includes the `Object` class, the `String` class, and the `System` class. It also contains the special classes for the primitive types (`Integer`, `Character`, `Float`, and so on).

- [ ] `java.util`: Utility classes, such as `Date`, as well as simple collection classes, such as `Vector` and `Hashtable`.

- [ ] `java.io`: Input and output classes for writing to and reading from streams (such as standard input and output) and for handling files.

- [ ] `java.net`: Classes for networking support, including `Socket` and `URL` (a class to represent references to documents on the World Wide Web).

- [ ] `java.awt`: *(the Abstract Window Toolkit):* Classes to implement a graphical user interface, including classes for `Window`, `Menu`, `Button`, `Font`, `CheckBox`, and so on. This package also includes classes for processing images (the `java.awt.Image` package).

- [ ] `java.applet`: Classes to implement Java applets, including the `Applet` class itself, as well as the `AudioClip` class.

In addition to the Java classes, your development environment may also include additional classes that provide other utilities or functionality. Although these classes may be useful, because they are not part of the standard Java library, they won't be available to other people trying to run your Java program. This is particularly important for applets, because applets are expected to be able to run on any platform, using any Java-aware browser. Only classes inside the java package are guaranteed to be available on all browsers and Java environments.

Summary

Objects, objects everywhere. Today, you learned all about how to deal with objects: how to create them, how to find out and change the values of their variables, and how to call their methods. You also learned how to copy and compare them, and how to convert them into other objects. Finally, you learned a bit about the Java class libraries—which give you a whole slew of classes to play with in your own programs.

You now have the fundamentals of how to deal with most simple things in the Java language. All you have left are arrays, conditionals, and loops, which you'll learn about tomorrow. Then you'll learn how to define and use classes in Java applications on Day 6, and launch directly into applets next week. With just about everything you do in your Java programs, you'll always come back to objects.

Q&A

Q I'm confused about the differences between objects and the primitive data types, such as `int` and `boolean`.

A The primitive types in the language (`byte`, `short`, `int`, `long`, `float`, `double`, and `char`) represent the smallest things in the language. They are not objects, although in many ways they can be handled like objects—they can be assigned to variables and passed in and out of methods. Most of the operations that work exclusively on objects, however, will not.

Objects usually represent instances of classes and as such, are much more complex data types than simple numbers and characters, often containing numbers and characters as instance or class variables.

Q In the section on calling methods, you had examples of calling a method with a different number of arguments each time—and it gave a different kind of result. How is that possible?

A That's called *method overloading*. Overloading enables the same function name to have different behavior based on the arguments it's called with—and the number and type of arguments can vary. When you define methods in your own classes, you define separate method signatures with different sets or arguments and different definitions. When that method is called, Java figures out which definition to execute based on the number and type of arguments with which you called it.

You'll learn all about this on Day 6.

Q No operator overloading in Java? Why not? I thought Java was based on C++, and C++ has operator overloading.

A Java was indeed based on C++, but it was also designed to be simple, so many of C++'s features have been removed. The argument against operator overloading is that because the operator can be defined to mean anything, it makes it very difficult to figure out what any given operator is doing at any one time. This can result in entirely unreadable code. Given the potential for abuse, the designers of Java felt it was one of the C++ features that was best left out.

Arrays, Conditionals, and Loops

by Laura Lemay

Although you could write Java programs using what you've learned so far, those programs would be pretty dull. Much of the good stuff in Java or in any programming language results when you have arrays to store values in and control-flow constructs (loops and conditionals) to execute different bits of a program based on tests. Today, you'll find out about the following:

☐ Arrays, one of the most useful objects in Java, which enable you to collect objects into an easy-to-manage list

☐ Block statements, for grouping together related statements

☐ `if` and `switch`, for conditional tests

☐ `for` and `while` loops, for iteration or repeating a statement or statements multiple times

Arrays

Arrays in Java are different than they are in other languages. Arrays in Java are actual objects that can be passed around and treated just like other objects.

NEW☞ TERM *Arrays* are a way to store a list of items. Each element of the array holds an individual item, and you can place items into and remove items from those slots as you need to.

Arrays can contain any type of value (base types or objects), but you can't store different types in a single array. You can have an array of integers, or an array of strings, or an array of arrays, but you can't have an array that contains, for example, both strings and integers.

To create an array in Java, you use three steps:

1. Declare a variable to hold the array.

2. Create a new array object and assign it to the array variable.

3. Store things in that array.

Declaring Array Variables

The first step to creating an array is creating a variable that will hold the array, just as you would any other variable. Array variables indicate the type of object the array will hold (just as they do for any variable) and the name of the array, followed by empty brackets (`[]`). The following are all typical array variable declarations:

```
String difficultWords[];

Point hits[];

int temps[];
```

An alternate method of defining an array variable is to put the brackets after the type instead of after the variable. They are equivalent, but this latter form is often much more readable. So, for example, these three declarations could be written like this:

```
String[] difficultWords;

Point[] hits;

int[] temps;
```

Creating Array Objects

The second step is to create an array object and assign it to that variable. There are two ways to do this:

☐ Using new
☐ Directly initializing the contents of that array

The first way is to use the new operator to create a new instance of an array:

```
String[] names = new String[10];
```

That line creates a new array of Strings with ten *slots*, or elements. When you create the new array object using new, you must indicate how many elements that array will hold.

Array objects can contain primitive types such as integers or booleans, just as they can contain objects:

```
int[] temps = new int[99];
```

When you create an array object using new, all its elements are initialized for you (0 for numeric arrays, false for boolean, '\0' for character arrays, and null for everything else). You can also create and initialize an array at the same time. Instead of using new to create the new array object, enclose the elements of the array inside braces, separated by commas:

```
String[] chiles = { "jalapeno", "anaheim", "serrano,"
    "habanero," "thai" };
```

Each of the elements inside the braces must be of the same type and must be the same type as the variable that holds that array. An array the size of the number of elements you've included will be automatically created for you. This example creates an array of String objects named chiles that contains five elements.

Accessing Array Elements

Once you have an array with initial values, you can test and change the values in each slot of that array. To get at a value stored within an array, use the array subscript expression:

```
myArray[subscript];
```

The *myArray* part of this expression is a variable holding an array object, although it can also be an expression that results in an array). The *subscript* is the slot within the array to access, which can also be an expression. Array subscripts start with 0, as they do in C and C++. So, an array with ten elements has array values from subscript 0 to 9.

Note that all array subscripts are checked to make sure that they are inside the boundaries of the array (greater than 0 but less than the array's length) either when your Java program is compiled or when it is run. It is impossible in Java to access or assign a value to an array element outside of the boundaries of the array. Note the following two statements, for example:

```
String arr[] = new String[10];
arr[10] = "eggplant";
```

A program with that last statement in it produces a compiler error at that line when you try to compile it. The array stored in arr has only ten elements numbered from 0, the element at subscript 10 doesn't exist, and the Java compiler will check for that.

If the array subscript is calculated at run-time (for example, as part of a loop) and ends up outside the boundaries of the array, the Java interpreter also produces an error (actually, to be technically correct, it throws an exception). You'll learn more about exceptions later on next week and on Day 18.

How can you keep from overrunning the end of an array accidentally in your own programs? You can test for the length of the array in your programs using the length instance variable—it's available for all array objects, regardless of type:

```
int len = arr.length // returns 10
```

Changing Array Elements

To assign a value to a particular array slot, merely put an assignment statement after the array access expression:

```
myarray[1] = 15;
sentence[0] = "The";
sentence[10] = sentence[0];
```

An important thing to note is that an array of objects in Java is an array of references to those objects (similar in some ways to an array of pointers in C or C++). When you assign a value to a slot in an array, you're creating a reference to that object, just as you do for a plain variable. When you move values around inside arrays (as in that last line), you just reassign the reference; you don't copy the value from one slot to another. Arrays of primitive types such as ints or floats do copy the values from one slot to another.

Arrays of references to objects, as opposed to the objects themselves, are particularly useful because it means you can have multiple references to the same objects both inside and outside arrays—for example, you can assign an object contained in an array to a variable and refer to that same object by using either the variable or the array position.

Multidimensional Arrays

Java does not support multidimensional arrays. However, you can declare and create an array of arrays (and those arrays can contain arrays, and so on, for however many dimensions you need), and access them as you would C-style multidimensional arrays:

```
int coords[][] = new int[12][12];
coords[0][0] = 1;
coords[0][1] = 2;
```

Block Statements

A block statement is a group of other statements surrounded by braces ({}). You can use a block anywhere a single statement would go, and the new block creates a new local scope for the statements inside it. This means that you can declare and use local variables inside a block, and those variables will cease to exist after the block is finished executing. For example, here's a block inside a method definition that declares a new variable y. You cannot use y outside the block in which it's declared:

```
void testblock() {
    int x = 10;
    { // start of block
      int y = 50;
      System.out.println("inside the block:");
      System.out.println("x:" + x);
      System.out.println("y:" + y);
    } // end of block
}
```

Blocks are not usually used in this way—alone in a method definition. You've mostly seen blocks up to this point surrounding class and method definitions, but another very common use of block statements is in the control flow constructs you'll learn about in the remainder of today's lesson.

if Conditionals

The if conditional, which enables you to execute different bits of code based on a simple test in Java, is nearly identical to if statements in C. if conditionals contain the keyword if, followed by a boolean test, followed by a statement (often a block statement) to execute if the test is true:

```
if (x < y)
    System.out.println("x is smaller than y");
```

An optional else keyword provides the statement to execute if the test is false:

```
if (x < y)
    System.out.println("x is smaller than y");
else System.out.println("y is bigger.");
```

Technical Note: The difference between `if` conditionals in Java and C or C++ is that the test must return a boolean value (true or false). Unlike in C, the test cannot return an integer.

```
if (engineState == true )
    System.out.println("Engine is already on.");
else {
    System.out.println("Now starting Engine");
    if (gasLevel >= 1)
        engineState = true;
    else System.out.println("Low on gas! Can't start engine.");
}
```

This example uses the test (`engineState == false`). For boolean tests of this type, a common shortcut is merely to include the first part of the expression, rather than explicitly testing its value against true or false:

```
if (engineState)
    System.out.println("Engine is on.");
else System.out.println("Engine is off");
```

The Conditional Operator

An alternative to using the `if` and `else` keywords in a conditional statement is to use the conditional operator, sometimes called the ternary operator.

NEW 🖝   A *conditional operator* is a *ternary operator* because it has three terms.
TERM

The conditional operator is an expression, meaning that it returns a value (unlike the more general `if`, which can result in any statement or block being executed). The conditional operator is most useful for very short or simple conditionals, and looks like this:

test ? trueresult : falseresult

The *test* is an expression that returns true or false, just like the test in the `if` statement. If the test is true, the conditional operator returns the value of *trueresult*; if it's false, it returns the value of *falseresult*. For example, the following conditional tests the values of x and y, returns the smaller of the two, and assigns that value to the variable `smaller`:

```
int smaller = x < y ? x : y;
```

The conditional operator has a very low precedence; that is, it's usually evaluated only after all its subexpressions are evaluated. The only operators lower in precedence are the assignment operators. See the precedence chart in Day 3's lesson for a refresher on precedence of all the operators.

switch Conditionals

A common practice in programming in any language is to test a variable against some value, and if it doesn't match that value, to test it again against a different value, and if it doesn't match that one to make yet another test, and so on. Using only `if` statements, this can become unwieldy, depending on how it's formatted and how many different options you have to test. For example, you might end up with a set of `if` statements something like this or longer:

```
if (oper == '+')
  addargs(arg1,arg2);
else if (oper == '=')
   subargs(arg1,arg2);
else if (oper == '*')
   multargs(arg1,arg2);
else if (oper == '/')
   divargs(arg1,arg2);
```

This form of `if` statement is called a nested `if`, because each `else` statement in turn contains yet another `if`, and so on, until all possible tests have been made.

A common shorthand mechanism for nested `if`s that you can use in some cases allows you tests and actions together in a single statement. This is the `switch` or `case` statement; in Java it's `switch` and behaves as it does in C:

```
switch (test) {
    case valueOne:
            resultOne;
      break;
    case valueTwo:
            resultTwo;
      break;
    case valueThree:
            resultThree;
      break;
    ...
    default: defaultresult;
}
```

In the `switch` statement, the test (a primitive type of `byte`, `char`, `short`, or `int`) is compared with each of the case values in turn. If a match is found, the statement, or statements after the test is executed. If no match is found, the `default` statement is executed. The `default` is optional, so if there isn't a match in any of the cases and `default` doesn't exist, the `switch` statement completes without doing anything.

Note that the significant limitation of the `switch` in Java is that the tests and values can be only simple primitive types (and then only primitive types that are castable to `int`). You cannot use larger primitive types (`long`, `float`) or objects within a `switch`, nor can you test for any relationship other than equality. This limits the usefulness of `switch` to all but the simplest cases; nested `if`s can work for any kind of test on any type.

Here's a simple example of a `switch` statement similar to the nested `if` shown earlier:

```
switch (oper) {
    case '+':
        addargs(arg1,arg2);
        break;
    case '*':
        subargs(arg1,arg2);
        break;
    case '-':
        multargs(arg1,arg2);
        break;
    case '/':
        divargs(arg1,arg2);
        break;
 }
```

Note the `break` statement included in every line. Without the explicit break, once a match is made, the statements for that match and also all the statements further down in the `switch` are executed until a `break` or the end of the `switch` is found (and then execution continues after the end of the `switch`). In some cases, this may be exactly what you want to do, but in most cases, you'll want to make sure to include the `break` so that only the statements you want to be executed are executed.

One handy use of falling through occurs when you want multiple values to execute the same statements. In this instance, you can use multiple case lines with no result, and the `switch` will execute the first statements it finds. For example, in the following `switch` statement, the string `"x is an even number."` is printed if x has values of 2, 4, 6, or 8. All other values of x print the string `"x is an odd number."`

```
switch (x) {
    case 2:
    case 4:
    case 6:
    case 8:
        System.out.println("x is an even number.");
        break;
    default: System.out.println("x is an odd number.");
}
```

for Loops

The `for` loop, as in C, repeats a statement or block of statements some number of times until a condition is matched. `for` loops are frequently used for simple iteration in which you repeat a block of statements a certain number of times and then stop, but you can use `for` loops for just about any kind of loop.

The `for` loop in Java looks roughly like this:

```
for (initialization; test; increment){
```

```
        statements;
}
```

The start of the for loop has three parts:

☐ initialization is an expression that initializes the start of the loop. If you have a loop index, this expression might declare and initialize it, for example, int i = 0. Variables that you declare in this part of the for loop are local to the loop itself; they cease existing after the loop is finished executing. (This is different from C or C++.)

☐ test is the test that occurs after each pass of the loop. The test must be a boolean expression or function that returns a boolean value, for example, i < 10. If the test is true, the loop executes. Once the test is false, the loop stops executing.

☐ increment is any expression or function call. Commonly, the increment is used to change the value of the loop index to bring the state of the loop closer to returning false and completing.

The statement part of the for loop is the statement that is executed each time the loop iterates. Just as with if, you can include either a single statement here or a block; the previous example used a block because that is more common. Here's an example of a for loop that initializes all the values of a String array to null strings:

```
String strArray[] = new String[10];
int i; // loop index

for (i = 0; i < strArray.length; i++)
    strArray[i] = "";
```

Any of the parts of the for loop can be empty statements, that is, you can simply include a semicolon with no expression or statement, and that part of the for loop will be ignored. Note that if you do use a null statement in your for loop, you may have to initialize or increment any loop variables or loop indices yourself elsewhere in the program.

You can also have an empty statement for the body of your for loop, if everything you want to do is in the first line of that loop. For example, here's one that finds the first prime number higher than 4000:

```
for (i = 4001; notPrime(i); i += 2)
    ;
```

Note that a common mistake in C that also occurs in Java is accidentally to put a semicolon after the first line of the for loop:

```
for (i = 0; i < 10; i++);
    System.out.println("Loop!");
```

Because the first semicolon ends the loop with an empty statement, the loop doesn't actually do anything. The println function will be printed only once, because it's actually outside the for loop entirely. Be careful not to make this mistake in your own Java programs.

5

while and *do* Loops

Finally, there are while and do loops. while and do loops, like for loops, enable a block of Java code to be executed repeatedly until a specific condition is met. Whether you use a for loop, a while, or a do is mostly a matter of your programming style.

while and do loops, like for, are exactly the same as those same constructions in C and C++.

while Loops

The while loop is used to repeat a statement or block of statements as long as a particular condition is true. while loops look like this:

```
while (condition){
    bodyOfLoop;
}
```

The *condition* is a boolean expression. If it returns true, the while loop executes the statements in bodyOfLoop and then tests the condition again, repeating until the condition is false. I've shown the while loop here with a block statement, because it's most commonly used, although you can use a single statement in place of the block.

Here's an example of a while loop that copies the elements of an array of integers (in array1) to an array of floats (in array2), casting each element to a float as it goes. The one catch is that if any of the elements in the first array is 0, the loop will immediately exit at that point. To cover both the cases wherein all the elements have been copied and an element is 0, you can use a compound test with the && operator:

```
while ((ch != ' ') && (ch != '\t') && (ch != '\n') && (ch != '\r')) {
    addChar(ch, theName);
    ch = instream.read();
}
```

Note that if the condition is initially false the first time it is tested (for example, if the first element in that first array is 0), the body of the while loop will never be executed. If you need to execute the loop at least once, you can do one of two things:

- ☐ Duplicate the body of the loop outside the while loop.
- ☐ Use a do loop (described below).

The do loop is considered the better solution of the two.

do...while Loops

The do loop is just like a while loop, except that do executes a given statement or block until a condition is false. The main difference is that while loops test the condition before looping, making it possible that the body of the loop will never execute if the condition is false the first time it's tested. do loops run the body of the loop at least once before testing the condition. do loops look like this:

```
do {
    bodyOfLoop;
} while (condition);
```

Here, the bodyOfLoop part is the statements that are executed with each iteration. It's shown here with a block statement because it's most commonly used that way, but you can substitute the braces for a single statement as you can with the other control-flow constructs. The condition is a boolean test. If it returns true, the loop is run again. If it returns false, the loop exits. Keep in mind that with do loops, the body of the loop executes at least once.

Here's a simple example of a do loop that prints a message each time the loop iterates:

```
int x = 1;
do {
    System.out.println("Looping, round " + x);
    x++;
} while (x <= 10);
```

Here's the output of these statements:

```
Looping, round 1
Looping, round 2
Looping, round 3
Looping, round 4
Looping, round 5
Looping, round 6
Looping, round 7
Looping, round 8
Looping, round 9
Looping, round 10
```

Breaking Out of Loops

In all the loops (for, while, and do), the loop ends when the condition you're testing for is met. What happens if something odd occurs within the body of the loop and you want to exit the loop early? For that, you can use the break and continue keywords.

You've already seen break as part of the switch statement; it stops execution of the switch, and the program continues. The break keyword, when used with a loop, does the same thing—it immediately halts execution of the current loop. If you've nested loops within loops, execution picks up in the next outer loop; otherwise, the program merely continues executing the next statement after the loop.

For example, suppose you have a while loop that copies elements from one array into another. Each element in the array should be copied until the end of the array is reached or if an element contains 0. You can test for that latter case inside the body of the while and then use a break to exit the loop:

```
while (count < array1.length) {
    if (array1[count] == 0) {
        break;
    }
    array2[count] = array1[count];
    count++;
    }
}
```

continue is similar to break except that instead of halting execution of the loop entirely, the loop starts over at the next iteration. For do and while loops, this means the execution of the clock starts over again; for for loops, the increment expression is evaluated and then block is executed. continue is useful when you want to special-case elements within a loop. With the previous example of copying one array to another, you can test for whether the current element is 0 and restart the loop if you find it so that the resulting array will never contain zero. Note that because you're skipping elements in the first array, you now have to keep track of two different array counters:

```
while (count < array1.length) {
    if (array1[count] == 0)
        continue;

    array2[count2++] = (float)array1[count++];
}
```

Labeled Loops

Both break and continue can have an optional label that tells Java where to break to. Without a label, break jumps outside the nearest loop (to an enclosing loop or to the next statement outside the loop), and continue restarts the enclosing loop. Using labeled breaks and continues enables you to break outside nested loops or to continue a loop outside the current loop.

To use a labeled loop, add the label before the initial part of the loop, with a colon between them. Then, when you use break or continue, add the name of the label after the keyword itself:

```
out:
    for (int i = 0; i <10; i++) {
        while (x < 50) {
            if (i * x == 400)
                break out;
            ...
        }
        ...
    }
```

In this snippet of code, the label out labels the outer for loop. Then, inside both the for and the while loop, if a particular condition is met inside both loops, a break causes the execution to creak out of both loops and restart back at the label (out).

Here's another example. the following program contains a nested for loop. Inside the innermost loop, if the sum values of the two counters is greater than four, both loops exit at once:

```
foo:
    for (int i = 1; i <= 5; i++)
        for (int j = 1; j <= 3; j++) {
            System.out.println("i is " + i + ", j is " + j);
            if ((i + j) > 4)
                break foo;
        }
System.out.println("end of loops");
```

Here's the output from this program:

```
i is 1, j is 1
i is 1, j is 2
i is 1, j is 3
i is 2, j is 1
i is 2, j is 2
i is 2, j is 3
end of loops
```

As you can see, the loop iterated until the sum of i and j was greater than 4, and then both loops exited back to the outer block and the final message was printed.

Summary

Today, you learned about three main topics that you'll most likely use quite often in your own Java programs: arrays, conditionals, and loops.

You learned how to declare an array variable, create and assign an array object to that variable, and access and change elements within that array.

Conditionals include the `if` and `switch` statements, with which you can branch to different parts of your program based on a boolean test.

Finally, you learned about the `for`, `while`, and `do` loops, each of which enable you to execute a portion of your program repeatedly until a given condition is met.

Now that you've learned the small stuff, all that's left is to go over the bigger issues of declaring classes and creating methods within which instances of those classes can communicate with each other by calling methods. Get to bed early tonight, because tomorrow is going to be a wild ride.

Q&A

Q **If arrays are objects, and you use `new` to create them, and they have an instance variable `length`, where is the `Array` class? I didn't see it in the Java class libraries.**

A Arrays are implemented kind of weirdly in Java. The `Array` class is constructed automatically when your Java program runs; `Array` provides the basic framework for arrays, including the `length` variable. Additionally, each primitive type and object has an implicit subclass of `Array` that represents an array of that class or object. When you create a new array object, it may not have an actual class, but it behaves as if it does.

Q **Does Java have `goto`s?**

A The Java language defines the keyword `goto`, but it is not currently used for anything. In other words, no, Java does not have `goto`s.

Q **I declared a variable inside a block statement for an `if`. When the `if` was done, the definition of that variable vanished. Where did it go?**

A In technical terms, block statements inside braces form a new lexical scope. What this means is that if you declare a variable inside a block, it's only visible and usable inside that block. Once the block finishes executing, all the variables you declared go away.

It's a good idea to declare most of your variables in the outermost block in which they'll be needed—usually at the top of a block statement. The exception might be very simple variables, such as index counters in `for` loops, where declaring them in the first line of the `for` loop is an easy shortcut.

You'll learn more about variables and scope tomorrow.

Q **What can't you use `switch` with strings?**

A Strings are objects, and `switch` in Java works only for the primitive types that can be cast to integers (`byte`, `char`, `short`, and `int`). To compare strings, you have to use nested `if`s, which enable more general expression tests, including string comparison.

Q It seems to me that a lot of `for` loops could be written as `while` loops, and vice versa.

A True. The `for` loop is actually a special case of `while` that enables you to iterate a loop a specific number of times. You could just as easily do this with a `while` and then increment a counter inside the loop. Either works equally well. This is mostly just a question of programming style and personal choice.

5

Creating Classes
and Applications
in Java

By Laura Lemay

In just about every lesson up to this point you've been creating Java applications—writing classes, creating instance variables and methods, and running those applications to perform simple tasks. Also up to this point, you've focused either on the very broad (general object-oriented theory) or the very minute (arithmetic and other expressions). Today, you pull it all together and learn how and why to create classes by using the following basics:

- ☐ The parts of a class definition
- ☐ Declaring and using instance variables
- ☐ Defining and using methods
- ☐ Creating Java applications, including the `main()` method and how to pass arguments to a Java program from a command line

Defining Classes

Defining classes is pretty easy; you've seen how to do it a bunch of times in previous lessons. To define a class, use the `class` keyword and the name of the class:

```
class MyClassName {
...
}
```

If this class is a subclass of another class, use `extends` to indicate the superclass of this class:

```
class myClassName extends mySuperClassName {
...
}
```

If this class implements a specific interface, use `implements` to refer to that interface:

```
class MyRunnableClassName implements Runnable {
...
}
```

Both `extends` and `implements` are optional. You'll learn about using and defining interfaces in Week 3.

Creating Instance and Class Variables

A class definition with nothing in it is pretty dull; usually, when you create a class, you have something you want to add to make that class different from its superclasses. Inside each class definition are declarations and definitions for variables or methods or both—for the class *and* for each instance. In this section, you'll learn all about instance and class variables; the next section talks about methods.

Defining Instance Variables

On Day 3, you learned how to declare and initialize local variables—that is, variables inside method definitions. Instance variables, fortunately, are declared and defined in exactly the same way as local variables; the only difference is their location in the class definition. Instance variables are considered instance variables if they are declared outside a method definition. Customarily, however, most instance variables are defined just after the first line of the class definition. For example, Listing 6.1 shows a simple class definition for the class `Bicycle`, which inherits from the class `PersonPoweredVehicle`. This class definition contains four instance variables:

☐ `bikeType`: the kind of bicycle this bicycle is—for example, `Mountain` or `Street`

☐ `chainGear`, the number of gears in the front

☐ `rearCogs`, the number of minor gears on the rear axle

☐ `currentGearFront` and `currentGearRear`: the gears the bike is currently in, both front and rear

Type **Listing 6.1. The bicycle class.**

```
1: class Bicycle extends PersonPoweredVehicle {
2:     String bikeType;
3:     int chainGear;
4:     int rearCogs;
5:     int currentGearFront;
6:     int currentGearRear;
7: }
```

Constants

Constants are useful for setting global states in a method or object, or for giving meaningful names to object-wide values that will never change. In Java, you can create constants only for instance or class variables, not for local variables.

NEW☞ A *constant variable* or *constant* is a variable whose value never changes (which may seem
TERM strange given the meaning of the word "variable").

To declare a constant, use the `final` keyword before the variable declaration and include an initial value for that variable:

```
final float pi = 3.141592;
final boolean debug = false;
final int maxsize = 40000;
```

Technical Note: The only way to define constants in Java is by using the `final` keyword. Neither the C and C++ constructs for `#define` nor `const` are available in Java.

Constants can be useful for naming various states of an object and then testing for those states. For example, suppose you have a test label that can be aligned left, right, or center. You can define those values as constant integers:

```
final int LEFT = 0;
final int RIGHT = 1;
final int CENTER = 2;
```

The variable alignment is then also declared as an `int`:

```
int alignment;
```

Then, later on in the body of a method definition, you can either set the alignment:

```
this.alignment = CENTER;
```

or test for a given alignment:

```
switch (this.alignment) {
    case LEFT: // deal with left alignment
            ...
            break;
    case RIGHT: // deal with right alignment
            ...
            break;
    case CENTER: // deal with center alignment
            ...
            break;
}
```

Class Variables

As you learned in previous lessons, class variables are global to a class and to all that class's instances. You can think of class variables as being even more global than instance variables. Class variables are good for communicating between different objects with the same class, or for keeping track of global states among a set of objects.

To declare a class variable, use the `static` keyword in the class declaration:

```
static int sum;
static final int maxObjects = 10;
```

Creating Methods

Methods, as you learned on Day 2, define an object's behavior—what happens when that object is created and the various operations that object can perform during its lifetime. In this section, you'll get a basic introduction to method definition and how methods work; tomorrow, you'll go into more detail about advanced things you can do with methods.

Defining Methods

Method definitions have four basic parts:

☐ The name of the method

☐ The type of object or base type this method returns

☐ A list of parameters

☐ The body of the method

NEW☞ TERM The method's *signature* is a combination of the name of the method, the type of object or base type this method returns, and a list of parameters.

> **Note:** To keep things simple today, I've left off two optional parts of the method definition: an access qualifier such as `public` or `private`, and the `throws` keyword, which indicates the exceptions a method can throw. You'll learn about these parts of a method definition in Week 3.

In other languages, the name of the method (or function, subroutine, or procedure) is enough to distinguish it from other methods in the program. In Java, you can have different methods that have the same name but a different return type or argument list. This is called method overloading, and you'll learn more about it tomorrow.

Here's what a basic method definition looks like:

```
returntype methodname (type1 arg1, type2 arg2, type3 arg3..) {
    ...
}
```

The `returntype` is the primitive type or class of the of the value this method returns. It can be one of the primitive types, a class name, or `void` if the method does not return a value at all.

Note that if this method returns an array object, the array brackets can go either after the return type or after the parameter list; because the former way is considerably easier to read, it is used in the examples today (and throughout this book):

```
int[] makeRange (int lower, int upper) {...}
```

The method's parameter list is a set of variable declarations, separated by commas, inside parentheses. These parameters become local variables in the body of the method, whose values are the objects or values of primitives passed in when the method is called.

Inside the body of the method you can have statements, expressions, method calls to other objects, conditionals, loops, and so on—everything you've learned about in the previous lessons.

If your method has a real return type (that is, it has not been declared to return void), somewhere inside the body of the method you need to return a value. Use the return keyword to do this. Listing 6.2 shows an example of a class that defines a makeRange() method. makeRange() takes two integers—a lower bound and an upper bound—and creates an array that contains all the integers between those two boundaries (inclusive).

 Listing 6.2. The RangeClass class.

```
1: class RangeClass {
2:     int[] makeRange (int lower, int upper) {
3:         int arr[] = new int[ (upper - lower) + 1 ];
4:
5:         for (int i = 0; i < arr.length; i++) {
6:             arr[i] = lower++;
7:         }
8:         return arr;
9:     }
10:
11:     public static void main (String arg[]) {
12:         int theArray[];
13:         RangeClass theRange = new RangeClass();
14:
15:         theArray = theRange.makeRange(1,10);
16:         System.out.print("The array: [ ");
17:         for (int i = 0; i < theArray.length; i++) {
18:             System.out.print(theArray[i] + " ");
19:         }
20:         System.out.println("]");
21:     }
22:
23: }
```

Here's the output of this program:

```
The array: [ 1 2 3 4 5 6 7 8 9 10 ]
```

The main() method in this class tests the makeRange() method by creating a range where the lower and upper boundaries of the range are 1 and 10, respectively (see line 6), and then uses a for loop to print the values of the new array.

The *this* Keyword

Sometimes, in the body of a method definition, you may want to refer to the current object—for example, to refer to that object's instance variables or to pass the current object as an argument to another method. To refer to the current object in these cases, you can use the this keyword. this refers to the current object, and you can use it anywhere that object might appear—in dot notation to refer to the object's instance variables, as an argument to a method, as the return value for the current method, and so on. Here's an example:

```
t = this.x             // the x instance variable for this object
this.myMethod(this)    // call the mymethod method, defined in
                       // this class, and pass it the current
                       // object
return this;           // return the current object
```

In many cases, however, you may be able to omit the this keyword. You can refer to both instance variables and method calls defined in the current class simply by name; the this is implicit in those references. So, the first two examples could be written like this:

```
t = x             // the x instance variable for this object
myMethod(this)    // call the myMethod method, defined in this
                  // class
```

> **Note:** Omitting the this keyword for instance variables depends on whether there are no variables of the same name declared in the local scope. See the next section for details.

Keep in mind that because this is a reference to the current instance of a class, it makes sense to use it only inside the body of an instance method definition. Class methods, that is, methods declared with the static keyword, cannot use this.

Variable Scope and Method Definitions

When you refer to a variable within your method definitions, Java checks for a definition of that variable first in the current scope (which may be a block), then in the outer scopes up to the current method definition. If that variable is not a local variable, Java then checks for a definition of that variable as an instance variable in the current class, and then, finally, in each superclass in turn.

Because of the way Java checks for the scope of a given variable, it is possible for you to create a variable in a lower scope such that a definition of that same variable "hides" the original value of that variable. This can introduce subtle and confusing bugs into your code.

For example, note this small Java program:

```
class ScopeTest {
    int test = 10;

    void printTest () {
        int test = 20;
        System.out.println("test = " + test);
    }
}
```

In this class, you have two variables with the same name and definition: the first, an instance variable, has the name test and is initialized to the value 10. The second is a local variable with the same name, but with the value 20. Because the local variable hides the instance variable, the println() method will print that test is 20.

You can get around this particular instance by using this.test to refer to the instance variable, and just test to refer to the local variable.

A more insidious example of this occurs when you redefine a variable in a subclass that already occurs in a superclass. This can create very insidious bugs in your code—for example, you may call methods that are intended to change the value of an instance variable, but that change the wrong one. Another bug might occur when you cast an object from one class to another—the value of your instance variable may mysteriously change (because it was getting that value from the superclass instead of from your class). The best way to avoid this behavior is to make sure that, when you define variables in a subclass, you're aware of the variables in each of that class's superclasses and you don't duplicate what is already there.

Passing Arguments to Methods

When you call a method with object parameters, the variables you pass into the body of the method are passed by reference, which means that whatever you do to those objects inside the method affects the original objects as well. This includes arrays and all the objects that arrays contain; when you pass an array into a method and modify its contents, the original array is affected. (Note that primitive types are passed by value.)

Here's an example to demonstrate how this works. First, you have a simple class definition, which includes a single method called OneToZero() (see Listing 6.3).

Type **Listing 6.3. The PassByReference class.**

```
1: class PassByReference {
2:     int OnetoZero (int arg[]) {
3:         int count = 0;
4:
5:         for (int i = 0; i < arg.length; i++) {
6:             if (arg[i] == 1) {
```

```
7:                    count++;
8:                    arg[i] = 0;
9:                }
10:         }
11:         return count;
12:     }
13: }
```

The OnetoZero() method does two things:

☐ It counts the number of ones in the array and returns that value.

☐ If it finds a one, it substitutes a zero in its place in the array.

Listing 6.4 shows the main() method for the PassByReference class, which tests the OnetoZero() method:

Listing 6.4. The main() method in PassByReference.

```
1: public static void main (String arg[]) {
2:     int arr[] = { 1, 3, 4, 5, 1, 1, 7 };
3:     PassByReference test = new PassByReference();
4:     int numOnes;
5:
6:     System.out.print("Values of the array: [ ");
7:     for (int i = 0; i < arr.length; i++) {
8:         System.out.print(arr[i] + " ");
9:     }
10:     System.out.println("]");
11:
12:     numOnes = test.OnetoZero(arr);
13:     System.out.println("Number of Ones = " + numOnes);
14:     System.out.print("New values of the array: [ ");
15:     for (int i = 0; i < arr.length; i++) {
16:         System.out.print(arr[i] + " ");
17:     }
18:     System.out.println("]");
19: }
```

Here is the output of this program:

```
Values of the array: [ 1 3 4 5 1 1 7 ]
Number of Ones = 3
New values of the array: [ 0 3 4 5 0 0 7 ]
```

Let's go over the main() method line by line so that you can see what is going on.

Lines 2 through 4 set up the initial variables for this example. The first one is an array of integers; the second one is an instance of the class PassByReference, which is stored in the variable test. The third is a simple integer to hold the number of ones in the array.

Lines 6 through 11 print out the initial values of the array; you can see the output of these lines in the first line of the output.

Line 12 is where the real work takes place; this is where you call the OnetoZero() method, defined in the object test, and pass it the array stored in arr. This method returns the number of ones in the array, which you'll then assign to the variable numOnes.

Got it so far? Line 13 prints out the number of ones, that is, the value you got back from the OnetoZero() method. It returns three, as you would expect.

The last bunch of lines print out the array values. Because a reference to the array object is passed to the method, changing the array inside that method changes that original copy of the array. Printing out the values in lines 14 through 18 proves this—that last line of output shows that all the 1s in the array have been changed to 0s.

Class Methods

Just as you have class and instance variables, you also have class and instance methods, and the difference between the two types of methods are analogous. Class methods are global to the class itself and available to any other classes or objects. Therefore, class methods can be used anywhere regardless of whether an instance of the class exists or not.

For example, the Java class libraries include a class called Math. The Math class defines a whole set of math operations that can be used in any program with the various number types:

```
float root = Math.sqrt(453.0);
System.out.print("The larger of x and y is" + Math.max(x,y));
```

To define class methods, use the static keyword in front of the method definition, just as you would create a class variable. For example, that max class method might have a signature like this:

```
static int max (int arg1, int arg2) { ... }
```

In a similar example, Java supplies "wrapper" classes for each of the base types—for example, classes for Integer, Float, and Boolean. Using class methods defined in those classes, you can convert to and from objects and base types. For example, the parseInt() class method in the Integer class takes a string and a radix (base) and returns the value of that string as an integer:

```
int count = Integer.parseInt("42", 10) // returns 42
```

Most methods that operate on a particular object, or that affect that object, should be defined as instance methods. Methods that provide some general utility but do not directly affect an instance of that class are better declared as class methods.

Creating Java Applications

Now that you know how to create classes, objects, and class and instance variables and methods, all that's left is to put it together into something that can actually run—in other words, to create a Java application.

Applications, to refresh your memory, are Java programs that run on their own. Applications are different from applets, which require HotJava or a Java-capable browser to view them. Much of what you've been using up to this point have been Java applications; next week you'll dive into how to create applets. (Applets require a bit more background in order to get them to interact with the browser and draw and update with the graphics system. You'll learn all of this next week.)

A Java application consists of one of more classes and can be as large or as small as you want it to be. HotJava is an example of a Java application. The only thing you need to make a Java application run is one class that serves as the "jumping-off" point for the rest of your Java program. If your program is small enough, it may need only the one class.

The jumping-off class for your program needs one thing: a main() method. When you run your compiled Java class (using the Java interpreter), the main() method is the first thing that gets called. None of this should be much of a surprise to you at this point; you've been creating Java applications with main() methods all along.

The signature for the main() method always looks like this:

```
public static void main (String arg[]) {...}
```

Here's a run-down of the parts of the main() method:

☐ public means that this method is available to other classes and objects. The main() method must be declared public. You'll learn more about public and private methods in Week 3.

☐ static means that this is a class method.

☐ void means the main() method doesn't return anything.

☐ main() takes one parameter: an array of strings. This argument is used for command-line arguments, which you'll learn about in the next section.

The body of the main() method contains any code you need to get your application started: initial variables or creating instances of any classes you may have declared.

When Java executes the main() method, keep in mind that main() is a class method—the class that holds it is not automatically instantiated when your program runs. If you want to treat that class as an object, you have to instantiate it in the main() method yourself (all the examples up to this point have done this).

Java Applications and Command-Line Arguments

Because Java applications are stand-alone programs, it's useful to be able to pass arguments or options to that program to determine how the program is going to run, or to enable a generic program to operate on many different kinds of input. Command-line arguments can be used for many different purposes—for example, to turn on debugging input, to indicate a filename to read or write from, or for any other information that you might want your Java program to know.

Passing Arguments to Java Programs

To pass arguments to a Java program, you merely append them to the command line when you run your Java program:

```
java Myprogram argumentOne 2 three
```

On this command line, you have three arguments: `argumentOne`, the number 2, and `three`. Note that a space separates arguments, so this command line produces three arguments:

```
java myprogram Java is cool
```

To group arguments, surround them with double-quotes. This command line produces one argument:

```
java myprogram "Java is cool"
```

The double-quotes are stripped off before the argument gets to your Java program.

Handling Arguments in Your Java Program

How does Java handle arguments? It stores them in an array of strings, which is passed to the `main()` method in your Java program. Remember the signature for `main()`:

```
public static void main (String arg[]) {...}
```

Here, `arg` is the name of the array of strings that contains the list of arguments. You can actually call it anything you want; `argv` is common (after the array of the same name from C and Unix shell scripting).

Inside your `main()` method, you can then handle the arguments your program was given by iterating over the array of arguments and handling those arguments any way you want. For example, Listing 6.5 is a really simple class that prints out the arguments it gets, one per line.

Listing 6.5. The `EchoArgs` class.

```
1: class EchoArgs {
2:     public static void main(String args[]) {
3:         for (int i = 0; i < args.length; i++) {
4:             System.out.println("Argument " + i + ": " + args[i]);
5:         }
6:     }
7: }
```

The following is some sample input and output from this program:

```
java EchoArgs 1 2 3 jump
```

Output

```
Argument 0: 1
Argument 1: 2
Argument 2: 3
Argument 3: jump
```

```
java EchoArgs "foo bar" zap twaddle 5
```

Output

```
Argument 0: foo bar
Argument 1: zap
Argument 2: twaddle
Argument 3: 5
```

Note how the arguments are grouped in the listing; putting quotes around foo bar causes that argument to be treated as one unit inside the argument array.

> **Technical Note:** The array of arguments in Java is not analogous to argv in C and Unix. In particular, arg[0], the first element in the array of arguments, is the first command-line argument after the name of the class—*not* the name of the program as it would be in C. Be careful of this as you write your Java programs.

6

An important thing to note about the arguments you pass into a Java program is that those arguments will be stored in an array of strings. This means that any arguments you pass to your Java program will be converted to strings so they can be stored in the argument array. To treat them as non-strings, you'll have to convert them to whatever type you want them to be.

For example, suppose you have a very simple Java program called SumAverage that takes any number of numeric arguments and returns the sum and the average of those arguments. Listing 6.6 shows a first pass at this program.

Listing 6.6. First try at the `SumAverage` class.

```
1: class SumAverage {
2:     public static void main (String args[]) {
3:         int sum = 0;
4:
5:         for (int i = 0; i < args.length; i++) {
6:             sum += args[i];
7:         }
8:
9:         System.out.println("Sum is: " + sum);
10:        System.out.println("Average is: " +
11:            (float)sum / (float)args.length);
12:    }
13: }
```

At first glance, this program seems rather straightforward—a `for` loop iterates over the array of arguments, summing them, and then the sum and the average are printed out as the last step.

What happens when you try and compile this? You get the following error:

```
SumAverage.java:9: Incompatible type for +=. Can't convert java.lang.String to int.
    sum += args[i];
```

You get this error because the argument array is an array of strings. Even though you passed integers into the program from the command line, those integers were converted to strings before they were stored in the array. To be able to sum those integers, you have to convert them back from strings to integers. There's a class method for the `Integer` class, called `parseInt`, that does just this. If you change line 7 to use that method, everything works just fine:

```
sum += Integer.parseInt(args[i]);
```

Now, compiling the program produces no errors and running it with various arguments returns the expected results. For example, `java SumAverage 1 2 3` returns the following output:

```
Sum is: 6
Average is: 2
```

Summary

Today, you put together everything you've come across in the preceding days of this week about how to create Java classes and use them in Java applications. This included the following:

☐ Instance and class variables, which hold the attributes of the class and its instances. You learned how to declare them, how they are different from regular local variables, and how to declare constants.

☐ Instance and class methods, which define a class's behavior. You learned how to define methods, including the parts of a method's signature, how to return values from a method, how arguments are passed in and out of methods, and the `this` keyword to refer to the current object

☐ Java applications—all about the `main()` method and how it works as well as how to pass arguments into a Java application from a command line.

Q&A

Q **I tried creating a constant variable inside a method, and I got a compiler error when I tried it. What was I doing wrong?**

A You can create only constant (`final`) class or instance variables; local variables cannot be constant.

Q **`static` and `final` are not exactly the most descriptive words for creating class variables, class methods, and constants. Why not use `class` and `const`?**

A `static` comes from Java's C++ heritage; C++ uses the `static` keyword to retain memory for class variables and methods (and, in fact, they aren't called class methods and variables in C++: `static` member functions and variables are more common terms).

`final`, however, is new. `final` is used in a more general way for classes and methods to indicate that those things cannot be subclassed or overridden. Using the `final` keyword for variables is consistent with that behavior. `final` variables are not quite the same as constant variables in C++, which is why the `const` keyword is not used.

Q **In my class, I have an instance variable called `name`. I also have a local variable called `name` in a method, which, because of variable scope, gets hidden by the local variable. Is there any way to get hold of the instance variable's value?**

A The easiest way is not to name your local variables the same names as your instance variables. If you feel you must, you can use `this.name` to refer to the instance variable and `name` to refer to the local variable.

Q **I want to pass command-line arguments to an applet. How do I do this?**

A You're writing applets already? Been skipping ahead, have you? The answer is that you use HTML attributes to pass arguments to an applet, not the command line (you don't have a command line for applets). You'll learn how to do this next week.

Q **I wrote a program to take four arguments, but if I give it too few arguments, it crashes with a run-time error.**

A Testing for the number and type of arguments your program expects is up to you in your Java program; Java won't do it for you. If your program requires four arguments, test that you have indeed been given four arguments, and return an error message if you haven't.

More About Methods

by Laura Lemay

Methods are arguably the most important part of any object-oriented language. Whereas classes and objects provide the framework, and class and instance variables provide a way of holding that class or object's attributes and state, it is the methods that actually provide an object's behavior and define how that object interacts with other objects in the system.

Yesterday, you learned a little about defining methods. With what you learned yesterday, you could create lots of Java programs, but you'd be missing some of the features of methods that make them really powerful, that make your objects and classes more efficient and easier to understand. Today, you'll learn about these additional features, including the following:

☐ Overloading methods, sometimes called creating polymorphic methods—that is, creating methods with multiple signatures and definitions but with the same name

☐ Creating constructor methods—methods that enable you to initialize objects to set up an initial state in the system when an object is created

☐ Overriding methods—creating a different definition for a method that has been defined in a superclass

☐ Finalizer methods—a way for an object to clean up after itself before it is removed from the system

Creating Methods with the Same Name, Different Arguments

Yesterday, you learned how to create methods with a single name and a single signature. Methods in Java can also be overloaded—that is, you can create methods that have the same name, but different signatures and different definitions. Method overloading enables instances of your class to have a simpler interface to other objects (no need for entirely different methods that do essentially the same thing) and to behave differently based on the input to that method.

When you call a method in an object, Java matches up the method name and the number and type of arguments to choose which method definition to execute.

To create an overloaded method, all you need to do is create several different method definitions in your class, all with the same name, but with different parameter lists (either in number or type of arguments) and with different bodies. Java can understand method overloading as long as each parameter list is unique for each method name.

Note that Java differentiates overloaded methods with the same name, based on the number and type of parameters to that method, not on its return type. That is, if you try to create two methods with the same name, same parameter list, but different return types, you'll get a compiler error. The variable names you choose for each parameter to the method are irrelevant—all that matters is the number and the type.

Here's an example of creating an overloaded method. Listing 7.1 shows a simple class definition for a class called MyRect, which defines a rectangular shape. The MyRect class has four instance variables to define the upper left and lower right corners of the rectangle: x1, y1, x2, and y2.

Note: Why did I call it MyRect? Java's awt package has a class called Rectangle that implements much of this same behavior. I called this class MyRect to prevent confusion between the two classes.

Type **Listing 7.1. The MyRect class.**

```
class MyRect {
    int x1 = 0;
    int y1 = 0;
    int x2 = 0;
    int y2 = 0;
}
```

When a new instance of the myRect class is initially created, all its instance variables are initialized to 0. Let's define a buildRect() method that takes four integer arguments and "resizes" the rectangle to have the appropriate values for its corners, returning the resulting rectangle object (note that because the arguments have the same names as the instance variables, you have to make sure to use this to refer to them):

```
MyRect buildRect(int x1, int y1, int x2, int y2) {
    this.x1 = x1;
    this.y1 = y1;
    this.x2 = x2;
    this.y2 = y2;
    return this;
}
```

What if you want to define a rectangle's dimensions in a different way—for example, by using Point objects rather than individual coordinates? You can overload buildRect() so that its parameter list takes two Point objects (note that you'll need to import the Point class at the top of your source file so Java can find it):

```
MyRect buildRect(Point topLeft, Point bottomRight) {
    x1 = topLeft.x;
    y1 = topLeft.y;
    x2 = bottomRight.x;
    y2 = bottomRight.y;
    return this;
}
```

113

Perhaps you want to define the rectangle using a top corner and a width and height. Just create a different definition for buildRect():

```
MyRect buildRect(Point topLeft, int w, int h) {
    x1 = topLeft.x;
    y1 = topLeft.y;
    x2 = (x1 + w);
    y2 = (y1 + h);
    return this;
}
```

To finish up this example, let's create a method to print out the rectangle's coordinates, and a main() method to test it all (just to prove that this does indeed work). Listing 7.2 shows the completed class definition with all its methods.

Type   **Listing 7.2. The complete MyRect class.**

```
import java.awt.Point;

class MyRect {
    int x1 = 0;
    int y1 = 0;
    int x2 = 0;
    int y2 = 0;

    MyRect buildRect(int x1, int y1, int x2, int y2) {
        this.x1 = x1;
        this.y1 = y1;
        this.x2 = x2;
        this.y2 = y2;
        return this;
    }

    MyRect buildRect(Point topLeft, Point bottomRight) {
        x1 = topLeft.x;
        y1 = topLeft.y;
        x2 = bottomRight.x;
        y2 = bottomRight.y;
        return this;
    }

    MyRect buildRect(Point topLeft, int w, int h) {
        x1 = topLeft.x;
        y1 = topLeft.y;
        x2 = (x1 + w);
        y2 = (y1 + h);
        return this;
    }

    void printRect(){
        System.out.print("MyRect: <" + x1 + ", " + y1);
        System.out.println(", " + x2 + ", " + y2 + ">");
    }
```

```
public static void main (String args[]) {
    MyRect rect = new MyRect();

    System.out.println("Calling buildRect with coordinates 25,25 50,50:");
    rect.buildRect(25, 25, 50, 50);
    rect.printRect();
    System.out.println("----------");

    System.out.println("Calling buildRect w/points (10,10), (20,20):");
    rect.buildRect(new Point(10,10), new Point(20,20));
    rect.printRect();
    System.out.println("----------");

    System.out.print("Calling buildRect w/1 point (10,10),");
    System.out.println(" width (50) and height (50)");

    rect.buildRect(new Point(10,10), 50, 50);
    rect.printRect();
    System.out.println("----------");

    }
}
```

Here's the output of this Java program:

Output
```
Calling buildRect with coordinates 25,25 50,50:
MyRect: <25, 25, 50, 50>
----------
Calling buildRect w/points (10,10), (20,20):
MyRect: <10, 10, 20, 20>
----------
Calling buildRect w/1 point (10,10), width (50) and height (50)
MyRect: <10, 10, 60, 60>
----------
```

As you can see from this example, all the buildRect() methods work based on the arguments with which they are called. You can define as many versions of a method as you need to in your own classes to implement the behavior you need for that class.

Constructor Methods

In addition to regular methods, you can also define constructor methods in your class definition.

NEW☞ A *constructor method* is a special kind of method that determines how an object is initialized
TERM when it's created.

Unlike regular methods, you can't call a constructor method by calling it directly; instead, constructor methods are called by Java automatically. Here's how it works: when you use new to create a new instance of a class, Java does three things:

☐ Allocates memory for the object

7

☐ Initializes that object's instance variables, either to their initial values or to a default (0 for numbers, `null` for objects, `false` for booleans)

☐ Calls the class's constructor method (which may be one of several methods)

If a class doesn't have any special constructor methods defined, you'll still end up with an object, but you'll have to set its instance variables or call other methods that object needs to initialize itself to that object afterward. All the examples you've created up to this point have behaved like this.

By defining constructor methods in your own classes, you can set initial values of instance variables, call methods based on those variables or call methods on other objects, or calculate initial properties of your object. You can also overload constructors, as you would regular methods, to create an object that has specific properties based on the arguments you give to new.

Basic Constructors

Constructors look a lot like regular methods, with two basic differences:

☐ Constructors always have the same name as the class.

☐ Constructors don't have a return type.

For example, Listing 7.3 shows a simple class called `Person`, with a constructor that initializes its instance variables based on the arguments to new. The class also includes a method for the object to introduce itself, and a `main()` method to test each of these things.

Type   **Listing 7.3. The `Person` class.**

```
class Person {
    String name;
    int age;

    Person(String n, int a) {
        name = n;
        age = a;
    }

    void printPerson() {
        System.out.print("Hi, my name is " + name);
        System.out.println(". I am " + age + " years old.");
    }

    public static void main (String args[]) {
        Person p;

        p = new Person("Laura", 20);
        p.printPerson();
        System.out.println("--------");
```

```
            p = new Person("Tommy", 3);
            p.printPerson();
            System.out.println("--------");
    }
}
```

Here's the output for this example program:

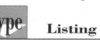

```
Hi, my name is Laura. I am 20 years old.
--------
Hi, my name is Tommy. I am 3 years old.
--------
```

Calling Another Constructor

Some constructors you write may be a superset of another constructor defined in your class; that is, they might have the same behavior plus a little bit more. Rather than duplicating identical behavior in multiple constructor methods in your class, it makes sense to be able to just call that first constructor from inside the body of the second constructor. Java provides a special syntax for doing this. To call a constructor defined on the current class, use this form:

```
this(arg1, arg2, arg3...);
```

The arguments to this are, of course, the arguments to the constructor.

Overloading Constructors

Like regular methods, constructors can also take varying numbers and types of parameters, enabling you to create your objects with exactly the properties you want it to have, or for it to be able to calculate properties from different kinds of input.

For example, the buildRect() methods you defined in the MyRect class earlier today would make excellent constructors, because what they're doing is initializing an object's instance variables to the appropriate objects. So, instead of the original buildRect() method you had defined (which took four parameters for the coordinates of the corners), you can create a constructor instead. Listing 7.4 shows a new class, called MyRect2, that has all the same functionality of the original MyRect, except with overloaded constructor methods instead of the buildRect() method.

Type   **Listing 7.4. The MyRect2 class (with constructors).**

```
import java.awt.Point;

class MyRect2 {
    int x1 = 0;
    int y1 = 0;
```

continues

117

Listing 7.4. continued

```
        int x2 = 0;
        int y2 = 0;

        MyRect2(int x1, int y1, int x2, int y2) {
            this.x1 = x1;
            this.y1 = y1;
            this.x2 = x2;
            this.y2 = y2;
        }

        MyRect2(Point topLeft, Point bottomRight) {
            x1 = topLeft.x;
            y1 = topLeft.y;
            x2 = bottomRight.x;
            y2 = bottomRight.y;
    }

        MyRect2(Point topLeft, int w, int h) {
            x1 = topLeft.x;
            y1 = topLeft.y;
            x2 = (x1 + w);
            y2 = (y1 + h);
    }

        void printRect(){
            System.out.print("MyRect: <" + x1 + ", " + y1);
            System.out.println(", " + x2 + ", " + y2 + ">");
        }

        public static void main (String args[]) {
            MyRect2 rect;

            System.out.println("Calling MyRect2 with coordinates 25,25 50,50:");
            rect = new MyRect2(25, 25, 50,50);
            rect.printRect();
            System.out.println("----------");

            System.out.println("Calling buildRect w/points (10,10), (20,20):");
            rect= new MyRect2(new Point(10,10), new Point(20,20));
            rect.printRect();
            System.out.println("----------");

            System.out.print("Calling buildRect w/1 point (10,10),");
            System.out.println(" width (50) and height (50)");
            rect = new MyRect2(new Point(10,10), 50, 50);
            rect.printRect();
            System.out.println("----------");

        }
    }
```

Here's the output for this example program (it's the same output from the previous example; only the code to produce it has changed):

```
Calling MyRect2 with coordinates 25,25 50,50:
MyRect: <25, 25, 50, 50>
----------
Calling buildRect w/points (10,10), (20,20):
MyRect: <10, 10, 20, 20>
----------
Calling buildRect w/1 point (10,10), width (50) and height (50)
MyRect: <10, 10, 60, 60>
----------
```

Overriding Methods

When you class a method in an object, Java looks for that method definition in the correct object, and if it doesn't find one, it passes the method call up the class hierarchy until a method definition is found. Method inheritance enables you to define and use methods repeatedly in subclasses without having to duplicate the code itself.

However, there may be times when you want an object to respond to the same methods but have different behavior when that method is called. In this case, you can override that method. Overriding a method involves defining a method in a subclass that has the same signature as a method in a superclass. Then, when that method is called, the method in the subclass is found and executed instead of the one in the superclass.

Creating Methods that Override Existing Methods

To override a method, all you have to do is create a method in your superclass that has the same signature (name, return type, and parameter list) as a method defined by one of your class's superclasses. Because Java executes the first method definition it finds that matches the signature, this effectively "hides" the original method definition. Here's a simple example; Listing 7.5 shows a simple class with a method called `printMe()`, which prints out the name of the class and the values of its instance variables.

Type

Listing 7.5. The `PrintClass` class.

```java
class PrintClass {
    int x = 0;
    int y = 1;

    void printMe() {
        System.out.println("X is " + x + ", Y is " + y);
        System.out.println("I am an instance of the class " +
        this.getClass().getName());
    }
}
```

7

Listing 7.6 shows a class called PrintSubClass that is a subclass of (extends) PrintClass. The only difference between PrintClass and PrintSubClass is that the latter has a z instance variable.

Type **Listing 7.6. The PrintSubClass class.**

```
class PrintSubClass extends PrintClass {
    int z = 3;

    public static void main (String args[]) {
        PrintSubClass obj = new PrintSubClass();
        obj.printMe();
    }
}
```

Here's the output from PrintSubClass:

Output
```
X is 0, Y is 1
I am an instance of the class PrintSubClass
```

Analysis In the main() method of PrintSubClass, you create a PrintSubClass object and call the printMe() method. Note that PrintSubClass doesn't define this method, so Java looks for it in each of PrintSubClass's superclasses—and finds it, in this case, in PrintClass. Unfortunately, because printMe() is still defined in PrintClass, it doesn't print the z instance variable.

Now, let's create a third class. PrintSubClass2 is nearly identical to PrintSubClass, but you override the printMe() method to include the z variable. Listing 7.7 shows this class.

Type **Listing 7.7. The PrintSubClass2 class.**

```
class PrintSubClass2 extends PrintClass {
    int z = 3;

    void printMe() {
        System.out.println("x is " + x + ", y is " + y +
                ", z is " + z);
        System.out.println("I am an instance of the class " +
                this.getClass().getName());
    }

    public static void main (String args[]) {
        PrintSubClass2 obj = new PrintSubClass2();
        obj.printMe();
    }
}
```

Now, when you instantiate this class and call the printMe() method, the version of printMe() you defined for this class is called instead of the one in the superclass PrintClass (as you can see in this output):

Output

```
x is 0, y is 1, z is 3
I am an instance of the class PrintSubClass2
```

Calling the Original Method

Usually, there are two reasons why you want to override a method that a superclass has already implemented:

- ☐ To replace the definition of that original method completely
- ☐ To augment the original method with additional behavior

You've already learned about the first one; by overriding a method and giving that method a new definition, you've hidden the original method definition. But sometimes you may just want to add behavior to the original definition rather than erase it altogether. This is particularly useful where you end up duplicating behavior in both the original method and the method that overrides it; by being able to call the original method in the body of the overridden method, you can add only what you need.

To call the original method from inside a method definition, use the super keyword to pass the method call up the hierarchy:

```
void myMethod (String a, String b) {
    // do stuff here
    super.myMethod(a, b);
    // maybe do more stuff here
}
```

The super keyword, like the this keyword, is a placeholder for this class's superclass. You can use it anywhere you want to refer to your superclass rather than to the current class.

For example, Listing 7.8 shows those printMe() methods used in the previous example.

Type

Listing 7.8. The printMe methods.

```
// from PrintClass
void printMe() {
        System.out.println("X is " + x + ", Y is " + y);
        System.out.println("I am an instance of the class" +
                this.getClass().getName());
    }
}

//from PrintSubClass2
    void printMe() {
        System.out.println("X is " + x + ", Y is " + y + ", Z is " + z);
        System.out.println("I am an instance of the class " +
                this.getClass().getName());
    }
```

Rather than duplicating most of the behavior of the superclass's method in the subclass, you can rearrange the superclass's method so that additional behavior can easily be added:

```
// from PrintClass
void printMe() {
    System.out.println("I am an instance of the class" +
                this.getClass().getName());
    System.out.println("X is " + x);
    System.out.println("Y is " + y);
    }
}
```

Then, in the superclass, when you override printMe, you can merely call the original method and then add the extra stuff:

```
// From PrintSubClass2
void printMe() {
    super.printMe();
    System.out.println("Z is " + z);
    }
}
```

Here's the output of calling printMe() on an instance of the superclass:

```
I am an instance of the class PrintSubClass2
X is 0
Y is 1
Z is 3
```

Overriding Constructors

Constructors cannot technically be overridden. Because they always have the same name as the current class, you're always creating new constructors instead of inheriting the ones you've got. Much of the time, this is fine, because when your class's constructor is called, the constructor with the same signature for all your superclass is also called, so initialization of all the parts of a class you inherit can happen.

However, when you're defining constructors for your own class, you may want to change how your object is initialized, not only by initializing the information your class adds, but also to change the information that is already there. You can do this by explicitly calling your superclass's constructors.

To call a regular method in a superclass, you use super.methodname(arguments). Because with constructors you don't have a method name to call, however, you have to use a different form:

```
super(arg1, arg2, ...);
```

Similar to using this(...) in a constructor, super(...) calls the constructor method for the immediate superclass (which may, in turn, call the constructor of its superclass, and so on).

For example, Listing 7.9 shows a class called NamedPoint, which extends the class Point from Java's awt package. The Point class has only one constructor, which takes an x and a y argument and returns a Point object. NamedPoint has an additional instance variable (a string for the name) and defines a constructor to initialize x, y, and the name.

Listing 7.9. The NamedPoint class.

```
1: import java.awt.Point;

2: class NamedPoint extends Point {
3:     String name;
4:
5:     NamedPoint(int x, int y, String name) {
6:         super(x,y);
7:          this.name = name;
8:     }
9: }
```

The constructor defined here for NamedPoint (lines 6 through 8) calls Point's constructor method to initialize Point's instance variables (x and y). Although you can just as easily initialize x and y yourself, you may not know what other things Point is doing to initialize itself, so it's always a good idea to pass constructors up the hierarchy to make sure everything is set up correctly.

Finalizer Methods

Finalizer methods are like the opposite of constructor methods; whereas a constructor method is used to initialize an object, finalizer methods are called just before the object is garbage-collected and its memory reclaimed.

To create a finalizer method, include a method with the following signature in your class definition:

```
void finalize() {
    ...
}
```

Inside the body of that finalize() method, include any cleaning up you want to do for that object.

Before you start using finalizer methods extensively in your Java programs, however, be aware that finalizer methods have several very important restrictions. First of all, the finalizer method is not guaranteed to be called until the object's memory is actually reclaimed, which may be some time after you've removed all references to that object.

You can always call the `finalize()` method yourself at any time; it's just a plain method like any other. However, calling `finalize()` does not trigger an object to be garbage-collected. Only removing all references to an object will cause it to be marked for deleting, and even then, Java may or may not call the `finalize()` method itself—regardless of whether or not you've already called it.

Finalizer methods are best used for optimizing the removal of an object—for example, by removing references to other objects, by cleaning up things that object may have touched, or for other optional behaviors that may make it easier for that object to be removed. In most cases, you may not need to use `finalize()` at all.

Summary

Today, you learned all kinds of techniques for using, reusing, defining, and redefining methods. You learned how to overload a method name so that the same method can have different behaviors based on the arguments with which it's called. You learned about constructor methods, which are used to initialize a new object when it's created. You learned about method inheritance and how to override methods that have been defined in a class's superclasses. Finally, you learned about finalizer methods, that can be used to clean up after an object just before that object is garbage-collected and its memory reclaimed.

Congratulations on completing your first week of *Teach Yourself Java in 21 Days*! Starting next week, you'll apply everything you've learned this week to writing Java applets and to working with more advanced concepts in putting together Java programs and working with the standard Java class libraries.

Q&A

Q I created two methods with the following signatures:

```
int total(int arg1, int arg2, int arg3) {...}
float total(int arg1, int arg2, int arg3) {...}
```

The Java compiler complains when I try to compile the class with these method definitions. But their signatures are different—what have I done wrong?

A Method overloading in Java works only if the parameter lists are different—either in number or type of arguments. Return type is not relevant for method overloading. Think about it—if you had two methods with exactly the same parameter list, how would Java know which one to call?

Q You described using the `this()` method (`this(arg, arg, ...)`) to call a constructor from inside another constructor. Are you limited to using the `this()` method call inside constructors?

A No, you can use that method anywhere to refer to the current object's constructor. On an existing object, calling a constructor is an easy way to reinitialize that object back to its default state (or to change it to have the state that you want it to have).

Q Can I overload overridden methods (that is, can I create methods that have the same name as an inherited method, but a different parameter list)?

A Sure! As long as a parameter lists vary, it doesn't matter whether you've defined a new method name or one that you've inherited from a superclass.

Q I created a finalizer method to decrement a class variable and print a message when my object gets garbage-collected. This way I can keep track of how many objects of this class are running at any given time. But sometimes `finalize()` gets called and sometimes it doesn't. How can I guarantee that `finalize()` will be called and my program will operate correctly?

A `finalize()` is provided as a convenience, to give an object a chance to clean up after itself. `finalize()` may or may not be called on any given object before it is garbage-collected, so you should not depend on its existence; you should be using `finalize()` only to provide program optimizations.

If you absolutely require that an object perform some operation before that object gets garbage-collected, you should create a specific method other than `finalize()` and explicitly call that method before discarding references to that object.

2

☐ Java Applet Basics
   Including an applet on a Web page
   Passing parameters
☐ Graphics, Fonts, and Color
   Graphics primitives
   The `Color` class
☐ Simple Animation and Threads
   `paint()` and `repaint()`
   Reducing animation flicker
   `stop` and `start`
☐ More Animation, Images, and Sound
   Scaling options, executing sound effectively
   Double-buffering
☐ Managing Simple Events and Interactivity
   `MouseDown` and `MouseUp`
   The Java event handler

- ☐ User Interfaces with the Java Abstract Windowing Toolkit
  Canvases, text components, widgets, and window construction components
- ☐ Windows, Networking, and Other Tidbits
  Programming menus and creating links inside applets

Java Applet Basics

by Laura Lemay

Much of Java's current popularity has come about because of Java-capable World Wide Web browsers and their support for applets: small programs that run inside a Web page and can be used to create dynamic, interactive Web designs. Applets, as I noted at the beginning of this book, are written in the Java language, and can be viewed in any browser that supports Java, including Sun's HotJava and Netscape's Navigator 2.0. Learning how to create applets is most likely the reason you bought this book, so let's waste no more time.

Last week, you focused on learning about the Java language itself, and most of the little programs you created were Java applications. This week, now that you have the basics down, you move on to creating and using applets, which includes a discussion of many of the classes in the standard Java class library.

Today, you'll start with the basics:

☐ A small review of differences between Java applets and applications

☐ Getting started with applets: the basics of how an applet works and how to create your own simple applets

☐ Including an applet on a Web page by using the <APPLET> tag, including the various features of that tag

☐ Passing parameters to applets

How Applets and Applications Are Different

Although you explored the differences between Java applications and Java applets in the early part of this book, let's review them.

In short, Java applications are stand-alone Java programs that can be run by using just the Java interpreter, for example, from a command line. Most everything you've used up to this point in the book has been a Java application, albeit a simple one.

Java applets, however, are run from inside a World Wide Web browser. A reference to an applet is embedded in a Web page using a special HTML tag. When a reader, using a Java-aware browser, loads a Web page with an applet in it, the browser downloads that applet from a Web server and executes it on the local system (the one the browser is running on).

Because Java applets run inside the Java browser, they have access to the same capabilities that the browser has: sophisticated graphics, drawing, and image processing packages; user interface elements; networking; and event handling. Java applications can also take advantage of these features, but they don't require them (you'll learn how to create Java applications that use applet-like graphics and UI features on Day 14).

The advantages applets have over applications in terms of graphics and UI capabilities, however, are hampered by restrictions on what applets can do. Given the fact that Java applets can be downloaded from anywhere and run on a client's system, restrictions are necessary to prevent an applet from causing system damage or security breaches. Without these restrictions in place, Java applets could be written to contain viruses or trojan horses (programs that seem friendly but do some sort of damage to the system), or be used to compromise the security of the system that runs them. The restrictions on what an applet can do include the following:

- Applets can't read or write to the reader's file system, except in specific directories (which are defined by the user through an access control list that, by default, is empty). Some browsers may not even allow an applet to read or write to the file system at all.

- Applets can't usually communicate with a server other than the one that had originally stored the applet. (This may be configurable by the browser; however, you should not depend on having this behavior available.)

- Applets can't run any programs on the reader's system. For Unix systems, this includes forking a process.

- Applets can't load programs native to the local platform, including shared libraries such as DLLs.

In addition, Java itself includes various forms of security and consistency checking in the Java compiler and interpreter to prevent unorthodox use of the language (you'll learn more about this on Day 21). This combination of restrictions and security features make it more difficult for a rogue Java applet to do damage to the client's system.

> **Note:** The most important words in the last sentence are "more difficult." These restrictions can prevent most of the more obvious ways of trying to cause damage to a client's system, but it's impossible to be absolutely sure that a clever programmer cannot somehow work around those restrictions. Sun has asked the Net at large to try to break Java's security and to create an applet that can work around the restrictions imposed on it. If a hole is found, Sun will patch it. You'll learn about more issues in Java security on Day 21.

Creating Applets

For the most part, all the Java programs you've created up to this point have been Java applications—simple programs with a single main() method that created objects, set instance variables, and ran methods. Today and in the days following, you'll be creating applets exclusively, so you should have a good grasp of how an applet works, the sorts of features an applet has, and where to start when you first create your own applets. Without further ado, let's get on with it.

To create an applet, you create a subclass of the class `Applet`, in the java.applet package. The `Applet` class provides behavior to enable your applet not only to work within the browser itself, but also to take advantage of the capabilities of AWT to include UI elements, to handle mouse and keyword events, and to draw to the screen. Although your applet can have as many "helper" classes as it needs, it's the main applet class that triggers the execution of the applet. That initial applet class always has a signature like this:

```
public class myClass extends java.applet.Applet {
    ...
}
```

Note the `public` keyword. Java requires that your applet subclass be declared `public`. Again, this is true only of your main applet class; any helper classes you create can be `public` or `private` as you wish. Public, private, and other forms of access control are described on Day 15.

When Java encounters your applet in a Web page, it loads your initial applet class over the network, as well as any other helper classes that first class uses. Unlike with applications, where Java calls the `main()` method directly on your initial class, when your applet is loaded, Java creates an instance of that class, and all the system-based methods are sent to that instance. Different applets on the same page, or on different pages that use the same class, use different instances, so each one can behave differently from other applets running on the same system.

Major Applet Activities

To create a basic Java application, your class has to have one method, `main()`, with a specific signature. Then, when your application starts up, `main` is executed, and from `main` you can set up the behavior that your programs need. Applets are similar but more complicated. Applets have many different activities that correspond to various major events in the life cycle of the applet—for example, initialization, painting, or mouse events. Each activity has a corresponding method, so when an event occurs, the browser or other Java-capable tool calls those specific methods.

By default, none of those activity methods have any definitions; to provide behavior for those events you must override the appropriate method in your applet's subclass. You don't have to override all of them, of course; different applet behavior requires different methods to be overridden.

You'll learn about the various important methods to override as the week progresses, but, for a general overview, here are five of the more important methods in an applet's execution: initialization, starting, stopping, destroying, and painting.

Initialization

Initialization occurs when the applet is first loaded (or reloaded). Initialization can include creating the objects it needs, setting up an initial state, loading images or fonts, or setting parameters. To provide behavior for the initialization of your applet, override the `init()` method:

```
public void init() {
    ...
}
```

Starting

After an applet is initialized, it is started. Starting can also occur if the applet was previously stopped. For example, an applet is stopped if the reader follows a link to a different page, and it is started again when the reader returns to this page. Note that starting can occur several times during an applet's life cycle, whereas initialization happens only once. To provide startup behavior for your applet, override the `start()` method:

```
public void start() {
    ...
}
```

Functionality that you put in the `start()` method might include starting up a thread to control the applet, sending the appropriate messages to helper objects, or in some way telling the applet to begin running. You'll learn more about starting applets on Day 10.

Stopping

Stopping and starting go hand in hand. Stopping occurs when the reader leaves the page that contains a currently running applet. By default, when the reader leaves a page, the applet continues running, using up system resources. By overriding `stop`, you can suspend execution of the applet and then restart it if the applet is viewed again. To stop an applet's execution, use the `stop()` method:

```
public void stop() {
    ...
}
```

Destroying

Destroying sounds more violent than it is. Destroying enables the applet to clean up after itself just before it or the browser exits—for example, to kill any running threads or to release any other running objects. Generally, you won't want to override `destroy` unless you have specific resources that need to be released—for example, threads that the applet has created. To provide clean up behavior for your applet, override the `destroy()` method:

```
public void destroy() {
    ...
}
```

> **Technical Note:** How is `destroy()` different from `finalize()`, which was described on Day 7? First, `destroy()` applies only to applets. `finalize()` is a more general-purpose way for a single object of any type to clean up after itself.
>
> The other difference is that `destroy()` is always called when the applet has finished executing, either because the browser is exiting or because the applet is being reloaded. `finalize()` is not guaranteed to be executed.

Painting

Painting is how an applet actually draws something on the screen, be it text, a line, a colored background, or an image. Painting can occur many hundreds of times during an applet's life cycle—for example, once after the applet is initialized, if the browser is placed behind another window on the screen and then brought forward again, if the browser window is moved to a different position on the screen, or perhaps repeatedly in the case of animations. You override the `paint()` method for your applet to have an actual appearance on the screen. The `paint()` method looks like this:

```
public void paint(Graphics g) {
    ...
}
```

Note that unlike the other major methods in this section, `paint()` takes an argument, an instance of the class `Graphics`. This object is created and passed to `paint` by the browser, so you don't have to worry about it. However, you will have to make sure that the `Graphics` class (part of the java.awt package) gets imported into your applet code, usually through an `import` statement at the top of your Java file:

```
import java.awt.Graphics;
```

A Simple Applet

On Day 2, you created a simple applet called HelloAgainApplet (this was the one with the big red `Hello Again`). There, you created and used that applet as an example of creating a subclass. Let's go over the code for that applet again, this time looking at it slightly differently in light of the things you just learned about applets. Listing 8.1 shows the code for that applet.

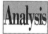

Listing 8.1. The Hello Again applet.

```
1:  import java.awt.Graphics;
2:  import java.awt.Font;
3:  import java.awt.Color;
4:
5:  public class HelloAgainApplet extends java.applet.Applet {
6:
7:      Font f = new Font("TimesRoman",Font.BOLD,36);
8:
9:      public void paint(Graphics g) {
10:         g.setFont(f);
11:         g.setColor(Color.red);
12:         g.drawString("Hello again!", 5, 50);
13:     }
14: }
```

Analysis

This applet overrides paint(), one of the major methods described in the previous section. Because the applet doesn't actually execute (all it does is print a couple of words to the screen), and there's not really anything to initialize, you don't need a start() or a stop() or an init() method.

The paint method is where the real work of this applet (what little work goes on) really occurs. The Graphics object passed into the paint() method holds that graphics state—that is, the current features of the drawing surface. Lines 10 and 11 set up the default font and color for this graphics state (here, the font object help in the f instance variable, and an object representing the color red that's stored in the Color class's variable red).

Line 12 then draws the string "Hello Again!" by using the current font and color at the position 5, 50. Note that the 0 point for y is at the top left of the applet's drawing surface, with positive y moving downward, so 50 is actually at the bottom of the applet. Figure 8.1 shows how the applet's bounding box and the string are drawn on the page.

Figure 8.1.
Drawing the applet.

Including an Applet on a Web Page

After you create a class or classes that contain your applet and compile them into class files as you would any other Java program, you have to create a Web page that will hold that applet by using the HTML language. There is a special HTML tag for including applets in Web pages; Java-capable browsers use the information contained in that tag to locate the compiled class files and execute the applet itself. In this section, you'll learn about how to put Java applets in a Web page and how to serve those files to the Web at large.

 Note: The following section assumes you have at least a passing understanding of writing HTML pages. If you need help in this area, you may find the book *Teach Yourself Web Publishing with HTML in 14 Days* useful. It is also from Sams.Net (and also written by one of the authors of this book).

The *<APPLET>* Tag

To include an applet on a Web page, use the <APPLET> tag. <APPLET> is a special extension to HTML for including applets in Web pages. Listing 8.2 shows a very simple example of a Web page with an applet included in it.

Type   **Listing 8.2. A simple HTML page.**

```
 1:  <HTML>
 2:  <HEAD>
 3:  <TITLE>This page has an applet on it</TITLE>
 4:  </HEAD>
 5:  <BODY>
 6:  <P>My second Java applet says:
 7:  <BR>
 8:  <APPLET CODE="HelloAgainApplet.class" WIDTH=200 HEIGHT=50>
 9:  There would be an applet here if your browser
10:  supported Java.
11:  </APPLET>
12:  </BODY>
13:  </HTML>
```

 There are three things to note about the <APPLET> tag in this page:

☐ The CODE attribute indicates the name of the class file that loads this applet, including the .class extension. In this case, the class file must be in the same directory as this

HTML file. To indicate applets are in a different directory, use CODEBASE, described later today.

☐ WIDTH and HEIGHT are required and used to indicate the bounding box of the applet—that is, how big a box to draw for the applet on the Web page. Be sure you set WIDTH and HEIGHT to be an appropriate size for the applet; depending on the browser, if your applet draws outside the boundaries of the space you've given it, you may not be able to see or get to those parts of the applet outside the bounding box.

☐ The text between the <APPLET> and </APPLET> tags is displayed by browsers that do not understand the <APPLET> tag (which includes most browsers that are not Java-capable). Because your page may be viewed in many different kinds of browsers, it is a very good idea to include alternate text here so that readers of your page who don't have Java will see something other than a blank line. Here, you include a simple statement that says There would be an applet here if your browser supported Java.

Note that the <APPLET> tag, like the <IMG> tag, is not itself a paragraph, so it should be enclosed inside a more general text tag, such as <P> or one of the heading tags (<H1> , <H2>, and so on).

Testing the Result

Now with a class file and an HTML file that refers to your applet, you should be able to load that HTML file into your Java-capable browser (using either the Open Local... dialog item or a file URL, or by indicating the filename on a command line). The browser loads and parses your HTML file, and then loads and executes your applet class.

Figure 8.2 shows the Hello Again applet, in case you've forgotten what it looks like.

Figure 8.2.
The Hello Again applet.

Making Java Applets Available to the Web

After you have an applet and an HTML file, and you've verified that everything is working correctly on your local system, the last step is making that applet available to the World Wide Web at large so that anyone with a Java-capable browser can view that applet.

Java applets are served by a Web server the same way that HTML files, images, and other media are. You don't need special server software to make Java applets available to the Web; you don't even need to configure your server to handle Java files. If you have a Web server up and running, or space on a Web server available to you, all you have to do is move your HTML and compiled class files to that server, as you would any other file.

If you don't have a Web server, you have to rent space on one or set one up yourself. (Web server setup and administration, as well as other facets of Web publishing in general, are outside the scope of this book.)

More About the *<APPLET>* Tag

In its simplest form, by using CODE, WIDTH, and HEIGHT, the <APPLET> tag merely creates a space of the appropriate size and then loads and plays the applet in that space. The <APPLET> tag, however, does include several attributes that can help you better integrate your applet into the overall design of your Web page.

Note: The attributes available for the <APPLET> tag are almost identical to those for the HTML <IMG> tag.

ALIGN

The ALIGN attribute defines how the applet will be aligned on the page. This attribute can have one of nine values: LEFT, RIGHT, TOP, TEXTTOP, MIDDLE, ABSMIDDLE, BASELINE, BOTTOM, and ABSBOTTOM.

In the case of ALIGN=LEFT and ALIGN=RIGHT, the applet is placed at the left or right margins of the page, respectively, and all text following that applet flows in the space to the right or left of that applet. The text will continue to flow in that space until the end of the applet, or you can use a line break tag (<BR>) with the CLEAR attribute to start the left line of text below that applet. The CLEAR attribute can have one of three values: CLEAR=LEFT starts the text at the next clear left margin, CLEAR=RIGHT does the same for the right margin, and CLEAR=ALL starts the text at the next line where both margins are clear.

For example, here's a snippet of HTML code that aligns an applet against the left margin, has some text flowing alongside it, and then breaks at the end of the paragraph so that the next bit of text starts below the applet:

```
<P><APPLET CODE="HelloAgainApplet" WIDTH=300 HEIGHT=200
ALIGN=LEFT>Hello Again!</APPLET>
To the left of this paragraph is an applet. It's a
simple, unassuming applet, in which a small string is
printed in red type, set in 36 point Times bold.
<BR CLEAR=ALL>
<P>In the next part of the page, we demonstrate how
under certain conditions, styrofoam peanuts can be
used as a healthy snack.
```

Figure 8.3 shows how this applet and the text surrounding it might appear in a Java-capable browser.

Figure 8.3.

An applet aligned left.

For smaller applets, you may want to include your applet within a single line of text. To do this, there are seven values for ALIGN that determine how the applet is vertically aligned with the text:

☐ ALIGN=TEXTTTOP aligns the top of the applet with the top of the tallest text in the line.

☐ ALIGN=TOP aligns the applet with the topmost item in the line (which may be another applet, or an image, or the top of the text).

☐ ALIGN=ABSMIDDLE aligns the middle of the applet with the middle of the largest item in the line.

☐ ALIGN=MIDDLE aligns the middle of the applet with the middle of the baseline of the text.

☐ ALIGN=BASELINE aligns the bottom of the applet with the baseline of the text. ALIGN=BASELINE is the same as ALIGN=BOTTOM, but ALIGN=BASELINE is a more descriptive name.

☐ ALIGN=ABSBOTTOM aligns the bottom of the applet with the lowest item in the line (which may be the baseline of the text or another applet or image).

Figure 8.4 shows the various alignment options, where the line is an image and the arrow is a small applet.

Figure 8.4.
Applet alignment options.

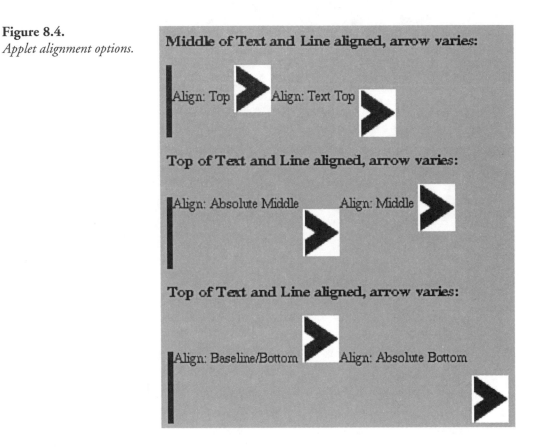

HSPACE and *VSPACE*

The HSPACE and VSPACE attributes are used to set the amount of space, in pixels, between an applet and its surrounding text. HSPACE controls the horizontal space (the space to the left and right of the applet). VSPACE controls the vertical space (the space above and below). For example, here's that sample snippet of HTML with vertical space of 10 and horizontal space of 50:

```
<P><APPLET CODE="HelloAgainApplet" WIDTH=300 HEIGHT=200
ALIGN=LEFT VSPACE=10 HSPACE=50>Hello Again!</APPLET>
To the left of this paragraph is an applet. It's a
simple, unassuming applet, in which a small string is
printed in red type, set in 36 point Times bold.
<BR CLEAR=ALL>
<P>In the next part of the page, we demonstrate how
under certain conditions, styrofoam peanuts can be
used as a healthy snack.
```

The result in a typical Java browser might look like that in Figure 8.5.

Figure 8.5.
Vertical and horizontal space.

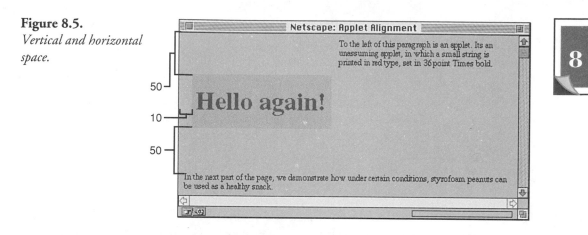

CODE and *CODEBASE*

CODE is used to indicate the name of the class file that holds the current applet. If CODE is used alone in the <APPLET> tag, the class file is searched for in the same directory as the HTML file that references it.

If you want to store your class files in a different directory than that of your HTML files, you have to tell the Java-capable browser where to find those class files. To do this, you use CODEBASE. CODE contains only the name of the class file; CODEBASE contains an alternate pathname where classes are contained. For example, if you store your class files in a directory called /classes, which is in the same directory as your HTML files, CODEBASE is the following:

```
<APPLET CODE="myclass.class" CODEBASE="classes"
    WIDTH=100 HEIGHT=100>
```

Passing Parameters to Applets

With Java applications, you can pass parameters to your main() routine by using arguments on the command line. You can then parse those arguments inside the body of your class, and the application acts accordingly based on the arguments it is given.

Applets, however, don't have a command line. How do you pass in different arguments to an applet? Applets can get different input from the HTML file that contains the <APPLET> tag through the use of applet parameters. To set up and handle parameters in an applet, you need two things:

☐ A special parameter tag in the HTML file
☐ Code in your applet to parse those parameters

141

Applet parameters come in two parts: a name, which is simply a name you pick, and a value, which determines the value of that particular parameter. So, for example, you can indicate the color of text in an applet by using a parameter with the name color and the value red. You can determine an animation's speed using a parameter with the name speed and the value 5.

In the HTML fie that contains the embedded applet, you indicate each parameter using the <PARAM> tag, which has two attributes for the name and the value, called (surprisingly enough), NAME and VALUE. The <PARAM> tag goes inside the opening and closing <APPLET> tags:

```
<APPLET CODE="MyApplet.class" WIDTH=100 HEIGHT=100>
<PARAM NAME=font VALUE="TimesRoman">
<PARAM NAME=size VALUE="36">
A Java applet appears here.</APPLET>
```

This particular example defines two parameters to the MyApplet applet: one whose name is font and whose value is TimesRoman, and one whose name is size and whose value is 36.

Those parameters are passed to your applet when it is loaded. In the init() method for your applet, you can then get hold of those parameters by using the getParameter method. getParameter takes one argument—a string representing the name of the parameter you're looking for—and returns a string containing the corresponding value of that parameter. (Like arguments in Java applications, all the parameter values are converted to strings.) To get the value of the font parameter from the HTML file, you might have a line such as this in your init() method:

```
String theFontName = getParameter("font");
```

> **Note:** The names of the parameters as specified in <PARAM> and the names of the parameters in getParameter must match identically, including having the same upper and lower case. In other words, <PARAM= NAME="name"> is different from <PARAM NAME="Name">. If your parameters are not being properly passed to your applet, make sure the parameter names match.

Note that if a parameter you expect has not been specified in the HTML file, getParameter returns null. Most often, you will want to test for a null parameter and supply a reasonable default:

```
if (theFontName == null)
    theFontName = "Courier"
```

Keep in mind also that because getParameter returns strings, if you want a parameter to be some other object or type, you have to convert it yourself. To parse the size parameter from that same HTML file and assign it to an integer variable called theSize, you might use the following lines:

```
int theSize;
String s = getParameter("size");
if (s == null)
    theSize = 12;
else theSize = Integer.parseInt(s);
```

Get it? Not yet? Let's create an example of an applet that uses this technique. You'll modify the HelloAgainApplet so that it says hello to a specific name, for example "Hello Bill" or "Hello Alice". The name is passed into the applet through an HTML parameter.

Let's start with the original HelloAgainApplet class:

```
import java.awt.Graphics;
import java.awt.Font;
import java.awt.Color;

public class MoreHelloApplet extends java.applet.Applet {

    Font f = new Font("TimesRoman",Font.BOLD,36);

    public void paint(Graphics g) {
        g.setFont(f);
        g.setColor(Color.red);
        g.drawString("Hello Again!", 5, 50);
    }
}
```

The first thing you need to add in this class is a place for the name. Because you'll need that name throughout the applet, let's add an instance variable for the name, just after the variable for the font:

```
String name;
```

To set a value for the name, you have to get the parameter. The best place to handle parameters to an applet is inside an init() method. The init() method is defined similarly to paint() (public, with no arguments, and a return type of void). Make sure when you test for a parameter that you test for a value of null. The default, in this case, if a name isn't indicated, is to say hello to "Laura":

```
public void init() {
this.name = getParameter("name");
    if (this.name == null)
        this.name = "Laura";
    }
```

One last thing to do now that you have the name from the HTML parameters is to modify the name so that it's a complete string—that is, to tack "Hello " onto the beginning, and an exclamation point onto the end. You could do this in the paint method just before printing the string to the screen. Here it's done only once, however, whereas in paint it's done every time the screen is repainted—in other words, it's slightly more efficient to do it inside init() instead:

```
this.name = "Hello " + this.name + "!";
```

And now, all that's left is to modify the paint() method. The original drawString method looked like this:

```
g.drawString("Hello Again!", 5, 50);
```

To draw the new string you have stored in the name instance variable, all you need to do is substitute that variable for the literal string:

```
g.drawString(this.name, 5, 50);
```

Listing 8.3 shows the final result of the MoreHelloApplet class. Compile it so that you have a class file ready.

Type **Listing 8.3. The MoreHelloApplet class.**

```
 1:  import java.awt.Graphics;
 2:  import java.awt.Font;
 3:  import java.awt.Color;
 4:
 5:  public class MoreHelloApplet extends java.applet.Applet {
 6:
 7:      Font f = new Font("TimesRoman",Font.BOLD,36);
 8:      String name;
 9:
10:     public void init() {
11:         this.name = getParameter("name");
12:         if (this.name == null)
13:             this.name = "Laura";
14:
15:         this.name = "Hello " + this.name + "!";
16:     }
17:
18:     public void paint(Graphics g) {
19:         g.setFont(f);
20:         g.setColor(Color.red);
21:         g.drawString(this.name, 5, 50);
22:     }
23: }
```

Now, let's create the HTML file that contains this applet. Listing 8.4 shows a new Web page for the MoreHelloApplet applet.

Type **Listing 8.4. The HTML file for the MoreHelloApplet applet.**

```
 1:  <HTML>
 2:  <HEAD>
 3:  <TITLE>Hello!</TITLE>
 4:  </HEAD>
 5:  <BODY>
```

```
 6:   <P>
 7:   <APPLET CODE="MoreHelloApplet.class" WIDTH=300 HEIGHT=50>
 8:   <PARAM NAME=name VALUE="Bonzo">
 9:    Hello to whoever you are!
10:  </APPLET>
11:  </BODY>
12:  </HTML>
```

 Note the <APPLET> tag, which points to the class file for the applet with the appropriate width and height (300 and 50). Just below it (line 8) is the <PARAM> tag, which you use to pass in the name. Here, the NAME parameter is simply name, and the value is the strong "Bonzo".

Loading up this HTML file produces the result shown in Figure 8.6.

Figure 8.6.
The result of MoreHelloApplet, first try.

Let's try a second example. Remember that in the code for MoreHelloApplet, if no name is specified, the default is the name "Laura". Listing 8.5 creates an HTML file with no parameter tag for name.

 Listing 8.5. Another HTML File for the MoreHelloApplet applet.

```
 1:  <HTML>
 2:  <HEAD>
 3:  <TITLE>Hello!</TITLE>
 4:  </HEAD>
 5:  <BODY>
 6:  <P>
 7:  <APPLET CODE="MoreHelloApplet.class" WIDTH=300 HEIGHT=50>
 8:   Hello to whoever you are!
 9:  </APPLET>
10:  </BODY>
11:  </HTML>
```

Here, because no name was supplied, the applet uses the default, and the result is what you might expect (see Figure 8.7).

Figure 8.7.
*The result of
MoreHelloApplet,
second try.*

Hello Laura!

Summary

Applets are probably the most common use of the Java language today. Applets are more complicated than many Java applications because they are executed and drawn inline with a Web page. Applets can more easily provide easy access to the graphics, user interface, and events systems in the Web browser itself. Today, you learned the basics of creating applets, including the following things:

- [ ] All applets you develop using Java inherit from the `Applet` class, part of the java.applet package. The `Applet` class provides basic behavior for how the applet will be integrated with and react to the browser and various forms of input from that browser and the person running it. By subclassing `Applet`, you have access to all that behavior.

- [ ] Applets have five main methods, which are used for the basic activities an applet performs during its life cycle: `init()`, `start()`, `stop()`, `destroy()`, and `paint()`. Although you don't need to override all these methods, these are the most common methods you'll see repeated in many of the applets you'll create in this book and in other sample programs.

- [ ] To run a compiled applet class file, you include it in an HTML Web page by using the `<APPLET>` tag. When a Java-capable browser comes across `<APPLET>`, it loads and plays the applet described in that tag. Note that to publish Java applets on the World Wide Web alongside HTML files you do not need special server software; any plain old Web server will do just fine.

- [ ] Unlike applications, applets do not have a common line on which to pass arguments, so those arguments must be passed into the applet through the HTML file that contains it. You indicate parameters in an HTML file by using the `<PARAM>` tag inside the opening and closing `<APPLET>` tags. `<PARAM>` has two attributes: `NAME` for the name of the parameter, and `VALUE` for its value. Inside the body of your applet (usually in `init()`), you can then gain access to those parameters using the `getParameter` method.

Q&A

Q In the first part of today's lesson, you say that applets are downloaded from random Web servers and run on the client's system. What's to stop an applet developer from creating an applet that deletes all the files on that system, or in some other way compromises the security of the system?

A Recall that Java applets have several restrictions that make it difficult for most of the more obvious malicious behavior to take place. For example, because Java applets cannot read or write files on the client system, they cannot delete files or read system files that might contain private information. Because they cannot run programs on the client's system, they cannot, for example, use the system's mail system to mail files to someone elsewhere on the network.

In addition, Java's very architecture makes it difficult to circumvent these restrictions. The language itself, the Java compiler, and the Java interpreter all have checks to make sure that no one has tried to sneak in bogus code or play games with the system itself. You'll learn more about these checks at the end of this book.

Of course, no system can claim to be entirely secure, and the fact that Java applets are run on the client's system makes them especially ripe for suspicion.

Q Wait a minute. If I can't read or write files or run programs on the system the applet is running on, doesn't that mean I basically can't do anything other than simple animations and flashy graphics? How can I save state in an applet? How can I create, say, a word processor or a spreadsheet as a Java applet?

A For everyone who doesn't believe that Java is secure enough, there is someone who believes that Java's security restrictions are too severe for just these reasons. Yes, Java applets are limited because of the security restrictions. But given the possibility for abuse, I believe that it's better to err on the side of being more conservative as far as security is concerned. Consider it a challenge.

Keep in mind, also, that Java applications have none of the restrictions that Java applets do, but because they are also compiled to bytecode, they are portable across platforms. It may be that the thing you want to create would make a much better application than an applet.

Q I have an older version of HotJava. I followed all the examples in this section, but HotJava cannot read my applets (it seems to ignore that they exist). What's going on?

A You most likely have an alpha version of HotJava. Recall that significant changes were made to the Java API and how Java applets are written between alpha and beta. The results of these changes are that browsers that support alpha applets cannot read beta applets, and vice versa. The HTML tags are even different, so an older browser just skips over newer applets, and vice versa.

By the time you read this, there may be a new version of HotJava with support for beta. If not, you can use Netscape 2.0 or the JDK's applet viewer to view applets written to the beta specification.

Q I noticed in a page about the <APPLET> tag that there's also a NAME attribute. You didn't discuss it here.

A NAME is used when you have multiple applets on a page that need to communicate with each other. You'll learn about this on Day 12.

Q I have an applet that takes parameters and an HTML file that passes it those parameters. But when my applet runs, all I get are null values. What's going on here?

A Do the names of your parameters (in the NAME attribute) match exactly with the names you're testing for in getParameter? They must be exact, including case, for the match to be made. Make sure also that your <PARAM> tags are inside the opening and closing <APPLET> tags, and that you haven't misspelled anything.

Graphics, Fonts, and Color

by Laura Lemay

Now you have a basic understanding of how applets work. For the remainder of this week you'll cover the sorts of things you can do with applets with the built-in Java class libraries, and how you can combine them to produce interesting effects. You'll start today with how to draw to the screen—that is, how to produce lines and shapes with the built-in graphics primitive, how to print text using fonts, and how to use and modify color in your applets. Today you'll learn, specifically:

☐ How the graphics system works in Java: the Graphics class, the coordinate system used to draw to the screen, and how applets paint and repaint

☐ Using the Java graphics primitives, including drawing and filling lines, rectangles, ovals, and arcs

☐ Creating and using fonts, including how to draw characters and strings and how to find out the metrics of a given font for better layout

☐ All about color in Java, including the Color class and how to set the foreground (drawing) and background color for your applet

Note: Today's lesson discusses many of the basic operations available to you with the Java class libraries regarding graphics, fonts, and color. However, today's lesson, as well as all of this book, is also intended to be more of an introduction and an overview than an exhaustive description of all the features available to you. Be sure to check out the Java API documentation for more information on the classes described today.

The Graphics Class

With Java's graphics capabilities, you can draw lines, shapes, characters, and images to the screen inside your applet. Most of the graphics operations in Java are methods defined in the Graphics class. You don't have to create an instance of Graphics in order to draw something in your applet; in your applet's paint() method (which you learned about yesterday), you are given a Graphics object. By drawing on that object, you draw onto your applet and the results appear on screen.

The Graphics class is part of the java.awt package, so if your applet does any painting (as it usually will), make sure you import that class at the beginning of your Java file:

```
import java.awt.Graphics;

public class MyClass extended java.applet.Applet {
...
}
```

The Graphics Coordinate System

To draw an object on the screen, you call one of the drawing methods available in the Graphics class. All the drawing methods have arguments representing endpoints, corners, or starting locations of the object as values in the applet's coordinate system—for example, a line starts at the points 10,10 and ends at the points 20,20.

Java's coordinate system has the origin (0,0) in the top left corner. Positive x values are to the right, and positive y values are down. All pixel values are integers; there are no partial or fractional pixels. Figure 9.1 shows how you might draw a simple square by using this coordinate system.

Figure 9.1.
The Java graphics coordinate system.

Java's coordinate system is different from many painting and layout programs that have their x and y in the bottom left. If you're not used to working with this upside-down graphics system, it may take some practice to get familiar with it.

Drawing and Filling

The Graphics class provides a set of simple built-in graphics primitives for drawing, including lines, rectangles, polygons, ovals, and arcs.

> **Note:** Bitmap images, such as GIF files, can also be drawn by using the Graphics class. You'll learn about this tomorrow.

Lines

To draw straight lines, use the `drawLine` method. `drawLine` takes four arguments: the x and y coordinates of the starting point and the x and y coordinates of the ending point.

```
public void paint(Graphics g) {
    g.drawLine(25,25,75,75);
}
```

Figure 9.2 shows the result of this snippet of code.

Figure 9.2.
Drawing lines.

Rectangles

The Java graphics primitives provide not just one, but three kinds of rectangles:

☐ Plain rectangles

☐ Rounded rectangles, which are rectangles with rounded corners

☐ Three-dimensional rectangles, which are drawn with a shaded border

For each of these rectangles, you have two methods to choose from: one that draws the rectangle in outline form, and one that draws the rectangle filled with color.

To draw a plain rectangle, use either the `drawRect` or `fillRect` methods. Both take four arguments: the x and y coordinates of the top left corner of the rectangle, and the width and height of the rectangle to draw. For example, the following `paint()` method draws two squares: the left one is an outline and the right one is filled (Figure 9.3 shows the result):

```
public void paint(Graphics g) {
    g.drawRect(20,20,60,60);
    g.fillRect(120,20,60,60);
}
```

Rounded rectangles are, as you might expect, rectangles with rounded edges. The `drawRoundRect` and `fillRoundRect` methods to draw rounded rectangles are similar to regular rectangles except that rounded rectangles have two extra arguments for the width and height of the angle of the corners. Those two arguments determine how far along the edges of the rectangle the arc for the corner will start; the first for the angle along the horizontal plane, the second for the vertical. Larger values for the angle width and height make the overall rectangle more rounded; values equal to the width and height of the rectangle itself produce a circle. Figure 9.4 shows some examples of rounded corners.

Figure 9.3.
Rectangles.

Figure 9.4.
Rounded corners.

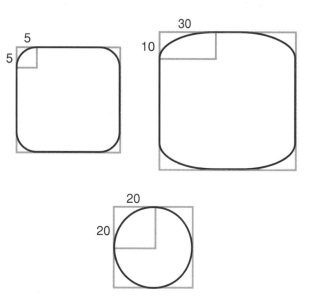

Here's a paint method that draws two rounded rectangles: one as an outline with a rounded corner 10 pixels square; the other, filled, with a rounded corner 20 pixels square (Figure 9.5 shows the resulting squares):

```
public void paint(Graphics g) {
    g.drawRoundRect(20,20,60,60,10,10);
    g.fillRoundRect(120,20,60,60,20,20);
}
```

Figure 9.5.
Rounded rectangles.

Finally, there are three-dimensional rectangles. These rectangles aren't really 3D; instead, they have a shadow effect that makes them appear either raised or indented from the surface of the applet. Three-dimensional rectangles have four arguments for the x and y of the start position and the width and height of the rectangle. The fifth argument is a boolean indicating whether the 3D effect is to raise the rectangle (`true`) or indent it (`false`). As with the other rectangles, there are also different methods for drawing and filling: `draw3DRect` and `fill3DRect`. Here's code to produce two of them—the left one indented, the right one raised (Figure 9.6 shows the result):

```
public void paint(Graphics g) {
    g.draw3DRect(20,20,60,60,true);
    g.draw3DRect(120,20,60,60,false);
}
```

Figure 9.6.
*Three-dimensional
rectangles.*

> **Note:** In the current beta version of the Java developer's kit, it is very difficult to see the 3D effect on 3D rectangles, due to a very small line width. (In fact, I enhanced Figure 9.6 to better show the effect.) If you are having troubles with 3D rectangles, this may be why. Drawing 3D rectangles in any color other than black makes them easier to see.

Polygons

Polygons are shapes with an unlimited number of sides. To draw a polygon, you need a set of x and y coordinates, and the drawing method then starts at one, draws a line to the second, then a line to the third, and so on.

As with rectangles, you can draw an outline or a filled polygon (the drawPolygon and fillPolygon methods, respectively). You also have a choice of how you want to indicate the list of coordinates—either as arrays of x and y coordinates or as an instance of the Polygon class.

Using the first method, the drawPolygon and fillPolygon methods take three arguments:

☐ An array of integers representing x coordinates

☐ An array of integers representing y coordinates

☐ An integer for the total number of points

The x and y arrays should, of course, have the same number of elements.

Here's an example of drawing a polygon's outline by using this method (Figure 9.7 shows the result):

```
public void paint(Graphics g) {
    int exes[] = { 39,94,97,142,53,58,26 };
    int whys[] = { 33,74,36,70,108,80,106 };
    int pts = exes.length;

    g.drawPolygon(exes,whys,pts);
}
```

Figure 9.7.
A polygon.

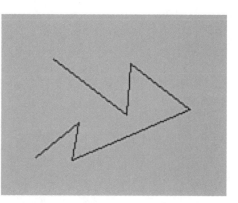

Note that Java does not automatically close the polygon; if you want to complete the shape, you have to include the starting point of the polygon at the end of the array. Drawing a filled polygon, however, joins the starting and ending points.

The second way of calling `drawPolygon` and `fillPolygon` is to use a `Polygon` object. The `Polygon` class is useful if you intend to add points to the polygon or if you're building the polygon on the fly. The `Polygon` class enables you to treat the polygon as an object rather than having to deal with individual arrays.

To create a polygon object you can either create an empty polygon:

```
Polygon poly = new Polygon();
```

or create a polygon from a set of points using integer arrays, as in the previous example:

```
int exes[] = { 39,94,97,142,53,58,26 };
int whys[] = { 33,74,36,70,108,80,106 };
int pts = exes.length;
Polygon poly = new Polygon(exes,whys,pts);
```

Once you have a polygon object, you can append points to the polygon as you need to:

```
poly.addPoint(20,35);
```

Then, to draw the polygon, just use the polygon object as an argument to `drawPolygon` or `fillPolygon`. Here's that previous example, rewritten this time with a `Polygon` object. You'll also fill this polygon rather than just drawing its outline (Figure 9.8 shows the output):

```
public void paint(Graphics g) {
    int exes[] = { 39,94,97,142,53,58,26 };
    int whys[] = { 33,74,36,70,108,80,106 };
    int pts = exes.length;
    Polygon poly = new Polygon(exes,whys,pts);
    g.fillPolygon(poly);
}
```

Figure 9.8.
Another polygon.

Ovals

Use ovals to draw ellipses or circles. Ovals are just like rectangles with overly rounded corners. In fact, you draw them using the same four arguments: the x and y of the top corner, and the width and height of the oval itself. Note that, because you're drawing an oval, the starting point is some distance to the left and up from the actual outline of the oval itself. Again, if you think of it as a rectangle, it's easier to place.

As with the other drawing operations, the drawOval method draws an outline of an oval, and the fillOval method draws a filled oval.

Here's an example of two ovals, a circle and an ellipse (Figure 9.9 shows how these two ovals appear on screen):

```
public void paint(Graphics g) {
    g.drawOval(20,20,60,60);
    g.fillOval(120,20,100,60);
}
```

Figure 9.9.
Ovals.

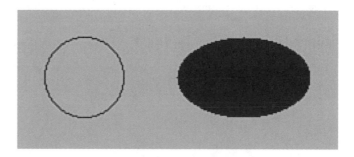

Arc

Of the drawing operations, arcs are the most complex to construct, which is why I saved them for last. An arc is a part of a oval; in fact, the easiest way to think of an arc is as a section of a complete oval. Figure 9.10 shows some arcs.

Figure 9.10.
Arcs.

The drawArc method takes six arguments: the starting corner, the width and height, the angle at which to start the arc, and the degrees to draw it before stopping. Once again, there is a drawArc method to draw the arc's outline and the fillArc to fill the arc. Filled arcs are drawn as if they were sections of a pie; instead of joining the two endpoints, both endpoints are joined to the center of the circle.

The important thing to understand about arcs is that you're actually formulating the arc as an oval and then drawing only some of that. The starting corner and width and height are not the starting point and width and height of the actual arc as drawn on the screen; they're the width and height of the full ellipse of which the arc is a part. Those first points determine the size and shape of the arc; the last two arguments (for the degrees) determine the starting and ending points.

Let's start with a simple arc, a C shape on a circle as shown in Figure 9.11.

Figure 9.11.
A C arc.

To construct the method to draw this arc, the first thing you do is think of it as a complete circle. Then you find the x and y coordinates and the width and height of that circle. Those four values are the first four arguments to the drawArc or fillArc methods. Figure 9.12 shows how to get those values from the arc.

Figure 9.12.
Constructing a circular arc.

To get the last two arguments, think in degrees around the circle. Zero degrees is at 3 o'clock, 90 degrees is at 12 o'clock, 180 at 9 o'clock, and 270 at 6 o'clock. The start of the arc is the degree value of the start of the arc. In this example, the starting point is the top of the C at 90 degrees; 90 is the fifth argument.

The sixth and last argument is another degree value indicating how far around the circle to sweep and the direction to go in (it's *not* the ending degree angle, as you might think). In this case, because you're going halfway around the circle, you're sweeping 180 degrees—and 180 is therefore the last argument in the arc. The important part is that you're sweeping 180 degrees counterclockwise, which is in the positive direction in Java. If you are drawing a backwards C, you sweep 180 degrees in the negative direction, and the last argument is -180. See Figure 9.13 for the final illustration of how this works.

Note: It doesn't matter which side of the arc you start with; because the shape of the arc has already been determined by the complete oval it's a section of, starting at either endpoint will work.

Figure 9.13.
Arcs on circles.

Here's the code for this example; you'll draw an outline of the C and a filled C to its right, as shown in Figure 9.14:

```
public void paint(Graphics g) {
    g.drawArc(20,20,60,60,90,180);
    g.fillArc(120,20,60,60,90,180);
}
```

Circles are an easy way to visualize arcs on circles; arcs on ellipses are slightly more difficult. Let's go through this same process to draw the arc shown in Figure 9.15.

Figure 9.14.
Two circular arcs.

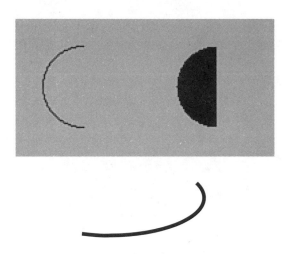

Figure 9.15.
An elliptical arc.

Like the arc on the circle, this arc is a piece of a complete oval, in this case, an elliptical oval. By completing the oval that this arc is a part of, you can get the starting points and the width and height arguments for the drawArc or fillArc method (Figure 9.16).

Figure 9.16.
Arcs on ellipses.

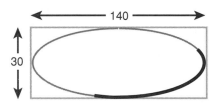

Then, all you need is to figure out the starting angle and the angle to sweep. This arc doesn't start on a nice boundary such as 90 or 180 degrees, so you'll need some trial and error. This arc starts somewhere around 25 degrees, and then sweeps clockwise about 130 degrees (Figure 9.17).

Figure 9.17.
Starting and ending points.

With all portions of the arc in place, you can write the code. Here's the Java code for this arc, both drawn and filled (note in the filled case how filled arcs are drawn as if they were pie sections):

```java
public void paint(Graphics g) {
    g.drawArc(10,20,150,50,25,-130);
    g.fillArc(10,80,150,50,25,-130);
}
```

Figure 9.18 shows the two elliptical arcs.

Figure 9.18.
Two elliptical arcs.

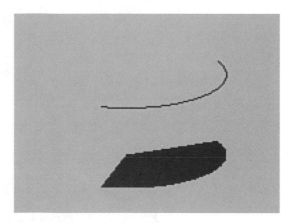

To summarize, here are the steps to take to construct arcs in Java:

- ☐ Think of the arc as a slice of a complete oval.
- ☐ Construct the full oval with the starting point and the width and height (it often helps to draw the full oval on the screen to get an idea of the right positioning).
- ☐ Determine the starting angle for the beginning of the arc.
- ☐ Determine how far to sweep the arc and in which direction (counterclockwise indicates positive values, clockwise indicates negatives).

A Simple Graphics Example

Here's an example of an applet that uses many of the built-in graphics primitives to draw a rudimentary shape. In this case, it's a lamp with a spotted shade (or a sort of cubist mushroom, depending on your point of view). Listing 9.1 has the complete code for the lamp; Figure 9.19 shows the resulting applet.

Figure 9.19.
The Lamp applet.

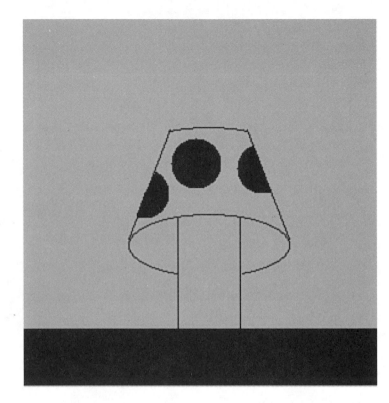

Type

Listing 9.1. The `Lamp` class.

```
1: import java.awt.*;
2:
3: public class Lamp extends java.applet.Applet {
4:
5:     public void paint(Graphics g) {
6:         // the lamp platform
7:         g.fillRect(0,250,290,290);
8:
9:         // the base of the lamp
10:        g.drawLine(125,250,125,160);
11:        g.drawLine(175,250,175,160);
12:
13:        // the lamp shade, top and bottom edges
14:        g.drawArc(85,157,130,50,-65,312);
15:        g.drawArc(85,87,130,50,62,58);
16:
17:        // lamp shade, sides
18:        g.drawLine(85,177,119,89);
19:        g.drawLine(215,177,181,89);
20:
21:        // dots on the shade
22:        g.fillArc(78,120,40,40,63,-174);
```

```
23:          g.fillOval(120,96,40,40);
24:          g.fillArc(173,100,40,40,110,180);
25:      }
26: }
```

Copying and Clearing

Once you've drawn a few things on the screen, you may want to move them around or clear the entire applet. The Graphics class provides methods for doing both these things.

The copyArea method copies a rectangular area of the screen to another area of the screen. copyArea takes six arguments: the x and y of the top corner of the rectangle to copy, the width and the height of that rectangle, and the distance in the x and y directions to which to copy it. For example, this line copies a square area 100 pixels on a side 100 pixels directly to its right:

```
g.copyArea(0,0,100,100,100,0);
```

To clear a rectangular area, use the clearRect method. clearRect, which takes the same four arguments as the drawRect and fillRect methods, fills the given rectangle with the current background color of the applet (you'll learn how to set the current background color later on today).

To clear the entire applet, you can use the size() method, which returns a Dimension object representing the width and height of the applet. You can then get to the actual values for width and height by using the width and height instance variables:

```
g.clearRect(0,0,this.size().width,this.height());
```

Text and Fonts

The Graphics class also enables you to print text on the screen, in conjunction with the Font class, and, sometimes, the Font metrics class. The Font class represents a given font—its name, style, and point size—and Font metrics gives you information about that font (for example, the actual height or width of a given character) so that you can precisely lay out text in your applet.

Note that the text here is static text, drawn to the screen once and intended to stay there. You'll learn about entering text from the keyboard later on this week.

Creating Font Objects

To draw text to the screen, first you need to create an instance of the Font class. Font objects represent an individual font—that is, its name, style (bold, italic), and point size. Font names are strings representing the family of the font, for example, "TimesRoman", "Courier", or

"Helvetica". Font styles are constants defined by the Font class; you can get to them using class variables—for example, Font.PLAIN, Font.BOLD, or Font.ITALIC. Finally, the point size is the size of the font, as defined by the font itself; the point size may or may not be the height of the characters.

To create an individual font object, use these three arguments to the Font class's new constructor:

```
Font f = new Font("TimesRoman", Font.BOLD, 24);
```

This example creates a font object for the TimesRoman BOLD font, in 24 points. Note that like most Java classes, you have to import this class before you can use it.

Font styles are actually integer constants that can be added to create combined styles; for example, Font.BOLD + Font.ITALIC produces a font that is both bold and italic.

The fonts you have available to you in your applet depend on the system on which the applet is running. Currently, although there is a mechanism in Java to get a list of fonts (see the getFontList method, defined in the java.awt.Toolkit class), it appears not to be working currently in the beta version of the JDK. Once these capabilities work, it is possible to get a list of fonts on the system and to be able to make choices based on that list; for now, to make sure your applet is completely compatible across systems, it's a very good idea to limit the fonts you use in your applets to "TimesRoman", "Helvetica", and "Courier". If Java can't find a font you want to use, it will substitute some default font, usually Courier.

Drawing Characters and Strings

With a font object in hand, you can draw text on the screen using the methods drawChars and drawString. First, though, you need to set the current font to your font object using the setFont method.

The current font is part of the graphics state that is kept track of by the Graphics object on which you're drawing. Each time you draw a character or a string to the screen, that text is drawn by using the current font. To change the font of the text, first change the current font. Here's a paint() method that creates a new font, sets the current font to that font, and draws the string "This is a big font.", starting from the point 10,100.

```
public void paint(Graphics g) {
    Font f = new Font("TimesRoman", Font.PLAIN,72);
    g.setFont(f);
    g.drawString("This is a big font.",10,100);
}
```

This should all look familiar to you; this is how the Hello applets throughout this book were produced.

The latter two arguments to drawString determine the point where the string will start. The x value is the start of the leftmost edge of the text; y is the baseline for the entire string.

Similar to `drawString` is the `drawChars` method that, instead of taking a string as an argument, takes an array of characters. `drawChars` has five arguments: the array of characters, an n integer representing the first character in the array to draw, another integer for the last character in the array to draw (all characters between the first and last are drawn), and the x and y for the starting point. Most of the time, `drawString` is more useful than `drawChars`.

Listing 9.2 shows an applet that draws several lines of text in different fonts; Figure 9.20 shows the result.

 Listing 9.2. Many different fonts.

```
 1: import java.awt.Font;
 2: import java.awt.Graphics;
 3:
 4: public class ManyFonts extends java.applet.Applet {
 5:
 6:     public void paint(Graphics g) {
 7:         Font f = new Font("TimesRoman", Font.PLAIN, 18);
 8:         Font fb = new Font("TimesRoman", Font.BOLD, 18);
 9:         Font fi = new Font("TimesRoman", Font.ITALIC, 18);
10:         Font fbi = new Font("TimesRoman", Font.BOLD + Font.ITALIC, 18);
11:
12:         g.setFont(f);
13:         g.drawString("This is a plain font", 10, 25);
14:         g.setFont(fb);
15:         g.drawString("This is a bold font", 10, 50);
16:         g.setFont(fi);
17:         g.drawString("This is an italic font", 10, 75);
18:         g.setFont(fbi);
19:         g.drawString("This is a bold italic font", 10, 100);
20:     }
21:
22: }
```

Figure 9.20.
The output of the ManyFonts applet.

This is a plain font
This is a bold font
This is an italic font
This is a bold italic font

165

Finding Out Information About a Font

Sometimes, you may want to make decisions in your Java program based on the qualities of the current font—for example, its point size, or the total height of its characters. You can find out some basic information about fonts and font objects by using simple methods on `Graphics` and on the `Font` objects. Table 9.1 shows some of these methods:

Table 9.1. Font methods.

Method Name	In Object	Action
getFont()	Graphics	Returns the current font object as previously set by setFont()
getName()	Font	Returns the name of the font as a string
getSize()	Font	Returns the current font size (an integer)
getStyle()	Font	Returns the current style of the font (styles are integer constants: 0 is plain, 1 is bold, 2 is italic, 3 is bold italic)
isPlain()	Font	Returns true or false if the font's style is plain
isBold()	Font	Returns true or false if the font's style is bold
isItalic()	Font	Returns true or false if the font's style is italic

For more detailed information about the qualities of the current font (for example, the length or height of given characters), you need to work with font metrics. The `FontMetrics` class describes information specific to a given font: the leading between lines, the height and width of each character, and so on. To work with these sorts of values, you create a `FontMetrics` object based on the current font by using the applet method `getFontMetrics`:

```
Font f = new Font("TimesRoman", Font.BOLD, 36);
FontMetrics fmetrics = getFontMetrics(f);
g.setfont(f);
```

Table 9.2 shows some of the things you can find out using font metrics. All these methods should be called on a `FontMetrics` object.

Table 9.2. Font metrics methods.

Method Name	Action
stringWidth()	Given a string, returns the full width of that string, in pixels
charWidth()	Given a character, returns the width of that character

Method Name	Action
getAscent()	Returns the ascent of the font, that is, the distance between the font's baseline and the top of the characters
getDescent()	Returns the descent of the font—that is, the distance between the font's baseline and the bottoms of the characters (for characters such as p and q that drop below the baseline)
getLeading()	Returns the leading for the font, that is, the spacing between the descent of one line and the ascent of another line
getHeight()	Returns the total height of the font, which is the sum of the ascent, descent, and leading value

As an example of the sorts of information you can use with font metrics, Listing 9.3 shows the Java code for an applet that automatically centers a string horizontally and vertically inside an applet. The centering position is different depending on the font and font size; by using font metrics to find out the actual size of a string, you can draw the string in the appropriate place.

Note the applet.size() method here, which returns the width and height of the overall applet area as a Dimension object. You can then get to the individual width and height by using the width and height instance variables.

Figure 9.21 shows the result (less interesting than if you actually compile and experiment with various applet sizes).

Type

Listing 9.3. Centering a string.

```
 1: import java.awt.Font;
 2: import java.awt.Graphics;
 3: import java.awt.FontMetrics;
 4:
 5: public class Centered extends java.applet.Applet {
 6:
 7:     public void paint(Graphics g) {
 8:         Font f = new Font("TimesRoman", Font.PLAIN, 36);
 9:         FontMetrics fm = getFontMetrics(f);
10:         g.setFont(f);
11:
12:         String s = "This is how the world ends.";
13:         int xstart = (this.size().width - fm.stringWidth(s)) / 2;
14:         int ystart = (this.size().height - fm.getHeight()) / 2;
15:
16:         g.drawString(s, xstart, ystart);
17:     }
18:}
```

Figure 9.21.
The centered text.

This is how the world ends.

Color

Drawing black lines and tests on a gray background is all very nice, but being able to use different colors is much nicer. Java provides methods and behaviors for dealing with color in general through the `Color` class, and also provides methods for setting the current foreground and background colors so that you can draw with the colors you created.

Java's abstract color model uses 24-bit color, wherein a color is represented as a combination of red, green, and blue values. Each component of the color can have a number between 0 and 255. 0,0,0 is black, 255,255,255 is white, and Java can represent millions of colors between as well.

Java's abstract color model maps onto the color model of the platform Java is running on, which usually has only 256 colors or fewer from which to choose. If a requested color in a color object is not available for display, the resulting color may be mapped to another or dithered, depending on how the browser viewing the color implemented it, and depending on the platform on which you're running. In other words, although Java gives the capability of managing millions of colors, very few may actually be available to you in real life.

Using Color Objects

To draw an object in a particular color, you must create an instance of the `Color` class to represent that color. The `Color` class defines a set of standard color objects, stored in class variables, that enable you quickly to get a color object for some of the more popular colors. For example, `Color.red` gives you a `Color` object representing red (RGB values of 255, 0, and 0), `Color.white` gives you a white color (RGB values of 255, 255, and 255), and so on. Table 9.3 shows the standard colors defined by variables in the `Color` class.

Table 9.3. Standard colors.

Color Name	RGB Value
`Color.white`	255,255,255
`Color.black`	0,0,0
`Color.lightGray`	192,192,192
`Color.gray`	128,128,128
`Color.darkGray`	64,64,64

Color Name	RGB Value
Color.red	255,0,0
Color.green	0,255,0
Color.blue	0,0,255
Color.yellow	255,255,0
Color.magenta	255,0,255
Color.cyan	0,255,255
Color.pink	255,175,175
Color.orange	255,200,0

If the color you want to draw in is not one of the standard color objects, fear not. You can create a color object for any combination of red, green, and blue, as long as you have the values of the color you want. Just create a new color object:

```
Color c = new Color(140,140,140);
```

This line of Java code creates a color object representing a dark grey. You can use any combination of red, green, and blue values to construct a color object.

Alternatively, you can also create a color object using three floats from 0.0 to 1.0:

```
Color c = new Color(0.34,1.0,0.25)
```

Testing and Setting the Current Colors

To draw an object or text using a color object, you have to set the current color to be that color object, just as you have to set the current font to the font in which you want to draw. Use the setColor method (a method for Graphics objects) to do this:

```
g.setColor(Color.green);
```

After setting the current color, all drawing operations will occur in that color.

In addition to setting the current color for the graphics context, you can also set the background and foreground colors for the applet itself by using the setBackground and setForeground methods. Both of these methods are defined in the java.awt.Component class, which Applet—and therefore your classes—automatically inherits.

The setBackground method sets the background color of the applet, which is usually a dark grey. It takes a single argument, a color object:

```
setBackground(Color.white);
```

The setForeground method also takes a single color as an argument, and affects everything that has been drawn on the applet, regardless of the color in which it has been drawn. You can use setForeground to change the color of everything in the applet at once, rather than having to redraw everything:

```
setForeground(Color.black);
```

In addition to the setColor, setForeground, and setBackground methods, there are corresponding "get" methods that enable you to retrieve the current graphics color, background, or foreground. Those methods are getColor (defined in Graphics objects), getForeground (defined in Applet), and getBackground (also in Applet). You can use these methods to choose colors based on existing colors in the applet:

```
setForeground(g.getColor());
```

A Single Color Example

Listing 9.4 shows the code for an applet that fills the applet's drawing area with square boxes, each of which has a randomly chosen color in it. It's written so that it can handle any size of applet and automatically fill the area with the right number of boxes.

 Listing 9.4. Random color boxes.

```
 1: import java.awt.Graphics;
 2: import java.awt.Color;
 3:
 4: public class ColorBoxes extends java.applet.Applet {
 5:
 6:     public void paint(Graphics g) {
 7:         int rval, gval, bval;
 8:
 9:         for (int j = 30; j < (this.size().height -25); j += 30)
10:           for (int i = 5; i < (this.size().width -25); i+= 30) {
11:               rval = (int)Math.floor(Math.random() * 256);
12:               gval = (int)Math.floor(Math.random() * 256);
13:               bval = (int)Math.floor(Math.random() * 256);
14:
15:               g.setColor(new Color(rval,gval,bval));
16:               g.fillRect(i,j,25,25);
17:               g.setColor(Color.black);
18:               g.drawRect(i-1,j-1,25,25);
19:           }
20:     }
21: }
```

Analysis The two for loops are the heart of this example; the first one draws the rows, and the second draws the individual boxes within the row. When a box is drawn, the random color is calculated first, and then the box is drawn. A black outline is drawn around each box, because some of them tend to blend into the background of the applet.

Because this `paint` method generates new colors each time the applet is painted, you can regenerate the colors by moving the window around or by covering the applet's window with another one. Figure 9.22 shows the final applet (although given that this picture is black and white, you can't get the full effect of the multicolored squares).

Figure 9.22.
The random colors applet.

Summary

You present something on the screen by painting inside your applet: shapes, graphics, text, or images. Today, you learned the basics of how to paint, including using the graphics primitives to draw rudimentary shapes, using fonts and font metrics to draw text, and using `Color` objects to change the color of what you're drawing on the screen. It's this foundation in painting that enables you to do animation inside an applet (which basically involves just painting repeatedly to the screen) and to work with images. These are topics you'll learn about tomorrow.

Q&A

Q In all the examples you show, and in all the tests I've made, the graphics primitives, such as `drawLine` and `drawRect`, produce lines that are one pixel wide. How can I draw thicker lines?

A In the current state of the Java Graphics class, you can't; no methods exist for changing the default line width. If you really need a thicker line, you have to draw multiple lines one pixel apart to produce that effect.

Q I wrote an applet to use Helvetica. It worked fine on my system, but when I run it on my friend's system, everything is in Courier. Why?

A Your friend most likely doesn't have the Helvetica font installed on his or her system. When Java can't find a font, it substitutes a default font instead—in your case, Courier. The best way to deal with this is to query the font list. As I'm writing this, however, querying the font list doesn't yet work, so your safest bet is to stick with either Times Roman or Courier in your applets.

Q **I tried out that applet that draws boxes with random colors, but each time it draws, a lot of the boxes are the same color. If the colors are truly random, why is it doing this?**

A Two reasons. The first is that the random number generator I used in that code (from the Math class) isn't a very good random number generator; in fact, the documentation for that method says as much. For a better random number generator, use the Random class from the java.util package.

The second, more likely, reason is that there just aren't enough colors available in your browser or on your system to draw all the colors that the applet is generating. If your system can't produce the wide range of colors available using the Color class, or if the browser has allocated too many colors for other things, you may end up with duplicate colors in the boxes, depending on how the browser and the system has been written to handle that. Usually your applet won't use quite so many colors, so you won't run into this problem quite so often.

Simple Animation and Threads

by Laura Lemay

The first thing I ever saw Java do was an animation: a large red `"Hi there!"` that ran across the screen from the right to left. Even that simple form of animation was enough to make me stop and think, "this is really cool."

That sort of simple animation takes only a few methods to implement in Java, but those few methods are the basis for any Java applet that you want to update the screen dynamically. Starting with simple animations is a good way to build up to the more complicated applets. Today, you'll learn the fundamentals of animation in Java: how the various parts of the system all work together so that you can create moving figures and dynamic updateable applets. Specifically, you'll explore the following:

☐ How Java animations work—the `paint()` and `repaint()` methods, starting and stopping dynamic applets, and how to use and override these methods in your own applets

☐ Threads—what they are and how they can make your applets more well-behaved with other applets and with the Java system in general

☐ Reducing animation flicker, a common problem with animation in Java

Throughout today, you'll also work with lots of examples of real applets that create animations or perform some kind of dynamic movement.

Creating Animation in Java

Animation in Java involves two steps: constructing a frame of animation, and then asking Java to paint that frame. Repeat as necessary to create the illusion of movement. The basic, static applets that you created yesterday taught you how to accomplish the first part; all that's left is how to tell Java to paint a frame.

Painting and Repainting

The `paint()` method, as you learned yesterday, is called by Java whenever the applet needs to be painted—when the applet is initially drawn, when the window containing it is moved, or when another window is moved from over it. You can also, however, ask Java to repaint the applet at a time you choose. So, to change the appearance of what is on the screen, you construct the image or "frame" you want to paint, and then ask Java to paint this frame. If you do this repeatedly, and fast enough, you get animation inside your Java applet. That's all there is to it.

Where does all this take place? Not in the `paint()` method itself. All `paint()` does is put dots on the screen. `paint()`, in other words, is responsible only for the current frame of the animation at a time. The real work of changing what `paint()` does, of modifying the frame for an animation, actually occurs somewhere else in the definition of your applet.

In that "somewhere else," you construct the frame (set variables for paint() to use, create color or font or other objects that paint() will need), and then call the repaint() method. repaint() is the trigger that causes Java to call paint() and causes your frame to get drawn.

> **Technical Note:** Because a Java applet can contain many different components that all need to be painted (as you'll learn later on this week), and in fact, applets are embedded inside a larger Java application that also paints to the screen in similar ways, when you call repaint() (and therefore paint()) you're not actually immediately drawing to the screen as you do in other window or graphics toolkits. Instead, repaint() is a *request* for Java to repaint your applet as soon as it can. Much of the time, the delay between the call and the actual repaint is negligible.

10

Starting and Stopping an Applet's Execution

Remember start() and stop() from Day 8? These are the methods that trigger your applet to start and stop running. You didn't use start() and stop() yesterday, because the applets on that day did nothing except paint once. With animations and other Java applets that are actually processing and running over time, you'll need to make use of start() and stop() to trigger the start of your applet's execution, and to stop it from running when you leave the page that contains that applet. For most applets, you'll want to override start and stop for just this reason.

The start() method triggers the execution of the applet. You can either do all the applet's work inside that method, or you can call other object's methods in order to do so. Usually, start() is used to create and begin execution of a thread so the applet can run in its own time.

stop(), on the other hand, suspects an applet's execution so when you move off the page on which the applet is displaying, it doesn't keep running and using up system resources. Most of the time when you create a start() method, you should also create a corresponding stop().

Putting It Together

Explaining how to do Java animation in text is more of a task than actually showing you how it works in code. An example or two will help make the relationship between all these methods clearer.

Listing 10.1 shows a sample applet that, at first glance, uses basic applet animation to display the date and time and constantly updates it every second, creating a very simple animated digital clock (a frame from that clock is shown in Figure 10.1).

The words "at first glance" in the previous paragraph are very important: this applet doesn't work! However, despite the fact that it doesn't work, you can still learn a lot about basic animation with it, so working through the code will still be valuable. In the next section, you'll learn just what's wrong with it.

See whether you can figure out what's going on with this code before you go on to the analysis.

Listing 10.1. The Date applet.

```
1:  import java.awt.Graphics;
2:  import java.awt.Font;
3:  import java.util.Date;
4:
5:  public class DigitalClock extends java.applet.Applet {
6:
7:      Font theFont = new Font("TimesRoman",Font.BOLD,24);
8:      Date theDate;
9:
10:     public void start() {
11:         while (true) {
12:             theDate = new Date();
13:             repaint();
14:             try { Thread.sleep(1000); }
15:             catch (InterruptedException e) { }
16:         }
17:     }
18:
19:     public void paint(Graphics g) {
20:         g.setFont(theFont);
21:         g.drawString(theDate.toString(),10,50);
22:     }
23: }
```

Figure 10.1.
The digital clock.

Sun Nov 05 20:43:02 PST 1995

Think you've got the basic idea? Let's go through it, line by line.

Lines 7 and 8 define two basic instance variables: theFont and theDate, which hold objects representing the current font and the current date, respectively. More about these later.

The start() method triggers the actual execution of the applet. Note the while loop inside this method; given that the test (true) always returns true, the loop never exits. A single animation frame is constructed inside that while loop, with the following steps:

☐ The Date class represents a date and time (Date is part of the java.util package—note that it was specifically imported in line three). Line 12 creates a new instance of the Date class, which holds the current date and time, and assigns it to the theDate instance variable.

☐ The repaint() method is called.

☐ Lines 14 and 15, as complicated as they look, do nothing except pause for 1000 milliseconds (one second) before the loop repeats. The sleep() method there, part of the Thread class, is what causes the applet to pause. Without a specific sleep() method, the applet would run as fast as it possibly could, which, for faster computer systems, might be too fast for the eye to see. Using sleep() enables you to control exactly how fast the animation takes place. The try and catch stuff around it enables Java to manage errors if they occur. try and catch are called exceptions and are described on Day 18, next week.

On to the paint() method. Here, inside paint(), all that happens is that the current font (in the variable theFont) is set, and the date itself is printed to the screen (note that you have to call the toString() method to convert the date to a string). Because paint() is called repeatedly with whatever value happens to be in theDate, the string is updated every second to reflect the new date.

There are a few things to note about this example. First, you might think it would be easier to create the new Date object inside the paint() method. That way you could use a local variable and not need an instance variable to pass the Date object around. Although doing things that way creates cleaner code, it also results in a less efficient program. The paint() method is called every time a frame needs to be changed. In this case, it's not that important(), but in an animation that needs to change frames very quickly, the paint() method has to pause to create that new object every time. By leaving paint() to do what it does best—painting the screen—and calculating new objects before hand, you can make painting as efficient as possible. This is precisely the same reason why the Font object is also in an instance variable.

Threads: What They Are and Why You Need Them

Depending on your experience with operating systems and with environments within those systems, you may or may not have run into the concept of threads. Let's start from the beginning with some definitions.

When a program runs, it starts executing, runs its initialization code, calls methods or procedures, and continues running and processing until it's complete or until the program is exited. That program uses a single thread—where the thread is a single locus of control for the program.

Multithreading, as in Java, enables several different execution threads to run at the same time inside the same program, in parallel, without interfering with each other.

Here's a simple example. Suppose you have a long computation near the start of a program's execution. This long computation may not be needed until later on in the program's execution—it's actually tangential to the main point of the program, but it needs to get done eventually. In a single-threaded program, you have to wait for that computation to finish before the rest of the program can continue running. In a multithreaded system, you can put that computation into its own thread, enabling the rest of the program to continue running independently.

Using threads in Java, you can create an applet so that it runs in its own thread, and it will happily run all by itself without interfering with any other part of the system. Using threads, you can have lots of applets running at once on the same page. Depending on how many you have, you may eventually exhaust the system so that all of them will run slower, but all of them will run independently.

Even if you don't have lots of applets, using threads in your applets is good Java programming practice. The general rule of thumb for well-behaved applets: whenever you have any bit of processing that is likely to continue for a long time (such as an animation loop, or a bit of code that takes a long time to execute), put it in a thread.

The Problem with the Digital Clock Applet

That Digital Clock applet in the last section doesn't use threads. Instead, you put the while loop that cycles through the animation directly into the start() method so that when the applet starts running it keeps going until you quit the browser or applet viewer. Although this may seem like a good way to approach the problem, the digital clock won't work because the while loop in the start() method is monopolizing all the resources in the system—including painting. If you try compiling and running the digital clock applet, all you get is a blank screen. You also won't be able to stop the applet, because there's no way a stop() method can ever be called.

The solution to this problem is to rewrite the applet to use threads. Threads enable this applet to animate on its own without interfering with other system operations, enable it to be started and stopped, and enable you to run it in parallel with other applets.

Writing Applets with Threads

How do you create an applet that uses threads? There are several things you need to do. Fortunately, none of them are difficult, and a lot of the basics of using threads in applets is just boilerplate code that you can copy and paste from one applet to another. Because it's so easy, there's almost no reason *not* to use threads in your applets, given the benefits.

There are four modifications you need to make to create an applet that uses threads:

☐ Change the signature of your applet class to include the words `implements Runnable`.

☐ Include an instance variable to hold this applet's thread.

☐ Modify your `start()` method to do nothing but spawn a thread and start it running.

☐ Create a `run()` method that contains the actual code that starts your applet running.

The first change is to the first line of your class definition. You've already got something like this:

```
public class MyAppletClass extends java.applet.Applet {
...
}
```

You need to change it to the following (I've put it on two lines so it'll fit on this page; it can be either like this or on one line depending on your preference):

```
public class MyAppletClass extends java.applet.Applet  implements Runnable {
...
}
```

What does this do? It includes support for the `Runnable` interface in your applet. If you think way back to Day 2, you'll remember that interfaces are a way to collect method names common to different classes, which can then be mixed in and implemented inside different classes that need to implement that behavior. Here, the `Runnable` interface includes the behavior your applet needs to run a thread; in particular, it gives you a default definition for the `run()` method.

The second step is to add an instance variable to hold this applet's thread. Call it anything you like; it's a variable of the type `Thread` (`Thread` is a class in `java.lang`, so you don't have to import it):

```
Thread runner;
```

Third, add a `start()` method or modify the existing one so that it does nothing but create a new thread and start it running. Here's a typical example of a `start()` method:

```
public void start() {
    if (runner == null); {
        runner = new Thread(this);
        runner.start();
    }
}
```

10

179

If you modify start() to do nothing but spawn a thread, where does the body of your applet go? It goes into a new method, run(), which looks like this:

```
public void run() {
    // what your applet actually does
}
```

run() can contain anything you want to run in the separate thread: initialization code, the actual loop for your applet, or anything else that needs to run in its own thread. You also can create new objects and call methods from inside run(), and they'll also run inside that thread. The run method is the real heart of your applet.

Finally, now that you've got threads running and a start method to start them, you should add a stop() method to suspend execution of that thread (and therefore whatever the applet is doing at the time) when the reader leaves the page. stop(), like start(), is usually something along these lines:

```
public void stop() {
        if (runner != null) {
            runner.stop();
            runner = null;
        }
    }
```

The stop() method here does two things: it stops the thread from executing and also sets the thread's variable (runner) to null. Setting the variable to null makes the Thread object it previously contained available for garbage collection so that the applet can be removed from memory after a certain amount of time. If the reader comes back to this page and this applet, the start method creates a new thread and starts up the applet once again.

And that's it! Four basic modifications, and now you have a well-behaved applet that runs in its own thread.

Fixing The Digital Clock

Remember the problems you had with the Digital Clock applet at the beginning of this section? Let's fix them so you can get an idea of how a real applet with threads looks. You'll follow the four steps outlined in the previous section.

First, modify the class definition to include the Runnable interface (the class is renamed to DigitalThreads instead of DigitalClock):

```
public class DigitalThreads extends java.applet.Applet
    implements Runnable {
    ...
```

Second, add an instance variable for the Thread:

```
Thread runner;
```

For the third step, swap the way you did things. Because the bulk of the applet is currently in a method called start(), but you want it to be in a method called run(), rather than do a lot of copying and pasting, just rename the existing start() to run():

```
public void run() {
        while (true) {
    ...
```

Finally, add the boilerplate start() and stop() methods:

```
public void start() {
        if (runner == null); {
            runner = new Thread(this);
            runner.start();
        }
    }

    public void stop() {
        if (runner != null) {
            runner.stop();
            runner = null;
        }
    }
```

You're finished! One applet converted to use threads in less than a minute flat. The code for the final applet appears in Listing 10.2.

Type   Listing 10.2. The fixed digital clock applet.

```
1:   import java.awt.Graphics;
2:   import java.awt.Font;
3:   import java.util.Date;
4:
5:   public class DigitalThreads extends java.applet.Applet
6:       implements Runnable {
7:
8:       Font theFont = new Font("TimesRoman",Font.BOLD,24);
9:       Date theDate;
10:      Thread runner;
11:
12:      public void start() {
13:          if (runner == null); {
14:              runner = new Thread(this);
15:              runner.start();
16:          }
17:      }
18:
19:      public void stop() {
20:          if (runner != null) {
21:              runner.stop();
22:              runner = null;
23:          }
24:      }
```

continues

Listing 10.2. continued

```
25:
26: public void run() {
27:        while (true) {
28:            theDate = new Date();
29:            repaint();
30:            try { Thread.sleep(1000); }
31:            catch (InterruptedException e) { }
32:        }
33:    }
34:
35:    public void paint(Graphics g) {
36:        g.setFont(theFont);
37:        g.drawString(theDate.toString(),10,50);
38:    }
39: }
40:
```

Reducing Animation Flicker

If you've been following along with this book and trying the examples as you go, rather than reading this book on the airplane or in the bathtub, you may have noticed that when the date program runs every once in a while, there's an annoying flicker in the animation. (Not that there's anything wrong with reading this book in the bathtub, but you won't see the flicker if you do that, so just trust me—there's a flicker.) This isn't a mistake or an error in the program; in fact, that flicker is a side effect of creating animations in Java. Because it is really annoying, however, you'll learn how to reduce flicker in this part of today's lesson so that your animations run cleaner and look better on the screen.

Flicker and How to Avoid It

Flicker is caused by the way Java paints and repaints each frame of an applet. At the beginning of today's lesson, you learned that when you call the repaint() method, repaint() calls paint(). That's not precisely true. A call to paint() does indeed occur in response to a repaint(), but what actually happens are the following steps:

1. The call to repaint() results in a call to the method update().

2. The update() method clears the screen of any existing contents (in essence, fills it with the current background color), and then calls paint().

3. The paint() method then draws the contents of the current frame.

It's Step 2, the call to update(), that causes animation flicker. Because the screen is cleared between frames, the parts of the screen that don't change alternate rapidly between being painted and being cleared. Hence, flickering.

There are two major ways to avoid flicker in your Java applets:

☐ Override `update()` either not to clear the screen at all, or to clear only the parts of the screen you've changed.

☐ Override both `update()` and `paint()`, and use double-buffering.

If the second way sounds complicated, that's because it is. Double-buffering involves drawing to an offscreen graphics surface and then copying that entire surface to the screen. Because it's more complicated, you'll explore that one tomorrow. Today, let's cover the easier solution: overriding `update`.

How to Override Update

The cause of flickering lies in the `update()` method. To reduce flickering, therefore, override both `update()` and `paint()`. Here's what the default version of `update()` does (in the `Component` class, which you'll learn more about on Day 13):

```
public void update(Graphics g) {
    g.setColor(getBackground());
    g.fillRect(0, 0, width, height);
    g.setColor(getForeground());
    paint(g);
}
```

Basically, `update()` clears the screen (or, to be exact, fills the applet's bounding rectangle with the background color), sets things back to normal, and then calls `paint()`. When you override `update()`, you have to keep these two things in mind and make sure that your version of `update()` does something similar. In the next two sections, you'll work through some examples of overriding `update()` in different cases to reduce flicker.

Solution One: Don't Clear the Screen

The first solution to reducing flicker is not to clear the screen at all. This works only for some applets, of course. Here's an example of an applet of this type. The ColorSwirl applet prints a single string to the screen (`"All the swirly colors"`), but that string is presented in different colors that fade into each other dynamically. This applet flickers terribly when it's run. Listing 10.3 shows the source for this applet, and Figure 10.2 shows the result.

 Listing 10.3. The ColorSwirl applet.

```
1:  import java.awt.Graphics;
2:  import java.awt.Color;
3:  import java.awt.Font;
4:
```

continues

Listing 10.3. continued

```
 5:  public class ColorSwirl extends java.applet.Applet
 6:      implements Runnable {
 7:
 8:      Font f = new Font("TimesRoman",Font.BOLD,48);
 9:      Color colors[] = new Color[50];
10:      Thread runThread;
11:
12:      public void start() {
13:          if (runThread == null) {
14:              runThread = new Thread(this);
15:              runThread.start();
16:          }
17:      }
18:
19:      public void stop() {
20:          if (runThread != null) {
21:              runThread.stop();
22:              runThread = null;
23:          }
24:      }
25:
26:      public void run() {
27:
28:          // initialize the color array
29:          float c = 0;
30:          for (int i = 0; i < colors.length; i++) {
31:              colors[i] =
32:              Color.getHSBColor(c, (float)1.0,(float)1.0);
33:              c += .02;
34:          }
35:
36:          // cycle through the colors
37:          int i = 0;
38:          while (true) {
39:              setForeground(colors[i]);
40:              repaint();
41:              i++;
42:              try { Thread.sleep(50); }
43:              catch (InterruptedException e) { }
44:              if (i == colors.length ) i = 0;
45:          }
46:      }
47:
48:      public void paint(Graphics g) {
49:          g.setFont(f);
50:          g.drawString("All the Swirly Colors", 15,50);
51:      }
52: }
```

Figure 10.2.
The ColorSwirl applet.

All the Swirly Colors

There are three new things to note about this applet that might look strange to you:

☐ When the applet starts, the first thing you do (in lines 28 through 34) is to create an array of Color objects that contains all the colors the text will display. By creating all the colors beforehand you can then just draw text in, one at a time; it's faster to precompute all the colors at once.

☐ To create the different colors, a method in the Color class called getHSBColor() creates a color object based on values for hue, saturation, and brightness, rather than the standard red, green, and blue. This is easier; by incrementing the hue value and keeping saturation and brightness constant you can create a range of colors without having to know the RGB for each one. If you don't understand this, don't worry about it; it's just an easy way to create the color array.

☐ The applet then cycles through the array of colors, setting the foreground to each one in turn and calling repaint. When it gets to the end of the array, it starts over again (line 44), so the process repeats over and over ad infinitum.

Now that you understand what the applet does, let's fix the flicker. Flicker here results because each time the applet is painted, there's a moment where the screen is cleared. Instead of the text cycling neatly from red to a nice pink to purple, it's going from red to grey, to pink to grey, to purple to grey, and so on—not very nice looking at all.

Because the screen clearing is all that's causing the problem, the solution is easy: override update() and remove the part where the screen gets cleared. It doesn't really need to get cleared anyhow, because nothing is changing except the color of the text. With the screen clearing behavior removed from update(), all update needs to do is call paint(). Here's what the update() method looks like in this applet:

```
public void update(Graphics g) {
     paint(g);
   }
```

With that—with one small three-line addition—no more flicker. Wasn't that easy?

Solution Two: Redraw Only What You Have To

For some applets, it won't be quite that easy. Here's another example. In this applet, called Checkers, a red oval (a checker piece) moves from a black square to a white square, as if on a checkerboard. Listing 10.4 shows the code for this applet, and Figure 10.3 shows the applet itself.

Type **Listing 10.4. The Checkers applet.**

```
 1:   import java.awt.Graphics;
 2:     import java.awt.Color;
 3:
 4:   public class Checkers extends java.applet.Applet
 5:       implements Runnable {
 6:
 7:       Thread runner;
 8:       int xpos;
 9:
10:       public void start() {
11:           if (runner == null); {
12:               runner = new Thread(this);
13:               runner.start();
14:           }
15:       }
16:
17:       public void stop() {
18:           if (runner != null) {
19:               runner.stop();
20:               runner = null;
21:           }
22:       }
23:
24:   public void run() {
25:           setBackground(Color.blue);
26:           while (true) {
27:               for (xpos = 5; xpos <= 105; xpos+=4) {
28:                   repaint();
29:                   try { Thread.sleep(100); }
30:                   catch (InterruptedException e) { }
31:               }
32:               for (xpos = 105; xpos > 5; xpos -=4) {
33:                   repaint();
34:                   try { Thread.sleep(100); }
35:                   catch (InterruptedException e) { }
36:               }
37:           }
38:       }
39:
40:       public void paint(Graphics g) {
41:           // Draw background
42:           g.setColor(Color.black);
```

```
43:              g.fillRect(0,0,100,100);
44:              g.setColor(Color.white);
45:              g.fillRect(101,0,100,100);
46:
47:              // Draw checker
48:              g.setColor(Color.red);
49:              g.fillOval(xpos,5,90,90);
50:      }
51:  }
```

Figure 10.3.
The Checkers applet.

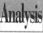 Here's a quick run-through of what this applet does: an instance variable, xpos, keeps track of the current starting position of the checker (because it moves horizontally, the y stays constant and the x changes). In the run() method, you change the value of x and repaint, waiting 50 milliseconds between each move. The checker moves from one side of the screen to the other and then moves back (hence the two for loops in that method).

In the actual paint() method, the background squares are painted (one black and one white), and then the checker is drawn at its current position.

This applet, like the Swirling Colors applet, also has a terrible flicker. (In line 25, the background is blue to emphasize it, so if you run this applet you'll definitely see the flicker.)

However, the solution to solving the flicker problem for this applet is more difficult than for the last one, because you actually want to clear the screen before the next frame is drawn. Otherwise, the red checker won't have the appearance of leaving one position and moving to another; it'll just leave a red smear from one side of the checkerboard to the other.

How do you get around this? You still clear the screen, in order to get the animation effect, but, rather than clearing the entire screen, you clear only the part that you actually changed. By limiting the redraw to only a small area, you can eliminate much of the flicker you get from redrawing the entire screen.

To limit what gets redrawn, you need a couple of things. First, you need a way to restrict the drawing area so that each time paint() is called, only the part that needs to get redrawn actually gets redrawn. Fortunately, this is easy by using a mechanism called clipping.

NEW☞ TERM *Clipping*, part of the graphics class, enables you to restrict the drawing area to a small portion of the full screen; although the entire screen may get instructions to redraw, only the portions inside the clipping area are actually drawn.

The second thing you need is a way to keep track of the actual area to redraw. Both the left and right edges of the drawing area change for each frame of the animation (one side to draw the new oval, the other to erase the bit of the oval left over from the previous frame), so to keep track of those two x values, you need instance variables for both the left side and the right.

With those two concepts in mind, let's start modifying the Checkers applet to redraw only what needs to be redrawn. First, you'll add instance variables for the left and right edges of the drawing area. Let's call those instance variables ux1 and ux2 (u for update), where ux1 is the left side of the area to draw and ux2 the right.

```
int ux1,ux2;
```

Now let's modify the run() method so that it keeps track of the actual area to be drawn, which you would think is easy—just update each side for each iteration of the animation. Here, however, things can get complicated because of the way Java uses paint() and repaint().

The problem with updating the edges of the drawing area with each frame of the animation is that for every call to repaint() there may not be an individual corresponding paint(). If system resources get tight (because of other programs running on the system or for any other reason), paint() may not get executed immediately and several calls to paint() may queue up waiting for their turn to change the pixels on the screen. In this case, rather than trying to make all those calls to paint() in order (and be potentially behind all the time), Java catches up by executing only the *most recent* call to paint() and skips all the others.

If you update the edges of the drawing area with each repaint(), and a couple of calls to paint() are skipped, you end up with bits of the drawing surface not being updated and bits of the oval left behind. There's a simple way around this: update the leading edge of the oval each time the frame updates, but only update the trailing edge if the most recent paint has actually occurred. This way, if a couple of calls to paint() get skipped, the drawing area will get larger for each frame, and when paint() finally gets caught up, everything will get repainted correctly.

Yes, this is horrifyingly complex. If I could have written this applet simpler, I would have, but without this mechanism the applet will not get repainted correctly. Let's step through it slowly in the code so you can get a better grasp of what's going on at each step.

Let's start with run(), where each frame of the animation takes place. Here's where you calculate each side of the drawing area based on the old position of the oval and the new position of the oval. When the oval is moving toward the left side of the screen, this is easy. The value of ux1 (the left side of the drawing area) is the previous oval's x position (xpos), and the value of ux2 is the x position of the current oval plus the width of that oval (90 pixels in this example).

Here's what the old run() method looked like, to refresh your memory:

```
public void run() {
    setBackground(Color.blue);
    while (true) {
        for (xpos = 5; xpos <= 105; xpos+=4) {
            repaint();
            try { Thread.sleep(100); }
            catch (InterruptedException e) { }
        }
        for (xpos = 105; xpos > 5; xpos -=4) {
            repaint();
            try { Thread.sleep(100); }
            catch (InterruptedException e) { }
        }
    }
}
```

In the first for loop in the run() method, where the oval is moving towards the right, you first update ux2 (the right edge of the drawing area):

```
ux2 = xpos + 90;
```

Then, after the repaint() has occurred, you update ux1 to reflect the old x position of the oval. However, you want to update this value only if the paint actually happened. How can you tell if the paint actually happened? You can reset ux1 in paint() to a given value (0), and then test to see whether you can update that value or whether you have to wait for the paint() to occur:

```
if (ux1 == 0) ux1 = xpos;
```

Here's the new, completed for loop for when the oval is moving to the right:

```
for (xpos = 5; xpos <= 105; xpos+=4) {
    ux2 = xpos + 90;
    repaint();
    try { Thread.sleep(100); }
    catch (InterruptedException e) { }
    if (ux1 == 0) ux1 = xpos;
}
```

When the oval is moving to the left, everything flips. ux1, the left side, is the leading edge of the oval that gets updated every time, and ux2, the right side, has to wait to make sure it gets updated. So, in the second for loop, you first update ux1 to be the x position of the current oval:

```
ux1 = xpos;
```

Then, after the repaint() is called, you test to make sure the paint happened and update ux2:

```
if (ux2 == 0) ux2 = xpos + 90;
```

Here's the new version of the secod for loop inside `run()`:

```
for (xpos = 105; xpos > 5; xpos -=4) {
    ux1 = xpos;
    repaint();
    try { Thread.sleep(100); }
    catch (InterruptedException e) { }
    if (ux2 == 0) ux2 = xpos + 90;
}
```

Those are the only modifications `run()` needs. Let's override `update` to limit the region that is being painted to the left and right edges of the drawing area that you set inside `run()`. To clip the drawing area to a specific rectangle, use the `clipRect()` method. `clipRect()`, like `drawRect()`, `fillRect()`, and `clearRect()`, is defined for graphics objects and takes four arguments: x and y starting positions, and width and height of the region.

Here's where `ux1` and `ux2` come into play. `ux1` is the x point of the top corner of the region; then use `ux2` to get the width of the region by subtracting `ux1` from that value. Finally, to finish `update()`, you call `paint()`:

```
public void update(Graphics g) {
        g.clipRect(ux1, 5, ux2 - ux1, 95);
        paint(g);
    }
```

Note that with the clipping region in place, you don't have to do anything to the actual `paint()` method. `paint()` goes ahead and draws to the entire screen each time, but only the areas inside the clipping region actually get changed on screen.

You need to update the trailing edge of each drawing area inside `paint()` in case several calls to `paint()` were skipped. Because you are testing for a value of 0 inside `run()`, you merely reset `ux1` and `ux2` to 0 after drawing everything:

```
ux1 = ux2 = 0;
```

Those are the only changes you have to make to this applet in order to draw only the parts of the applet that changed (and to manage the case where some frames don't get updated immediately). Although this doesn't totally eliminate flickering in the animation, it does reduce it a great deal. Try it and see. Listing 10.5 shows the final code for the Checkers applet.

Type **Listing 10.5. The final Checkers applet.**

```
1: import java.awt.Graphics;
2: import java.awt.Color;
3:
4: public class Checkers2 extends java.applet.Applet implements Runnable {
5:
6:     Thread runner;
7:     int xpos;
```

```
 8:     int ux1,ux2;
 9:
10:     public void start() {
11:         if (runner == null); {
12:             runner = new Thread(this);
13:             runner.start();
14:         }
15:     }
16:
17:     public void stop() {
18:         if (runner != null) {
19:             runner.stop();
20:             runner = null;
21:         }
22:     }
23:
24:     public void run() {
25:         setBackground(Color.blue);
26:         while (true) {
27:             for (xpos = 5; xpos <= 105; xpos+=4) {
28:                 ux2 = xpos + 90;
29:                 repaint();
30:                 try { Thread.sleep(100); }
31:                 catch (InterruptedException e) { }
32:                 if (ux1 == 0) ux1 = xpos;
33:             }
34:             for (xpos = 105; xpos > 5; xpos -=4) {
35:                 ux1 = xpos;
36:                 repaint();
37:                 try { Thread.sleep(100); }
38:                 catch (InterruptedException e) { }
39:                 if (ux2 == 0) ux2 = xpos + 90;
40:             }
41:         }
42:     }
43:     public void update(Graphics g) {
44:         g.clipRect(ux1, 5, ux2 - ux1, 95);
45:         paint(g);
46:     }
47:
48:     public void paint(Graphics g) {
49:         // Draw background
50:         g.setColor(Color.black);
51:         g.fillRect(0,0,100,100);
52:         g.setColor(Color.white);
53:         g.fillRect(101,0,100,100);
54:
55:         // Draw checker
56:         g.setColor(Color.red);
57:         g.fillOval(xpos,5,90,90);
58:
59:         // reset the drawing area
60:         ux1 = ux2 = 0;
61:     }
62:}
```

10

Summary

Congratulations on getting through Day 10! This day was a bit rough; you've learned a lot, and it all might seem overwhelming. You learned about a plethora of methods to use and override: `start()`, `stop()`, `paint()`, `repaint()`, `run()`, and `update()`—and you got a solid foundation in creating and using threads.

After today, you're over the worst hurdles in terms of understanding applets. Other than handling bitmap images, which you'll learn about tomorrow, you now have the basic background to create just about any animation you want in Java.

Q&A

Q Why all the indirection with paint and repaint and update and all that? Why not have a simple paint method that just puts stuff on the screen when you want it there?

A The Java AWT toolkit enables you to nest drawable surfaces within other drawable surfaces. When a paint takes place, all the parts of the system are redrawn, starting from the outermost surface and moving downward into the most nested one. Because the drawing of your applet takes place at the same time everything else is drawn, your applet doesn't get any special treatment. Your applet will be painted when everything else is painted. Although with this system you sacrifice some of the immediacy of instant painting, it enables your applet to co-exist with the rest of the system more cleanly.

Q Are Java threads like threads on other systems?

A Java threads have been influenced by other thread systems, and if you're used to working with threads, many of the concepts in Java threads will be very familiar to you. You learned the basics today; you'll learn more next week on Day 17.

Q When an applet uses threads, I just have to tell the thread to start and it starts, and tell it to stop and it stops? That's it? I don't have to test anything in my loops or keep track of its state? Is just stops?

A It just stops. When you put your applet into a thread, Java can control the execution of your applet much more readily. By causing the thread to stop, your applet just stops running, and then resumes when the thread starts up again. Yes, it's all automatic. Neat, isn't it?

Q The Swirling Colors applet seems to display only five or six colors. What's going on here?

A This is the same problem that you ran into yesterday wherein, on some systems, there might not be enough colors to be able to display all of them reliably. If you're running into this problem, other than upgrading your hardware, you might try quitting other applications running on your system that use color. Other browsers or color tools in particular might be hogging colors that Java wants to be able to use.

Q Even with the changes you made, the Checkers applet still flickers.

A And, unfortunately, it will continue to do so. Reducing the size of the drawing area by using clipping does significantly reduce the flickering, but it doesn't stop it entirely. For many applets, using either of the methods described today may be enough to reduce animation flicker to the point where your applet works right. To get totally flicker-free animation, you'll use a technique called double-buffering, which you'll learn about tomorrow.

2

More Animation, Images, and Sound

by Laura Lemay

Animations are fun and easy to do in Java, but there's only so much you can do with the built-in Java methods for lines and fonts and colors. For really interesting animations, you have to provide your own images for each frame of the animation—and having sounds is nice, as well. Today, you'll do more with animations, incorporating images and sounds into Java applets.

Specifically, you'll explore the following topics:

☐ Using images—getting them from the server, loading them into Java, and displaying them in your applet

☐ Creating animations by using images, including an extensive example

☐ Using sounds—getting them and playing them at the appropriate times

☐ Sun's Animator applet—an easy way to organize animations and sounds in Java

☐ Double-buffering—hardcore flicker avoidance

Retrieving and Using Images

Basic image handling in Java is easy. The Image class in java.awt provides abstract methods to represent common image behavior, and special methods defined in Applet and Graphics give you everything you need to load and display images in your applet as easily as drawing a rectangle. In this section, you'll learn about how to get and draw images in your Java applets.

Getting Images

To display an image in your applet, you first must load that image over the net into your Java program. Images are stored as separate files from your Java class files, so you have to tell Java where to find them.

The Applet class provides a method called getImage, which loads an image and automatically creates an instance of the Image class for you. To use it, all you have to do is import the java.awt.Image class, and then give getImage the URL of the image you want to load. There are two ways of doing the latter step:

☐ The getImage method with a single argument (an object of type URL) retrieves the image at that URL.

☐ The getImage method with two arguments: the base URL (also a URL object) and a string representing the path or filename of the actual image (relative to the base).

Although the first way may seem easier (just plug in the URL as a URL object), the second is more flexible. Remember, because you're compiling Java files, if you include a hard-coded URL of an image and then move your files around to a different location, you have to recompile all your Java files.

The latter form, therefore, is usually the one to use. The `Applet` class also provides two methods that will help with the base URL argument to `getImage`:

- [ ] The `getDocumentBase()` method returns a URL object representing the directory of the HTML file that contains this applet. So, for example, if the HTML file is located at `http://www.myserver.com/htmlfiles/javahtml/`, `getDocumentBase` returns a URL pointing to that path.

- [ ] The `getCodeBase()` method returns a string representing the directory in which this applet is contained—which may or may not be the same directory as the HTML file, depending on whether the `CODEBASE` attribute in `<APPLET>` is set or not.

Whether you use `getDocumentBase()` or `getCodebase()` depends on whether your images are relative to your HTML files or relative to your Java class files. Use whichever one applies better to your situation. Note that either of these methods is more flexible than hard-coding a URL or pathname into the `getImage` method; using either `getDocumentBase` or `getCodeBase` enables you to move your HTML files and applets around and Java can still find your images.

Here are a few examples of `getImage`, to give you an idea of how to use it. This first call to `getImage` retrieves the file at that specific URL (`"http://www.server.com/files/image.gif"`). If any part of that URL changes, you have to recompile your Java applet to take the new path into account:

```
Image img = getImage(
    new URL("http://www.server.com/files/image.gif"));
```

In the following form of `getImage`, the image.gif file is in the same directory as the HTML files that refer to this applet:

```
Image img = getImage(getDocumentBase(), "image.gif")
```

In this similar form, the file image.gif is in the same directory as the applet itself:

```
Image img = getImage(getCodeBase(), "image.gif")
```

If you have lots of image files, it's common to put them into their own subdirectory. This form of `getImage` looks for the file image.gif in the directory images, which, in turn, is in the same directory as the Java applet:

```
Image img = getImage(getCodeBase(), "images/image.gif")
```

If Java can't find the file you've indicated, `getImage` returns `null`. Your program will continue to run—you just won't see that image on your screen when you try to draw it.

> **Note:** Currently, Java supports images in the GIF and JPEG formats. Other image formats may be available later; however, for now, your images should be in either GIF or JPEG.

Drawing Images

All that stuff with `getImage` does nothing except go off and retrieve an image and stuff it into an instance of the `Image` class. Now that you have an image, you have to do something with it.

The most likely thing you're going to want to do is display it as you would a rectangle or a text string. The `Graphics` class provides two methods to do just that, both called `drawImage`.

The first version of `drawImage` takes four arguments: the image to display, the x and y positions of the top left corner, and `this`:

```
void paint() {
    g.drawImage(img, 10, 10, this);
}
```

This first form does what you would expect it to: it draws the image in its original dimensions with the top left corner at the given x and y positions. Listing 11.1 shows the code for a very simple applet that loads in an image called ladybug.gif and displays it. Figure 11.1 shows the obvious result.

Type

Listing 11.1. The Ladybug applet.

```
 1: import java.awt.Graphics;
 2: import java.awt.Image;
 3:
 4: public class LadyBug extends java.applet.Applet {
 5:
 6:     Image bugimg;
 7:
 8:     public void init() {
 9:         bugimg = getImage(getCodeBase(),
10:             "images/ladybug.gif");
11:     }
12:
13:     public void paint(Graphics g) {
14:         g.drawImage(bugimg,10,10,this);
15:     }
16: }
```

Analysis

The second form of `drawImage` takes six arguments: the image to draw, the x and y coordinates, a width and height of the image bounding box, and `this`. If the width and height arguments for the bounding box are smaller or larger than the actual image, the image is automatically scaled to fit. Using those extra arguments enables you to squeeze and expand images into whatever space you need them to fit in (keep in mind, however, that there may be some image degradation from scaling it smaller or larger than its intended size).

One helpful hint for scaling images is to find out the size of the actual image that you've loaded, so you can then scale it to a specific percentage and avoid distortion in either direction. Two methods defined for the `Image` class enable you do this: `getWidth()` and `getHeight()`. Both take

198

a single argument, an instance of `ImageObserver`, which is used to track the loading of the image (more about this later). Most of the time, you can use just `this` as an argument to either `getWidth()` or `getHeight()`.

Figure 11.1.
The `Ladybug` *image.*

If you stored the ladybug image in a variable called `bugimg`, for example, this line returns the width of that image, in pixels:

```
theWidth = bugimg.getWidth(this);
```

Listing 11.2 shows another use of the ladybug image, this time scaled several times to different sizes (Figure 11.2 shows the result).

 Listing 11.2. More `Ladybugs`, scaled.

```
1:  import java.awt.Graphics;
2:  import java.awt.Image;
3:
4:  public class LadyBug2 extends java.applet.Applet {
5:
6:      Image bugimg;
7:
8:      public void init() {
9:          bugimg = getImage(getCodeBase(),
10:             "images/ladybug.gif");
11:     }
12:
13:     public void paint(Graphics g) {
14:         int iwidth = bugimg.getWidth(this);
15:         int iheight = bugimg.getHeight(this);
16:         int xpos = 10;
17:
18:         // 25 %
```

continues

199

Listing 11.2. continued

```
19:        g.drawImage(bugimg,xpos,10,
20:            iwidth / 4, iheight / 4, this);
21:
22:        // 50 %
23:        xpos += (iwidth / 4) + 10;
24:        g.drawImage(bugimg, xpos , 10,
25:            iwidth / 2, iheight / 2, this);
26:
27:        // 100%
28:        xpos += (iwidth / 2) + 10;
29:        g.drawImage (bugimg, xpos, 10, this);
30:
31:        // 150% x, 25% y
32:        g.drawImage(bugimg, 10, iheight + 30,
33:            (int)(iwidth * 1.5), iheight / 4, this);
34:    }
35: }
```

Figure 11.2.
The second Ladybug applet.

Analysis I've been steadfastly ignoring mentioning that last argument to drawImage: the mysterious this, which also appears as an argument to getWidth() and getHeight(). Why is this argument used? Its official use is to pass in an object that functions as an ImageObserver (that is, an object that implements the ImageObserver interface). Image observers enable you to watch the progress of how far along an image is in the loading process and to make decisions when the image is only fully or partially loaded. The `Applet` class, which your applet inherits from, contains default behavior for watching for images that should work in the majority of cases—hence, the `this` argument to `drawImage()`, `getWidth()`, and `getHeight()`. The only reason you'll want to use an alternate argument in its place is if you are tracking lots of images loading synchronously. See the `java.awt.image.ImageObserver` class for more details.

Modifying Images

In addition to the basics and handling images described in this section, the java.awt.image package provides more classes and interfaces that enable you to modify images and their internal colors, or to create bitmap images by hand. Most of these classes require background knowledge in image processing, including a good grasp of color models and bitwise operations. All these things are outside the scope of an introductory book on Java, but if you have this background (or you're interested in trying it out), the classes in java.awt.image will be helpful to you. Take a look at the example code for creating and using images that comes with the Java development kit for examples of how to use the image classes.

Creating Animation Using Images

Creating animations by using images is much the same as creating images by using fonts, colors, or shapes—you use the same methods, the same procedures for painting, repainting, and reducing flicker that you learned about yesterday. The only difference is that you have a stack of images to flip through rather than a set of painting methods.

Probably the best way to show you how to use images for animation is simply to walk through an example. Here's an extensive one of an animation of a small cat called Neko.

An Example: Neko

Neko was a small Macintosh animation/game written and drawn by Kenji Gotoh in 1989. "Neko" is Japanese for "cat," and the animation is of a small kitten that chases the mouse pointer around the screen, sleeps, scratches, and generally acts cute. The Neko program has since been ported to just about every possible platform, as well as rewritten as a popular screensaver.

For this example, you'll implement a small animation based on the original Neko graphics. Because the original Neko the cat was autonomous (it could "sense" the edges of the window and turn and run in a different direction), this applet merely causes Neko to run in from the left side of the screen, stop in the middle, yawn, scratch its ear, sleep a little, and then run off to the right.

> **Note:** This is by far the largest of the applets discussed in this book, and if I either print it here and then describe it, or build it up line by line, you'll be here for days. Instead, I'm going to describe the parts of this applet independently, and I'm going to leave out the basics—the stuff you learned yesterday about starting and stopping threads, what the run() method does, and so on. All the code is printed later today so that you can put it all together.

Before you begin writing Java code to construct an animation, you should have all the images that form the animation itself. For this version of Neko there are nine of them (the original has 36), as shown in Figure 11.3.

Figure 11.3.
The images for Neko.

I've stored these images in a subdirectory of my applet directory called, appropriately, images. Where you store your images isn't all the important, but you should take note of where you've put them because you'll need that information

Now, onto the applet. The basic idea of animation by using images is that you have a set of images, and you display them one at a time, rapidly, so they give the appearance of movement. The easiest way to manage this in Java is to store the images in an array of class Image, and then to have a special variable that stores a reference to the current image.

> **Technical Note:** The java.util class contains a class (HashTable) that implements a hash table. For large amounts of images, a hash table is faster to find and retrieve images from than an array is. Because you have a relatively small amount of images here, and because arrays are easier to deal with, I'll use an array here.

For the Neko applet, you'll include instance variables to implement both these things: an array to hold the images called nekopics, and a variable of type Image to hold the current image:

```
Image nekopics[] = new Image[9];
Image currentimg;
```

Because you'll need to pass the position of the current image around between the methods in this applet, you'll also need to keep track of the current x and y positions. The y stays constant for this particular applet, but the x may vary. let's add two instance variables for those two positions:

```
int xpos;
int ypos = 50;
```

Now, onto the body of the applet. During the applet's initialization, you'll read in all the images and store them in the nekopics array. This is the sort of operation that works especially well in an init() method.

Given that you have nine images with nine different filenames, you could do a separate call to getImage for each one. You can save at least a little typing, however, by creating an array of the file names (nekosrc, an array of strings) and then just using a for loop to iterate over each one. Here's the init() method for the Neko applet that loads all the images into the nekopics array:

```
public void init() {

    String nekosrc[] = { "right1.gif", "right2.gif",
            "stop.gif", "yawn.gif", "scratch1.gif",
            "scratch2.gif","sleep1.gif", "sleep2.gif",
            "awake.gif" };
    for (int i=0; i < nekopics.length; i++) {
        nekopics[i] = getImage(getCodeBase(),
            "images/" + nekosrc[i]);
    }
}
```

Note here in the call to getImage that the directory these images are stored in is included as part of the path.

With the images loaded, the next step is to start animating the bits of the applet. You do this inside the applet's thread's run() method. In this applet, Neko does five main things:

- [ ] Runs in from the left side of the screen
- [ ] Stops in the middle and yawns
- [ ] Scratches four times
- [ ] Sleeps
- [ ] Wakes up and runs off to the right side of the screen

Because you could animate this applet by merely painting the right image to the screen at the right time, it makes more sense to write this applet so that many of Neko's activities are contained in individual methods. This way, you can reuse some of the activities (the animation of Neko running, in particular) if you want Neko to do things in a different order.

Let's start by creating a method to make Neko run. Because you're going to be using this one twice, making it generic is a good plan. Let's create the nekorun method, which takes two arguments: the x position to start, and the x position to end. Neko then runs between those two positions (the y remains constant).

There are two images that represent Neko running; so, to create the running effect, you need to alternate between those two images (stored in positions 0 and 1 of the image array), as well as move them across the screen. The moving part is a simple `for` loop between the `start` and `end` arguments, setting the global `x` position to the current loop value. Swapping the images means merely testing to see which one is active at any turn of the loop and assigning the other one to the current image. Finally, at each new frame, you'll call `repaint` and `sleep` for a bit.

Actually, given that during this animation there will be a lot of sleeping of various intervals, it makes sense to create a method that does the sleeping for the appropriate time interval. Call it pause—here's its definition:

```
void pause(int time) {
    try { Thread.sleep(time); }
    catch (InterruptedException e) { }
}
```

Back to the `nekorun` method. To summarize, `nekorun` iterates from the `start` position to the `end` position. For each turn of the loop, it sets the current `x` position, sets `currentimg` to the right animation frame, calls `repaint`, and pauses. Got it? Here's the definition of `nekorun`:

```
void nekorun(int start, int end) {
    for (int i = start; i < end; i+=10) {
        this.xpos = i;
        // swap images
        if (currentimg == nekopics[0])
            currentimg = nekopics[1];
        else if (currentimg == nekopics[1])
            currentimg = nekopics[0];
        repaint();
        pause(150);
    }
}
```

Note that in that second line you increment the loop by ten pixels. Why ten pixels, and not, say, five or eight? The answer is determined mostly through trial and error to see what looks right. Ten seems to work best for the animation. When you write your own animations, you have to play with both the distances and the sleep times until you get an animation you like.

Speaking of `repaint`, let's cover the `paint()` method, which paints each frame. Here the `paint` method is trivially simple; all `paint` is responsible for is painting the current image at the current `x` and `y` positions. All that information is stored in global variables, so the paint method has only a single line in it:

```
public void paint(Graphics g) {
    g.drawImage(currentimg, xpos, ypos, this);
}
```

Now let's back up to the `run()` method, where the main processing of this animation is happening. You've created the `nekorun` method; in `run` you'll call that method with the appropriate values to make Neko run from the right edge of the screen to the center:

```
// run from one side of the screen to the middle
nekorun(0, this.size().width / 2);
```

The second major thing Neko does in this animation is stop and yawn. You have a single frame for each of these things (in positions 2 and 3 in the array), so you don't really need a separate method for them. All you need to do is set the appropriate image, call repaint(), and pause for the right amount of time. This example pauses for a second each time for both stopping and yawning—again, using trial and error. Here's the code:

```
// stop and pause
currentimg = nekopics[2];
repaint();
pause(1000);

// yawn
currentimg = nekopics[3];
repaint();
pause(1000);
```

Let's move on to the third part of the animation: scratching. There's no horizontal for this part of the animation. You alternate between the two scratching images (stored in positions 4 and 5 of the image array). Because scratching is a distinct action, however, let's create a separate method for it.

The nekoscratch method takes a single argument: the number of times to scratch. With that argument, you can iterate, and then, inside the loop, alternate between the two scratching images and repaint each time:

```
void nekoscratch(int numtimes) {
    for (int i = numtimes; i > 0; i--) {
        currentimg = nekopics[4];
        repaint();
        pause(150);
        currentimg = nekopics[5];
        repaint();
        pause(150);
    }
}
```

Inside the run method, you can then call nekoscratch with an argument of four:

```
// scratch four times
nekoscratch(4);
```

Onward! After scratching, Neko sleeps. Again, you have two images for sleeping (in positions 6 and 7 of the array), which you'll alternate a certain number of times. Here's the nekosleep method, which takes a single number argument, and animates for that many "turns":

```
void nekosleep(int numtimes) {
    for (int i = numtimes; i > 0; i--) {
        currentimg = nekopics[6];
```

11

```
        repaint();
        pause(250);
        currentimg = nekopics[7];
        repaint();
        pause(250);
    }
}
```

Call `nekosleep` in the `run()` method like this:

```
// sleep for 5 "turns"
nekosleep(5);
```

Finally, to finish off the applet, Neko wakes up and runs off to the right side of the screen. wake up is your last image in the array (position eight), and you can reuse the `nekorun` method to finish:

```
// wake up and run off
currentimg = nekopics[8];
repaint();
pause(500);
nekorun(xpos, this.size().width + 10);
```

There's one more thing left to do to finish the applet. The images for the animation all have white backgrounds. Drawing those images on the default applet background (a medium grey) means an unsightly white box around each image. To get around the problem, merely set the applet's background to white at the start of the `run()` method:

```
setBackground(Color.white);
```

Got all that? There's a lot of code in this applet, and a lot of individual methods to accomplish a rather simple animation, but it's not all that complicated. The heart of it, as in the heart of all Java animations, is to set up the frame and then call `repaint()` to enable the screen to be drawn.

Note that you don't do anything to reduce the amount of flicker in this applet. It turns out that the images are small enough, and the drawing area also small enough, that flicker is not a problem for this applet. It's always a good idea to write your animations to do the simplest thing first, and then add behavior to make them run cleaner.

To finish up this section, Listing 11.3 shows the complete code for the Neko applet.

Type

Listing 11.3. The final Neko applet.

```
36: import java.awt.Graphics;
37: import java.awt.Image;
38: import java.awt.Color;
39:
40: public class Neko extends java.applet.Applet
41:     implements Runnable {
42:
43:     Image nekopics[] = new Image[9];
44:     Image currentimg;
45:     Thread runner;
46:     int xpos;
```

```
47:        int ypos = 50;
48:
49:        public void init() {
50:                String nekosrc[] = { "right1.gif", "right2.gif",
51:                "stop.gif", "yawn.gif", "scratch1.gif",
52:                "scratch2.gif","sleep1.gif", "sleep2.gif",
53:                "awake.gif" };
54:
55:            for (int i=0; i < nekopics.length; i++) {
56:                nekopics[i] = getImage(getCodeBase(),
57:                "images/" + nekosrc[i]);
58:            }
59:
60:        public void start() {
61:            if (runner == null) {
62:                runner = new Thread(this);
63:                runner.start();
64:            }
65:        }
66:
67:        public void stop() {
68:            if (runner != null) {
69:                runner.stop();
70:                runner = null;
71:            }
72:        }
73:
74:        public void run() {
75:
76:            setBackground(Color.white);
77:
78:            // run from one side of the screen to the middle
79:            nekorun(0, this.size().width / 2);
80:
81:            // stop and pause
82:            currentimg = nekopics[2];
83:            repaint();
84:            pause(1000);
85:
86:            // yawn
87:            currentimg = nekopics[3];
88:            repaint();
89:            pause(1000);
90:
91:            // scratch four times
92:            nekoscratch(4);
93:
94:            // sleep for 5 "turns"
95:            nekosleep(5);
96:
97:            // wake up and run off
98:            currentimg = nekopics[0];
99:            repaint();
100:             pause(500);
101:             nekorun(xpos, this.size().width + 10);
```

continues

Listing 11.3. continued

```
102:        }
103:
104:        void nekorun(int start, int end) {
105:            for (int i = start; i < end; i+=10) {
106:                this.xpos = i;
107:                // swap images
108:                if (currentimg == nekopics[0])
109:            currentimg = nekopics[1];
110:                else if (currentimg == nekopics[1])
111:            currentimg = nekopics[0];
112:                else currentimg = nekopics[0];
113:
114:                repaint();
115:                pause(150);
116:            }
117:        }
118:
119:        void nekoscratch(int numtimes) {
120:            for (int i = numtimes; i > 0; i--) {
121:                currentimg = nekopics[4];
122:                repaint();
123:                pause(150);
124:                currentimg = nekopics[5];
125:                repaint();
126:                pause(150);
127:            }
128:        }
129:
130:        void nekosleep(int numtimes) {
131:            for (int i = numtimes; i > 0; i--) {
132:                currentimg = nekopics[6];
133:                repaint();
134:                pause(250);
135:                currentimg = nekopics[7];
136:                repaint();
137:                pause(250);
138:            }
139:
140:        void pause(int time) {
141:            try { Thread.sleep(time); }
142:            catch (InterruptedException e) { }
143:        }
144:
145:        public void paint(Graphics g) {
146:          g.drawImage(currentimg, xpos, ypos, this);
147:        }
148: }
```

Retrieving and Using Sounds

Java has built-in support for playing sounds in conjunction with running animations or for sounds on their own. In fact, support for sound, like support for images, is built into the Applet and awt classes, so using sound in your Java applets is as easy as loading and using images.

Currently, the only sound format that Java supports is Sun's AU format, sometimes called μ-law format. AU files tend to be smaller than sound files in other formats, but the sound quality is not very good. If you're especially concerned with sound quality, you may want your sound clips to be references in the traditional HTML way (as links to external files) rather than included in a Java applet.

The simplest way to retrieve and play a sound is through the play() method, part of the Applet class and therefore available to you in your applets. The play() method is similar to the getImage method in that it takes one of two forms:

☐ play with one argument, a URL object, loads and plays the given audio clip at that URL.

☐ play() with two arguments, one a base URL and one a pathname, loads and plays that audio file. The first argument can most usefully be either a call to getDocumentBase() or getCodeBase().

For example, the following line of code retrieves and plays the sound meow.au, which is contained in the audio directory. The audio directory, in turn, is located in the same directory as this applet:

```
play(getCodeBase(), "audio/meow.au");
```

The play method retrieves and plays the given sound as soon as possible after it is called. If it can't find the sound, you won't get an error; you just won't get any audio when you expect it.

If you want to play a sound repeatedly, start and stop the sound clip, or run the clip as a loop (play it over and over), things are slightly more complicated—but not much more so. In this case, you use the applet method getAudioClip() to load the sound clip into an instance of the class AudioClip (part of java.applet—don't forget to import it) and then operate directly on that AudioClip object.

Suppose, for example, that you have a sound loop that you want to play in the background of your applet. In your initialization code, you can use this line to get the audio clip:

```
AudioClip clip = getAudioClip(getCodeBase(),
    "audio/loop.au");
```

Then, to play the clip once, use the play method:

```
clip.play();
```

To stop a currently playing sound clip, use the `stop()` method:

```
clip.stop();
```

To loop the clip (play it repeatedly), use the `loop()` method:

```
clip.loop();
```

If the `getAudioClip` method can't find the sound you indicate, or can't load it for any reason, the `AudioClip` variable is set to `null`. It's a good idea to test for this case in your code before trying to play the audio clip—, because trying to call the `play()`, `stop()`, and `loop()` methods on a `null` object will result in an error (actually, an exception).

In your applet, you can play as many audio clips as you need; all the sounds you use play concurrently as your applet executes.

Note that if you use a background sound—a sound clip that loops repeatedly—that sound clip will not stop playing automatically when you suspend the applet's thread. This means that even if your reader moves to another page, the first applet's sounds will continue to play. You can fix this problem by stopping the applet's background sound in your `stop()` method:

```
public void stop() {
    if (runner != null) {
        if (bgsound!= null)
            bgsound.stop();
        runner.stop();
        runner = null;
    }
}
```

Listing 11.4 shows a simple framework for an applet that plays two sounds: the first, a background sound called loop.au, plays repeatedly. The second, a horn honking (beep.au) plays every five seconds. (I won't bother giving you a picture of this applet, because it doesn't actually display anything other than a simple string to the screen).

Type   **Listing 11.4. The AudioLoop applet.**

```
 1: import java.awt.Graphics;
 2: import java.applet.AudioClip;
 3:
 4: public class AudioLoop extends java.applet.Applet
 5:   implements Runnable {
 6:
 7:   AudioClip bgsound;
 8:   AudioClip beep;
 9:     Thread runner;
10:
11:     public void start() {
12:         if (runner == null) {
13:             runner = new Thread(this);
14:             runner.start();
```

```
15:        }
16:    }
17:
18:    public void stop() {
19:        if (runner != null) {
20:            if (bgsound != null) bgsound.stop();
21:            runner.stop();
22:            runner = null;
23:        }
24:    }
25:
26:    public void init() {
27:        bgsound = getAudioClip(getCodeBase(),"audio/loop.au");
28:        beep = getAudioClip(getCodeBase(), "audio/beep.au");
29:    }
30:
31:    public void run() {
32:        if (bgsound != null) bgsound.loop();
33:        while (runner != null) {
34:            try { Thread.sleep(5000); }
35:            catch (InterruptedException e) { }
36:            if (bgsound != null) beep.play();
37:        }
38:    }
39:
40:    public void paint(Graphics g) {
41:        g.drawString("Playing Sounds....", 10, 10);
42:    }
43: }
```

Sun's Animator Applet

Because most Java animations have a lot of code in common, being able to reuse all that code as much as possible makes creating animations with images and sounds much easier, particular for Java developers who aren't as good at the programming side of Java. For just this reason, Sun provides an Animator class as part of the standard Java release.

The Animator applet provides a simple, general-purpose animation interface. You compile the code and create an HTML file with the appropriate parameters for the animation. Using the Animator applet, you can do the following:

☐ Create an animation loop, that is, an animation that plays repeatedly.

☐ Add a soundtrack to the applet.

☐ Add sounds to be played at individual frames.

☐ Indicate the speed at which the animation is to occur.

☐ Specify the order of the frames in the animation—which means that you can reuse frames that repeat during the course of the animation.

Even if you don't intend to use Sun's Animator code, it's a great example of how animations work in Java and the sorts of clever tricks you can use in a Java applet.

The Animator class is part of the Java distribution (in the demo directory), or you can find out more information about it at the Java home page, http://java.sun.com.

More About Flicker: Double-Buffering

Yesterday, you learned two simple ways to reduce flickering in animations. Although you learned specifically about animations using drawing, flicker can also result from animations using images. In addition to the two flicker-reducing methods described yesterday, there is one other way to reduce flicker in an application: double-buffering.

NEW☞ TERM With *double-buffering*, you create a second surface (offscreen, so to speak), do all your painting to that offscreen surface, and then draw the whole surface at once onto the actual applet (and onto the screen) at the end—rather than drawing to the applet's actual graphics surface. Because all the work actually goes on behind the scenes, there's no opportunity for interim parts of the drawing process to appear accidentally and disrupt the smoothness of the animation.

Double-buffering isn't always the best solution. If your applet is suffering from flicker, try overriding update and drawing only portions of the screen first; that may solve your problem. Double-buffering is less efficient than regular buffering, and also takes up more memory and space, so if you can avoid it, make an effort to do so. In terms of nearly eliminating animation flicker, however, double-buffering works exceptionally well.

Creating Applets with Double-Buffering

To execute double-buffering, you need two things: an image to draw on and a graphics context for that image. Those two together mimic the effect of the applet's drawing surface: the graphics context (an instance of Graphics) to provide the drawing methods, such as drawImage and drawString, and the Image to hold the dots that get drawn.

There are four major steps to adding double-buffering to your applet. First, your offscreen image and graphics context need to be stored in instance variables so that you can pass them to the paint() method. Declare the following instance variables in your class definition:

```
Image offscreenImage;
Graphics offscreenGraphics;
```

Second, during the initialization of the applet, you'll create an Image and a Graphics object and assign them to these variables (you have to wait until initialization so you know how big they're going to be). The createImage method gives you an instance of Image, which you can then send the getGraphics() method in order to get a new graphics context for that image:

```
offscreenImage = createImage(this.size().width,
    this.size().height);
offscreenGraphics = offscreenImage.getGraphics();
```

Now, whenever you have to draw to the screen (usually in your `paint` method), rather than drawing to paint's graphics, draw to the offscreen graphics. For example, to draw an image called img at position 10,10, use this line:

```
offscreenGraphics.drawImage(img,10,10,this);
```

Finally, at the end of your `paint` method, after all the drawing to the offscreen image is done, add the following line to print the offscreen buffer to the real screen:

```
g.drawImage(offscreenImage, 0, 0, this);
```

Of course, you most likely will want to override `update` so that it doesn't clear the screen between paintings:

```
public void update(Graphics g) {
    paint(g);
}
```

Let's review those four steps:

- ☐ Add instance variables to hold the image and graphics contexts for the offscreen buffer.
- ☐ Create an image and a graphics context when your applet is initialized.
- ☐ Do all your applet painting to the offscreen buffer, not the applet's drawing surface.
- ☐ At the end of your `paint` method, draw the offscreen buffer to the real screen.

An Example: Checkers Revisited

Yesterday's example featured the animated moving red oval to demonstrate animation flicker and how to reduce it. Even with the operations you did yesterday, however, the Checkers applet still flashed occasionally. Let's revise that applet to include double-buffering.

First, add the instance variables for the offscreen image and its graphics context:

```
Image offscreenImg;
Graphics offscreenG;
```

Second, add an `init` method to initialize the offscreen buffer:

```
public void init() {
    offscreenImg = createImage(this.size().width,
    this.size().height);
    offscreenG = offscreenImg.getGraphics();
}
```

Third, modify the paint method to draw to the offscreen buffer instead of to the main graphics buffer:

```
public void paint(Graphics g) {
    // Draw background
    offscreenG.setColor(Color.black);
    offscreenG.fillRect(0,0,100,100);
    offscreenG.setColor(Color.white);
    offscreenG.fillRect(100,0,100,100);

    // Draw checker
    offscreenG.setColor(Color.red);
    offscreenG.fillOval(xpos,5,90,90);

    g.drawImage(offscreenImg,0,0,this);
}
```

Note that you're still clipping the main graphics rectangle in the update method, as you did yesterday; you don't have to change that part. The only part that is relevant is that final paint method wherein everything is drawn offscreen before finally being displayed.

Summary

Three major topics were the focus of today's lesson. First, you learned about using images in your applets—locating them, loading them, and using the drawImage method to display them, either at their normal size or scaled to different sizes. You also learned how to create animations using images.

Secondly, you learned how to use sounds, which can be included in your applets any time you need them—at specific moments, or as background sounds that can be repeated while the applet executes. You learned how to locate, load, and play sounds both using the play() and the getAudioClip() methods.

Finally, you learned about double-buffering, a technique that enables you virtually to eliminate flicker in animations, at some expense of animation efficiency and speed. Using images and graphics contexts, you can create an offscreen buffer to draw to, the result of which is then displayed to the screen at the last possible moment.

Q&A

Q In the Neko program, you put the image loading into the `init()` method. It seems to me that it might take Java a long time to load all those images, and because `init()` isn't in the main thread of the applet, there's going to be a distinct pause there. Why not put the image loading at the beginning of the `run()` method instead?

A There are sneaky things going on behind the scenes. The `getImage` method doesn't actually load the image; in fact, it returns an `Image` object almost instantaneously, so it isn't taking up a large amount of processing time during initialization. The image data that `getImage` points to isn't actually loaded until the image is needed. This way, Java doesn't have to keep enormous images around in memory if the program is going to use only a small piece. Instead, it can just keep a reference to that data and retrieve what it needs later.

Q I wrote an applet to do a background sound using the `getAudioClip()` and `loop()` methods. The sounds works great, but it won't stop. I've tried suspending the current thread and killing, but the sound goes on.

A I mentioned this as a small note in the section on sounds; background sounds don't run in the main thread of the applet, so if you stop the thread, the sound keeps going. The solution is easy—in the same method where you stop the thread, also stop the sound, like this:

```
runner.stop() //stop the thread
bgsound.stop() //also stop the sound
```

Q If I use double-buffering, do I still have to clip to a small region of the screen? Because double-buffering eliminates flicker, it seems easier to draw the whole frame every time.

A Easier, yes, but less efficient. Drawing only part of the screen not only reduces flicker, it also limits the amount of work your applet has to do in the `paint()` method. The faster the `paint()` method works, the faster and smoother your animation will run. Using clip regions and drawing only what is necessary is a good practice to follow in general—not just if you have a problem with flicker.

11

Managing Simple Events and Interactivity

by Laura Lemay

Java events are part of the Java AWT (Abstract Windowing Toolkit) package. An event is the way that the AWT communicates to you, as the programmer, and to other Java AWT components that *something* has happened. That something can be input from the user (mouse movements or clicks, keypresses), changes in the system environment (a window opening or closing, the window being scrolled up or down), or a host of other things that might, in some way, be interesting to the operation of the program.

> **Note:** Java's Abstract Windowing Toolkit is a package of classes that implements most common UI components, such as windows, buttons, menus, and so on. It is also specifically the AWT, and not Java, that generates and manages events.

In other words, whenever just about anything happens to a Java AWT component, including an applet, an event is generated. Some events are handled by the AWT or by the browser without your needing to do anything. paint() methods, for example, are generated and handled by the browser—all you have to do is tell the AWT what you want painted when it gets to your part of the window. Some events, however—for example, a mouse click inside the boundaries of your applet—you may need to know about. Writing your Java programs to handle these kinds of events enables you to get input from the user and have your applet change its behavior based on that input.

Today, you'll learn about managing simple events, including the following basics:

☐ Mouse clicks

☐ Mouse movements, including mouse dragging

☐ Keyboard actions

You'll also learn about the handleEvent() method, which is the basis for collecting, handling, and passing on events of all kinds from your applet to other UI components in the window or in your applet itself. Tomorrow, you'll learn how to combine events with the AWT to create a complete interface for your applet.

Mouse Clicks

Let's start with the most common event you might be interested in: mouse clicks. Mouse-click events occur when your user clicks the mouse somewhere in the body of your applet. You can intercept mouse clicks to do very simple things—for example, to toggle the sound on and off in your applet, to move to the next slide in a presentation, or to clear the screen and start over—or you can use mouse clicks in conjunction with mouse movements to perform more complex motions inside your applet.

mouseDown and *mouseUp*

When you click the mouse once, the AWT generates two events: a `mouseDown` event when the mouse button is pressed, and a `mouseUp` event when the button is released. Why two individual events for a single mouse action? Because you may want to do different things for the "down" and the "up." For example, look at a pull-down menu. The `mouseDown` extends the menu, and the `mouseUp` selects an item (with `mouseDrags` between—but you'll learn about that one later). If you have only one event for both actions (`mouseUp` and `mouseDown`), you cannot implement that sort of user interaction.

Handling mouse events in your applet is easy—all you have to do is override the right method definition in your applet. That method will be called when that particular event occurs. Here's an example of the method signature for a `mouseDown` event:

```
public boolean mouseDown(Event evt, int x, int y) {
...
}
```

The `mouseDown()` method (and the `mouseUp()` method as well) takes three parameters: the event itself and the x and y coordinates where the `mouseDown` or `mouseUp` event occurred.

The event argument is an instance of the class `Event`. All system events generate an instance of the `Event` class, which contains information about where and when the event took place, the kind of event it is, and other information that you might want to know about this event. Sometimes having a handle to that event object is useful, as you'll discover later on in this section.

The x and the y coordinates of the event, as passed in through the x and y arguments, are particularly nice to know because you can use them to determine precisely where the mouse click took place.

For example, here's a simple method that prints out information about a `mouseDown` when it occurs:

```
public boolean mouseDown(Event evt, int x, int y) {
    System.out.println("Mouse down at " + x + "," + y);
    return true;
}
```

By including this method in your applet, every time your user clicks the mouse inside your applet, this message will get printed.

Note that this method, unlike the other system methods you've studied this far, returns a boolean value instead of not returning anything (`void`). This will become important tomorrow when you create user interfaces and then manage input to these interfaces; having an event handler return `true` or `false` determines whether a given UI component can intercept an event or whether it needs to pass it on to the enclosing component. The general rule is that if your method deals with the event, it should return `true`, which for the focus of today's lesson is almost always the case.

The second half of the mouse click is the `mouseUp()` method, which is called when the mouse button is released. To handle a `mouseUp` event, add the `mouseUp()` method to your applet. `mouseUp()` looks just like `mouseDown()`:

```
public boolean mouseUp(Event evt, int x, int y) {
    ....
}
```

An Example: Spots

In this section, you'll create an example of an applet that uses mouse events—`mouseDown` events in particular. The Spots applet starts with a blank screen and then sits and waits. When you click the mouse on that screen, a blue dot is drawn. You can place up to ten dots on the screen. Figure 12.1 shows the Spots applet.

Figure 12.1.
The Spots applet.

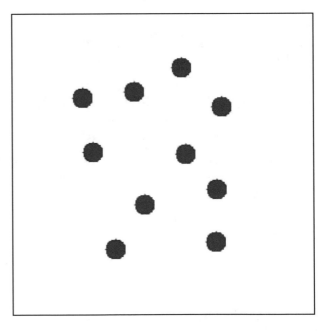

Let's start from the beginning and build this applet, starting from the initial class definition:

```
import java.awt.Graphics;
import java.awt.Color;
import java.awt.Event;

public class Spots extends java.applet.Applet {

    final int MAXSPOTS = 10;
    int xspots[] = new int[MAXSPOTS];
```

```
int yspots[] = new int[MAXSPOTS];
int currspots = 0;
}
```

This class uses three other AWT classes: Graphics, Color, and Event. That last class, Event, needs to be imported in any applets that use events. The class has four instance variables: a constant to determine the maximum number of spots that can be drawn, two arrays to store the x and y coordinates of the spots that have already been drawn, and an integer to keep track of the number of the current spot.

> **Note:** This class doesn't include the implements Runnable words in its definition. As you'll see later on as you build this applet, it also doesn't have a run() method. Why not? Because it doesn't actually do anything on its own—all it does is wait for input and then do stuff when input happens. There's no need for threads if your applet isn't actively doing something all the time.

Let's start with the init() method, which has one line, to set the background to white:

```
public void init() {
        setBackground(Color.white);
}
```

Set the background here, instead of in paint(), because paint() is called repeatedly each time a new spot is added. Because you really need to set the background only once, putting it in the paint() method unnecessarily slows down that method. Putting it here is a much better idea.

The main action of this applet occurs on the mouseDown() method, so let's add that one now:

```
public boolean mouseDown(Event evt, int x, int y) {
    if (currspots < MAXSPOTS)
            addspot(x,y);
        else System.out.println("Too many spots.");
        return true;
}
```

When the mouse click occurs, the mouseDown() method tests to see whether there are less than ten spots. If so, it calls the addspot() method (which you'll write soon). If not, it just prints an error message. Finally, it returns true, because all the event methods have to return a boolean value (usually true).

What does addspot() do? It adds the coordinates of the spot to the arrays that store the coordinates, increments the currspots variable, and then calls repaint():

```
void addspot(int x,int y) {
        xspots[currspots] = x;
        yspots[currspots] = y;
```

```
        currspots++;
        repaint();
    }
```

You may be wondering why you have to keep track of all the past spots in addition to the current spot. The reason is because of repaint(): each time you paint the screen, you have to paint all the old spots in addition to the newest spot. Otherwise, each time you painted a new spot, the older spots would get erased. Now, on to the paint() method:

```
public void paint(Graphics g) {
        g.setColor(Color.blue);
        for (int i = 0; i < currspots; i++) {
            g.fillOval(xspots[i] -10, yspots[i] -10,20,20);
        }
    }
```

Inside paint, you just loop through the spots you've stored in the xspots and yspots arrays, painting each one (actually, painting them a little to the right and upward so that the spot is painted around the mouse pointer rather than below and to the right).

That's it! That's all you need to create an applet that handles mouse clicks. Everything else is handled for you. You have to add the appropriate behavior to mouseDown() or mouseUp() to intercept and handle that event. Listing 12.1 shows the full text for the Spots applet.

Type

Listing 12.1. The Spots applet.

```
1: import java.awt.Graphics;
2: import java.awt.Color;
3: import java.awt.Event;
4:
5: public class Spots extends java.applet.Applet {
6:
7: final int MAXSPOTS = 10;
8:     int xspots[] = new int[MAXSPOTS];
9:     int yspots[] = new int[MAXSPOTS];
10:     int currspots = 0;
11:
12:     public void init() {
13:         setBackground(Color.white);
14:     }
15:
16:     public boolean mouseDown(Event evt, int x, int y) {
17:         if (currspots < MAXSPOTS)
18:             addspot(x,y);
19:         else System.out.println("Too many spots.");
20:         return true;
21: }
22:
23:     void addspot(int x,int y) {
24:         xspots[currspots] = x;
25:         yspots[currspots] = y;
26:         currspots++;
27:         repaint();
```

```
28:    }
29:
30:    public void paint(Graphics g) {
31:        g.setColor(Color.blue);
32:        for (int i = 0; i < currspots; i++) {
33:            g.fillOval(xspots[i] -10, yspots[i] -10,20,20);
34:        }
35:    }
36: }
```

Mouse Movements

Every time the mouse is moved a single pixel in any direction, a mouse move event is generated. There are two mouse movement events: mouse drags, where the movement occurs with the mouse button pressed down, and plain mouse movements, where the mouse button isn't pressed.

To manage mouse movement events, use the mouseDrag() and mouseMove() methods.

mouseDrag and *mouseMove*

The mouseDrag() and mouseMove() methods, when included in your applet code, intercept and handle mouse movement events. The mouseMove() method, for plain mouse pointer movements without the mouse button pressed, looks much like the mouse-click methods:

```
public boolean mouseMove(Event evt, int x, int y) {
    ...
}
```

The mouseDrag() method handles mouse movements made with the mouse button pressed down (a complete dragging movement consists of a mouseDown event, a series of mouseDrag events for each pixel the mouse is moved, and a mouseUp even when the button is released). The mouseDrag() method looks like this:

```
public boolean mouseDrag(Event evt, int x, int y) {
    ...
}
```

mouseEnter and *mouseExit*

Finally, there are the mouseEnter() and mouseExit() methods. These two methods are called when the mouse pointer enters the applet or when it exits the applet. (In case you're wondering why you might need to know this, it's more useful on components of user interfaces that you might put inside an applet. You'll learn more about UI tomorrow).

Both `mouseEnter()` and `mouseExit()` have similar signatures—three arguments: the event object and the x and y coordinates of the point where the mouse entered or exited the applet.

```
public boolean mouseEnter(Event evt, int x, int y) {
    ...
}

public boolean mouseExit(Event evt, int x, int y) {
    ...
}
```

An Example: Drawing Lines

Examples always help to make concepts more concrete. In this section you'll create an applet that enables you to draw straight lines on the screen by dragging from the startpoint to the endpoint. Figure 12.2 shows the applet at work.

Figure 12.2.

Drawing `Lines`.

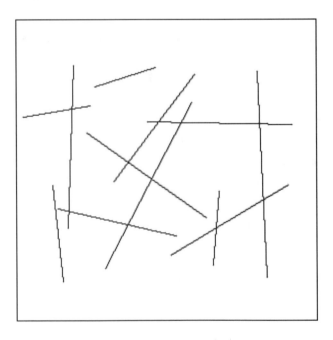

As with the Spots applet (on which this applet is based), let's start with the basic definition and work our way through it. Listing 12.2 shows the top of the Lines applet.

Type

Listing 12.2. The top of the Lines applet.

```
1: import java.awt.Graphics;
2: import java.awt.Color;
3: import java.awt.Event;
```

```
 4: import java.awt.Point;
 5:
 6: public class Lines extends java.applet.Applet {
 7:
 8:     final int MAXLINES = 10;
 9:     Point starts[] = new Point[MAXLINES]; // starting points
10:     Point ends[] = new Point[10];     // ending points
11:     Point anchor;    // start of current line
12:     Point currentpoint; // current end of line
13:     int currline = 0; // number of lines
14:
15:     public void init() {
16:         setBackground(Color.white);
17:     }
18:
```

Analysis Compared to Spots, this applet added a few extra things. Unlike Spots, which keeps track of individual integer coordinates, this one keeps track of Point objects. Points represent an x and a y coordinate, encapsulated in a single object. To deal with points, you import the Point class (line 4) and set up a bunch of instance variables that hold points:

☐ The starts array holds points representing the starts of lines already drawn.

☐ The ends array holds the endpoints of those same lines.

☐ anchor holds the starting point of the line currently being drawn.

☐ currentpoint holds the current endpoint of the line currently being drawn.

☐ currline holds the current number of lines (to make sure you don't go over MAXLINES).

Finally, the init() method (lines 15 through 17), as in the Spots applet, sets the background of the applet to white.

The three main events this applet deals with are mouseDown(), to set the anchor point for the current line, mouseDrag(), to animate the current line as it's being drawn, and mouseUp(), to set the ending point for the new line. Given that you have instance variables to hold each of these values, it's merely a matter of plugging the right variables into the right methods. Here's mouseDown(), which sets the anchor point:

```
public boolean mouseDown(Event evt, int x, int y) {
    anchor = new Point(x,y);
    return true;
}
```

While the mouse is being dragged to draw the line, the applet animates the line being drawn. As you draw the mouse around, the new line moves with it from the anchor point to the tip of the mouse. The mouseDrag event contains the current point each time the mouse moves, so use that method to keep track of the current point (and to repaint for each movement so the line "animates"):

12

```
public boolean mouseDrag(Event evt, int x, int y) {
    currentpoint = new Point(x,y);
    repaint();
    return true;
}
```

The new line doesn't get added to the arrays of old lines until the mouse button is released. Here's mouseUp(), which tests to make sure you haven't exceeded the maximum number of lines before calling the addline() method (described next):

```
public boolean mouseUp(Event evt, int x, int y) {
    if (currline < MAXLINES)
        addline(x,y);
    else System.out.println("Too many lines.");
    return true;
}
```

The addline() method is where the arrays of lines get updated and where the applet is repainted to take the new line into effect:

```
void addline(int x,int y) {
    starts[currline] = anchor;
    ends[currline] = new Point(x,y);
    currline++;
    currentpoint = null;
    repaint();
}
```

Note that in this line you also set currentpoint to null. Why? Because the current line in process is over. By setting currentpoint to null, you can test for that value in the paint() method.

Painting the applet means drawing all the old lines stored in the starts and ends arrays, as well as drawing the current line in process (whose endpoints are in anchor and currentpoint, respectively). To show the animation of the current line, draw it in blue. Here's the paint() method for the Lines applet:

```
public void paint(Graphics g) {

    // Draw existing lines
    for (int i = 0; i < currline; i++) {
        g.drawLine(starts[i].x, starts[i].y,
            ends[i].x, ends[i].y);
    }

    // draw current line
    g.setColor(Color.blue);
    if (currentpoint != null)
        g.drawLine(anchor.x,anchor.y,
            currentpoint.x,currentpoint.y);
}
```

In paint, when you're drawing the current line, you test first to see whether currentpoint is null. If it is, the applet isn't in the middle of drawing a line, so there's no reason to try drawing a line that doesn't exist. By testing for currentpoint (and by setting currentpoint to null in the addline() method), you can paint only what you need.

That's it—just 60 lines of code and a few basic methods, and you have a very basic drawing application in your Web browser. Listing 12.3 shows the full text of the Lines applet so that you can put the pieces together.

Type

Listing 12.3. The Lines applet.

```
 1: import java.awt.Graphics;
 2: import java.awt.Color;
 3: import java.awt.Event;
 4: import java.awt.Point;
 5:
 6: public class Lines extends java.applet.Applet {
 7:
 8:     final int MAXLINES = ;
 9:     Point starts[] = new Point[MAXLINES]; // starting points
10:     Point ends[] = new Point[10];    // endingpoints
11:     Point anchor;    // start of current line
12:     Point currentpoint; // current end of line
13:     int currline = 0; // number of lines
14:
15:     public void init() {
16:         setBackground(Color.white);
17:     }
18:
19:     public boolean mouseDown(Event evt, int x, int y) {
20:         anchor = new Point(x,y);
21:         return true;
22:     }
23:
24:     public boolean mouseUp(Event evt, int x, int y) {
25:         if (currline < MAXSPOTS)
26:             addline(x,y);
27:         else System.out.println("Too many lines.");
28:         return true;
29:     }
30:
31:     public boolean mouseDrag(Event evt, int x, int y) {
32:         currentpoint = new Point(x,y);
33:         repaint();
34:         return true;
35:     }
36:
37:     void addline(int x,int y) {
38:         starts[currline] = anchor;
39:         ends[currline] = new Point(x,y);
40:         currline++;
41:         currentpoint = null;
42:         repaint();
43:     }
44:
45:     public void paint(Graphics g) {
```

12

227

Listing 12.3. continued

```
46:
47:            // Draw existing lines
48:            for (int i = 0; i < currline; i++) {
49:                g.drawLine(starts[i].x, starts[i].y,
50:                    ends[i].x, ends[i].y);
51:            }
52:
53:            // draw current line
54:        g.setColor(Color.blue);
55:        if (currentpoint != null)
56:            g.drawLine(anchor.x,anchor.y,
57:            currentpoint.x,currentpoint.y);
58:    }
59: }
```

Keyboard Events

Keyboard events are generated whenever users press a key on the keyboard. By using key events, you can get hold of the values of the keys they pressed to perform an action or merely to get character input from the users of your applet.

The *keyDown* Method

To capture a keyboard event, use the keyDown() method:

```
public boolean keyDown(Event evt, int key) {
    ...
}
```

The keys generated by keyDown events (and passed into keyDown() as the key argument) are integers representing ASCII character values, which include alphanumeric characters, function keys, tabs, returns, and so on. To use them as characters (for example, to print them), you need to cast them to characters:

```
currentchar = (char)key;
```

Here's a simple example of a keyDown() method that does nothing but print the key you just typed in both its ASCII and character representation:

```
public boolean keyDown(Event evt, int key) {
    System.out.println("ASCII value: " + key);
    System.out.println("Character: " + (char)key);
    return true;
}
```

Default Keys

The Event class provides a set of class variables that refer to several standard nonalphanumeric keys, such as the arrow keys. If your interface uses these keys, you can provide more readable code by testing for these names in your keyDown() method rather than testing for their numeric values. For example, to test whether the up arrow was pressed, you might use the following snippet of code:

```
if (key == Event.UP) {
    ...
}
```

Because the values these class variables hold are integers, you also can use the switch statement to test for them.

Table 12.1 shows the standard event class variables for various keys and the actual keys they represent.

Table 12.1. Standard keys defined by the event class.

Class Variable	Represened Key
Event.HOME	The Home key
Event.END	The End key
Event.PGUP	The Page Up key
Event.PGDN	The Page Down key
Event.UP	The up arrow
Event.DOWN	The down arrow
Event.LEFT	The left arrow
Event.RIGHT	The right arrow

An Example: Entering, Displaying, and Moving Characters

Let's look at an applet that demonstrates keyboard events. This one enables you to type a character, and it displays that character in the center of the applet window. You then can move that character around on the screen by using the arrow keys. Typing another character at any time changes the character as it's currently displayed. Figure 12.3 shows an example.

Figure 12.3.

The Keys applet.

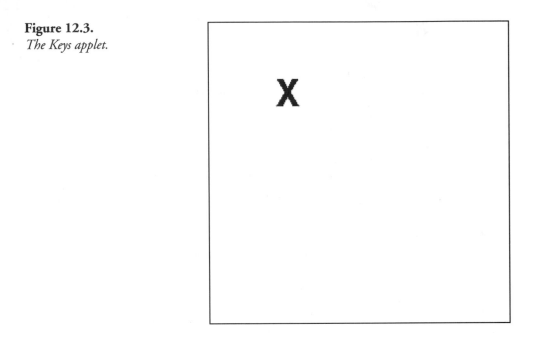

This applet is actually less complicated than the previous applets you've used. This one has only three methods: `init()`, `keyDown()`, and `paint()`. The instance variables are also simpler, because the only things you need to keep track of are the x and y positions of the current character and the values of that character itself. Here's the top of this class definition:

```
import java.awt.Graphics;
import java.awt.Event;
import java.awt.Font;

public class Keys extends java.applet.Applet {

    char currkey;
    int currx;
    int curry;
```

The `init()` method is responsible for three things: setting the background color, setting the applet's font (here, 36 point Helvetica bold), and setting the beginning position for the character (the middle of the screen, minus a few points to nudge it up and to the right):

```
public void init() {
    currx = (this.size().width / 2) -8;   // default
    curry = (this.size().height / 2) -16;
    setBackground(Color.white);
    setFont(new Font("Helvetica",Font.BOLD,36));
}
```

Because this applet's behavior is based on keyboard input, the keyDown() method is where most of the work of the applet takes place:

```
public boolean keyDown(Event evt, int key) {
        switch (key) {
        case Event.DOWN:
            curry += 5;
            break;
        case Event.UP:
            curry -= 5;
            break;
        case Event.LEFT:
            currx -= 5;
            break;
        case Event.RIGHT:
            currx += 5;
            break;
    default:
            currkey = (char)key;
        }
        repaint();
        return true;
    }
```

In the center of the keyDown() applet is a switch statement that tests for different key events. If the event is an arrow key, the appropriate change is made to the character's position. If the event is any other key, the character itself is changed. The method finishes up with a repaint() and returns true.

The paint() method here is almost trivial; just display the current character at the current position. However, note that when the applet starts up, there's no initial character and nothing to draw, so you have to take that into account. The currkey variable is initialized to 0, so you paint the applet only if currkey has an actual value:

```
    public void paint(Graphics g) {
        if (currkey != 0) {
            g.drawString(String.valueOf(currkey), currx,curry);
        }
    }
```

Listing 12.4 shows the complete source for the Keys applet:

Listing 12.4. The Keys applet.

```
1: import java.awt.Graphics;
2: import java.awt.Event;
3: import java.awt.Font;
4:
5: public class Keys extends java.applet.Applet {
6:
7:     char currkey;
8:     int currx;
```

continues

Listing 12.4. continued

```
 9:    int curry;
10:
11:    public void init() {
12:        currx = (this.size().width / 2) -8;   // default
13:        curry = (this.size().height / 2) -16;
14:
15:        setBackground(Color.white);
16:        setFont(new Font("Helvetica",Font.BOLD,36));
17:    }
18:
19:    public boolean keyDown(Event evt, int key) {
20:        switch (key) {
21:        case Event.DOWN:
22:            curry += 5;
23:            break;
24:        case Event.UP:
25:            curry -= 5;
26:            break;
27:        case Event.LEFT:
28:            currx -= 5;
29:            break;
30:        case Event.RIGHT:
31:            currx += 5;
32:            break;
33:    default:
34:            currkey = (char)key;
35:        }
36:
37:        repaint();
38:        return true;
39:    }
40:
41:    public void paint(Graphics g) {
42:        if (currkey != 0) {
43:            g.drawString(String.valueOf(currkey), currx,curry);
44:        }
45:    }
46: }
```

Testing for Modifier Keys

Shift, control, and meta are modifier keys. They don't generate key events themselves, but when you get an ordinary mouse or keyboard event, you can test to see whether those keys were held down when the event occurred. Sometimes it may be obvious—shifted alphanumeric keys produce different key events than unshifted ones, for example. For other events, however—mouse events in particular—you may want to handle an event with a modifier key held down differently from a regular version of that event.

The Event class provides three methods for testing whether or not a modifier key is held down: shiftDown(), metaDown(), and controlDown(). All return boolean values based on whether that modifier key is indeed held down. You can use these three methods in any of the event handling methods (mouse or keyboard) by calling them on the event object passed into that method:

```
public boolean mouseDown(Event evt, int x, int y ) {
    if (evt.shiftDown)
        // handle shift-click
    else // handle regular click
}
```

The AWT Event Handler

The default methods you've learned about today for handling basic events in applets are actually called by a generic event handler method called handleEvent(). The handleEvent() method is how the AWT generically deals with events that occur between application components and events based on user input.

In the default handleEvent() method, basic events are processed and the methods you learned about today are called. To handle events other than those mentioned here, to change the default event handling behavior, or to create and pass around your own events, you need to override handleEvent in your own Java programs. The handleEvent() method looks like this:

```
public boolean handleEvent(Event evt) {
    ...
}
```

To test for specific events, examine the ID instance variable of the Event object that gets passed in. The event ID is an integer, but fortunately, the Event class defines a whole set of event IDs as class variables that you can test for in the body of the handleEvent. Because these class variables are integer constants, a switch statement works particularly well. For example, here's a simple handleEvent() method to print out debugging information about mouse events:

```
public boolean handleEvent(Event evt) {
    switch (evt.id) {
    case Event.MOUSE_DOWN:
        System.out.println("MouseDown: " +
                evt.x + "," + evt.y);
        return true;
    case Event.MOUSE_UP:
        System.out.println("MouseUp: " +
                evt.x + "," + evt.y);
        return true;
    case Event.MOUSE_MOVE:
        System.out.println("MouseMove: " +
                evt.x + "," + evt.y);
        return true;
    case Event.MOUSE_DRAG:
        System.out.println("MouseDown: " +
                evt.x + "," + evt.y);
```

12

233

```
        return true;
    default:
        return false;
    }
}
```

You can test for the following keyboard events:

- [ ] `Event.KEYPRESS` is generated when a key is pressed (the same as the `keyDown()` method).

- [ ] `Event.KEYRELEASE` is generated when a key is released.

- [ ] `Event.KEYACTION` is generated when a key action (a press and a release) occurs.

You can test for these mouse events:

- [ ] `Event.MOUSE_DOWN` is generated when the mouse button is pressed (the same as the `mouseDown()` method).

- [ ] `Event.MOUSE_UP` is generated when the mouse button is released (the same as the `mouseUp()` method).

- [ ] `Event.MOUSE_MOVE` is generated when the mouse is moved (the same as the `mouseMove()` method).

- [ ] `Event.MOUSE_DRAG` is generated when the mouse is moved with the button pressed (the same as the `mouseDrag()` method).

- [ ] `Event.MOUSE_ENTER` is generated when the mouse enters the applet (or a component of that applet). You can also use the `mouseEnter()` method.

- [ ] `Event.MOUSE_EXIT` is generated when the mouse exits the applet. You can also use the `mouseExit()` method.

In addition to these events, the `Event` class has a whole suite of methods for handling UI components. You'll learn more about these events tomorrow.

Note that if you override `handleEvent()` in your class, none of the default event handling methods you learned about today will get called unless you explicitly call them in the body of `handleEvent()`, so be careful if you decide to do this. One way to get around this is to test for the event you're interested in, and if that event isn't it, to call `super.handleEvent()` so that the superclass that defines `handleEvent()` can process things. Here's an example of how to do this:

```
public boolean handleEvent(Event evt) {
    if (evt.id == Event.MOUSE_DOWN) {
        // process the mouse down
        return true;
    } else {
        return super.handleEvent(evt);
    }
}
```

Summary

Handling events in Java's Abstract Windowing Toolkit (AWT) is easy. Most of the time, all you need to do is stick the right method in your applet code, and your applet intercepts and handles that method. Here are some of the basic events you can manage in this way:

☐ Mouse clicks—`mouseUp()` and `mouseDown()` methods for each part of a mouse click.

☐ Mouse movements—`mouseMove()` and `mouseDrag()` for mouse movement with the mouse button released and pressed, respectively, as well as `mouseEnter()` and `mouseExit()` for when the mouse enters and exits the applet area.

☐ `keyDown` for when a key on the keyboard is pressed.

All events in the AWT generate an `Event` object; inside that object, you can find out information about the event, when it occurred, and its x and y coordinates (if applicable). You can also test that event to see whether a modifier key was pressed when the event occurred, by using the `shiftDown()`, `controlDown()`, and `metaDown()` methods.

Finally, there is the `handleEvent()`, the "parent" of the individual event methods. The `handleEvent()` method is actually what the Java system calls to manage events; the default implementation calls the individual method events where necessary. To override how methods are managed in your applet, override `handleEvent`.

Q&A

Q **In the Spots applet, the spot coordinates are stored in arrays, which have a limited size. How can I modify this applet so that it will drawn an unlimited number of spots?**

A You can do one of a couple things:

The first thing to do is test, in your `addspot()` method, whether the number of spots has exceeded `MAXSPOTS`. Then create a bigger array, copy the elements of the old array into that bigger array (use the `System.arraycopy()` method to do that), and reassign the x and y arrays to that new, bigger array.

The second thing to do is to use the `Vector` class. `Vector`, part of the java.util package, implements an array that is automatically growable—sort of like a linked list is in other languages. The disadvantage of `Vector` is that to put something into `Vector`, it has to be an actual object. This means you'll have to cast integers to `Integer` objects, and then extract their values from `Integer` objects to treat them as integers again. The `Vector` class enables you to add and remove objects to the end of `Vector` just as you can in an array (by using method calls, rather than array syntax). Check it out.

Q `mouseDown()` and `mouseUp()` seem to apply to only a single mouse button. How can I determine which button on the mouse has been pressed?

A At the moment, you can't. AWT assumes that you're using only one mouse button, or if you have a mouse with multiple buttons, that you're using only the left one. Although this provides some limitations on the kinds of actions you can perform in your applet, it does provide a cross-platform solution. Remember— different systems have different mice, so writing your applet to do something specific with the right mouse button isn't a good idea if the people running your applet are using Macintoshes and have only one mouse button. If you really want to have different mouse actions perform different things, test for modifier keys in your `mouseDown()` and `mouseUp()` methods.

Q What's a meta key?

A It's popular in Unix systems, and often mapped to Alt on most keyboards. Because Shift and Ctrl are much more popular and widespread, it's probably a good idea to base your interfaces on those modifier keys if you can.

Q How do I test to see whether the Return key has been pressed?

A Return (line feed) is character 10; Enter (carriage return) is character 13. Note that different platforms may send different keys for the actual key marked Return. In particular, Unix systems send line feeds, Macintoshes send carriage returns, and DOS systems send both. So, to provide a cross-platform behavior, you may want to test for both line feed and carriage return.

The word from the Java team is that a Return is a Return is a Return regardless of the platform. However, at the time of this writing, it is questionable whether or not this is currently true in the Java developer's kit. You may want to check the API documentation for the `Event` class to see whether this has changed in the interim.

Q I looked at the API for the `Event` class, and there are many more event types listed there than the ones you mention today.

A Yes. The `Event` class defines many different kinds of events, both for general user input, such as the mouse and keyboard events you learned about here, and also events for managing changes to the state of user interface components, such as windows and scroll bars. Tomorrow, you'll learn about those other events.

The Java Abstract
Windowing Toolkit

by Laura Lemay

For the past five days you've concentrated on creating applets that do very simple things: display text, play an animation or a sound, or enable very basic interactions with the user. Once you get past that point, however, you may want to start creating more complex applets that behave like real applications, embedded in a Web page—applets that start to look like real GUI applications with buttons, menus, text fields and other elements of a real application.

It's this sort of real work in Java applets and applications that Java's Abstract Windowing Toolkit, or AWT, was designed for. You've actually been using the AWT all along, as you might have guessed from the classes you've been importing. The `Applet` class and most of the classes you've been using this week are all integral parts of the AWT. In fact, the HotJava browser is also written in Java and uses the AWT as well.

The AWT provides the following:

- [ ] A full set of UI widgets and other components, including windows, menus, buttons, checkboxes, text fields, scrollbars, and scrolling lists
- [ ] Support for UI "containers," which can contain other embedded containers or UI widgets
- [ ] An event system for managing system and user events between and among parts of the AWT
- [ ] Mechanisms for laying out components in a way that enables platform-independent UI design

Today, you'll learn about how to use all these things in your Java applets. Tomorrow, you'll learn about creating windows, menus, and dialogs, which enable you to pop up separate windows from the browser window. In addition, you can use the AWT in stand-alone applications, so everything you've learned so far this week can still be used. If you find the framework of the Web browser too limiting, you can take your AWT background and start writing full-fledged Java applications.

Today, however, you'll continue focusing on applets.

> **Note:** This is by far the most complex lesson so far. There's a lot to cover and a lot of code to go through today, so if it starts becoming overwhelming, you might want to take two days (or more) for this one.

An AWT Overview

The basic idea behind the AWT is that a Java window is a set of nested components, starting from the outermost window all the way down to the smallest UI component. Components can include things you can actually see on the screen, such as windows, menubars, buttons, and text fields, and they can also include containers, which in turn can contain other components. Figure 13.1 shows how a sample page in a Java browser might include several different components, all of which are managed through the AWT.

This nesting of components within containers within other components creates a hierarchy of components, from the smallest checkbox inside an applet to the overall window on the screen. The hierarchy of components determines the arrangement of items on the screen and inside other items, the order in which they are painted, and how events are passed from one component to another.

Figure 13.1.
AWT components.

These are the major components you can work with in the AWT:

- ☐ *Containers.* Containers are generic AWT components that can contain other components, including other containers. The most common form of container is the panel, which represents a container that can be displayed on screen. Applets are a form of panel (in fact, the Applet class is a subclass of the Panel class).
- ☐ *Canvases.* A canvas is a simple drawing surface. Although you can draw on panels (as you've been doing all along), canvases are good for painting images or other graphics operations.
- ☐ *UI components.* These can include buttons, lists, simple popup menus, checkboxes, test fields, and other typical elements of a user interface.

☐ *Window construction components.* These include windows, frames, menubars, and dialogs. These are listed separately from the other UI components because you'll use these less often—particularly in applets. In applets, the browser provides the main window and menubar, so you don't have to use these. Your applet may create a new window, however, or you may want to write your own Java application that uses these components.

The classes inside the java.awt package are written and organized to mirror the abstract structure of containers, components, and individual UI components. Figure 13.2 shows some of the class hierarchy that makes up the main classes in the AWT. The root of most of the AWT components is the class Component, which provides basic display and event handling features. The classes Container, Canvas, TextComponent, and many of the other UI components inherit from Component. Inheriting from the Container class are objects that can contain other AWT components—the Panel and Window classes, in particular. Note that the java.applet.Applet class, even though it lives in its own package, inherits from Panel, so your applets are an integral part of the hierarchy of components in the AWT system.

Figure 13.2.
A partial AWT class hierarchy.

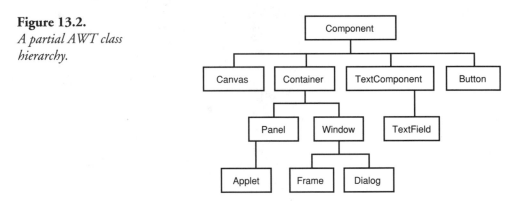

A graphical user interface-based application that you write by using the AWT can be as complex as you like, with dozens of nested containers and components inside each other. AWT was designed so that each component can play its part in the overall AWT system without needing to duplicate or keep track of the behavior of other parts in the system.

The Basic User Interface Components

The simplest form of AWT component is the basic UI component. You can create and add these to your applet without needing to know anything about creating containers or panels—your applet, even before you start painting and drawing and handling events, is already an AWT container. Because an applet is a container, you can put other AWT components—such as UI components or other containers—into it.

In this section, you'll learn about the basic UI components: labels, buttons, checkboxes, choice menus, and text fields. In each case, the procedure for creating the component is the same—you first create the component, and then add it to the panel that holds it, at which point it is displayed on the screen. To add a component to a panel (such as your applet, for example), use the add() method:

```
public void init() {
    Button b = new Button("OK");
    add(b);
}
```

Note that where the component appears in the panel depends on the layout that panel is defined to have. The default layout for panels such as applets is FlowLayout, with a centered alignment, which means that components are added from left to right in rows, and then row by row as they fit, with each row centered. This explains why some of the examples in this section look a little funny. You'll learn more about panels and layouts in the next section.

Note also that each of these components has an action associated with it—that is, something that component does when it's activated. Actions generally trigger events or other activities in your applet (often called callbacks in other window toolkits). In this section, you'll focus on creating the components themselves; you'll learn about adding actions to them later in today's lesson.

On to the components!

Labels

The simplest form of UI component is the label.

NEW TERM *Labels* are, effectively, text strings that you can use to label other UI components.

The advantages that a label has over an ordinary text string is that it follows the layout of the given panel, and you don't have to worry about repainting it every time the panel is redrawn. Labels also can be easily aligned within a panel, enabling you to attach labels to other UI components without knowing exact pixel positions.

To create a label, use one of the following constructors:

☐ Label() creates an empty label, with its text aligned left.

☐ Label(*String*) creates a label with the given text string, also aligned left.

☐ Label(*String*, *int*) creates a label with the given text string and the given alignment. The available alignments are stored in class variables in Label, making them easier to remember: Label.RIGHT, Label.LEFT, and Label.CENTER.

The label's font is determined by the overall font for the component (as set by the setFont() method).

Here's some simple code to create a few labels. Figure 13.3 shows how this looks on screen:

```
add(new Label("aligned left "));
add(new Label("aligned center", Label.CENTER));
add(new Label(" aligned right", Label.RIGHT));
```

Figure 13.3.
Labels.

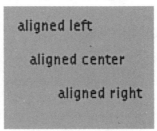

Once you have a label object, you can use methods defined in the `Label` class to get and set the values of the text as shown in Table 13.1.

Table 13.1. Label methods.

Method	Action
getText()	Returns a string containing this label's text
setText(String)	Changes the text of this label
getAlignment()	Returns an integer representing the alignment of this label: `0` is `Label.LEFT`, 1 is `Label.CENTER`, 2 is `Label.RIGHT`
setAlignment(int)	Changes the alignment of this label to the given integer or class variable

Buttons

The second user interface component to explore is the button.

NEW☞
TERM *Buttons* are simple UI components that trigger some action in your interface when they are pressed. For example, a calculator applet might have buttons for each number and operator, or a dialog box might have buttons for "OK" and "Cancel."

To create a button, use one of the following constructors:

☐ `Button()` creates an empty button with no label.

☐ `Button(String)` creates a button with the given string object as a label.

Once you have a button object, you can get the value of the button's label by using the getLabel() method and set the label using the setLabel(String) methods.

Figure 13.4 shows some simple buttons, created using the following code:

```
add(new Button("Rewind"));
add(new Button("Play"));
add(new Button("Fast Forward"));
add(new Button("Stop"));
```

Figure 13.4.
Buttons.

Checkboxes

Checkboxes can be selected or deselected to provide options.

NEW☞ TERM *Checkboxes* are user interface components that have two states: on and off (or checked and unchecked, selected and unselected, true and false, and so on). Unlike buttons, checkboxes usually don't trigger direct actions in a UI but, instead, are used to indicate optional features of some other action.

Checkboxes can be used in two ways:

☐ Nonexclusive, meaning that given a series of checkboxes, any of them can be selected.

☐ Exclusive, meaning that within one series, only one checkbox can be selected at a time.

The latter kind of checkboxes are called radio buttons or checkbox groups, and are described in the next section.

Nonexclusive checkboxes can be created by using the Checkbox class. You can create a checkbox by using one of the following constructors:

☐ Checkbox() creates an empty checkbox, unselected.

☐ Checkbox(*String*) creates a checkbox with the given string as a label.

☐ Checkbox(*String*, *null*, *boolean*) creates a checkbox that is either selected or unselected based on whether the boolean argument is true or false, respectively. (The null is used as a placeholder for a group argument. Only radio buttons have groups, as you'll learn in the next section).

Table 13.2 lists the checkbox methods; Figure 13.5 shows a few simple checkboxes (only Underwear is selected), generated using the following code:

```
add(new Checkbox("Shoes"));
add(new Checkbox("Socks"));
add(new Checkbox("Pants"));
add(new Checkbox("Underwear", null, true));
add(new Checkbox("Shirt"));
```

Figure 13.5.
Checkboxes.

Red

Blue

Yellow

Green

Orange

Purple

Table 13.2. Checkbox methods.

Method	Action
getLabel()	Returns a string containing this checkbox's label
setLabel(String)	Changes the text of the checkbox's label
getState()	Returns true or false, based on whether the checkbox is selected or not
setState(boolean)	Changes the checkbox's state to selected (true) or unselected (false)

Radio Buttons

Radio buttons are a variation on the checkbox.

NEW☞ TERM *Radio buttons* have the same appearance as checkboxes, but only one in a series can be selected at a time.

To create a series of radio buttons, first create an instance of CheckboxGroup:

```
CheckboxGroup cbg = new CheckboxGroup();
```

Then create and add the individual checkboxes, using the group as the second argument, and whether or not that checkbox is selected (only one in the series can be selected):

```
add(new Checkbox("Yes", cbg, true);
add(new Checkbox("no", cbg, false);
```

Here's a simple example (the results of which are shown in Figure 13.6):

```
CheckboxGroup cbg = new CheckboxGroup();

add(new Checkbox("Red", cbg, true));
add(new Checkbox("Blue", cbg, false));
add(new Checkbox("Yellow", cbg, false));
add(new Checkbox("Green", cbg, false));
add(new Checkbox("Orange", cbg, false));
add(new Checkbox("Purple", cbg, false));
```

Figure 13.6.
Radio buttons.

All the checkbox methods defined in the previous section can be used with the checkboxes in the group. In addition, you can use the getCheckboxGroup() and setCheckboxGroup() methods to access and change the group of any given checkbox.

Finally, the getCurrent() and setCurrent(Checkbox) methods, defined in the checkbox group, can be used to get or set the currently selected checkbox.

Choice Menus

The choice menu is a more complex UI component than labels, buttons, or checkboxes.

NEW TERM *Choice menus* are popup (or pulldown) menus that enable you to select an item from that menu. The menu then displays that choice on the screen.

To create a choice menu, create an instance of the Choice class, and then use the addItem() method to add individual items to it in the order in which they should appear:

```
Choice c = new Choice();

c.addItem("Apples");
c.addItem("Oranges");
c.addItem("Strawberries");
c.addItem("Blueberries");
c.addItem("Bananas");
```

Finally, add the entire choice menu to the panel in the usual way:

```
add(c);
```

Figure 13.7 shows a simple choice menu generated from code in the previous example:

Figure 13.7.
Choice menus.

 Tip: Choice menus enable only one selection per menu. If you want to select multiple items, use a scrolling list instead.

Once your choice menu is created, regardless of whether it's added to a panel, you can continue to add items to that menu by using the `addItem()` method. Table 13.3 shows some other methods that may be useful in working with choice menus.

Table 13.3. Choice menu methods.

Method	Action
getItem(int)	Returns the string item at the given position (items inside a choice begin at 0, same as arrays)
countItems()	Returns the number of items in the menu
getSelectedIndex()	Returns the index position of the item that's selected

Method	Action
getSelectedItem()	Returns the currently selected item as a string
select(int)	Selects the item at the given position
select(String)	Selects the item with that string

Text Fields

Unlike the UI components up to this point, which enable you to select only among several options to perform an action, text fields allow you to enter any values.

Text fields enable your reader to enter text.

To create a text field, use one of the following constructors:

☐ `TextField()` creates an empty `TextField` 0 characters wide.

☐ `TextField(int)` creates an empty text field with the given width in characters.

☐ `TextField(String)` creates a text field 0 characters wide, initialized with the given string.

☐ `TextField(String, int)` creates a text field with the given width in characters and containing the given string. If the string is longer than the width, you can select and drag portions of the text within the field and the box will scroll left or right.

For example, the following line creates a text field 30 characters wide with the string "Enter Your Name" as its initial contents.

```
TextField tf = new TextField("Enter Your Name",30);
add(tf);
```

Tip: Text fields include only the editable field itself. You usually need to include a label with a text field to indicate what belongs in that text field.

Note: Text fields are different from text areas; text fields are limited in size and are best used for one-line items, whereas text areas have scrollbars and are better for larger text windows. Both can be edited and enable selections with the mouse. You'll learn about text areas later today.

You can also create a text field that obscures the characters typed into it—for example, for password fields. To do this, first create the text fields itself, and then use the `setEchoCharacter()` method to set the character that is echoed on the screen. Here is an example:

```
TextField tf = new TextField(30);
tf.setEchoCharacter('*');
```

Figure 13.8 shows three text boxes (and labels) that were created by using the following code:

```
add(new Label("Enter your Name"));
add(new TextField("your name here",45));
add(new Label("Enter your phone number"));
add(new TextField(12));
add(new Label("Enter your password"));
TextField t = new TextField(20);
t.setEchoCharacter('*');
add(t);
```

Figure 13.8.
Text fields.

Text fields inherit from the class `TextComponent` and have a whole suite of methods, both inherited from that class and defined in its own class, that may be useful to you in your Java programs. Table 13.4 shows a selection of those methods.

Table 13.4. Text field methods.

Method	Action
getText()	Returns the text this text field contains (as a string)
setText(String)	Puts the given text string into the field
getColumns()	Returns the width of this text field
select(int, int)	Selects the text between the two integer positions (positions start from 0)
selectAll()	Selects all the text in the field

Method	Action
isEditable()	Returns `true` or `false` based on whether the text is editable or not
setEditable(boolean)	`True` (the default) enables text to be edited; `false` freezes the text
getEchoChar()	Returns the character used for masking input
echoCharIsSet()	Returns `true` or `false` whether the field has a masking character or not

Panels and Layout

You know at this point that an AWT panel can contain UI components or other panels. The question now is how those components are actually arranged and displayed on the screen.

In other windowing systems, UI components are often arranged using hard-coded pixel measurements—put text field tf at 10,30, for example—the same way you used the graphics operations to paint squares and ovals on the screen. In the AWT, the window may be displayed on many different windowing systems on many different screens and with many different kinds of fonts with different font metrics. Therefore, you need a more flexible method of arranging components on the screen so that a layout that looks nice on one platform isn't a jumbled unusable mess on another.

For just this purpose, Java has layout managers, insets, and hints that each component can provide for helping lay out the screen.

Note that the nice thing about AWT components and user interface items is that you don't have to paint them—the AWT system manages all that for you. If you have graphical components or images, or you want to create animations inside panels, you still have to do that by hand, but for most of the basic components, all you have to do is put them on the screen and Java will handle the rest.

Layout Managers

The actual appearance of the AWT components on the screen is determined by two things: the order in which they are added to the panel that holds them, and the layout manager that panel is currently using to lay out the screen. The layout manager determines how portions of the screen will be sectioned and how components within that panel will be placed.

Note that each panel on the screen can have its own layout manager. By nesting panels within panels, and using the appropriate layout manager for each one, you can often arrange your UI to group and arrange components in a way that is both functionally useful and also looks good on a variety of platforms and windowing systems. You'll learn about nesting panels in a later section.

The AWT provides four basic layout managers: FlowLayout, GridLayout, BorderLayout, and CardLayout. To create a layout manager for a given panel, use the setLayout() method for that panel:

```java
public void init() {
    this.setLayout(new FlowLayout());
}
```

Setting the default layout manager, like defining the user interface components, is best done during the applet or class's initialization, which is why it's included here.

Once the layout manager is set, you can start adding components to the panel. The order in which components are added is often significant, depending on which layout manager is currently active. Read on for information about the specific layout managers and how they present components within the panel to which they apply.

The following sections describe the four basic Java AWT layout managers.

The *FlowLayout* Class

The FlowLayout class is the most basic of layouts. Using the flow layout, components are added to the panel one at a time, row by row. If a component doesn't fit onto a row, it's wrapped onto the next row. The flow layout also has an alignment, which determines the alignment of each row. By default, each row is aligned centered. Figure 13.9 shows a flow layout at its best—a simple row of buttons, centered on a line.

Figure 13.9.
Flow layout.

To create a basic flow layout with a centered alignment, use the following line of code in your panel's initialization (because this is the default pane layout, you don't need to include this line if that is your intent):

```
setLayout(new FlowLayout());
```

To create a flow layout with an alignment other than centered, add the FlowLayout.RIGHT or FlowLayout.LEFT class variable as an argument:

```
setLayout(new FlowLayout(FlowLayout.LEFT));
```

You can also set horizontal and vertical gap values by using flow layouts. The gap is the number of pixels between components in a panel; by default, the horizontal and vertical gap values are three pixels, which can be very close indeed. Horizontal gap spreads out components to the left and to the right, vertical gap to the top and bottom of each component. Add integer arguments to the flow layout constructor to increase the gap (a layout gap of 10 points in both the horizontal and vertical directions is shown in Figure 13.10):

```
setLayout(new FlowLayout(FlowLayout.LEFT),10,10);
```

Figure 13.10.
Flow layout with a gap of 10 points.

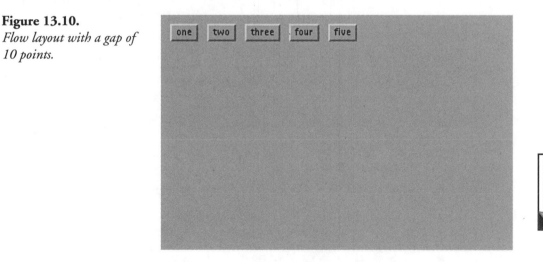

Grid Layouts

Grid layouts use a layout that offers more control over the placement of components inside a panel. Using a grid layout, you portion off the area of the panel into rows and columns. Each component you then add to the panel is placed in a "cell" of the grid, starting from the top row and progressing through each row from left to right (here's where the order of calls to the add() method are very relevant to how the screen is laid out). By using grid layouts and nested grids, you can often approximate the use of hard-coded pixel values to place your UI components precisely where you want them. Figure 13.11 shows a grid layout with three columns and three rows.

Figure 13.11.
Grid layout.

To create a grid layout, indicate the number of rows and columns you want the grid to have when you create a new instance of the `GridLayout` class:

```
setLayout(new GridLayout(3,3));
```

Grid layouts can also have a horizontal and vertical gap between components; to create gaps, add those pixel values:

```
setLayout(new GridLayout(3,3,10,15));
```

Figure 13.12 shows a grid layout with a 10-pixel horizontal gap and a 15-pixel vertical gap.

Grid bag layouts, as implemented by the `GridBagLayout` class, are variations on grid layouts. Grid bag layouts also enable you to lay out your user interface elements in a rectangular grid, but with grid bag layouts you have much more control over the presentation of each element in the grid. Grid bag layouts use a helper class, `GridBagConstraints`, to indicate how each cell in the grid is to be formatted.

Note: The `GridBagLayout` and `GridBagConstraints` classes were added to the Java Developer's Kit just before this book went to press. For a much better description of grid bag layouts, see the API documentation for those classes that comes with the JDK.

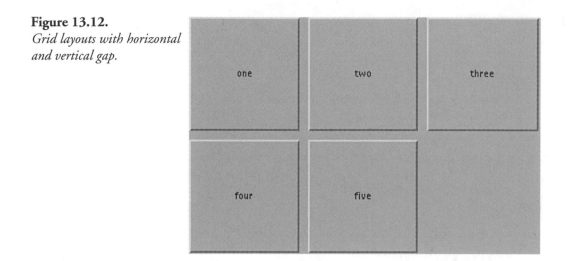

Figure 13.12.
Grid layouts with horizontal and vertical gap.

Border Layouts

Border layouts behave differently from flow and grid layouts. When you add a component to a panel that uses a border layout, you indicate its placement as a geographic direction: north, south, east, west, and center (see Figure 13.13). The components around all the edges are laid out with as much size as they need; the component in the center, if any, gets any space left over.

Figure 13.13.
Border layout.

13

To use a border layout, you create it as you do the other layouts:

```
setLayout(new BorderLayout());
```

Then you add the individual components by using a special `add()` method: the first argument to `add()` is a string indicating the position of the component within the layout:

```
add("North", new TextField("Title",50));
add("South", new TextField("Status",50));
```

You can also use this form of `add()` for the other layout managers; the string argument will just be ignored if it's not needed.

Border layouts can also have horizontal and vertical gaps. Note that the north and south components extend all the way to the edge of the panel, so the gap will result in less space for the east, right, and center components. To add gaps to a border layout, include those pixel values as before:

```
setLayout(new BorderLayout(10,10));
```

Card Layouts

Card layouts are different from the other layouts. Unlike with the other three layouts, when you add components to a card layout, they are not all displayed on the screen at once. Card layouts are used to produce slide shows of components, one at a time. If you've ever used the HyperCard program on the Macintosh, you've worked with the same basic idea.

Generally when you create a card layout, the components you add to it will be other container components—usually panels. You can then use different layouts for those individual "cards" so that each screen has its own look.

When you add each "card" to the panel, you can give it a name. Then you can use methods defined on the `CardLayout` class to move back and forth between different cards in the layout.

For example, here's how to create a card layout containing three cards:

```
setLayout(new CardLayout());
Panel one = new Panel()
add("first", one);
Panel two = new Panel()
add("second", two);
Panel three = new Panel()
add("third", three);
show(this, "second");
```

Insets

Whereas horizontal gap and vertical gap are used to determine the amount of space between components in a panel, insets are used to determine the amount of space around the panel itself. The insets class provides values for the top, bottom, left, and right insets, which are then used when the panel itself is drawn. Figure 13.14 shows an inset in a `GridLayout`.

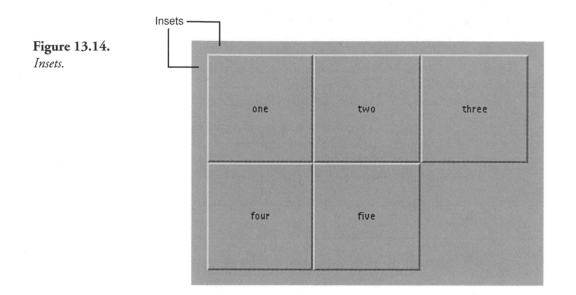

Figure 13.14.
Insets.

Insets

one   two   three

four   five

To include an inset, override the `insets()` method in your class (your `Applet` class or other class that serves as a panel):

```
public Insets insets() {
        return new Insets(10,10,10,10);
}
```

The arguments to the Insets constructor provide pixel insets for the top, bottom, left, and right edges of the panel. This particular example provides an inset of 10 pixels on all four sides of the panel.

Handling UI Actions and Events

If you stopped reading today's lesson right now, you could go out and create an applet that had lots of little UI components, nicely laid out on the screen with the proper layout manager, gap, and insets. If you did stop right here, however, your applet would be really dull, because none of your UI components would actually do anything when they were pressed or typed into or selected.

For your UI components to do something when they are activated, you need to hook up the UI's action with an operation.

Testing for an action by a UI component is a form of event management—the things you learned yesterday about events will come in handy here. In particular, UI components produce the special kind of event called an action. To intercept an action by any UI component, you define an `action()` method in your applet or class:

```
public boolean action(Event evt, Object arg) {
    ...
}
```

The `action()` method should look familiar to the basic mouse and keyboard event methods. Like those methods, it gets passed the event object that represents this event. It also gets an extra object, which can be of any type of object. What's that second argument for?

The second argument to the action method depends on the UI component that's generating the event. The basic definition is that it's any arbitrary argument—when a component generates an event, it can pass along any extra information that might later be needed. Because that extra information may be useful for you, it's passed on through the `action()` method.

All the basic UI components (except for labels, which have no action) have different actions and arguments:

☐ Buttons create actions when they are selected, and a button's argument is the label of the button.

☐ Checkboxes, both exclusive and nonexclusive, generate actions when a box is checked. The argument is always `true`.

☐ Choice menus generate an action when a menu item is selected, and the argument is that item.

☐ Text fields create actions when the user presses Return inside that text field. Note that if the user tabs to a different text field or uses the mouse to change the input focus, an action is *not* generated. Only a Return triggers the action.

Note that with actions, unlike with ordinary events, you can have many different kinds of objects generating the event, as opposed to a single event such as a `mouseDown`. To deal with those different UI components and the actions they generate, you have to test for the type of object that called the event in the first place inside the body of your `action()` method. That object is stored in the event's `target` instance variable, and you can use the `instanceof` operator to find out what kind of UI component sent it:

```
public boolean action(Event evt, Object arg) {
    if (evt.target instanceof TextField)
        handleText(evt.target);
    else if (evt.target instanceof Choice)
        handleChoice(arg);
...
}
```

Although you can handle UI actions in the body of the `action()` method, it's much more common simply to define a handler method and call that method from `action()` instead. Here, there are two handler methods: one to handle the action on the text field (`handleText()`) and one to handle the action on the choice menu (`handleChoice()`). Depending on the action you want to handle, you may also want to pass on the argument from the action, the UI component that sent it, or any other information that the event might contain.

Here's a simple applet that has five buttons labeled with colors. The action() method tests for a button action and then passes off the word to a method called changeColor(), which changes the background color of the applet based on which button was pressed (see Figure 13.15 to see the applet in action):

```java
import java.awt.*;

public class ButtonActionsTest extends java.applet.Applet {

    public void init() {
        setBackground(Color.white);

        add(new Button("Red"));
        add(new Button("Blue"));
        add(new Button("Green"));
        add(new Button("White"));
        add(new Button("Black"));
    }

    public boolean action(Event evt, Object arg) {
        if (evt.target instanceof Button)
            changeColor((String)arg);
        return true;
    }

    void changeColor(String bname) {
        if (bname.equals("Red")) setBackground(Color.red);
        else if (bname.equals("Blue")) setBackground(Color.blue);
        else if (bname.equals("Green")) setBackground(Color.green);
        else if (bname.equals("White")) setBackground(Color.white);
        else setBackground(Color.black);
    }
}
```

Figure 13.15.
The ButtonAction applet.

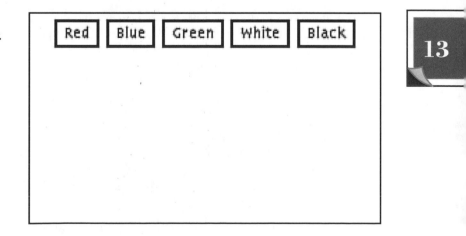

13

Nesting Panels and Components

Adding UI components to individual applets is fun, but applets begin to turn into lots of fun when you begin working with nested panels. By nesting different panels inside your applet, and panels inside those panels, you can create different layouts for different parts of the overall applet area, isolate background and foreground colors and fonts to individual parts of an applet, and manage the design of your UI components much more cleanly and simply. The more complex the layout of your applet, the more likely you're going to want to use nested panels.

Nested Panels

Panels, as you've already learned, are components that can be actually displayed on screen; Panel's superclass Container provides the generic behavior for holding other components inside it. The Applet class, which your applets all inherit from, is a subclass of Panel. To nest other panels inside an applet, you merely create a new panel and add it to the applet, just as you would add any other UI component:

```
setLayout(new GridLayout(1,2,10,10));
Panel panel1 = new Panel();
Panel panel2 = new Panel();
add(panel1);
add(panel2);
```

You can then set up an independent layout for those subpanels and add AWT components to them (including still more subpanels) by calling the add() method in the appropriate panel:

```
panel1.setLayout(new FlowLayout());
panel1.add(new Button("Up"));
panel1.add(new Button("Down"));
```

Although you can do all this in a single class, it's common in applets that make heavy use of the panels to factor out the layout and behavior of the subpanels into separate classes, and to communicate between the panels by using method calls. You'll look at an extensive example of this later on in today's lesson.

Events and Nested Panels

When you create applets with nested panels, those panels form a hierarchy from the outermost panel (the applet, usually), to the innermost UI component. This hierarchy is important to how each component in an applet interacts with the other components in the applet or with the browser that contains that applet; in particular, the component hierarchy determines the order in which components are painted to the screen.

More importantly, the hierarchy also affects event handling, particularly for user input events such as mouse and keyboard events.

Events are received by the innermost component in the component hierarchy and passed up the chain to the root. Suppose, for example, that you have an applet with a subpanel that can handle mouse events (using the mouseDown() and mouseUp() methods) and that panel contains a button. Clicking on the button means that the button receives the event before the panel does; if the button isn't interested in that mouseDown(), the event gets passed to the panel, which can then process it or pass it further up the hierarchy.

Remember the discussion about the basic event methods yesterday? You learned that the basic event methods all return boolean values. Those boolean values become important when you're talking about handling events or passing them on.

An event handling method, whether it is the set of basic event methods or the more generic handleEvent(), can do one of three things, given any random event:

☐ Not be interested in the event (this is usually true only for handleEvent(), which receives all the events generated by the system). If this is the case, the event is passed on up the hierarchy until a component processes it (or it is ignored altogether). In this case, the event handling method should return false.

☐ Intercept the event, process it, and return true. In this case, the event stops with that event method. Recall that this is the case with the basic mouseDown() and keyDown() methods that you learned about yesterday.

☐ Intercept the method, process it, and pass it on to the next event handler. This is a more unusual case, but you may create a user interface by using nested components that will want to do this. In this case, the event method should return false to pass the event on to the next handler in the chain.

More UI Components

Once you master the basic UI components and how to add them to panels and manage their events, you can add more UI components. In this section, you'll learn about text areas, scrolling lists, scrollbars, and canvases.

13

Note that the UI components in this section do not produce actions, so you can't use the action() method to handle their behavior. Instead, you have to use a generic handleEvent() method to test for specific events that these UI components generate. You'll learn more about this in the next section.

Text Areas

Text areas are like text fields, except they have more functionality for handling large amounts of text. Because text fields are limited in size and don't scroll, they are better for one-line responses and text entry; text areas can be any given width and height and have scrollbars in default, so you can deal with larger amounts of text more easily.

To create a text area, use one of the following constructors:

☐ `TextArea()` creates an empty text area 0 rows long and 0 characters wide. Given that a text area with no dimensions can't be displayed, you should make sure you change the dimensions of this new text area before adding it to a panel (or just use the next constructor instead).

☐ `TextArea(int, int)` creates an empty text area with the given rows and columns (characters).

☐ `TextArea(String)` creates a text area displaying the given string, 0 rows by 0 columns.

☐ `TextArea(String, int, int)` creates a text area by displaying the given string and with the given dimensions.

Figure 13.16 shows a simple text area generated from the following code:

```
String str = "Once upon a midnight dreary, while I pondered, weak and weary,\n" +
    "Over many a quaint and curious volume of forgotten lore,\n" +
    "While I nodded, nearly napping, suddenly there came a tapping,\n" +
    "As of some one gently rapping, rapping at my chamber door.\n" +
    "\"'Tis some visitor,\" I muttered, \"tapping at my chamber door-\n";

add(new TextArea(str,10,60));
```

Figure 13.16.

A text area.

Once upon a midnight dreary, while I pondered, weak and weary,
Over many a quaint and curious volume of forgotten lore,
While I nodded, nearly napping, suddenly there came a tapping,
As of some one gently rapping, rapping at my chamber door.
"'Tis some visitor," I muttered, "tapping at my chamber door-
Only this, and nothing more."

Ah, distinctly I remember it was in the bleak December,
And each separate dying ember wrought its ghost upon the floor.
Eagerly I wished the morrow;- vainly I had sought to borrow

Both text areas and text fields inherit from the `TextComponent` class, so a lot of the behavior for text fields (particularly getting and setting text and selections) is usable on text areas as well (refer to Table 13.4). Text areas also have a number of their own methods that you may find useful. Table 13.5 shows a sampling of those methods.

Table 13.5. Text area methods.

Method	Action
getColumns()	Returns the width of the text area, in characters or columns
getRows()	Returns the number of rows in the text area (not the number of rows of text that the text area contains)
insertText(String, int)	Inserts the string at the given position in the text (text positions start at 0)
replaceText(String, int, int)	Replace the text between the given integer positions with the new string

Scrolling Lists

Remember the choice menu, which enables you to choose one of several different options? A scrolling list is functionally similar to a choice menu in that it lets you pick several options from a list. Scrolling lists differ in two significant ways:

☐ Scrolling lists are not popup menus. They're lists of items in which you can choose one or more items from a list. If the number of items is larger than the list box, a scrollbar is automatically provided so that you can see the other items.

☐ A scrolling list can be defined to accept only one item at a time (exclusive), or multiple items (nonexclusive).

To create a scrolling list, create an instance of the List class and then add individual items to that list. The List class has two constructors:

☐ List() creates an empty scrolling list that enables only one selection at a time.

☐ List(int, boolean) creates a scrolling list with the given number of visible lines on the screen (you're unlimited as to the number of actual items you can add to the list). The boolean argument indicates whether this list enables multiple selections (true) or not (false).

After creating a List object, add items to it using the addItem() method and then add the list itself to the panel that contains it. Here's an example, the result of which is shown in Figure 13.17:

```
List lst = new List(5, true);

lst.addItem("Hamlet");
lst.addItem("Claudius");
```

13

```
lst.addItem("Gertrude");
lst.addItem("Polonius");
lst.addItem("Horatio");
lst.addItem("Laertes");
lst.addItem("Ophelia");

add(lst);
```

Figure 13.17.
A scrolling list.

Table 13.6 shows some of the methods available to scrolling lists. See the API documentation for a complete set.

Table 13.6. Scrolling list methods.

Method	Action
getItem(int)	Returns the string item at the given position
countItems()	Returns the number of items in the menu
getSelectedIndex()	Returns the index position of the item that's selected (used for lists that enable only single selections)
getSelectedIndexes()	Returns an array of index positions (used for lists that enable multiple selections)
getSelectedItem()	Returns the currently selected item as a string
getSelectedItems()	Returns an array of strings containing all the selected items
select(int)	Selects the item at the given position
select(String)	Selects the item with that string

Scrollbars and Sliders

Text areas and scrolling lists come with their own scrollbars, which are built into those UI components and enable you to manage both the body of the area or the list and its scrollbar as a single unit. You can also create individual scrollbars, or sliders, to manipulate a range of values.

Scrollbars are used to select a value between a maximum and a minimum value. To change the current value of that scrollbar, you can use three different parts of the scrollbar (see Figure 13.18):

☐ Arrows on either end, which increment or decrement the values by some small unit (1 by default).

☐ A range in the middle, which increments or decrements the value by a larger amount (10 by default).

☐ A box in the middle, often called an *elevator* or *thumb*, whose position shows where in the range of values the current value is located. Moving this box with the mouse causes an absolute change in the value, based on the position of the box within the scrollbar.

Figure 13.18.
Scrollbar parts.

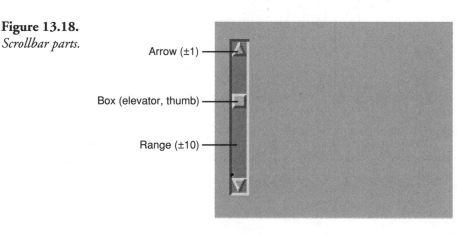

Arrow (±1)

Box (elevator, thumb)

Range (±10)

Choosing any of these visual elements causes a change in the scrollbar's value; you don't have to update anything or handle any events. All you have to do is give the scrollbar a maximum and minimum, and Java will handle the rest.

13

To create a scrollbar, you can use one of three constructors:

☐ `Scrollbar()` creates a scrollbar with 0, 0 as its initial maximum and initial minimum values, in a vertical orientation.

☐ `Scrollbar(int)` creates a scrollbar with 0, 0 as its initial maximum and initial minimum values. The argument represents an orientation, for which you can use the class variables `Scrollbar.HORIZONTAL` and `Scrollbar.VERTICAL`.

☐ `Scrollbar(int, int, int, int, int)` creates a scrollbar with the following arguments (each one is an integer, and must be presented in this order):

The first argument is the orientation of the scrollbar: `Scrollbar.HORIZONTAL` and `Scrollbar.VERTICAL`.

The second argument is the initial value of the scrollbar, which should be a value between the scrollbar's maximum and minimum values.

The third argument is the the overall width (or height, depending on the orientation) of the scrollbar's box. In user interface design, a larger box implies that a larger amount of the total range is currently showing (applies best to things such as windows and text areas).

The fourth and fifth arguments are the minimum and maximum values for the scrollbar.

Here's a simple example of a scrollbar that increments a single value (see Figure 13.19). The label to the left of the scrollbar is updated each time the scrollbar's value changes:

```java
import java.awt.*;

public class SliderTest extends java.applet.Applet {
    Label l;

    public void init() {
        l = new Label("0");
        add(l);
        add(new Scrollbar(Scrollbar.HORIZONTAL, 1, 0, 1, 100));
    }

    public boolean handleEvent(Event evt) {
        if (evt.target instanceof Scrollbar) {
            int v = ((Scrollbar)evt.target).getValue();
            l.setText(String.valueOf(v));
        }
        return true;
    }
}
```

Figure 13.19.
A scrollbar.

0

The Scrollbar class provides several methods for managing the values within scrollbars (see Table 13.7).

Table 13.7. Scrollbar methods.

Method	Action
getMaximum()	Returns the maximum value
getMinimum()	Returns the minimum value

Method	Action
getOrientation()	Returns the orientation of this scrollbar: 0 for vertical, 1 for horizontal
getValue()	Returns the scrollbar's current value
setValue(int)	Sets the current value of the scrollbar

Canvases

Although you can draw on most AWT components, such as panels, canvases do little *except* let you draw on them. They can't contain other components, but they can accept events, and you can create animations and display images on them. Canvases, in other words, should be used for much of the stuff you learned about earlier this week.

NEW☞ TERM   A *canvas* is a component that you can draw on.

To create a canvas, use the Canvas class and add it to a panel as you would any other component:

```
Canvas can = new Canvas();
add(can);
```

More UI Events

Yesterday, you learned about some basic event types that are generated from user input to the mouse or the keyboard. These event types are stored in the Event object as the event ID, and can be tested for in the body of a handleEvent() method by using class variables defined in Event. For many basic events, such as mouseDown() and keyDown(), you can define methods for those events to handle the event directly. You learned a similar mechanism today for UI actions where creating an action() method handled a specific action generated by a UI component.

The most general way of managing events, however, continues to be the handleEvent() method. For events relating to scrollbars and scrolling lists, the only way to intercept these events is to override handleEvent().

To intercept a specific event, test for that event's ID. The available IDs are defined as class variables in the Event class, so you can test them by name. You learned about some of the basic events yesterday; Table 13.8 shows additonal events that may be useful to you for the components you've learned about today (or that you might find useful in general).

13

Table 13.8. Additional events.

Event ID	What It Represents
ACTION_EVENT	Generated when a UI component action occurs
KEY_ACTION	Generated when text field action occurs
LIST_DESELECT	Generated when an item in a scrolling list is deselected
LIST_SELECT	Generated when an item in a scrolling list is selected
SCROLL_ABSOLUTE	Generated when a scrollbar's box has been moved
SCROLL_LINE_DOWN	Generated when a scrollbar's bottom endpoint (or left endpoint) is selected
SCROLL_LINE_UP	Generated when a scrollbar's top endpoint (or right endpoint) is selected
SCROLL_PAGE_DOWN	Generated when the scrollbar's field below (or to the left of) the box is selected
SCROLL_PAGE_UP	Generated when the scrollbar's field above (or to the right of) the box is selected

A Complete Example: RGB to HSB Converter

Let's take a break here from theory and smaller examples to create a larger, more complex example that puts together much of what you've learned so far. The following applet example demonstrates layouts, nesting panels, creating user interface components, and catching and handling actions, as well as using multiple classes to put together a single applet. In short, it's probably the most complex applet you'll create so far.

Figure 13.20 shows the applet you'll be creating in this example. The ColorTest applet enables you to pick colors based on RGB (red, green, and blue) and HSB (hue, saturation, and brightness) values.

Figure 13.20.
The ColorTest applet.

The ColorTest applet has three main parts: a colored box on the left side and two groups of text fields on the right. The first group indicates RGB values, the right, HSB. By changing any of the values in any of the text boxes, the colored box is updated to the new color, as are the values in the other group of text boxes.

This applet uses two classes:

☐ ColorTest, which inherits from Applet. This is the controlling class for the applet itself.

☐ ColorControls, which inherits from Panel. You'll create this class to represent a group of three text fields and to handle actions from those text fields. Two instances of this class, one for the RGB values and one for the HSB ones, will be created and added to the applet.

Let's work through this step by step, because it's very complicated and can get confusing. All the code for this applet will be shown at the end of this section.

Create the Applet Layout

The best way to start creating an applet that uses AWT components is to worry about the layout first and then worry about the functionality. When dealing with the layout, you also should start with the outermost panel first and work inward.

Making a sketch of your UI design can help you figure out how to organize the panels inside your applet or window to best take advantage of layout and space. Figure 13.21 shows the ColorTest applet with a grid drawn over it so that you can get an idea of how the panels and embedded panels work.

Figure 13.21.
The ColorTest applet panels and components.

Create the Panel Layout

Let's start with the outermost panel—the applet itself. This panel has three parts: the color box on the left, the RGB text fields in the middle, and the HSB fields on the right.

Because this is the applet, your ColorTest class will be the applet class and inherit from Applet. You'll also import the AWT classes here (note that because you use so many of them in this program, it's easiest to just import the entire package):

```
import java.awt.*;

public class ColorTest extends java.applet.Applet {
...
}
```

Let's start with the `init()` method, where all the basic initialization and layout takes place. There are four major steps:

1. Set the layout for the big parts of the panel. Although a flow layout would work, a grid layout with one row and three columns is a much better idea.

2. Create the three components of this applet: a canvas for the color box and two subpanels for the text fields.

3. Add those components to the applet.

4. Finally, initialize the default color and update all the panels to reflect that default color.

Before you do any of that, let's set up instance variables to hold the three major components of this applet. You need to keep hold of these objects so you can update things when a value changes.

The color box is easy—it's just a canvas. Call it `swatch`.

```
Canvas swatch;
```

Now onto the subpanels. There are two of them, and although they have different labels and values, they're essentially the same panel. You could just create code for each one here, but you'd end up duplicating a lot of the same code. This is a perfect opportunity, therefore, to create another class to represent the subpanels with the text fields on them. Call them `ColorControls` (you'll get around to creating the class later) and define two variables, `RGBcontrols` and `HSBcontrols`, to hold them:

```
ColorControls RGBcontrols, HSBcontrols;
```

Back to the `init()` method. Step one is the layout. Let's use a grid layout and a gap of ten points to separate each of the components:

```
setLayout(new GridLayout(1,3,10,10));
```

Step two is creating the components, the canvas first. You have an instance variable to hold that one:

```
swatch = new Canvas();
```

You need to create two instances of your as-of-yet nonexistent `ColorControls` panels here as well, but you don't know exactly what you need to create them yet, so let's put in some basic constructors and fill in the details later:

```
RGBcontrols = new ColorControls()
HSBcontrols = new ColorControls();
```

Step three is adding them to the panel.

```
add(swatch);
add(RGBcontrols);
add(HSBcontrols);
```

While you're working on layout, add an inset just for fun—ten points along all the edges:

```
public Insets insets() {
    return new Insets(10,10,10,10);
}
```

Got it so far? Now you have a skeleton `init()` method and an `insets()` method in your `ColorTest` class. Let's move on now to creating the subpanel layout—to creating that `ColorControls` class.

Define the Subpanels

The `ColorControls` class will have behavior for laying out and handling the subpanels that represent the RGB and HSB values for the color. `ColorControls` doesn't need to be a subclass of `Applet` because it isn't actually an applet, it's just a panel. Define it to inherit from `Panel`:

```
class ColorControls extends Panel {
    ...
}
```

Note: You can put the `ColorControls` class in the same file as the `ColorTest` class. You haven't been doing this so far because the applets and applications you've been creating had only one class. If you remember way back to Day 1, however, you learned that you can have multiple class definitions in a single file as long as only one of those definitions is declared `public`. In this case, the `ColorTest` class is `public` (it's an applet, so it has to be), but the `ColorControls` class doesn't need to be, so everything works out fine.

13

You need a couple of instance variables in this class. The first thing you need is a hook back up to the applet class that contains this panel. Why? The applet class is the class that oversees how the subcomponents work, so it's going to be the class that updates everything. Eventually, you're going to have to call a method in that class to indicate that something in this panel has changed. Without an actual reference to that outer class, there's no way to do this. So, instance variable number one is a reference to the class `ColorTest`:

```
ColorTest outerparent;
```

If you figure that the applet class is the one that's going to be updating everything, that class is going to need a way to get hold of the pieces inside this class. In particular, it's going to be interested in the individual text fields, so you're going to need instance variables to hold those. This creates three of them:

```
TextField f1, f2, f3;
```

Now for the constructor for this class. Again, this isn't an applet, so you don't use `init()`; all you need is a constructor method.

What do you need inside that constructor? You need to set the layout for the subpanel, create the text fields, and add them to the panel. The goal here is to make the `ColorControls` class generic enough so that you can use it for both the RGB fields and the HSB fields.

The two different panels differ in two respects: the labels for the text fields, and the initial values for the text fields. That's six values to get before you can create the object. You can pass those six values in through the constructors in `ColorTest`. You also need one more. Because you need that hook back to the applet class, you should also pass in a reference to that object as part of the constructor.

You now have seven arguments to the basic constructor for the `ColorControls` class. Here's the signature for that constructor:

```
ColorControls(ColorTest target,
        String l1, String l2, String l3,
        int v1, int v2, int v3) {
}
```

Given those arguments, you can assign the right values to your instance variables:

```
outerparent = target;

f1 = new TextField(String.valueOf(v1),10);
f2 = new TextField(String.valueOf(v2),10);
f3 = new TextField(String.valueOf(v3),10);
```

Note that because the first argument to the `TextField` constructor is a string, and the values that you passed in were integers, you have to use the `valueOf()` class method (defined in `String`) to convert the integer to a string before creating each text field.

Next, you create the layout for this panel. You also use a grid layout for these subpanels, as you did for the applet panel, but this time the grid will have three rows (one for each of the text field and label pairs) and two columns (one for the labels and one for the fields).

Given the 3-by-2 grid, you can now add the text fields and labels to that panel. Note that by separating the labels and the text fields into separate cells in the grid, you can align the labels, creating a nice aligned layout.

```
add(new Label(l1, Label.RIGHT));
add(f1);
add(new Label(l2, Label.RIGHT));
add(f2);
```

```
add(new Label(l3, Label.RIGHT));
add(f3);
```

Finally (because I like insets), you'll inset the contents of the subpanel a bit—only on the top and bottom edges—by including an insets() method:

```
public Insets insets() {
       return new Insets(10,10,0,0);
 }
```

You're almost there. You have 98 percent of the layout in place and ready to go, but you're missing two things: creating the ColorControls objects in ColorTest, and initializing everything so that all the components have the right values.

For both, you need to go back to the ColorTest class and the init() method you defined there. Let's start with the initialization part, because that's easy. The default color is black. Set up a local variable to hold that color object:

```
Color theColor = new Color(0,0,0);
```

To set the initial color of the color box, all you need to do is set its background:

```
swatch.setBackground(theColor);
```

Now, let's finally tackle initializing those subpanels. The constructor for ColorControls has seven arguments: the ColorTest object, three labels (strings), and three initial values for the text fields (integers). Let's do the RGB controls first, because you can easily extract the initial red, green, and blue values out of the Color object:

```
RGBcontrols = new ColorControls(this, "Red", "Green", "Blue",
        theColor.getRed(), theColor.getGreen(),
        theColor.getBlue());
```

Things get complicated on the HSB side of the panel. The Color class provides you with a method to get the HSB values out of a Color object, but there are two problems:

☐ The RGBtoHSB() method is a single class method that insists on returning an array of the three values.

☐ The HSB values are measured in floating-point values. I prefer to think of HSB as integers, wherein the hue is a degree value around a color wheel (0 through 360), and saturation and brightness are percentages from 0 to 100. Having HSB as integer values also enables you to have a generic subpanel, as was the intent.

Initializing the HSB subpanel is going to be a little difficult.

First, let's extract those HSB values. Given that the method takes three RGB arguments—an array of three floats—and returns an array of three floats, you have to go through this process to get those values:

```
float[] HSB = Color.RGBtoHSB(theColor.getRed(),
    theColor.getGreen(), theColor.getBlue(),(new float[3]));
```

271

Now you have an array of floats, where HSB[0] is the hue, HSB[1] is the saturation, and HSB[2] is the brightness. You can now (finally!) initialize the HSB side of the applet, making sure that when you pass those HSB values into the subpanel, you multiply them by the right values (360 for the hues, 100 for the saturation and the brightness) and convert them to integers:

```
HSBcontrols = new ColorControls(this,
       "Hue", "Saturation", "Brightness",
       (int)(HSB[0] * 360), (int)(HSB[1] * 100),
       (int)(HSB[2] * 100));
```

Ready to give up? Fear not—you've done the hard part. From here, it's (mostly) easy. Once you have your layout working, you can compile your Java program and see how it looks. None of your UI components actually does anything, but perfecting the layout is half the battle.

Handle the Actions

After creating the layout, you set up actions with the UI components so that when the user interacts with the applet, the applet can respond.

The action of this applet occurs when the user changes a value in any of the text fields. By causing an action in a text field, the color changes, the color box updates to the new color, and the values of the fields in the opposite subpanel change to reflect the new color.

The ColorTest class is responsible for actually doing the updating, because it keeps track of all the subpanels. You should be tracking and intercepting events in the subpanel in which they occur, however. Because the action of the applet is an actual text action, you can use an action() method to intercept it:

```
public boolean action(Event evt, Object arg) {
       if (evt.target instanceof TextField) {
           this.outerparent.update(this);
           return true;
       }
       else return false;
   }
```

In the action() method, you test to make sure the action was indeed generated by a text field (because there are only text fields available, that's the only action you'll get, but it's a good idea to test for it anyhow). If so, call the update() method, defined in ColorTest, to update the applet to reflect all the new values. Because the outer applet is responsible for doing all the updating, this is precisely why you need that hook back to the applet—so you can call the right method at the right time.

Update the Result

The only part left now is to update all the values and the color swatch if one of the values changes. For this, you define the update() method in the ColorTest class. This update() method takes a single argument—the `ColorControls` instance that contains the changed value (you get that argument from the `action()` method in the subpanel).

> **Note:** Won't this `update()` method interfere with the system's `update()` method? Nope. Remember, methods can have the same names, but different signatures and definitions. Because this `update()` has a single argument of type `ColorControls`, it doesn't interfere with the other version of `update()`.

The `update()` method is responsible for updating all the panels in the applet. To know which panel to update, you need to know which panel changed. You can find out by testing to see whether the argument you got passed is the same as the subpanels you have stored in the `RGBcontrols` and `HSBcontrols` instance variables:

```
void update(ColorControls in) {

    if (in == RGBcontrols) { // the change was in RGB
        ...
    }
    else { // change was in HSB
}
```

This test is the heart of the `update()` method. Let's start with that first case—a number has been changed in the RGB text fields. So now, based on those new RGB values, you have to generate a new color object and update the values on the HSB panel. To reduce some typing, you create a few local variables to hold some basic values. In particular, the values of the text fields are strings, and you get into them by accessing the text field instance variables for the `ColorControls` panel (`f1`, `f2`, `f3`) and then using the `getText()` method to extract the actual values. Extract those values and store them in string variables so that you don't have to keep typing:

```
String v1 = in.f1.getText();
String v2 = in.f2.getText();
String v3 = in.f3.getText();
```

Given those string values for RGB, you now create a color object by converting those strings to integers:

```
Color c;
c = new Color(Integer.parseInt(v1),Integer.parseInt(v2),
                    Integer.parseInt(v3));
```

> **Note:** This part of the example isn't very robust; it assumes that the user has indeed entered real numbers into the text fields. A better version of this would test to make sure that no parsing errors had occurred (I was trying to keep this example small).

13

When you have a color object, you can update the color swatch:

```
swatch.setBackground(c);
```

The next step is to update the HSB panel to the new HSB values. Doing this in the init()
method is no fun at all, and it's even less fun here. To do this, you call RGBtoHSB to get the floating-
point values, convert them to integers with the right values, convert them to strings, and then
put them back into the text fields for the HSB subpanel. Got all that? Here's the code:

```
float[] HSB = Color.RGBtoHSB(c.getRed(),c.getGreen(),
          c.getBlue(), (new float[3]));
HSB[0] *= 360;
HSB[1] *= 100;
HSB[2] *= 100;
HSBcontrols.f1.setText(String.valueOf((int)HSB[0]));
HSBcontrols.f2.setText(String.valueOf((int)HSB[1]));
HSBcontrols.f3.setText(String.valueOf((int)HSB[2]));
```

The second part of the update() method is called when a value on the HSB side of the panel is
changed. This is the "else" in the if-else that determines what to update, given a change.

Believe it or not, it's easier to update RGB values given HSB than it is to do it the other way
around. First, convert the string values from the HSB text fields to integers by using these lines:

```
int f1 = Integer.parseInt(v1);
int f2 = Integer.parseInt(v2);
int f3 = Integer.parseInt(v3);
```

There's a class method in the Color class that creates a new color object when given three HSB
values. The catch is that those values are floats, and they're not the values you currently have.
To call getHSBColor() (that's the name of the method), convert the integers to floats and divide
by the right amounts:

```
c = Color.getHSBColor((float)f1 / 360, (float)f2 / 100, (float)f3/100);
```

Now that you have a color object, the rest is easy. Set the color swatch:

```
swatch.setBackground(c);
```

Then update the RGB text fields with the new RGB values from the color object:

```
RGBcontrols.f1.setText(String.valueOf(c.getRed()));
RGBcontrols.f2.setText(String.valueOf(c.getGreen()));
RGBcontrols.f3.setText(String.valueOf(c.getBlue()));
```

The Complete Source Code

Listing 13.1 shows the complete source code; often it's easier to figure out what's going on in
this applet when it's all in one place and you can follow the method calls and how values are
passed back and forth. Start with the init() method in applet, and go from there.

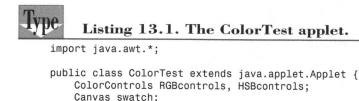

Listing 13.1. The ColorTest applet.

```java
import java.awt.*;

public class ColorTest extends java.applet.Applet {
    ColorControls RGBcontrols, HSBcontrols;
    Canvas swatch;

    public void init() {
        Color theColor = new Color(0,0,0);
        float[] HSB = Color.RGBtoHSB(theColor.getRed(),
            theColor.getGreen(), theColor.getBlue(),
            (new float[3]));

        setLayout(new GridLayout(1,3,10,10));

        // The color swatch
        swatch = new Canvas();
        swatch.setBackground(theColor);

        // the control panels
        RGBcontrols = new ColorControls(this,
            "Red", "Green", "Blue",
            theColor.getRed(), theColor.getGreen(),
            theColor.getBlue());

        HSBcontrols = new ColorControls(this,
            "Hue", "Saturation", "Brightness",
            (int)(HSB[0] * 360), (int)(HSB[1] * 100),
            (int)(HSB[2] * 100));

        add(swatch);
        add(RGBcontrols);
        add(HSBcontrols);

    }

    public Insets insets() {
        return new Insets(10,10,10,10);
    }

    void update(ColorControls in) {
        Color c;
        String v1 = in.f1.getText();
        String v2 = in.f2.getText();
        String v3 = in.f3.getText();

        if (in == RGBcontrols) {     // change to RGB
            c = new Color(Integer.parseInt(v1),
                    Integer.parseInt(v2),
                    Integer.parseInt(v3));
            swatch.setBackground(c);
```

continues

Listing 13.1. continued

```
            float[] HSB = Color.RGBtoHSB(c.getRed(),c.getGreen(),
                    c.getBlue(), (new float[3]));
            HSB[0] *= 360;
            HSB[1] *= 100;
            HSB[2] *= 100;
            HSBcontrols.f1.setText(String.valueOf((int)HSB[0]));
            HSBcontrols.f2.setText(String.valueOf((int)HSB[1]));
            HSBcontrols.f3.setText(String.valueOf((int)HSB[2]));
        }
        else {     // change to HSB
            int f1 = Integer.parseInt(v1);
            int f2 = Integer.parseInt(v2);
            int f3 = Integer.parseInt(v3);
            c = Color.getHSBColor((float)f1 / 360,
                    (float)f2 / 100, (float)f3/100);
            swatch.setBackground(c);
            RGBcontrols.f1.setText(String.valueOf(c.getRed()));
            RGBcontrols.f2.setText(String.valueOf(
                c.getGreen()));
            RGBcontrols.f3.setText(String.valueOf(c.getBlue()));
        }
    }
}


class ColorControls extends Panel {
    TextField f1, f2, f3;
    ColorTest outerparent;

    ColorControls(ColorTest target,
            String l1, String l2, String l3,
            int v1, int v2, int v3) {

        this.outerparent = target;
        setLayout(new GridLayout(3,4,10,10));

        f1 = new TextField(String.valueOf(v1),10);
        f2 = new TextField(String.valueOf(v2),10);
        f3 = new TextField(String.valueOf(v3),10);

        add(new Label(l1, Label.RIGHT));
        add(f1);
        add(new Label(l2, Label.RIGHT));
        add(f2);
        add(new Label(l3, Label.RIGHT));
        add(f3);
    }

    public Insets insets() {
        return new Insets(10,10,0,0);
    }

    public boolean action(Event evt, Object arg) {
        if (evt.target instanceof TextField) {
```

```
            this.outerparent.update(this);
            retrue true;
        }
        else return false;
    }
}
```

Summary

The Java AWT, or Abstract Windowing Toolkit, is a package of Java classes and interfaces for creating full-fledged access to a window-based graphical user interface system, with mechanisms for graphics display, event management, text and graphics primitives, user interface components, and cross-platform layout. The AWT is used by the HotJava browser itself for all its functionality. Applets are also an integral part of the AWT toolkit.

Today has been a big day; the lesson has brought together everything you've learned up to this point about simple applet management and added a lot more about creating applets, panels, and user interface components and managing the interactions between all of them. With the information you got today and the few bits that you'll learn tomorrow, you can create cross-platform Java applications that do just about anything you want.

Q&A

Q You've mentioned a lot about the Component and Container classes, but it looks like the only Container objects that ever get created are Panels. What do the Component and Container classes give me?

A Those classes factor out the behavior for components (generic AWT components) and containers (components that can contain other components). Although you don't necessarily create direct instances of these classes, you can create subclasses of them if you want to add behavior to the AWT that the default classes do not provide. As with most of the Java classes, any time you need a superclass's behavior, don't hesitate to extend that class by using your own subclass.

Q Can I put a UI component at a specific x and y position on the screen?

A By using the existing layout managers supplied with the AWT toolkit, no. This is actually a good thing because you don't know what kind of display environment your applet will be run under, what kind of fonts are installed, or what kind of fonts are being currently used. By using the layout managers provided with the AWT, you can be sure that every portion of your window will be viewable and readable and usable. You can't guarantee that with hard-coded layouts.

13

Q I was exploring the AWT package, and I saw this subpackage called `peer`. There's also references to the peer classes sprinkled throughout the API documentation. What do peers do?

A Peers are responsible for the platform-specific parts of the AWT. For example, when you create a Java AWT window, you have an instance of the `Window` class that provides generic Window behavior, and then you have an instance of `WindowPeer` that creates the very specific window for that platform—a motif window under X windows, a Macintosh-style window under the Macintosh, or a Windows 95 window under Windows 95. The peers also handle communication between the window system and the Java window itself. By separating the generic component behavior (the AWT classes) from the actual system implementation and appearance (the peer classes), you can focus on providing behavior in your Java application and let the Java implementation deal with the platform-specific details.

Q There's a whole lot of functionality in the AWT that you haven't talked about here. Why?

A Given that even a basic introduction took this long, I figured that if I put in even more detail than I already have that this book would turn into *Teach Yourself Java in 21 Days Plus a Few Extra for the AWT Stuff.*

As it is, I've left windows, menus, and dialog until tomorrow, so you'll have to wait for those. But you can find out about a lot of the other features of AWT merely by exploring the API documentation. Start with the `Applet` class and examine the sorts of methods you can call. Then look at `Panel`, from which applet inherits—you have all that class's functionality as well. The superclass of `Panel` is `Container`, which provides still more interesting detail. `Component` comes next. Explore the API and see what you can do with it. You might find something interesting.

Windows, Networking, and Other Tidbits

by Laura Lemay

Here you are on the last day of the second week, and you're just about finished with applets and the AWT. With the information you'll learn today, you can create a wide variety of applets and applications using Java. Next week's lessons provide more of the advanced stuff that you'll need if you start doing really serious work in Java.

Today, to finish up this week, there are three very different topics:

☐ Windows, menus, and dialog boxes—the last of the AWT classes that enable you to pop up real windows from applets, and to create stand-alone Java applications that have their own windows

☐ Networking—how to load new HTML files from an applet-capable browser, how to retrieve files from Web sites, and some basics on how to work with generic sockets in Java

☐ Extra tidbits—the smaller stuff that didn't fit in anywhere else, but that might be useful to you as you write your Java applets and applications

Windows, Menus, and Dialog Boxes

Today, you'll finish up the last bits of the AWT that didn't fit into yesterday's lesson. In addition to all the graphics, events, UI, and layout mechanisms that the AWT provides, it also provides windows, menus, and dialog boxes, enabling to you create fully featured applications either as part of your applet or independently for stand-alone Java applications.

Frames

The AWT `Window` class enables you to create windows that are independent of the browser window containing the applet—that is, separate popup windows with their own titles, resize handles, and menubars.

The `Window` class provides basic behavior for windows. Most commonly, instead of using the `Window` class, you'll use `Window`'s subclasses, `Frame` and `Dialog`. The `Frame` class enables you to create a fully functioning window with a menubar. `Dialog` is a more limited window for dialog boxes. You'll learn more about dialog boxes later on in this section.

To create a frame, use one of the following constructors:

☐ `new Frame()` creates a basic frame without a title.

☐ `new Frame(String)` creates a basic frame with the given title.

Frames are containers, just like panels are, so you can add other components to them just as you would regular panels, using the `add()` method. The default layout for windows is `BorderLayout`:

```
win = new Frame("My Cool Window");
win.setLayout(new BorderLayout(10,20));
```

```
win.add("North", new Button("start"));
win.add("Center", new Button("Move"));
```

To set a size for the new window, use the resize() method. To set a location for where the window appears, use the move() method. Note that the location() method can tell you where the applet window is on the screen so that you can pop up the extra window in a relative position to that window (all these methods are defined for all containers, so you can use them for applets, windows, and the components inside them, subject to the current layout):

```
win.resize(100,200);
Dimension d = location();
win.move(d.width + 50, d.height + 50);
```

When you initially create a window, it's invisible. You need to use the show() method to make the window appear on the screen (you can use hide() to hide it again):

```
win.show();
```

Listing 14.1 shows an example of a simple applet with a popup window (both the applet and the window are shown in Figure 14.1). The applet has two buttons: one to show the window, and one to hide the window. The window itself, created from a subclass called MyFrame has a single label: "This is a Window." You'll use this basic window and applet all through this section, so the more you understand what's going on here the easier it will be later.

Type **Listing 14.1. A popup window.**

```
public class GUI extends java.applet.Applet {
    Frame window;

    public void init() {
        add(new Button("Open Window"));
        add(new Button("Close Window"));

        window = new MyFrame("A Popup Window");
        window.resize(150,150);
        window.show();
    }

    public boolean action(Event evt, Object arg) {
        if (evt.target instanceof Button) {
            String label = (String)arg;
            if (label.equals("Open Window")) {
                if (!window.isShowing())
                    window.show();
            }
            else if (label == "Close Window") {
                if (window.isShowing())
                    window.hide();
            }
            return true;
        }
```

14

continues

Listing 14.1. continued

```
            else return false;
    }
}

class MyFrame extends Frame {
    Label l;

    MyFrame(String title) {
        super(title);
        setLayout(new GridLayout(1,1));
        l = new Label("This is a Window", Label.CENTER);
        add(l);
}
```

Figure 14.1.
Windows.

Menus

Each new window you create can have its own menubar along the top of the screen. Each menubar can have a number of menus, and each menu, in turn, can have menu items. The AWT provides classes for all these things called, respectively, `MenuBar`, `Menu`, and `MenuItem`.

Menus and Menubars

To create a menubar for a given window, create a new instance of the class `MenuBar`:

```
MenuBar mb = new MenuBar();
```

To set this menubar as the default menu for the window, use the `setMenuBar()` method on the window:

```
window.setMenuBar(mb);
```

Add individual menus (File, Edit, and so on) to the menubar by creating them and then adding them to the menubar:

```
Menu m = new Menu("File");
mb.add(m);
```

Some systems enable you to indicate a special help menu, which may be drawn on the right side of the menubar. You can indicate that a specific menu is the help menu by using the setHelpMenu() method. The given menu should already be added to the menu itself:

```
Menu hm = new Menu("Help");
mb.add(hm);
mb.setHelpMenu(hm);
```

If, for any reason, you want to prevent a user from selecting a menu, you can use the disable() command on that menu (and the enable() command to make it available again):

```
m.disable();
```

Menu Items

There are four kinds of items you can add to individual menus:

- [ ] Instances of the class MenuItem, for regular menu items
- [ ] Instances of the class CheckBoxMenuItem, for toggled menu items
- [ ] Other menus, with their own menu items
- [ ] Separators, for lines that separate groups of items on menus

Regular menu items are added by using the MenuItem class. Add them to a menu using the add() method:

```
Menu m = new Menu("Tools");
m.add(new MenuItem("Info"));
m.add(new MenuItem("Colors"));
m.add(new MenuItem("Sizes"));
```

Submenus can be added simply by creating a new instance of Menu and adding it to the first menu. You can then add items to *that* menu:

```
Menu sb = new Menu("Sizes");
m.add(sb);
sb.add(new MenuItem("Small"));
sb.add(new MenuItem("Medium"));
sb.add(new MenuItem("Large"));
```

The CheckBoxMenuItem class creates a menu item with a checkbox on it, enabling the menu state to be toggled on and off (selecting it once makes the checkbox appear selected; selecting it again unselects the checkbox). Create and add a checkbox menu item the same way you create and add regular menu items:

14

```
CheckboxMenuItem coords =
    new CheckboxMenuItem("Show Coordinates");
m.add(coords);
```

Finally, to add a separator to a menu (a line used to separate groups of items in a menu), create and add a menu item with the label "-".

```
MenuItem msep = new MenuItem("-");
m.add(msep);
```

Any menu item can be disabled by using the `disable()` method and enabled again using `enable()`. Disabled menu items cannot be selected:

```
MenuItem mi = new MenuItem("Fill");
m.addItem(mi);
mi.disable();
```

Menu Actions

The act of selecting a menu item causes an action event to be generated. You can handle that action the same way you handle other `action` methods—by overriding `action()`. Both regular menu items and checkbox menu items have actions that generate an extra argument representing the label for that menu. You can use that label to determine which action to take. Note, also, that because `CheckBoxMenuItem` is a subclass of `MenuItem`, you don't have to treat that menu item as a special case:

```
public boolean action(Event evt, Object arg) {
    if (evt.target instanceof MenuItem) {
        String label = (String)arg;
        if (label.equals("Show Coordinates")) toggleCoords();
        else if (label.equals("Fill")) fillcurrentArea();
        return true;
    }
    else return false;
}
```

An Example

Let's add a menu to the window you created in the previous section. Add it to the constructor method in the `MyFrame` class (Figure 14.2 shows the resulting menu):

```
MyFrame(String title) {
    super(title);
    MenuBar mb = new MenuBar();
    Menu m = new Menu("Colors");
    m.add(new MenuItem("Red"));
    m.add(new MenuItem("Blue"));
    m.add(new MenuItem("Green"));
    m.add(new MenuItem("-"));
    m.add(new CheckboxMenuItem("Reverse Text"));
    mb.add(m);
```

```
    mb.setHelpMenu(m);
    setMenuBar(mb);
...
}
```

This menu has four items: one each for the colors red, blue, and green (which, when selected, change the background of the window), and one checkbox menu item for reversing the color of the text (to white). To handle these menu items, you need an `action()` method:

```
public boolean action(Event evt, Object arg) {
    if (evt.target instanceof MenuItem) {
        String label = (String)arg;
        if (label.equals("Red")) setBackground(Color.red);
        else if (label.equals("Blue")) setBackground(Color.blue);
        else if (label.equals("Green")) setBackground(Color.green);
        else if (label.equals("Reverse Text")) {
            if (getForeground() == Color.black)
                setForeground(Color.white);
            else setForeground(Color.black);
        }
        return true;
    }
    else return false;
}
```

Figure 14.2.
A menu.

Dialog Boxes

Dialog boxes are functionally similar to frames in that they pop up new windows on the screen. However, dialog boxes are intended to be used for transient windows—for example, windows that let you know about warnings, windows that ask you for specific information, and so on. Dialogs don't usually have titlebars or many of the more general features that windows have (although you can create one with a titlebar), and they can be made nonresizable or modal.

NEW☞ TERM A *modal dialog* prevents input to any of the other windows on the screen until that dialog is dismissed.

The AWT provides two kinds of dialog boxes: the Dialog class, which provides a generic dialog, and FileDialog, which produces a platform-specific dialog to choose files to save or open.

To create a generic dialog, use one of these constructors:

- [ ] Dialog(Frame, boolean) creates an initially invisible dialog, attached to the current frame, which is either modal (true) or not (false).

- [ ] Dialog(Frame, String, boolean) is the same as the previous constructor, with the addition of a titlebar and a title indicated by the string argument.

Note that because you have to give a dialog a Frame argument, you can attach dialogs only to windows that already exist independently of the applet itself.

The dialog window, like the frame window, is a panel on which you can lay out and draw UI components and perform graphics operations, just as you would any other panel. Like other windows, the dialog is initially invisible, but you can show it with show() and hide it with hide().

Let's add a dialog to that same example with the popup window. You'll add a menu item for changing the text of the window, which brings up the Enter Text dialog box (see Figure 14.3).

Figure 14.3.
The Enter Text dialog.

To add this dialog, first add a menu item to that window (the constructor method for the MyFrame class) to change the text the popup window displays:

```
m.add(new MenuItem("Set Text..."));
```

In that same method, you can create the dialog and lay out the parts of it (it's invisible by default, so you can do whatever you want to it and it won't appear on screen until you show it):

```
dl = new Dialog(this, "Enter Text",true);
dl.setLayout(new GridLayout(2,1,30,30));
```

```
tf = new TextField(l.getText(),20);
dl.add(tf);
dl.add(new Button("OK"));
dl.resize(150,75);
```

The action of choosing the menu item you just added brings up the dialog; choosing the OK button dismisses it. So you need to add behavior to this class's action method so that the dialog works right. To the menu item tests, add a line for the new menu item:

```
if (evt.target instanceof MenuItem) {
    if (label.equals("Red")) setBackground(Color.red);
    if (label.equals("Blue")) setBackground(Color.blue);
    if (label.equals("Green")) setBackground(Color.green);
    if (label.equals("Set Text...")) dl.show();
}
```

Then, because OK is a button, you have to add a special case for that button separate from the menu items. In this special case, set the text of the window to the text that was typed into the text field, and then hide the dialog again:

```
if (evt.target instanceof Button) {
    if (label.equals("OK")) {
        l.setText(tf.getText());
        dl.hide();
    }
}
```

File Dialogs

FileDialog provides a basic file open/save dialog box that enables you to access the file system. The FileDialog class is system-independent, but depending on the platform, the standard Open File dialog is brought up.

> **Note:** For applets, you can bring up the file dialog, but due to security restrictions you can't do anything with it (or, if you can, access to any files on the local system is severely restricted). FileDialog is much more useful in stand-alone applications.

To create a file dialog, use the following constructors:

14

- [ ] FileDialog(*Frame*, *String*) creates an Open File dialog, attached to the given frame, with the given title. This form creates a dialog to load a file.

- [ ] FileDialog(*Frame*, *String*, *int*) also creates a file dialog, but that integer argument is used to determine whether the dialog is for loading a file or saving a file (the only difference is the labels on the buttons; the file dialog does not actually open or save anything). The possible options for the mode argument are FileDialog.LOAD and FileDialog.SAVE.

After you create a `FileDialog` instance, use `show()` to display it:

```
FileDialog fd = new FileDialog(this, "FileDialog");
fd.show();
```

When the reader chooses a file in the file dialog and dismisses it, you can then get to the file they chose by using the `getDirectory()` and `getFile()` methods; both return strings indicating the values the reader chose. You can then open that file by using the stream and file handling methods (which you'll learn about next week) and then read from or write to that file.

Window Events

Yesterday, you learned about writing your own event handler methods, and you noted that the `Event` class defines many standard events for which you can test. Window events are part of that list, so if you use windows, these events may be of interest to you. Table 14.1 shows those events.

Table 14.1: Window Events from the `Event` Class.

`WINDOW_DESTROY`	Generated when a window is destroyed (for example, when the browser or applet viewer has quit)
`WINDOW_EXPOSE`	Generated when the window is brought forward from behind other windows
`WINDOW_ICONIFY`	Generated when the window is iconified
`WINDOW_DEICONIFY`	Generated when the window is restored from an icon
`WINDOW_MOVED`	Generated when the window is moved

Using AWT Windows in Stand-Alone Applications

Because frames are general-purpose mechanisms for creating AWT windows with panels, you can use them in your stand-alone Java applications and easily take advantage of all the applet capabilities you learned about this week. To do this, write your application as if it were an applet (inheriting from the `Applet` class and using threads, graphics, and UI components as necessary), and then add a `main()` method. Here's one for a class called `MyAWTClass`:

```
public static void main(String args[]) {
    Frame f = new Frame("My Window");
    MyAWTClass mac = new MyAWTClass();
    mac.init();
    mac.start();

    f.add("Center", mac);
```

```
    f.resize(300, 300);
    f.show();
}
```

This `main()` method does five things:

- [ ] It creates a new frame to hold the applet.
- [ ] It creates an instance of the class that defines that method.
- [ ] It duplicates the applet environment calls to `init()` and `start()`.
- [ ] It adds the applet to the frame and resizes the frame to be 300 pixels square.
- [ ] It shows the frame on the screen.

By using this mechanism, you can create a Java program that can function equally well as an applet or an application—just include `init()` for applets and `main()` for applications.

If you do create an application that uses this mechanism, be careful of your `init()` methods that get parameters from an HTML file. When you run an applet as an application, you don't have the HTML parameters passed into the `init()` method. Pass them in as command-line arguments, instead, and handle them in your `main()` method. Then set a flag so that the `init()` method doesn't try to read parameters that don't exist.

Networking in Java

Networking is the capability of making connections from your applet or application to a system over the network. Networking in Java involves classes in the `java.net` package, which provide cross-platform abstractions for simple networking operations, including connecting and retrieving files by using common Web protocols and creating basic Unix-like sockets. Used in conjunction with input and output streams (which you'll learn much more about next week), reading and writing files over the network becomes as easy as reading or writing to files on the local disk.

There are restrictions, of course. Java applets cannot read or write from the disk on the machine that's running them. Depending on the browser, Java applets may not be able to connect to systems other than the one upon which they were originally stored. Even given these restrictions, you can still accomplish a great deal and take advantage of the Web to read and process information over the net.

This section describes three ways you can communicate with systems on the net:

- [ ] `showDocument()`, which enables an applet to tell the browser to load and link to another page on the Web
- [ ] `openStream()`, a method that opens a connection to a URL and enables you to extract data from that connection

14

☐ The socket classes, `Socket` and `ServerSocket`, which enable you to open standard socket connections to hosts and read to and write from those connections

Creating Links Inside Applets

Probably the easiest way to use networking inside an applet is to tell the browser running that applet to load a new page. You can use this, for example, to create animated image maps that, when clicked, load a new page.

To link to a new page, you create a new instance of the class URL. You saw some of this when you worked with images, but let's go over it a little more thoroughly here.

The URL class represents a uniform resource locator. To create a new URL, you can use one of four different forms:

☐ `URL(String, String, int, String)` creates a new URL object, given a protocol (http, ftp, gopher, file), a host name (`www.lne.com`, `ftp.netcom.com`), a port number (`80` for http), and a filename or pathname.

☐ `URL(String, String, String)` does the same thing as the previous form, minus the port number.

☐ `URL(URL, String)` creates a URL, given a base path and a relative path. For the base, you can use `getDocumentBase()` for the URL of the current HTML file, or `getCodeBase` for the URL of the Java class file. The relative path will be tacked onto the last directory in those base URLs (just like with images and sounds).

☐ `URL(String)` creates a URL object from a URL string (which should include the protocol, hostname, and filename).

For that last one (creating a URL from a string), you have to catch a malformed URL exception, so surround the URL constructor with a `try...catch`:

```
String url = "http://www.yahoo.com/";
try { theURL = new URL(url); }
catch ( MalformedURLException e) {
    System.out.println("Bad URL: " + theURL);
}
```

Getting a URL object is the hard part. Once you have one, all you have to do is pass it to the browser. Do this by using this single line of code, where `theURL` is the URL object to link to:

```
getAppletContext().showDocument(theURL);
```

The browser that contains your URL will then load and display the document at that URL.

Listing 14.2 shows a simple applet that displays three buttons that represent important Web locations (the buttons are shown in Figure 14.4). Clicking on the buttons causes the document to be loaded to the locations to which those buttons refer.

Listing 14.2. Bookmark buttons.

```java
import java.awt.*;
import java.net.URL;
import java.net.MalformedURLException;

public class ButtonLink extends java.applet.Applet {

    Bookmark bmlist[] = new Bookmark[3];

    public void init() {
        bmlist[0] = new Bookmark("Laura's Home Page",
            "http://www.lne.com/lemay/");
        bmlist[1] = new Bookmark("Yahoo",
            "http://www.yahoo.com");
        bmlist[2]= new Bookmark("Java Home Page",
            "http://java.sun.com");

        setLayout(new GridLayout(bmlist.length,1,10,10));
        for (int i = 0; i < bmlist.length; i++) {
            add(new Button(bmlist[i].name));
        }
    }

    public boolean action(Event evt, Object arg) {
        if (evt.target instanceof Button) {
            LinkTo((String)arg);
            return true;
        }
    else retrurn false;
    }

    void LinkTo(String name) {
        URL theURL = null;
        for (int i = 0; i < bmlist.length; i++) {
            if (name.equals(bmlist[i].name))
                theURL = bmlist[i].url;
        }
        if (theURL != null)
            getAppletContext().showDocument(theURL);
    }
}

class Bookmark {
    String name;
    URL url;

    Bookmark(String name, String theURL) {
        this.name = name;
        try { this.url = new URL(theURL); }
        catch ( MalformedURLException e) {
            System.out.println("Bad URL: " + theURL);
        }
    }
}
```

14

Figure 14.4.
Bookmark buttons.

 Two classes make up this applet: the first implements the actual applet itself, the second is a class representing a bookmark. Bookmarks have two parts: a name and a URL.

This particular applet creates three bookmark instances and stores them in an array of bookmarks (this applet could be easily modified to make bookmarks as parameters from an HTML file). For each bookmark, a button is created whose label is the value of the bookmark's name.

When the buttons are pressed, the linkTo() method is called, which tells the browser to load the URL referenced by that bookmark.

Opening Web Connections

Rather than asking the browser to just load the contents of a file, sometimes you might want to get hold of that file's contents so that your applet can use them. If the file you want to grab is stored on the Web, and can be accessed using the more common URL forms (http, ftp, and so on), your applet can use the URL class to get it.

Note that for security reasons, applets can connect back only to the same host from which they originally loaded. This means that if you have your applets stored on a system called www.myhost.com, the only machine your applet can open a connection to will be that same host (and that same host *name*, so be careful with host aliases). If the file the applet wants to retrieve is on that same system, using URL connections is the easiest way to get it.

openStream()

URL defines a method called openStream(), which opens a network connection using the given URL and returns an instance of the class InputStream (part of the java.io package). If you convert that stream to a DataInputStream (with a BufferedInputStream in the middle for better performance), you can then read characters and lines from that stream (you'll learn all about streams on Day 19). For example, these lines open a connection to the URL stored in the variable theURL, and then read and echo each line of the file to the standard output:

```
try {
    InputStream in = theURL.openStream();
    DataInputStream data = new DataInputStream(
        new BufferedInputStream(in);

    String line;
    while ((line = data.readLine()) != null) {
        System.out.println("line");
    }
}
catch (IOException e) {
    System.out.println("IO Error: " + e.getMessage());
}
```

> **Note:** You need to wrap all those lines in a try...catch statement to catch IOException exceptions.

Here's an example of an applet that uses the openStream() method to open a connection to a Web site, reads a file from that connection (Edgar Allen Poe's poem "The Raven"), and displays the result in a text area. Listing 14.3 shows the code; Figure 14.5 shows the result after the file has been read.

Type

Listing 14.3. The GetRaven class.

```
 1: import java.awt.*;
 2: import java.io.DataInputStream;
 3: import java.io.BufferedInputStream;
 4: import java.io.IOException;
 5: import java.net.URL;
 6: import java.net.URLConnection;
 7: import java.net.MalformedURLException;
 8:
 9: public class GetRaven extends java.applet.Applet
10:     implements Runnable {
```

continues

14

Listing 14.3. continued

```
11:
12:      URL theURL;
13:      Thread runner;
14:      TextArea ta = new TextArea("Getting text...",30,70);
15:
16:      public void init() {
17:
18:          String url = "http://www.lne.com/Web/Java/raven.txt";
19:          try { this.theURL = new URL(url); }
20:          catch ( MalformedURLException e) {
21:              System.out.println("Bad URL: " + theURL);
22:          }
23:          add(ta);
24:      }
25:
26:      public Insets insets() {
27:          return new Insets(10,10,10,10);
28:      }
29:
30:      public void start() {
31:          if (runner == null) {
32:              runner = new Thread(this);
33:              runner.start();
34:          }
35:      }
36:
37:      public void stop() {
38:          if (runner != null) {
39:              runner.stop();
40:              runner = null;
41:          }
42:      }
43:
44:      public void run() {
45:          InputStream conn = null;
46:          DataInputStream data = null;
47:          String line;
48:          StringBuffer buf = new StringBuffer();
49:
50:          try {
51:              conn = this.theURL.openStream();
52:              data = new DataInputStream(new BufferedInputStream(
53:                  conn));
54:
55:              while ((line = data.readLine()) != null) {
56:                  buf.append(line + "\n");
57:              }
58:
59:              ta.setText(buf.toString());
60:          }
61:          catch (IOException e) {
62:              System.out.println("IO Error:" + e.getMessage());
63:          }
64:      }
65: }
```

Figure 14.5.

The GetRaven *class.*

Analysis The init() method (lines 16 to 24) sets up the URL and the text area in which that file will be displayed. The URL could be easily passed into the applet via an HTML parameter; here, it's just hard-coded for simplicity.

Because it might take some time to load the file over the network, you put that routine into its own thread and use the familiar start(), stop(), and run() methods to control that thread.

Inside run() (lines 44 to 64), the work takes place. Here, you initialize a bunch of variables and then open the connection to the URL (using the openStream() method in line 51). Once the connection is open, you set up an input stream in lines 52 to 56 and read from it, line by line, putting the result into an instance of StringBuffer (a string buffer is a modifiable string).

Once all the data has been read, line 59 converts the StringBuffer object into a real string and then puts that result in the text area.

One other thing to note about this example is that the part of the code that opened a network connection, read from the file, and created a string is surrounded by a try and catch statement. If any errors occur while you're trying to read or process the file, these statements enable you to recover from them without the entire program crashing (in this case, the program exits with an error, because there's little else to be done if the applet can't read the file). try and catch give you the capability of handling and recovering from errors. You'll learn more about exceptions on Day 18.

14

The *URLconnection* Class

URL's openStream() method is actually a simplified use of the URLconnection class. URLconnection provides a way to retrieve files by using URLs—on Web or FTP sites, for example. URLconnection also enables you to create output streams if the protocol allows it.

To use a URL connection, you first create a new instance of the class URLconnection, set its parameters (whether it enables writing, for example), and then use the connect() method to open the connection. Keep in mind that, with a URL connection, the class handles the protocol for you based on the first part of the URL, so you don't have to make specific requests to retrieve a file; all you have to do is read it.

Sockets

For networking applications beyond what the URL and URLconnection classes offer (for example, for other protocols or for more general networking applications), Java provides the Socket and ServerSocket classes as an abstraction of standard socket programming techniques.

Note: I don't have the space to give you a full explanation of how socket programming works. If you haven't worked with sockets before, see whether openStream() will meet your needs. If you really need to do more, any book that discusses socket programming will give you the background you need to work with Java's sockets.

The Socket class provides a client-side socket interface similar to standard Unix sockets. To open a connection, create a new instance of Socket (where *hostname* is the host to connect to, and *portnum* is the port number):

```
Socket connection = new Socket(hostname, portnum);
```

Note: If you use sockets in an applet, you are still subject to the security restrictions about where you can connect.

Once the socket is open, you can use input and output streams to read and write from that socket (you'll learn all about input and output streams on Day 19):

```
DataInputStream in = new DataInputStream(
    new BufferedInputStream(connection.getInputStream()));
DataOutputStream out= new DataOutputStream(
    new BufferedOutputStream(connection.getOutputStream()));
```

Once you're done with the socket, don't forget to close it (this also closes all the input and ouput streams you may have set up for that socket):

```
connection.close();
```

Server-side sockets work similarly, with the exception of the accept() method. A server socket listens on a TCP port for a connection for a client; when a client connects to that port, the accept() method accepts a connection from that client. By using both client and server sockets, you can create applications that communicate with each other over the network.

To create a server socket and bind it to a port, create a new instance of ServerSocket with the port number:

```
ServerSocket sconnection = new ServerSocket(8888);
```

To listen on that port (and to accept a connection from any clients if one is made), use the accept() method:

```
sconnection.accept();
```

Once the socket connection is made, you can use input and output streams to read to and write from the client.

See the java.net package for more information about Java sockets.

Other Applet Hints

On this, the last section of the last day of the second week, let's finish up with some small hints that didn't fit in anywhere else: using showStatus() to print messages in the browser' status window, providing applet information, and communicating between multiple applets on the same page.

The *showStatus* Method

The showStatus() method, available in the applet class, enables you to display a string in the status bar of the browser, which contains the applet. You can use this for printing error, link, help, or other status messages:

```
getAppletContext().showStatus("Change the color");
```

The getAppletContext() method enables your applet to access features of the browser that contains it. You already saw a use of this with links, wherein you could use the showDocument() method to tell the browser to load a page. showStatus() uses that same mechanism to print status messages.

14

297

> **Note:** showStatus() may not be supported in all browsers, so do not depend on it for your applet's functionality or interface. It is a useful way of communicating optional information to your user—if you need a more reliable method of communication, set up a label in your applet and update it to reflect changes in its message.

Applet Information

The AWT gives you a mechanism for associating information with your applet. Usually, there is a mechanism in the browser viewing the applet to view display information. You can use this mechanism to sign your name or your organization to your applet, or to provide contact information so that users can get hold of you if they want.

To provide information about your applet, override the getAppletInfo() method:

```
public String getAppletInfo() {
    return "GetRaven copyright 1995 Laura Lemay";
}
```

Communicating Between Applets

Sometimes you want to have an HTML page that has several different applets on it. To do this, all you have to do is include several different iterations of the applet tag—the browser will create different instances of your applet for each one that appears on the HTML page.

What if you want to communicate between those applets? What if you want a change in one applet to affect the other applets in some way?

The best way to do this is to use the applet context to get to different applets on the same page. You've already seen the use of the getAppletContext() method for several other uses; you can also use it to get hold of the other applets on the page. For example, to call a method in all the applets on a page (including the current applet), use the getApplets() method and a for loop that looks something like this:

```
for (Enumeration e = getAppletContext().getApplets();
        e.hasMoreElements();) {
    Applet current = (Applet)(e.nextElement());
    sendMessage(current);
}
```

The getApplets() method returns an Enumeration object with a list of the applets on the page. Iterating over the Enumeration object in this way enables you to access each element in the Enumeration in turn.

If you want to call a method in a specific applet, it's slightly more complicated. To do this, you give your applets a name and then refer to them by name inside the body of code for that applet.

To give an applet a name, use the NAME parameter in your HTML file:

```
<P>This applet sends information:
<APPLET CODE="MyApplet.class" WIDTH=100 HEIGHT=150
    NAME="sender"> </APPLET>
<P>This applet receives information from the sender:
<APPLET CODE="MyApplet.class" WIDTH=100 HEIGHT=150
    NAME="receiver"> </APPLET>
```

To get a reference to another applet on the same page, use the getApplet() method from the applet context with the name of that applet. This gives you a reference to the applet of that name. You can then refer to that applet as if it were just another object: call methods, set its instance variables, and so on:

```
// get ahold of the receiver applet
Applet receiver = getAppletContext().getApplet("receiver");
// tell it to update itself.
reciever.update(text, value);
```

In this example, you use the getApplet() method to get a reference to the applet with the name receiver. Given that reference, you can then call methods in that applet as if it were just another object in your own environment. Here, for example, if both applets have an update() method, you can tell receiver to update itself by using the information the current applet has.

Naming your applets and then referring to them by using the methods described in this section enables your applets to communicate and stay in sync with each other, providing uniform behavior for all the applets on your page.

Summary

Congratulations! Take a deep breath—you're finished with Week 2. This week has been full of useful information about creating applets and using the Java AWT classes to display, draw, animate, process input, and create fully fledged interfaces in your applets.

Today, you finished exploring applets and the AWT by learning about three concepts.

First, you learned about windows, frames, menus, and dialogs, which enable you to create a framework for your applets—or enable your Java applications to take advantage of applet features.

Second, you head a brief introduction to Java networking through some of the classes in the java.net package. Applet networking includes things as simple as pointing the browser to another page from inside your applet, but can also include retrieving files from the Web by using

14

standard Web protocols (`http`, `ftp`, and so on). For more advanced networking capabilities, Java provides basic socket interfaces that can be used to implement many basic network-oriented applets—client-server interactions, chat sessions, and so on.

Finally, you finished up with the tidbits—small features of the Java AWT and of applets that didn't fit anywhere else, including `showStatus()`, producing information for your applet, and communicating between multiple applets on a single page.

Q&A

Q When I create popup windows using the `appletviewer`, they all show up with this big red bar that says `Warning: applet window`. What does this mean?

A The warning is to tell you (and the users of your applet) that the window being displayed was generated by an applet, and not by the browser itself. This is a security feature to keep an applet programmer from popping up a window that masquerades as a browser window and, for example, asks users for their passwords.

There's nothing you can do to hide or obscure the warning.

Q What good is having a file dialog box if you can't read or write files from the local file system?

A Applets can't read or write from the local file system, but because you can use AWT components in Java applications as well as applets, the file dialog box is very useful for that purpose.

Q How can I mimic an HTML form submission in a Java applet?

A Currently, applets make it difficult to do this. The best (and easiest way) is to use GET notation to get the browser to submit the form contents for you.

HTML forms can be submitted in two ways: by using the GET request, or by using POST. If you use GET, your form information is encoded in the URL itself, something like this:

```
http://www.blah.com/cgi-bin/myscript?foo=1&bar=2&name=Laura
```

Because the form input is encoded in the URL, you can write a Java applet to mimic a form, get input from the user, and then construct a new URL object with the form data included on the end. Then just pass that URL to the browser by using `getAppletContext().showDocument()`, and the browser will submit the form results itself. For simple forms, this is all you need.

Q How can I do POST form submissions?

A You'll have to mimic what a browser does to send forms using POST: open a socket to the server and send the data, which looks something like this (the exact format is determined by the HTTP protocol; this is only a subset of it):

```
POST /cgi-bin/mailto.cgi HTTP/1.0
Content-type: application/x-www-form-urlencoded
Content-length: 36

{your encoded form data here}
```

If you've done it right, you get the CGI form output back from the server. It's then up to your applet to handle that output properly. Note that if the output is in HTML, there really isn't a way to pass that output to the browser that is running your applet. If you get back a URL, however, you can redirect the browser to that URL.

Q showStatus doesn't work in my browser. How can I give my readers status information?

A As you learned in the section on showStatus(), whether or not a browser supports showStatus() is up to that browser. If you must have status-like behavior in your applet, consider creating a status label in the applet itself that is updated with the information you need to present.

14

- ☐ Modifiers
  Method and variable access control
- ☐ Packages and Interfaces
  Hiding classes
  Design versus implementation inheritance
- ☐ Exceptions
  Proper `throw` statements
  Using the `finally` clause
- ☐ Multithreading
  Synchronization problems
  More about `Point`
- ☐ Java Streams
  Input and output, `flush()` and `close()`
- ☐ Native Methods and Libraries
  Built-in optimizations
  Generating header and stub files

Week 3 at a Glance

☐ Under the Hood
Java bytecodes
Security and consistency checking
Garbage collection

Modifiers

by Charles L. Perkins

Once you begin to program Java for a while, you'll discover that making all your classes, methods, and variables `public` can become quite annoying. The larger your program becomes, and the more you reuse your classes for new projects, the more you will want some sort of control over their visibility. One of the large-scale solutions to this problem, packages, must wait until tomorrow, but today you'll explore what you can do within a class.

Today, you'll learn how to create and use the following:

- ☐ Methods and variables that control their access by other classes
- ☐ Class variables and methods
- ☐ Constant variables, classes that cannot be subclassed, and methods that cannot be overridden
- ☐ Abstract classes and methods

NEW 🖝 *Modifiers* are prefixes that can be applied in various combinations to the methods and **TERM** variables within a class and, some, to the class itself.

There is a long and varied list of modifiers. The order of modifiers is irrelevant to their meaning—your order can vary and is really a matter of taste. Pick a style and then be consistent with it throughout all your classes. Here is the recommended order:

```
<access> static abstract synchronized <unusual> final native
```

where `<access>` can be `public`, `protected`, or `private`, and `<unusual>` includes `volatile` and `transient`.

> **Note:** As of the beta release, `threadsafe` has been replaced by `volatile`. Both have to do with multithreading; no more will be said about them here (see Day 18). `transient` is a special modifier used to declare a variable to be outside the persistent part of an object. This makes persistent object storage systems easier to implement in Java, and though the compiler supports it, it is not used by the current Java system. Several reserved keywords (`byvalue`, `future`, and `generic`, for example) may end up being `<unusual>` modifiers in later releases of Java. In the beta system, *none* of these unusual modifiers appears in the source code for the standard Java library classes.

All the modifiers are essentially optional; none have to appear in a declaration. Good style suggests adding as many as are needed to best describe the intended use of, and restrictions on, what you're declaring. In some special situations (inside an interface, for example, as described tomorrow), certain modifiers are implicitly defined for you, and you needn't type them—they will be assumed to be there.

The synchronized modifier is covered on Day 18; it has to do with multithreaded methods. The native modifier is covered on Day 20; it specifies that a method is implemented in the native language of your computer (usually C), rather than in Java. How <access> modifiers apply to classes is covered tomorrow.

Method and Variable Access Control

Access control is about controlling visibility. When a method or variable is visible to another class, its methods can reference (call or modify) that method or variable. To "protect" a method or variable from such references, you use the four levels of visibility described in the next sections. Each, in turn, is more restrictive, and thus provides more protection than the one before it.

The Four P's of Protection

Learning your four P's (public, package, protected, and private) comes down to understanding the fundamental relationships that a method or variable within a class can have to the other classes in the system.

public

Because any class is an island unto itself, the first of these relationships builds on the distinction between the inside and the outside of the class. Any method or variable is visible to the class in which it is defined, but what if you want to make it visible to *all* the classes outside this class?

The answer is obvious: simply declare the method or variable to have public access. Almost every method and variable defined in the rest of this book has been declared, for simplicity's sake, public. When you use any of the examples provided in your own code, you'll probably decide to restrict this access further. Because you're just learning now, it's not a bad idea to begin with the widest possible access you can imagine and then narrow it down as you gain design experience, until the access that each of your variables and methods should have becomes second nature. Here are some examples of public declarations:

```
public class  APublicClass {
    public int     aPublicInt;
    public String  aPublicString;

    public float   aPublicMethod() {
        . . .
    }
}
```

> **Note:** The two (or more) spaces after the prefix of modifiers and type in these declarations are intentional. They make finding the variable or method name within each line a little easier. Further in the book, you'll see that the type and the name are sometimes separately lined up in a column to make it even more evident what is what. When you get enough modifiers on a line, you'll begin to appreciate these small touches.

A variable or method with `public` access has the widest possible visibility. Anyone can see it. Anyone can use it. Of course, this may not always be what you want—which brings us to the next level of protection.

package

In C, there is the notion of hiding a name so that only the functions within a given source file can see it. In Java, source files are replaced by the more explicit notion of packages, which can group classes (you learn about these tomorrow). For now, all you need to know is that the relationship you want to support is of a class to its fellow implementors of one piece of a system, library, or program (or to any other grouping of related classes). This defines the next level of increased protection and narrowed visibility.

Due to an idiosyncrasy of the Java language, this next level of access has no precise name. It is indicated by the lack of any access modifier in a declaration. Historically, it has been called various suggestive names, including "friendly" and "package." The latter usage seems most appropriate and is the one used here. Perhaps in a later release of the system, it will be possible to say `package` explicitly, but for now it is simply the default protection when none has been specified.

> **Note:** Why would anyone want to make more typing for themselves and explicitly say `package`? It is a matter of consistency and clarity. If you have a pattern of declarations with varying access modifier prefixes, you may always want the modifier to be stated explicitly, both for the reader's benefit and because, in some contexts, different "default" levels of protection are being assumed, and you want the compiler to notice your intentions and warn you of any conflicts.

Most of the declarations you've seen in the past two weeks have used this default level of protection. Here's a reminder of what they look like:

```
public class  ALessPublicClass {
    int     aPackageInt    = 2;
    String  aPackageString = "a 1 and a ";

    float   aPackageMethod() {     // no access modifier means "package"
        . . .
    }
}

public class  AClassInTheSamePackage {
    public void  testUse() {
        ALessPublicClass  aLPC = new ALessPublicClass();

        System.out.println(aLPC.aPackageString + aLPC.aPackageInt);
        aLPC.aPackageMethod();               // all of these are A.O.K.
    }
}
```

> **Note:** If a class from any other package tried to access aLPC the way that AClassInTheSamePackage does in this example, it would generate compile-time errors. (You'll learn how to create such classes tomorrow.)

Why was package made a default? When you're designing a large system and you partition your classes into work groups to implement smaller pieces of that system, the classes often need to share a lot more with one another than with the outside world. The need for this level of sharing is common enough that it was made the default level of protection.

What if you have some details of your implementation that you don't want to share with these "friends"? The answer to this question leads us naturally to the next level of protection.

protected

The third relationship is between a class and its present and future subclasses. These subclasses are much closer to a parent class than to any other "outside" classes for the following reasons:

☐ Subclasses are usually more intimately aware of the internals of a parent class.

☐ Subclasses are often written by you or by someone to whom you've given your source code.

☐ Subclasses frequently need to modify or enhance the representation of the data within a parent class.

No one else is allowed the privilege of this level of access; they must be content with the public face that the class presents.

To support the level of intimacy reserved for subclasses, modern programming languages have invented an intermediate level of access between the previous two levels and full privacy. This level gives more protection and narrows visibility still further, but still allows subclasses full access. In Java, this level of protection is called, appropriately enough, `protected`:

```
public class  AProtectedClass {
    protected int      aProtectedInt    = 4;
    protected String  aProtectedString = "and a 3 and a ";

    protected float   aProtectedMethod() {
        . . .
    }
}

public class  AProtectedClassSubclass extends AProtectedClass {
    public void  testUse() {
        AProtectedClass  aPC = new AProtectedClass();

        System.out.println(aPC.aProtectedString + aPC.aProtectedInt);
        aPC.aProtectedMethod();            // all of these are A.O.K.
    }
}

public class  AnyClassInTheSamePackage {
    public void  testUse() {
        AProtectedClass  aPC = new AProtectedClass();

        System.out.println(aPC.aProtectedString + aPC.aProtectedInt);
        aPC.aProtectedMethod();            // NONE of these are legal
    }
}
```

Even though `AnyClassInTheSamePackage` is in the same package as `AProtectedClass`, it is not a subclass of it (it's a subclass of `Object`). Only subclasses are allowed to see, and use, `protected` variables and methods.

One of the most striking examples of the need for this special level of access is when you are supporting a public abstraction with your class. As far as the outside world is concerned, you have a simple, public interface (via methods) to whatever abstraction you've built for your users. A more complex representation, and the implementation that depends on it, is hidden inside. When subclasses extend and modify this representation, or even just your implementation of it, they need to get to the underlying, concrete representation and not simply to the abstraction:

```
public class  SortedList {
    protected BinaryTree  theBinaryTree;

    . . .
    public Object[]  theList() {
        return theBinaryTree.asArray();
```

```
    }
    public void      add(Object o) {
        theBinaryTree.addObject(o);
    }
}

public class  InsertSortedList extends SortedList {
    public void      insert(Object o, int position) {
        theBinaryTree.insertObject(o,      position);
    }
}
```

Without being able to access theBinaryTree directly, the insert() method has to get the list as an array of Objects, via the public method theList(), allocate a new, bigger array, and insert the new object by hand. By "seeing" that its parent is using a BinaryTree to implement the sorted list, it can call upon BinaryTree's built-in method insertObject() to get the job done.

Some languages, such as CLU, have experimented with more explicit ways of "raising" and "lowering" your level of abstraction to solve this same problem in a more general way. In Java, protected solves only a part of the problem, by allowing you to separate the concrete from the abstract; the rest is up to you.

private

The final relationship comes full circle, back to the distinction between the inside and outside of the class. private is the most narrowly visible, highest level of protection that you can get—the diametric opposite of public. private methods and variables cannot be seen by any class other than the one in which they are defined:

```
public class  APrivateClass {
    private int      aPrivateInt;
    private String   aPrivateString;

    private float    aPrivateMethod() {
        . . .
    }
}
```

This may seem extremely restrictive, but it is, in fact, a commonly used level of protection. Any private data, internal state, or representations unique to your implementation—anything that shouldn't be directly shared with subclasses—is private. Remember that an an object's primary job is to encapsulate its data—to hide it from the world's sight and limit its manipulation. The best way to do that is to make as much data as private as possible. Your methods can always be less restrictive, as you'll see below, but keeping a tight rein on your internal representation is important. It separates design from implementation, minimizes the amount of information one class needs to know about another to get its job done, and reduces the extent of the code changes you need when your representation changes.

The Conventions for Instance Variable Access

A good rule of thumb is that unless an instance variable is constant (you'll soon see how to specify this), it should almost certainly be `private`. If you don't do this, you have the following problem:

```
public class  AFoolishClass {
    public String  aUsefulString;
    . . .  // set up the useful value of the string
}
```

This class may have thought of setting up `aUsefulString` for the use of other classes, expecting them to (only) read it. Because it isn't `private`, however, they can say:

```
AFoolishClass  aFC = new AFoolishClass();

aFC.aUsefulString = "oops!";
```

Because there is no way to specify separately the level of protection for reading from and writing to instance variables, they should almost always be `private`.

> **Note:** The careful reader may notice that this rule is violated in many examples in this book. Most of these were just for clarity's sake and to make the examples shorter and pithier. (You'll see soon that it takes more space to do the right thing.) One use cannot be avoided: the `System.out.print()` calls scattered throughout the book *must* use the `public` variable `out` directly. You cannot change this `final` system class (which you might have written differently). You can imagine the disastrous results if anyone accidentally modifies the contents of this (global) `public` variable!

Accessor Methods

If instance variables are `private`, how do you give access to them to the outside world? The answer is to write "accessor" methods:

```
public class  ACorrectClass {
    private    String  aUsefulString;

    public    String  aUsefulString() {            // "get" the value
        return aUsefulString;
    }

    protected void    aUsefulString(String s) {    // "set" the value
        aUsefulString = s;
    }
}
```

Using methods to access an instance variable is one of the most frequently used idioms in object-oriented programs. Applying it liberally throughout all your classes repays you numerous times over with more robust and reusable programs. Notice how separating the reading and writing of the instance variable allows you to specify a `public` method to return its value and a `protected` method to set it. This is often a useful pattern of protections, because everyone probably needs to be able to ask for the value, but only you (and your subclasses) should be able to change it. If it is a particularly private piece of data, you could make its "set" method `private` and its "get" method `protected`, or any other combination that suits the data's sensitivity to the light of the outside world.

> **Warning:** According to the beta language specification, it is not legal to have an instance variable and method by the same name. However, the beta compiler allows it! Because it is unclear what the final ruling on this conflict will be, use the simple naming scheme used previously for your programs. In a later release, if the compiler begins complaining, you can always change the method names to something less clear.
>
> One of the alternate conventions for the naming of accessor methods is to prepend the variable name with the prefixes `get` and `set`. Besides making you type more—for a little *less* clarity—this style forces you (by the capitalization conventions of Java) to write methods names such as `setAnnoyingFirstCapitalLetter()`. All this is, of course, a matter of taste—just be consistent in using whatever convention you adopt.

Whenever you want to append to your own instance variable, try writing this:

```
aUsefulString(aUsefulString() + " some appended text");
```

Just like someone outside the class, you're using accessor methods to change `aUsefulString`. Why do this?

You protected the variable in the first place so that changes to your representation would not affect the use of your class by others, but it still will affect the use of your class by you! As in the abstract versus concrete discussion earlier, you should be protected from knowing too much about your own representation, except in those few places that actually need to know about it. Then, if you must change something about `aUsefulString`, it will not affect every use of that variable in your class (as it would without accessor methods); rather, it affects only the implementations of its accessor.

One of the powerful side effects of maintaining this level of indirection in accessing your own instance variables is that if, at some later date, some special code needs to be performed each time aUsefulString is accessed, you can put that code in one place, and all the other methods in your class (and in everyone else's) will correctly call that special code. Here's an example:

```
protected void  aUsefulString(String s) {   // the "set" method
    aUsefulString = s;
    performSomeImportantBookkeepingOn(s);
}
```

It may seem a little difficult to get used to saying this:

```
x(12 + 5 * x());
```

rather than this:

```
x = 12 + 5 * x;
```

but the minor inconvenience will reward you with a rosy future of reusability and easy maintenance.

Class Variables and Methods

What if you want to create a shared variable that all your instances can see and use? If you use an instance variable, each instance has its own copy of the variable, defeating its whole purpose. If you place it in the class itself, however, there is only one copy, and all the instances of the class share it. This is called a class variable:

```
public class  Circle {
    public static float  pi = 3.14159265F;

    public float  area(float r) {
        return  pi * r * r;
    }
}
```

Tip: Because of its historical ties, Java uses the word static to declare class variables and methods. Whenever you see the word static, remember to substitute mentally the word "class."

Instances can refer to their own class variables as though they were instance variables, as in the last example. Because it's public, methods in other classes can also refer to pi:

```
float  circumference = 2 * Circle.pi * r;
```

Note: Instances of `Circle` can also use this form of access. In most cases, for clarity, this is the preferred form, even for instances. It clarifies that a class variable is being used, and helps the reader to know instantly where it's used and that the variable is global to all instances. This may seem pedantic, but if you try it yourself, you'll see that it can make things clearer.

By the way, if you might change your mind later about how a class variable is accessed, created, and so forth, you should create instance (or even class) accessor methods to hide any uses of it from these changes.

Class methods are defined analogously. They can be accessed in the same two ways by instances of their class, but only via the full class name by instances of other classes. Here's a class that defines class methods to help it count its own instances:

```
public class   InstanceCounter {
    private    static int    instanceCount = 0;    // a class variable

    protected static int    instanceCount() {    // a class method
        return instanceCount;
    }

    private    static void   incrementCount() {
        ++instanceCount;
    }

    InstanceCounter() {
        InstanceCounter.incrementCount();
    }
}
```

In this example, an explicit use of the class name calls the method `incrementCount()`. Though this may seem verbose, in a larger program it immediately tells the reader which object (the class, rather than the instance) is expected to handle the method. This is especially useful if the reader needs to find where that method is declared in a large class that places all its class methods at the top (the recommended practice, by the way).

Note the initialization of `instanceCount` to `0`. Just as an instance variable is initialized when its instance is created, a class variable is initialized when its class is created. This class initialization happens essentially before anything else can happen to that class, or its instances, so the class in the example will work as planned.

Finally, the conventions you learned for accessing an instance variable are applied in this example to access a class variable. The accessor methods are therefore class methods. (There is no "set" method here, just an increment method, because no one is allowed to set `instanceCount` directly.) Note that only subclasses are allowed to ask what the `instanceCount` is, because that is a (relatively) intimate detail. Here's a test of `InstanceCounter` in action:

```
public class  InstanceCounterTester extends InstanceCounter {
    public static void  main(String args[]) {
        for (int i = 0;  i < 10;  ++i)
            new InstanceCounter();
        System.out.println("made " + InstanceCounter.instanceCount());
    }
}
```

Not shockingly, this example prints the following:

```
made 10
```

The *final* Modifier

Although it's not the final modifier discussed, the `final` modifier is very versatile:

☐ When the `final` modifier is applied to a class, it means that the class cannot be subclassed.

☐ When it is applied to a variable, it means that the variable is constant.

☐ When it is applied to a method, it means that the method cannot be overridden by subclasses.

final Classes

Here's a `final` class declaration:

```
public final class  AFinalClass {
    . . .
}
```

You declare a class `final` for only two reasons. The first is security. You expect to use its instances as unforgeable capabilities, and you don't want anyone else to be able to subclass and create new and different instances of them. The second is efficiency. You want to count on instances of only that one class (and no subclasses) being around in the system so that you can optimize for them.

> **Note:** The Java class library uses `final` classes extensively. You can flip through the class hierarchy diagrams in Appendix B to see them (`final` classes are shaded darker than `public` classes). Examples of the first reason to use `final` are the classes: `java.lang.System` and, from the package `java.net`, `InetAddress` and `Socket`. A good example of the second reason is `java.lang.String`. Strings are so common in Java, and so central to it, that the run-time handles them specially.

It will be a rare event for you to create a `final` class yourself, although you'll have plenty of opportunity to be upset at certain system classes being `final` (thus making extending them annoyingly difficult). Oh well, such is the price of security and efficiency. Let's hope that efficiency will be less of an issue soon, and some of these classes will become `public` once again.

final Variables

To declare constants in Java, use `final` variables:

```
public class  AnotherFinalClass {
    public static final int     aConstantInt    = 123;
    public          final String aConstantString = "Hello world!";
}
```

> **Note:** The unusual spacing in the last line of the example makes it clearer that the top variable is a class variable and the bottom isn't, but that both are `public` and `final`.

`final` class and instance variables can be used in expressions just like normal class and instance variables, but they cannot be modified. As a result, `final` variables must be given their (constant) value at the time of declaration. These variables function like a better, typed version of the `#define` constants of C. Classes can provide useful constants to other classes via `final` class variables such as the one discussed previously. Other classes reference them just as before: `AnotherFinalClass.aConstantInt`.

Local variables (those inside blocks of code surrounded by braces, for example, in `while` or `for` loops) can't be declared `final`. (This would be just a convenience, really, because `final` instance variables work almost as well in this case.) In fact, local variables can have no modifiers in front of them at all:

```
{
    int  aLocalVariable;    // I'm so sad without my modifiers...
    . . .
}
```

final Methods

Here's an example of using `final` methods:

```
public class  MyPenultimateFinalClass {
    public static final void  aUniqueAndReallyUsefulMethod() {
        . . .
    }
```

317

```
    public       final void  noOneGetsToDoThisButMe() {
        . . .
    }
}
```

`final` methods cannot be overridden by subclasses. It is a rare thing that a method truly wants to declare itself the final word on its own implementation, so why does this modifier apply to methods?

The answer is efficiency. If you declare a method `final`, the compiler can then "in-line" it right in the middle of methods that call it, because it "knows" that no one else can ever subclass and override the method to change its meaning. Although you might not use `final` right away when writing a class, as you tune the system later, you may discover that a few methods have to be `final` to make your class fast enough. Almost all your methods will be fine, however, just as they are.

The Java class library declares a lot of commonly used methods `final` so that you'll benefit from the speed-up. In the case of classes that are already `final`, this makes perfect sense and is a wise choice. The few `final` methods declared in non-`final` classes will annoy you—your subclasses can no longer override them. When efficiency becomes less of an issue for the Java environment, many of these `final` methods can be "unfrozen" again, restoring this lost flexibility to the system.

> **Note:** `private` methods are effectively `final`, as are all methods declared in a `final` class. Marking these latter methods `final` (as the Java library sometimes does) is legal, but redundant; the current compiler already treats them as `final`.
>
> It's possible to use `final` methods for some of the same security reasons you use `final` classes, but it's a much rarer event.

If you use accessor methods a lot (as recommended) and are worried about efficiency, here's a rewrite of `ACorrectClass` that's much faster:

```
public class  ACorrectFinalClass {
    private         String  aUsefulString;

    public    final String  aUsefulString() {     // now faster to use
        return aUsefulString;
    }

    protected final void    aUsefulString(String s) {  // also faster
        aUsefulString = s;
    }
}
```

Note: Future Java compilers will almost certainly be smart enough to "in-line" simple methods automatically, so you probably won't need to use `final` in such cases for much longer.

abstract **Methods and Classes**

Whenever you arrange classes into an inheritance hierarchy, the presumption is that "higher" classes are more abstract and general, whereas "lower" subclasses are more concrete and specific. Often, as you design a set of classes, you factor out common design and implementation into a shared superclass. If the primary reason that a superclass exists is to act as this common, shared repository, and if only its subclasses expect to be used, that superclass is called an `abstract` class.

`abstract` classes can create no instances, but they can contain anything a normal class can contain and, in addition, are allowed to prefix any of their methods with the modifier `abstract`. Non-abstract classes are not allowed to use this modifier; using it on even one of your methods requires that your whole class be declared `abstract`. Here's an example:

```
public abstract class  MyFirstAbstractClass {
    int  anInstanceVariable;

    public abstract int  aMethodMyNonAbstractSubclassesMustImplement();

    public void  doSomething() {
        . . .    // a normal method
    }
}

public class  AConcreteSubClass extends MyFirstAbstractClass {
    public int  aMethodMyNonAbstractSubclassesMustImplement() {
        . . .    // we *must* implement this method
    }
}
```

and some attempted uses of these classes:

```
Object  a = new MyFirstAbstractClass();    // illegal, is abstract
Object  c = new AConcreteSubClass();       // OK, a concrete subclass
```

Notice that abstract methods need no implementation; it is required that non-abstract subclasses provide an implementation. The `abstract` class simply provides the template for the methods, which are implemented by others later. In fact, in the Java class library, there are several `abstract` classes that have no documented subclasses in the system, but simply provide a base from which you can subclass in your own programs. If you look at the diagrams in Appendix B, `abstract` classes are shaded even darker than `final` classes and are quite common in the library.

Using an abstract class to embody a pure design—that is, nothing but abstract methods—is better accomplished in Java by using an interface (discussed tomorrow). Whenever a design calls for an abstraction that includes instance state and/or a partial implementation, however, an abstract class is your only choice. In previous object-oriented languages, abstract classes were simply a convention. They proved so valuable that Java supports them not only in the form described here, but in the purer, richer form of interfaces, which will be described tomorrow.

Summary

Today, you learned how variables and methods can control their visibility and access by other classes via the four P's of protection: public, package, protected, and private. You also learned that, although instance variables are most often declared private, declaring accessor methods allows you to control the reading and writing of them separately. Protection levels allow you, for example, to separate cleanly your public abstractions from their concrete representations.

You also learned how to create class variables and methods, which are associated with the class itself, and how to declare final variables, methods, and classes to represent constants, fast or secure methods, and classes, respectively.

Finally, you discovered how to declare and use abstract classes, which cannot be instantiated, and abstract methods, which have no implementation and must be overridden in subclasses. Together, they provide a template for subclasses to fill in and act as a variant of the powerful interfaces of Java that you'll study tomorrow.

Q&A

Q Why are there so many different levels of protection in Java?

A Each level of protection, or visibility, provides a different view of your class to the outside world. One view is tailored for everyone, one for classes in your own package, another for your class and its subclasses only, and the final one for just within your class. Each is a logically well-defined and useful separation that Java supports directly in the language (as opposed to, for example, accessor methods, which are a convention you must follow).

Q Won't using accessor methods everywhere slow down my Java code?

A Not always. Soon, Java compilers will be smart enough to make them fast automatically, but if you're concerned about speed, you can always declare accessor methods to be final, and they'll be just as fast as direct instance variable accesses.

Q **Are class (`static`) methods inherited just like instance methods?**

A Yes, and no. The beta compiler still allows you to inherit them, but according to one of the oddest changes in the beta language specifications, `static` (class) methods are now `final` by default. How, then, can you ever declare a non-`final` class method? The answer is that you can't! Inheritance of class methods is not allowed, breaking the symmetry with instance methods. Because this goes against a part of Java's philosophy (of making everything as simple as possible) perhaps it will be reversed in a later release. For now, follow the compiler and assume that class methods are inherited normally.

Q **Based on what I've learned, it seems like `final abstract` or `private abstract` methods or classes don't make sense. Are they legal?**

A Nope, they're compile-time errors, as you have guessed. To be useful, `abstract` methods must be overridden, and `abstract` classes must be subclassed, but neither of those two operations would be legal if they were also `public` or `final`.

Q **What about `static transient` or `final transient`?**

A Those are also compile-time errors. Because a "transient" part of an object's state is assumed to be changing within each instance, it can not be `static` or `final`. This restriction matters only in the future, though, when `transient` is actually used by Java.

Packages and Interfaces

by Charles L. Perkins

When you examine a new language feature, you should ask yourself two questions:

1. How can I use it to better organize the methods and classes of my Java program?
2. How can I use it while writing the Java code in my methods?

The first is often called programming in the large, and the second, programming in the small. Bill Joy, a founder of Sun Microsystems, likes to say that Java feels like C when programming in the small and like Smalltalk when programming in the large. What he means by that is that Java is familiar and powerful like any C-like language while you're coding, but has the extensibility and expressive power of a pure object-oriented language like Smalltalk while you're designing.

The separation of "designing" from "coding" was one of the most fundamental advances in programming in the past few decades, and object-oriented languages such as Java implement a strong form of this separation. The first part of this separation has already been described on previous days: when you develop a Java program, first you design the classes and decide on the relationships between these classes, and then you implement the Java code needed for each of the methods in your design. If you are careful enough with both these processes, you can change your mind about aspects of the design without affecting anything but small, local pieces of your Java code, and you can change the implementation of any method without affecting the rest of the design.

As you begin to explore more advanced Java programming, however, you'll find that this simple model becomes too limiting. Today, you'll explore these limitations, for programming in the large and in the small, to motivate the need for packages and interfaces. Let's start with packages.

Packages

Packages are Java's way of doing large-scale design and organization. They are used both to categorize and group classes. Let's explore why you might need to use packages.

Programming in the Large

When you begin to develop Java programs that use a large number of classes, you will quickly discover some limitations in the model presented thus far for designing and building them.

For one thing, as the number of classes you build grows, the likelihood of your wanting to reuse the short, simple name of some class increases. If you use classes that you've built in the past, or that someone else has built for you (such as the classes in the Java library), you may not remember—or even know—that these class names are in conflict. Being able to "hide" a class inside a package becomes useful.

Here's a simple example of the creation of a package in a Java source file:

```
package  myFirstPackage;

public class  MyPublicClass extends ItsSuperclass {
    . . .
}
```

> **Note:** If a `package` statement appears in a Java source file, it must be the first thing in that file (except for comments and white space, of course).

You first declare the name of the package by using a `package` statement. Then you define a class, just as you would normally. That class, and any other classes also declared inside this same package name, are grouped together. (These other classes are usually located in other, separate source files.)

Packages can be further organized into a hierarchy somewhat analogous to the inheritance hierarchy, where each "level" usually represents a smaller, more specific grouping of classes. The Java class library itself is organized along these lines (see the diagrams in Appendix B). The top level is called `java`; the next level includes names such as `io`, `net`, `util`, and `awt`. The last has an even lower level, which includes the package `image`. The `ColorModel` class, located in the package `image`, can be uniquely referred to anywhere in your Java code as `java.awt.image.ColorModel`.

> **Note:** By convention, the first level of the hierarchy specifies the (globally unique) name of the company that developed the Java package(s). For example, Sun Microsystem's classes, which are not part of the standard Java environment, all begin with the prefix `sun`. The standard package, `java`, is an exception to this rule because it is so fundamental and because it might someday be implemented by multiple companies.
>
> Starting with the beta release, Sun has specified a more formal procedure for package naming to be followed in the future. The top-level package name space now reserves, for the use of this procedure, all the uppercase abbreviations used for top-level domains on the Internet (EDU, COM, GOV, FR, US, and so on). These reserved names form the first part of all new package names, which are prefixed by a reversed version of your domain name. By this procedure, the sun packages would be called `COM.sun`. If you're further down in your company's or university's domain tree, you can keep reversing to your heart's content: `EDU.harvard.cs.projects.ai.learning.myPackage`. Because domain names are already guaranteed to be unique globally, this nicely solves that thorny problem,

and as a bonus, the applets and packages from the potentially millions of Java programmers out there will automatically be stored into a growing hierarchy below your classes directory, giving you a way to find and categorize them all in a comprehensible manner.

Because each Java class should be located in a separate source file, the grouping of classes provided by a hierarchy of packages is analogous to the grouping of files into a hierarchy of directories on your file system. The Java compiler reinforces this analogy by requiring you to create a directory hierarchy under your classes directory that exactly matches the hierarchy of the packages you have created, and to place a class into the directory with the same name (and level) as the package in which it's defined.

For example, the directory hierarchy for the Java class library exactly mirrors its package hierarchy. On UNIX, for example, the class referenced as `java.awt.image.ColorModel` is stored in a file named ColorModel.class in the directory named .../classes/java/awt/image (the ... is the path where Java was installed on your computer). In particular, if you have created a package within `myFirstPackage` called `mySecondPackage`, by declaring a class:

```
package  myFirstPackage.mySecondPackage;

public class  AnotherPublicClass extends AnotherSuperclass {
   . . .
}
```

the Java source file (called AnotherPublicClass.java) must be located in a directory below the current directory called classes/myFirstPackage/mySecondPackage for the compiler (javac) to find it. When the compiler generates the file AnotherPublicClass.class, it places it into this same directory so that the java interpreter can find it. Both the compiler and the interpreter expect (and enforce) the hierarchy.

Note: This also means that, for today's first example, the source file would be named APublicClass.java and located in the directory called classes/myFirstPackage. What happens when, as in earlier examples in the book, classes are defined without a `package` statement? The compiler places such classes in a default, unnamed package, and their .java and .class files can be located in the current directory or in the classes directory below it.

To be more precise, any occurrence of the phrase "the current directory" in this section should be replaced by "any of the directories listed in the class path." The compiler and interpreter both search this list of paths to find any classes you reference.

You can specify a class path on the command line when running javac or java, or more permanently, by changing a special environment variable called CLASSPATH. (For more details, read the documentation in your Java release.)

Programming in the Small

When you refer to a class by name in your Java code, you are using a package. Most of the time you aren't aware of it because many of the most commonly used classes in the system are in a package that the Java compiler automatically imports for you, called java.lang. So whenever you saw this, for example:

```
String  aString;
```

something more interesting than you might have thought was occurring. What if you want to refer to the class you created at the start of this section, the one in the package myFirstPackage? If you try this:

```
MyPublicClass  someName;
```

the compiler complains—the class MyPublicClass is not defined in the package java.lang. To solve this problem, Java allows any class name to be prefixed by the name of the package in which it was defined to form a unique reference to the class:

```
myFirstPackage.MyPublicClass  someName;
```

Note: Recall that by convention, package names tend to begin with a lowercase letter to distinguish them from class names. Thus, for example, in the full name of the built-in String class, java.lang.String, it's easier to separate the package name from the class name visually.

Suppose you want to use a lot of classes from a package, a package with a long name, or both. You don't want to have to refer to your classes as that.really.long.package.name.ClassName. Java allows you to "import" the names of those classes into your program. They then act just as java.lang classes do, and you can refer to them without a prefix. For example, to use the really long class name in the last example more easily, you can write the following:

```
import that.really.long.package.name.ClassName;

ClassName  anObject;
// and you can use ClassName directly as many times as you like
```

> **Note:** All `import` statements must appear after any `package` statement but before any class definitions. Thus, they are "stuck" at the top of your source file.

What if you want to use several classes from that same package? Here's an attempt from a (soon-to-be-tired) programmer:

```
that.really.long.package.name.ClassOne     first;
that.really.long.package.name.ClassTwo     second;
that.really.long.package.name.ClassThree   andSoOn;
```

Here's one from a more savvy programmer, who knows how to import a whole package of public classes:

```
import that.really.long.package.name.*;

ClassOne     first;
ClassTwo     second;
ClassThree   andSoOn;
```

> **Warning:** The asterisk (*) in this example is not exactly the one you might use at a command prompt to specify the contents of a directory. For example, if you ask to list the contents of the directory classes/java/awt/*, that list includes all the .class files and subdirectories such as image and peer. Writing `import java.awt.*` does *not* import subpackages such as `image` and `peer`. To import all the classes in a complex package hierarchy, you must explicitly `import` each level of the hierarchy by hand.

If you plan to use a class or a package only a few times in your source file, it's probably not worth importing it. The rule of thumb is to ask yourself: "Does the loss in clarity I'd introduce by referring to just the class name outweigh the convenience of not having to type the extra characters?" If it does, don't use `import`. Remember that the package name lets the reader know where to find more information about the class *right at the place you're using it*, rather than at the top of the file, where the `import` statements are located.

What if you have the following in class A's source file?

```
package  packageA;

public class  ClassName {
    . . .
}

public class  ClassA {
    . . .
}
```

and in class B's source file you have this:

```
package  packageB;

public class  ClassName {
    . . .
}

public class  ClassB {
    . . .
}
```

Then you the write the following, somewhere else:

```
import packageA;
import packageB;

ClassName  anObject;        // which ClassName did you mean?
```

There are two possible interpretations for the class you intended, one in `packageA` and one in `packageB`. Because this is ambiguous, what should the poor compiler do? It generates an error, of course, and you have to be more explicit about which one you intended. Here's an example:

```
import packageA.*;
import packageB.*;

packageA.ClassName  anObject;       // now OK
packageB.ClassName  anotherObject;  // also OK

ClassA  anAObject;        // was never a problem
ClassB  aBObject;         // ditto
```

> **Note:** You may wonder about the numerous declarations that appear as examples in today's lesson. Declarations are good examples because they're the simplest possible way of referencing a class name. Any use of a class name (in your `extends` clause, for example, or in `new ClassName()`) obeys the same rules.

Hiding Classes

The astute reader may have noticed that the discussion of importing with an asterisk (*) stated that it imported a whole package of `public` classes. Why would you want to have classes of any other kind? Take a look at this:

```
package  collections;

public class  LinkedList {
    private Node  root;
```

```
    public  void  add(Object o) {
        root = new Node(o, root);
    }
    . . .
}

class  Node {                    // not public
    private Object  contents;
    private Node    next;

    Node(Object o, Node n) {
        contents = o;
        next     = n;
    }
    . . .
}
```

> **Note:** If this were all in one file, you might be violating one of the compiler's conventions: only one class should be located in each Java source file. Actually, the compiler cares only about every `public` class being in a separate file (although it still is good style to use separate files for each class).

The goal of the `LinkedList` class is to provide a set of useful public methods (such as `add()`) to any other classes that might want to use them. These other classes could care less about any support classes `LinkedList` needs to get its job done, and would prefer to not "see" them when using `LinkedList`. In addition, `LinkedList` may feel that the `Node` class is local to its implementation and should not be seen by any other classes.

For methods and variables, this would be addressed by the four Ps of protection discussed yesterday: `private`, `protected`, `package`, and `public`, listed in order of increasing visibility. You've already explored many `public` classes, and because both `private` and `protected` really make sense only when you're inside a class definition, you cannot put them outside of one as part of defining a new class. `LinkedList` might really like to say "only classes in my source file can see this class," but because, by convention, each class is located in a separate source file, this would be a little-needed, over-narrow approach.

Instead, `LinkedList` declares no protection modifier, which is equivalent to saying `package`. Now the class can be seen and used only by other classes in the same package in which it was defined. In this case, it's the `collections` package. You might use `LinkedList` as follows:

```
import collections.*;          // only imports public classes

LinkedList  aLinkedList;
/* Node  n; */            // would generate a compile-time error

aLinkedList.add(new Integer(1138));
aLinkedList.add("THX-");
. . .
```

Note: You also can import or declare a `LinkedList` as `collections.LinkedList` in this example. Because `LinkedList` refers to `Node`, that class is automatically loaded and used, and the compiler verifies that `LinkedList` (as part of package `collections`) has the right to create and use the `Node` class. You still do not have that right, though, just as in the example.

One of the great powers of hidden classes is that even if you use them to introduce a great deal of complexity into the implementation of some `public` class, all the complexity is hidden when that class is `imported`. Thus, creating a good package consists of defining a small, clean set of `public` classes and methods for other classes to use, and then implementing them by using any number of hidden (`package`) support classes. You'll see another use for hidden classes later today.

Interfaces

Interfaces, like the abstract classes and methods you saw yesterday, provide templates of behavior that other classes are expected to implement, but they are much more powerful. Let's see why you might need such power.

Programming in the Large

When you first begin to design object-oriented programs, the class hierarchy seems almost miraculous. Within that single tree you can express a hierarchy of numeric types (number, complex, float, rational, integer), many simple-to-moderately-complex relationships between objects and processes in the world, and any number of points along the axis from abstract/general to concrete/specific. After some deeper thought or more complex design experience, this wonderful tree begins to feel restrictive—at times, like a straitjacket. The very power and discipline you've achieved by carefully placing only one copy of each idea somewhere in the tree can come back to haunt you whenever you need to cross-fertilize disparate parts of that tree.

Some languages address these problems by introducing more flexible run-time power, such as the code block and the `perform:` method of Smalltalk; others choose to provide more complex inheritance hierarchies, such as multiple-inheritance. With the latter complexity comes a host of confusing and error-prone ambiguities and misunderstandings, and with the former, a harder time implementing safety and security and a harder language to explain and teach. Java has chosen to take neither of these paths but, in the spirit of objective-C's protocols, has adopted a separate hierarchy altogether to gain the expressive power needed to loosen the straitjacket.

This new hierarchy is a hierarchy of interfaces. Interfaces are not limited to a single superclass, so they allow a form of multiple-inheritance. But they pass on only method descriptions to their children, not method implementations nor instance variables, which helps to eliminate many of the complexities of full multiple-inheritance.

Interfaces, like classes, are declared in source files, one interface to a file. Like classes, they also are compiled into .class files. In fact, almost everywhere that this book has a class name in any of its examples or discussions, you can substitute an interface name. Java programmers often say "class" when they actually mean "class or interface." Interfaces complement and extend the power of classes, and the two can be treated almost exactly the same. One of the few differences between them is that an interface cannot be instantiated: new can create only an instance of a class. Here's the declaration of an interface:

```
package  myFirstPackage;

public interface  MyFirstInterface extends Interface1, Interface2, ... {
    . . .
    // all methods in here will be public and abstract
    // all variables will be public, static, and final
}
```

This example is a rewritten version of the first example in today's lesson. It now adds a new public interface to the package myFirstPackage, instead of a new public class. Note that multiple parents can be listed in an interface's extends clause.

 Note: If no extends clause is given, interfaces do not default to inheriting from Object, because Object is a class. In fact, interfaces have no "topmost" interface from which they are all guaranteed to descend.

Any variables or methods defined in a public interface are implicitly prefixed by the modifiers listed in the comments. Exactly those modifiers can (optionally) appear, but no others:

```
public interface  MySecondInterface {
    public static final int  theAnswer = 42;  // both lines OK
    public abstract     int  lifeTheUniverseAndEverything();

    long  bingBangCounter = 0;  // OK, becomes public, static, final
    long  ageOfTheUniverse();   // OK, becomes public and abstract

    protected int  aConstant;   // not OK
    private   int  getAnInt();  // not OK
}
```

 Note: If an interface is declared non-public (that is, package), no public modifiers are implicitly prefixed. If you say public inside such an interface, you're making a real statement of public-ness, not simply a redundant statement. It's not often, though, that an interface is shared only by the classes inside a package, and not by the classes using that package as well.

Design Versus Implementation Revisited

One of the most powerful things interfaces add to Java is the capability of separating *design* inheritance from *implementation* inheritance. In the single-class inheritance tree, these two are inextricably bound. Sometimes, you want to be able to describe an interface to a class of objects abstractly, without having to implement a particular implementation of it yourself. You could create an `abstract` class, such as those described yesterday. In order for a new class to use this type of "interface," however, it has to become a subclass of the `abstract` class and accept its position in the tree. If this new class also needs to be a subclass of some other class in the tree, for implementation reasons, what could it do? What if it wants to use two such "interfaces" at once? Watch this:

```
class  FirstImplementor extends SomeClass implements MySecondInterface {
    . . .
}

class  SecondImplementor implements MyFirstInterface, MySecondInterface {
    . . .
}
```

The first class above is "stuck" in the single inheritance tree just below the class `SomeClass` but is free to implement an interface as well. The second class is stuck just below `Object` but has implemented two interfaces (it could have implemented any number of them). Implementing an interface means promising to implement all the methods specified in it.

> **Note:** Although an `abstract` class is allowed to ignore this strict requirement, and can implement any subset of the methods (or even none of them), all its non-abstract subclasses must still obey it.

Because interfaces are in a separate hierarchy, they can be "mixed-in" to the classes in the single inheritance tree, allowing the designer to sprinkle an interface anywhere it is needed throughout the tree. The single-inheritance class tree can thus be viewed as containing only the implementation hierarchy; the design hierarchy (full of `abstract` methods, mostly) is contained in the multiple-inheritance interface tree. This is a powerful way of thinking about the organization of your program, and though it takes a little getting used to, it's also a highly recommended one.

Let's examine one simple example of this separation—creating the new class `Orange`. Suppose you already have a good implementation of the class `Fruit`, and an interface, `Fruitlike`, that represents what `Fruits` are expected to be able to do. You want an orange to be a fruit, but you also want it to be a spherical object that can be tossed, rotated, and so on. Here's how to express it all:

```
interface  Fruitlike extends Foodlike {
    void  decay();
    void  squish();
    . . .
}

class  Fruit extends Food implements Fruitlike {
    private Color  myColor;
    private int    daysTilIRot;
    . . .
}

interface  Spherelike {
    void  toss();
    void  rotate();
    . . .
}

class  Orange extends Fruit implements Spherelike {
    . . .  // toss()ing may squish() me (unique to me)
}
```

You'll use this example again later today. For now, notice that class `Orange` doesn't have to say `implements Fruitlike` because, by extending `Fruit`, it already has!

> **Note:** The reverse is not true, however. Implementing an interface implies nothing about the implementation hierarchy of a class. By the way, if you had used a more traditional way of designing classes (though not necessarily better), the class `Fruit` would be the interface description, as well as being the implementation.

One of the nice things about this structure is that you can change your mind about what class `Orange` extends (if a really great `Sphere` class is suddenly implemented, for example), yet class `Orange` will still understand the same two interfaces:

```
class  Sphere implements Spherelike {   // extends Object
    private float   radius;
    . . .
}

class  Orange extends Sphere implements Fruitlike {
    . . .       // users of Orange never need know about the change!
}
```

The canonical use of the "mix-in" capability of interfaces is to allow several classes, scattered across the single-inheritance tree, to implement the same set of methods (or even just one).

Although these classes share a common superclass (at worst, Object), it is likely that below this common parent are many subclasses that are not interested in this set of methods. Adding the methods to the parent class, or even creating a new abstract class to hold them and inserting it into the hierarchy above the parent, is not an ideal solution.

Instead, use an interface to specify the method(s). It can be implemented by every class that shares the need and by none of the other classes that would have been forced to "understand" them in the single-inheritance tree. (Design is applied only where needed.) Users of the interface can now specify variables and arguments to be of a new interface type that can refer to any of the classes that implement the interface (as you'll see below)—a powerful abstraction. Some examples of "mix-in" facilities are object persistence (via read() and write() methods), producing or consuming something (the Java library does this for images), and providing generally useful constants. The last of these might look like this:

```
public interface  PresumablyUsefulConstants {
    public static final int     oneOfThem   = 1234;
    public static final float   another     = 1.234F;
    public static final String  yetAnother  = "1234";
    . . .
}

public class  AnyClass implements PresumablyUsefulConstants {
    public static void  main(String argV[]) {
        double  calculation = oneOfThem * another;

        System.out.println("hello " + yetAnother + calculation);
        . . .
    }
}
```

This outputs the thoroughly meaningless hello 12341522.756, but in the process demonstrates that the class AnyClass can refer directly to all the variables defined in the interface PresumablyUsefulConstants. Normally, you refer to such variables and constants via the class, as for the constant Integer.MIN_VALUE, which is provided by the Integer class. If a set of constants is large or is widely used, the shortcut of being able to refer to them directly (as oneOfThem rather than as PresumablyUsefulConstants.oneOfThem) makes it worth placing them into an interface and implementing it widely.

Programming in the Small

How do you actually use these interfaces? Remember that almost everywhere that you can use a class, you can use an interface instead. Let's try to make use of the interface MySecondInterface defined previously:

```
MySecondInterface  anObject = getTheRightObjectSomehow();

long  age = anObject.ageOfTheUniverse();
```

Once you declare anObject to be of type MySecondInterface, you can use anObject as the receiver of any message that the interface defines (or inherits). What does the previous declaration really mean?

When a variable is declared to be of an interface type, it simply means that any object the variable refers to is expected to have implemented that interface—that is, it is expected to understand all the methods that interface specifies. It assumes that a promise made between the designer of the interface and its eventual implementors has been kept. Although this is a rather abstract notion, it allows, for example, the previous code to be written long before any classes that qualify are actually implemented (or even created!). In traditional object-oriented programming, you are forced to create a class with "stub" implementations to get the same effect.

Here's a more complicated example:

```
Orange      anOrange    = getAnOrange();
Fruit       aFruit      = (Fruit) getAnOrange();
Fruitlike   aFruitlike  = (Fruitlike) getAnOrange();
Spherelike  aSpherelike = (Spherelike) getAnOrange();

aFruit.decay();           // fruits decay
aFruitlike.squish();      //  and squish

aFruitlike.toss();        // not OK
aSpherelike.toss();       // OK

anOrange.decay();         // oranges can do it all
anOrange.squish();
anOrange.toss();
anOrange.rotate();
```

Declarations and casts are used in this example to restrict an orange to act more like a mere fruit or sphere, simply to demonstrate the flexibility of the structure built previously. If the second structure built (the one with the new Sphere class) were being used instead, most of this code would still work. (In the line bearing Fruit, all instances of Fruit need to be replaced by Sphere. The later use of aFruit.decay() could be replaced by, for example, aSphere.rotate(). Everything else is the same.)

Note: The direct use of (implementation) class names is for demonstration purposes only. Normally, you would use only interface names in those declarations and casts so that none of the code in the example would have to change to support the new structure.

Interfaces are implemented and used throughout the Java class library, whenever a behavior is expected to be implemented by a number of disparate classes. In Appendix B you'll find, for example, the interfaces `java.lang.Runnable`, `java.util.Enumeration`, `java.util.Observable`, `java.awt.image.ImageConsumer`, and `java.awt.image.ImageProducer`. Let's use one of these interfaces, `Enumeration`, to revisit the `LinkedList` example—and to tie together today's lesson—by demonstrating a good use of packages and interfaces together:

```java
package  collections;

public class  LinkedList {
    private Node  root;

    . . .
    public Enumeration  enumerate() {
        return new LinkedListEnumerator(root);
    }
}

class  Node {
    private Object  contents;
    private Node    next;

    . . .
    public  Object  contents() {
        return contents;
    }

    public  Node    next() {
        return next;
    }
}

class  LinkedListEnumerator implements Enumeration {
    private Node  currentNode;

    LinkedListEnumerator(Node  root) {
        currentNode = root;
    }

    public boolean  hasMoreElements() {
        return currentNode != null;
    }

    public Object   nextElement() {
        Object  anObject = currentNode.contents();

        currentNode = currentNode.next();
        return  anObject;
    }
}
```

Here is a typical use of the enumerator:

```
collections.LinkedList  aLinkedList = createLinkedList();
java.util.Enumeration   e = aLinkedList.enumerate();

while (e.hasMoreElements()) {
    Object  anObject = e.nextElement();
    // do something useful with anObject
}
```

Notice that although you are using the Enumeration e as though you know what it is, you actually do not. In fact, it is an instance of a hidden class (LinkedListEnumerator) that you cannot see or use directly. By a combination of packages and interfaces, the LinkedList class has managed to provide a transparent public interface to some of its most important behavior (via the already defined interface java.util.Enumeration) while still encapsulating (hiding) its two implementation (support) classes.

Handing out an object like this is sometime called vending. Often, the "vendor" gives out an object that a receiver can't create itself, but that it knows how to use. By giving it back to the vendor, the receiver can prove it has a certain capability, authenticate itself, or do any number of useful tasks—all without knowing much about the vended object. This is a powerful metaphor that can be applied in a broad range of situations.

Summary

Today, you learned how packages can be used to collect and categorize classes into meaningful groups. Packages are arranged in a hierarchy, which not only better organizes your programs, but allows you and the millions of Java programmers out on the Net to name and share their projects uniquely with one another.

You also learned how to use packages, both your own and the many preexisting ones in the Java class library.

You then discovered how to declare and use interfaces, a powerful mechanism for extending the traditional single-inheritance of Java's classes and for separating the design inheritance from the implementation inheritance in your programs. Interfaces are often used to call shared methods when the exact class involved is not known. You'll see further uses of interfaces tomorrow and the day after.

Finally, packages and interfaces can be combined to provide useful abstractions, such as Enumeration, that appear simple yet are actually hiding almost all their (complex) implementation from their users. This is a powerful technique.

Q&A

Q **What will happen to package/directory hierarchies when some sort of archiving is added to Java?**

A Being able to download over the Net a whole archive of packages, classes, and resources is something that Java systems may soon be able to do. When this happens, the simple mapping between directory hierarchy and package hierarchy will break down, and you will not be able to tell as easily where each class is stored (that is, in which archive). Presumably these new, advanced Java systems will provide tools that make this task (and compiling and linking your program in general) much easier.

Q **Can you say `import some.package.B*` to import all the classes in that package that begin with `B`?**

A No, the `import` asterisk (*) does not act like a command-line asterisk.

Q **Then what exactly does `import`-ing with an `*` mean?**

A Combining everything said previously, this precise definition emerges: it imports all the `public` classes that are *directly* inside the package named, and not inside one of its subpackages. (You can only `import` exactly this set of classes, or exactly one explicitly named class, from a given package.) By the way, Java only "loads" the information for a class when you actually refer to that class in your code, so the `*` form of `import` is no less efficient than naming each class individually.

Q **Is there any way that a hidden (`package`) class can somehow be forced out of hiding?**

A A bizarre case in which a hidden class can be forced into visibility occurs if it has a `public` superclass and someone casts an instance of it to the superclass. Any `public` methods of that superclass can now be called via your hidden class instance, even if those methods were not thought of by you as `public` when overridden in the hidden class. Usually, these `public` methods are ones you don't mind having your instances perform, or you wouldn't have declared them to have that `public` superclass. This isn't always the case. Many of the system's built-in classes are `public`—you may have no choice. Luckily, this is a rare event.

Q **Why is full multiple-inheritance so complex that Java abandoned it?**

A It's not so much that it is too complex, but that it makes the language overly complicated—and as you'll learn on the final day, this can cause larger systems to be less trustworthy and thus less secure. For example, if you were to inherit from two different parents, each having an instance variable with the same name, you would be forced to allow the conflict and explain how the exact same references to that variable name in each of your superclasses, and in you (all three), are now different. Instead of being able to call "super" methods to get more abstract behavior accomplished, you would always need to worry about which of the (possibly many) identical methods you actually wished to call in which parent. Java's run-time method dispatching would have to be more complex as well. Finally, because so many people would be providing classes for reuse on the Net, the normally manageable conflicts that would arise in your own program would be confounded by millions of users mixing and matching these fully multi-inherited classes at will. In the future, if all these issues are resolved, more powerful inheritance may be added to Java, but its current capabilities are already sufficient for 99 percent of your programs.

Q abstract classes don't have to implement all the methods in an interface themselves, but do all their subclasses have to?

A Actually, no. Because of inheritance, the precise rule is that an implementation must be provided by some class for each method, but it doesn't have to be your class. This is analogous to when you are the subclass of a class that implements an interface for you. Whatever the abstract class doesn't implement, the first nonabstract class below it must implement. Then, any further subclasses need do nothing further.

Q You didn't mention callbacks. Aren't they an important use of interfaces?

A Yes, but I didn't mention them because a good example would be too bulky in the text. These callbacks are often used in user interfaces (such as window systems) to specify what set of methods are going to be sent whenever the user does a certain set of things (such as clicking the mouse somewhere, typing, and so forth). Because the user interface classes should not "know" anything about the classes using them, an interface's ability to specify a set of methods separate from the class tree is crucial in this case. Callbacks using interfaces are not as general as using, for example, the perform: method of Smalltalk, however, because a given object can request that a user interface object "call it back" only by using a single method name. Suppose that object wanted two user interfaces objects of the same class to call it back, using different names to tell them apart? It cannot do this in Java, and it is forced to use special state and tests to tell them apart. (I warned you that it was complicated!). So, although interfaces are quite valuable in this case, they are not the ideal callback facility.

Exceptions

by Charles L. Perkins

Today, you'll learn about exceptional conditions in Java:

☐ How to declare when you are expecting one

☐ How to handle them in your code

☐ How to create them

☐ How your code is limited, yet made more robust by them

Let's begin by motivating why new ways of handling exceptions were invented.

Programming languages have long labored to solve the following common problem:

```
int   status = callSomethingThatAlmostAlwaysWorks();

if (status == FUNNY_RETURN_VALUE) {
    . . .            // something unusual happened, handle it
    switch(someGlobalErrorIndicator) {
        . . .            // handle more specific problems
    }
} else {
    . . .            // all is well, go your merry way
}
```

Somehow this seems like a lot of work to do to handle a rare case. What's worse, if the function called returns an `int` as part of its normal answer, you must distinguish one special integer (`FUNNY_RETURN_VALUE`) to indicate an error. What if that function really needs all the integers? You must do something even more ugly.

Even if you manage to find a distinguished value (such as `NULL` in C for pointers, `-1` for integers, and so forth), what if there are multiple errors that must be produced by the same function? Often, some global variable is used as an error indicator. The function stores a value in it and prays that no one else changes it before the caller gets to handle the error. Multiple errors propagate badly, if at all, and there are numerous problems with generalizing this to large programs, complex errors, and so forth.

Luckily, there is an alternative: using exceptions to help you handle exceptional conditions in your program, making the normal, nonexceptional code cleaner and easier to read.

NEW☞
TERM
An *exception* is any object that is an instance of the class `Throwable` (or any of its subclasses).

Programming in the Large

When you begin to build complex programs in Java, you discover that after designing the classes and interfaces, and their methods descriptions, you still have not defined all the behavior of your objects. After all, an interface describes the normal way to use an object and doesn't include any strange, exceptional cases. In many systems, the documentation takes care of this problem by explicitly listing the distinguished values used in "hacks" like the previous example. Because the system knows nothing about these hacks, it cannot check them for consistency. In fact, the compiler can do nothing at all to help you with these exceptional conditions, in contrast to the helpful warnings and errors it produces if a method is used incorrectly.

More importantly, you have not captured in your design this important aspect of your program. Instead, you are forced to make up a way to describe it in the documentation and hope you have not made any mistakes when you implement it later. What's worse, everyone else makes up a different way of describing the same thing. Clearly, you need some uniform way of declaring the intentions of classes and methods with respect to these exceptional conditions. Java provides just such a way:

```
public class  MyFirstExceptionalClass {
    public void  anExceptionalMethod() throws MyFirstException {
       . . .
    }
}
```

Here, you warn the reader (and the compiler) that the code . . . may throw an exception called MyFirstException.

You can think of a method's description as a contract between the designer of that method (or class) and you, the caller of the method. Usually, this description tells the types of a method's arguments, what it returns, and the general semantics of what it normally does. You are now being told, as well, what abnormal things it can do. This is a promise, just like the method promises to return a value of a certain type, and you can count on it when writing your code. These new promises help to tease apart and make explicit all the places where exceptional conditions should be handled in your program, and that makes large-scale design easier.

Because exceptions are instances of classes, they can be put into a hierarchy that can naturally describe the relationships among the different types of exceptions. In fact, if you take a moment to glance in Appendix B at the diagrams for java.lang-errors and java.lang-exceptions, you'll see that the class Throwable actually has two large hierarchies of classes beneath it. The roots of these two hierarchies are subclasses of Throwable called Exception and Error. These hierarchies embody the rich set of relationships that exist between exceptions and errors in the Java run-time environment.

When you know that a particular kind of error or exception can occur in your method, you are supposed to either handle it yourself or explicitly warn potential callers about the possibility via the throws clause. Not all errors and exceptions must be listed; instances of either class Error or RuntimeException (or any of their subclasses) do not have to be listed in your throws clause. They get special treatment because they can occur anywhere within a Java program and are usually conditions that you, as the programmer, did not directly cause. One good example is the OutOfMemoryError, which can happen anywhere, at any time, and for any number of reasons.

> **Note:** You can, of course, choose to list these errors and run-time exceptions if you like, and the callers of your methods will be forced to handle them, just like a non-run-time exception.
>
> Whenever you see the word "exception" by itself, it almost always means "exception or error" (that is, an instance of `Throwable`). The previous discussion makes it clear that `Exceptions` and `Errors` actually form two separate hierarchies, but except for the `throws` clause rule, they act exactly the same.

If you examine the diagrams in Appendix B more carefully, you'll notice that there are only five types of exceptions (in `java.lang`) that must be listed in a `throws` clause (remember that all `Errors` and `RuntimeExceptions` are exempt):

- ☐ `ClassNotFoundException`
- ☐ `IllegalAccessException`
- ☐ `InstantiationException`
- ☐ `InterrupedException`
- ☐ `NoSuchMethodException`

Each of these names suggests something that is explicitly caused by the programmer, not some behind-the-scenes event such as `OutOfMemoryError`.

If you look further in Appendix B, near the bottom of the diagrams for `java.util` and `java.io`, you'll see that each package adds some new exceptions. The former is adding two exceptions somewhat akin to `ArrayStoreException` and `IndexOutOfBoundsException`, and so decides to place them under `RuntimeException`. The latter is adding a whole new tree of `IOExceptions`, which are more explicitly caused by the programmer, and so they are rooted under `Exception`. Thus, `IOExceptions` must be described in `throws` clauses. Finally, package java.awt defines one of each style, implicit and explicit.

The Java class library uses exceptions everywhere, and to good effect. If you examine the detailed API documentation in your Java release, you see that many of the methods in the library have `throws` clauses, and some of them even document (when they believe it will make something clearer to the reader) when they may throw one of the implicit errors or exceptions. This is just a nicety on the documenter's part, because you are not required to catch conditions like that. If it wasn't obvious that such a condition could happen there, and for some reason you really cared about catching it, this would be useful information.

Programming in the Small

Now that you have a feeling for how exceptions can help you design a program and a class library better, how do you actually use exceptions? Let's try to use anExceptionalMethod() defined in today's first example:

```
public void  anotherExceptionalMethod() throws MyFirstException {
    MyFirstExceptionalClass  aMFEC = new MyFirstExceptionalClass();

    aMFEC.anExceptionalMethod();
}
```

Let's examine this example more closely. If you assume that MyFirstException is a subclass of Exception, it means that if you don't handle it in anotherExceptionalMethod()'s code, you must warn your callers about it. Because your code simply calls anExceptionalMethod() without doing anything about the fact that it may throw MyFirstException, you must add that exception to your throws clause. This is perfectly legal, but it does defer to your caller something that perhaps you should be responsible for doing yourself. (It depends on the circumstances, of course.)

Suppose that that you feel responsible today and decide to handle the exception. Because you're now declaring a method without a throws clause, you must "catch" the expected exception and do something useful with it:

```
public void  responsibleMethod() {
    MyFirstExceptionalClass  aMFEC = new MyFirstExceptionalClass();

    try {
        aMFEC.anExceptionalMethod();
    } catch (MyFirstException m) {
        . . .      // do something terribly significant and responsible
    }
}
```

The try statement says basically: "Try running the code inside these braces, and if there are exceptions thrown, I will attach handlers to take care of them." (You first heard about these on Day 10.) You can have as many catch clauses at the end of a try as you need. Each allows you to handle any and all exceptions that are instances: of the class listed in parentheses, of any of its subclasses, or of a class that implements the interface listed in parentheses. In the catch in this example, exceptions of the class MyFirstException (or any of its subclasses) are being handled.

What if you want to combine both the approaches shown so far? You'd like to handle the exception yourself, but also reflect it up to your caller. This can be done, by explicitly rethrowing the exception:

```
public void  responsibleExceptionalMethod() throws MyFirstException {
    MyFirstExceptionalClass  aMFEC = new MyFirstExceptionalClass();

    try {
        aMFEC.anExceptionalMethod();
```

```
    } catch (MyFirstException m) {
        . . .              // do something responsible
        throw m;       // re-throw the exception
    }
}
```

This works because exception handlers can be nested. You handle the exception by doing something responsible with it, but decide that it is too important to not give an exception handler that might be in your caller a chance to handle it as well. Exceptions float all the way up the chain of method callers this way (usually not being handled by most of them) until at last, the system itself handles any uncaught ones by aborting your program and printing an error message. In a stand-alone program, this is not such a bad idea; but in an applet, it can cause the browser to crash. Most browsers protect themselves from this disaster by catching all exceptions themselves whenever they run an applet, but you can never tell. If it's possible for you to catch an exception and do something intelligent with it, you should.

Let's see what throwing a new exception looks like. How about fleshing out today's first example:

```
public class  MyFirstExceptionalClass {
    public void  anExceptionalMethod() throws MyFirstException {
        . . .
        if (someThingUnusualHasHappened()) {
            throw new MyFirstException();
            // execution never reaches here
        }
    }
}
```

Note: throw is a little like a break statement—nothing "beyond it" is executed.

This is the fundamental way that all exceptions are generated; someone, somewhere, had to create an exception object and throw it. In fact, the whole hierarchy under the class Throwable would be worth much less if there were not throw statements scattered throughout the code in the Java library at just the right places. Because exceptions propagate up from any depth down inside methods, any method call you make might generate a plethora of possible errors and exceptions. Luckily, only the ones listed in the throws clause of that method need be thought about; the rest travel silently past on their way to becoming an error message (or being caught and handled higher in the system).

Here's an unusual demonstration of this, where the throw, and the handler that catches it, are very close together:

```
System.out.print("Now ");
try {
    System.out.print("is ");
    throw new MyFirstException();
```

```
    System.out.print("a ");
} catch (MyFirstException m) {
    System.out.print("the ");
}
System.out.print("time.");
```

It prints out Now is the time.

Exceptions are really a quite powerful way of partitioning the space of all possible error conditions into manageable pieces. Because the first catch clause that matches is executed, you can build chains such as the following:

```
try {
    someReallyExceptionalMethod();
} catch (NullPointerException n) {   // a subclass of RuntimeException
    . . .
} catch (RuntimeException r) {       // a subclass of Exception
    . . .
} catch (IOException i) {            // a subclass of Exception
    . . .
} catch (MyFirstException m) {       // our subclass of Exception
    . . .
} catch (Exception e) {              // a subclass of Throwable
    . . .
} catch (Throwable t) {
    . . .  // Errors, plus anything not caught above are caught here
}
```

By listing subclasses before their parent classes, the parent catches anything it would normally catch that's also not one of the subclasses above it. By juggling chains like these, you can express almost any combination of tests. If there's some really obscure case you can't handle, perhaps you can use an interface to catch it instead. That allows you to design your (peculiar) exceptions hierarchy using multiple inheritance. Catching an interface rather than a class can also be used to test for a property that many exceptions share but that cannot be expressed in the single-inheritance tree alone.

Suppose, for example, that a scattered set of your exception classes require a reboot after being thrown. You create an interface called NeedsReboot, and all these classes implement the interface. (None of them needs to have a common parent exception class.) Then, the highest level of exception handler simply catches classes that implement NeedsReboot and performs a reboot:

```
public interface  NeedsReboot { }   // needs no contents at all

try {
    someMethodThatGeneratesExceptionsThatImplementNeedsReboot();
} catch (NeedsReboot n) {    // catch an interface
    . . .                          // cleanup
    SystemClass.reboot();        // reboot using a made-up system class
}
```

By the way, if you need really unusual behavior during an exception, you can place the behavior into the exception class itself! Remember that an exception is also a normal class, so it can contain instance variables and methods. Although using them is a little peculiar, it might be valuable on a few bizarre occasions. Here's what this might look like:

```
try {
    someExceptionallyStrangeMethod();
} catch (ComplexException e) {
    switch (e.internalState()) {     // probably an instance variable value
        case e.COMPLEX_CASE:         // a class variable of the exception
            e.performComplexBehavior(myState, theContext, etc);
            break;
        . . .
    }
}
```

The Limitations Placed on the Programmer

As powerful as all this sounds, isn't it a little limiting, too? For example, suppose you want to override one of the standard methods of the Object class, toString(), to be smarter about how you print yourself:

```
public class  MyIllegalClass {
    public String  toString() {
        someReallyExceptionalMethod();
        . . .            // returns some String
    }
}
```

Because the superclass (Object) defined the method declaration for toString() without a throws clause, any implementation of it in any subclass must obey this restriction. In particular, you cannot just call someReallyExceptionalMethod(), as you did previously, because it will generate a host of errors and exceptions, some of which are not exempt from being listed in a throws clause (such as IOException and MyFirstException). If all the exceptions thrown were exempt, you would have no problem, but because some are not, you have to catch at least those few exceptions for this to be legal Java:

```
public class  MyLegalClass {
    public String  toString() {
        try {
            someReallyExceptionalMethod();
        } catch (IOException e) {
        } catch (MyFirstException m) {
        }
        . . .            // returns some String
    }
}
```

In both cases, you elect to catch the exceptions and do absolutely nothing with them. Although this is legal, it is not always the right thing to do. You may need to think for a while to come up with the best, nontrivial behavior for any particular catch clause. This extra thought and care makes your program more robust, better able to handle unusual input, and more likely to work correctly when used by multiple threads (you'll see this tomorrow).

MyIllegalClass's toString() method produces a compiler error to remind you to reflect on these issues. This extra care will richly reward you as you reuse your classes in later projects and in larger and larger programs. Of course, the Java class library has been written with exactly this degree of care, and that's one of the reasons it's robust enough to be used in constructing all your Java projects.

The *finally* Clause

Finally, for finally. Suppose there is some action that you absolutely must do, no matter what happens. Usually, this is to free some external resource after acquiring it, to close a file after opening it, or so forth. To be sure that "no matter what" includes exceptions as well, you use a clause of the try statement designed for exactly this sort of thing, finally:

```
SomeFileClass  f = new SomeFileClass();

if (f.open("/a/file/name/path")) {
    try {
        someReallyExceptionalMethod();
    } finally {
        f.close();
    }
}
```

This use of finally behaves very much like the following:

```
SomeFileClass  f = new SomeFileClass();

if (f.open("/a/file/name/path")) {
    try {
        someReallyExceptionalMethod();
    } catch (Throwable t) {
        f.close();
        throw t;
    }
}
```

except that finally can also be used to clean up not only after exceptions but after return, break, and continue statements as well. Here's a complex demonstration:

```
public class  MyFinalExceptionalClass extends ContextClass {
    public static void  main(String argv[]) {
        int  mysteriousState = getContext();

        while (true) {
            System.out.print("Who ");
            try {
                System.out.print("is ");
                if (mysteriousState == 1)
```

```
                        return;
                    System.out.print("that ");
                    if (mysteriousState == 2)
                        break;
                    System.out.print("strange ");
                    if (mysteriousState == 3)
                        continue;
                    System.out.print("but kindly ");
                    if (mysteriousState == 4)
                        throw new UncaughtException();
                    System.out.print("not at all ");
                } finally {
                    System.out.print("amusing ");
                }
                System.out.print("yet compelling ");
            }
            System.out.print("man?");
        }
    }
```

Here is the output produced depending on the value of `mysteriousState`:

```
1    Who is amusing
2    Who is that amusing man?
3    Who is that strange amusing Who is that strange amusing . . .
4    Who is that strange but kindly amusing
5    Who is that strange but kindly not at all amusing yet compelling man?
```

> **Note:** In case 3, the output never ends until you press Ctrl+C. In 4, an error message generated by the `UncaughtException` is also printed.

Summary

Today, you learned about how exceptions aid your program's design, robustness, and multithreading capability (more on this tomorrow).

You also learned about the vast array of exceptions defined and `thrown` in the Java class library, and how to `try` methods while `catch`-ing any of a hierarchically ordered set of possible exceptions and errors. Java's reliance on strict exception handling does place some restrictions on the programmer, but you learned that these restrictions are light compared to the rewards.

Finally, the `finally` clause was discussed, which provides a fool-proof way to be certain that something is accomplished, no matter what.

Q&A

Q I'd like to test the last example you gave, but where does `getContext()` come from?

A That example wasn't meant to be an executable program as it stands, but you can turn it into one as follows. First, remove the clause extends `ContextClass` from line one. Then, replace `getContext()` in the third line with `Integer.parseInt(args[0])`. You can now compile, then run, the example via the following:

```
java.MyFinalExceptionClass N
```

where N is the mysterious state you want.

Q I'm still not sure I understand the differences between `Exceptions`, `Errors`, and `RuntimeExceptions`. Is there another way of looking at them?

A Errors are caused by dynamic linking, or virtual machine problems, and are thus too low-level for most programs to care about (although sophisticated development libraries and environments probably care a great deal about them). RuntimeExceptions are generated by the normal execution of Java code, and though they occasionally reflect a condition you will want to handle explicitly, more often they reflect a coding mistake by the programmer and simply need to print an error to help flag that mistake. Exceptions that are not `RuntimeExceptions` (`IOExceptions`, for example) are conditions that, because of their nature, should be explicitly handled by any robust and well-thought-out code. The Java class library has been written using only a few of these, but they are extremely important to using the system safely and correctly. The compiler helps you handle these exceptions properly via its throws clause checks and restrictions.

Q Is there any way to "get around" the strict restrictions placed on methods by the `throws` clause?

A Yes. Suppose you thought long and hard and have decided that you need to circumvent this restriction. This is almost never the case, because the right solution is to go back and redesign your methods to reflect the exceptions that you need to throw. Imagine, however, that for some reason a system class has you in a straitjacket. Your first solution is to subclass `RuntimeException` to make up a new, exempt exception of your own. Now you can throw it to your heart's content, because the `throws` clause that was annoying you does not need to include this new exception. If you need a lot of such exceptions, an elegant approach is to mix in some novel exception interfaces to your new `Runtime` classes. You're free to choose whatever subset of these new interfaces you want to `catch` (none of the normal `Runtime` exceptions need be caught), while any leftover (new) `Runtime` exceptions are (legally) allowed to go through that otherwise annoying standard method in the library.

Q I'm still a little confused by long chains of catch clauses. Can you label the previous example with which exceptions are handled by each line of code?

A Certainly, here it is:

```
try {
    someReallyExceptionalMethod();
} catch (NullPointerException n) {
    . . .  // handles NullPointerExceptions
} catch (RuntimeException r) {
    . . .  // handles RuntimeExceptions that are not NullPointerExceptions
} catch (IOException i) {
    . . .  // handles IOExceptions
} catch (MyFirstException m) {
    . . .  // handles MyFirstExceptions
} catch (Exception e) {  // handles Exceptions that are not RuntimeExceptions
    . . .                 //            nor IOExceptions nor MyFirstExceptions
} catch (Throwable t) {
    . . .  // handles Throwables that are not Exceptions (i.e., Errors)
}
```

Q Given how annoying it can sometimes be to handle exceptional conditions properly, what's stopping me from surrounding any method with a `throws` clause as follows:

```
try { thatAnnoyingMethod(); } catch (Throwable t) { }
```

and simply ignoring all exceptions?

A Nothing, other than your own conscience. In some cases, you *should* do nothing, because it is the correct thing to do for your method's implementation. Otherwise, you should struggle through the annoyance and gain experience. Good style is a struggle even for the best programmer, but the rewards are rich indeed.

Multithreading

by Charles L. Perkins

Today, you'll learn more about the threads mentioned briefly in Week 2:

☐ How to "think multithreaded"

☐ How to protect your methods and variables from unintended thread conflicts

☐ How to create, start, and stop threads and threaded classes

☐ How the scheduler works in Java

First, let's begin by motivating the need for threads.

Threads are a relatively recent invention in the computer science world. Although processes, their larger parent, have been around for decades, threads have only recently been accepted into the mainstream. What's odd about this is that they are very valuable, and programs written with them are noticeably better, even to the casual user. In fact, some of the best individual, Herculean efforts over the years have involved implementing a threads-like facility by hand to give a program a more friendly feel to its users.

Imagine that you're using your favorite text editor on a large file. When it starts up, does it need to examine the entire file before it lets you edit? Does it need to make a copy of the file? If the file is huge, this can be a nightmare. Wouldn't it be nicer for it to show you the first page, enabling you to begin editing, and somehow (in the background) complete the slower tasks necessary for initialization? Threads allow exactly this kind of within-the-program parallelism.

Perhaps the best example of threading (or lack of it) is a WWW browser. Can your browser download an indefinite number of files and Web pages at once while still enabling you to continue browsing? While these pages are downloading, can your browser download all the pictures, sounds, and so forth in parallel, interleaving the fast and slow download times of multiple Internet servers? HotJava can do all of these things—and more—by using the built-in threading of the Java language.

The Problem with Parallelism

If threading is so wonderful, why doesn't every system have it? Many modern operating systems have the basic primitives needed to create and run threads, but they are missing a key ingredient. The rest of their environment is not thread-safe. Imagine that you are in a thread, one of many, and each of you is sharing some important data managed by the system. If you were managing that data, you could take steps to protect it (as you'll see later today), but the system is managing it. Now visualize a piece of code in the system that reads some crucial value, thinks about it for a while, and then adds 1 to the value:

```
if (crucialValue > 0) {
    . . .                    // think about what to do
    crucialValue += 1;
}
```

Remember that any number of threads may be calling upon this part of the system at once. The disaster occurs when two threads have both executed the `if` test before either has incremented the `crucialValue`. In that case, the value is clobbered by them both with the same `crucialValue` + 1, and one of the increments has been lost. This may not seem so bad to you, but imagine instead that the crucial value affects the state of the screen as it is being displayed. Now, unfortunate ordering of the threads can cause the screen to be updated incorrectly. In the same way, mouse or keyboard events can be lost, databases can be inaccurately updated, and so forth.

This disaster is inescapable if any significant part of the system has not been written with threads in mind. Therein lies the barrier to a mainstream threaded environment—the large effort required to rewrite existing libraries for thread safety. Luckily, Java was written from scratch with this is mind, and every Java class in its library is thread-safe. Thus, you now have to worry only about your own synchronization and thread-ordering problems, because you can assume that the Java system will do the right thing.

NEW☞
TERM *Atomic operations* are operations that appear to happen "all at once"—exactly at the same time—to other threads.

> **Note:** Some readers may wonder what the fundamental problem really is. Can't you just make the ... area in the example smaller and smaller to reduce or eliminate the problem? Without atomic operations, the answer is no. Even if the ... took zero time, you must first look at the value of some variable to make any decision and then change something to reflect that decision. These two steps can never be made to happen at the same time without an atomic operation. Unless you're given one by the system, it's literally impossible to create your own.
>
> Even the one line `crucialValue += 1` involves three steps: get the current value, add one to it, and store it back. (Using `++crucialValue` doesn't help either.) All three steps need to happen "all at once" (atomically) to be safe. Special Java primitives, at the lowest levels of the language, provide you with the basic atomic operations you need to build safe, threaded programs.

Thinking Multithreaded

Getting used to threads takes a little while and a new way of thinking. Rather than imagining that you always know exactly what's happening when you look at a method you've written, you have to ask yourself some additional questions. What will happen if more than one thread calls into this method at the same time? Do you need to protect it in some way? What about your class as a whole? Are you assuming that only one of its methods is running at the same time?

Often you make such assumptions, and a local instance variable will be messed up as a result. Let's make a few mistakes and then try to correct them. First, the simplest case:

```
public class  ThreadCounter {
    int  crucialValue;

    public void  countMe() {
        crucialValue += 1;
    }

    public int    howMany() {
        return crucialValue;
    }
}
```

This code suffers from the most pure form of the "synchronization problem:" the += takes more than one step, and you may miscount the number of threads as a result. (Don't worry about how threads are created yet, just imagine that a whole bunch of them are able to call countMe(), at once, at slightly different times.) Java allows you to fix this:

```
public class  SafeThreadCounter {
    int  crucialValue;

    public synchronized void  countMe() {
        crucialValue += 1;
    }

    public              int   howMany() {
        return crucialValue;
    }
}
```

The synchronized keyword tells Java to make the block of code in the method thread safe. Only one thread will be allowed inside this method at once, and others have to wait until the currently running thread is finished with it before they can begin running it. This implies that synchronizing a large, long-running method is almost always a bad idea. All your threads would end up stuck at this bottleneck, waiting in single file to get their turn at this one slow method.

It's even worse than you might think for most unsynchronized variables. Because the compiler can keep them around in registers during computations, and a thread's registers can't be seen by other threads (especially if they're on another processor in a true multiprocessor computer), a variable can be updated in such a way that *no possible order* of thread updates could have produced the result. This is completely incomprehensible to the programmer. To avoid this bizarre case, you can label a variable volatile, meaning that you know it will be updated asynchronously by multiprocessor-like threads. Java then loads and stores it each time it's needed and does not use registers.

Note: In earlier releases, variables that were safe from these bizarre effects were labeled `threadsafe`. Because most variables are safe to use, however, they are now assumed to be thread-safe unless you mark them `volatile`. Using `volatile` is an extremely rare event. In fact, in the beta release, the Java library does not use `volatile` anywhere.

Points About *Points*

The method `howMany()` in the last example doesn't need to be `synchronized`, because it simply returns the current value of an instance variable. Someone higher in the call chain may need to be `synchronized`, though—someone who uses the value returned from the method. Here's an example:

```
public class  Point {
    private float  x, y;

    public  float  x() {          // needs no synchronization
        return x;
    }

    public  float  y() {          // ditto
        return y;
    }
    . . .      // methods to set and change x and y
}

public class  UnsafePointPrinter {
    public void  print(Point p) {
        System.out.println("The point's x is " + p.x()
                            + " and y is " + p.y() + ".");
    }
}
```

The analogous methods to `howMany()` are `x()` and `y()`. They need no synchronization, because they just return the values of instance variables. It is the responsibility of the caller of `x()` and `y()` to decide whether it needs to synchronize itself—and in this case, it does. Although the method `print()` simply reads values and prints them out, it reads *two* values. This means that there is a chance that some other thread, running between the call to `p.x()` and the call to `p.y()`, could have changed the value of x and y stored inside the `Point` p. Remember, you don't know how many other threads have a way to reach and call methods in this `Point` object! "Thinking multithreaded" comes down to being careful any time you make an assumption that something has *not* happened between two parts of your program (even two parts of the same line, or the same expression, such as the string + expression in this example).

TryAgainPointPrinter

You could try to make a safe version of print() by simply adding the synchronized keyword modifier to it, but instead, let's try a slightly different approach:

```
public class  TryAgainPointPrinter {
    public void  print(Point p) {
        float  safeX, safeY;

        synchronized(this) {
            safeX = p.x();       // these two lines now
            safeY = p.y();       // happen atomically
        }
        System.out.print("The point's x is " + safeX
                               + " y is " + safeY);
    }
}
```

The synchronized statement takes an argument that says what object you would like to lock to prevent more than one thread from executing the enclosed block of code at the same time. Here, you use this (the instance itself), which is exactly the object that would have been locked by the synchronized method as a whole if you had changed print() to be like your safe countMe() method. You have an added bonus with this new form of synchronization: you can specify exactly what part of a method needs to be safe, and the rest can be left unsafe.

Notice how you took advantage of this freedom to make the protected part of the method as small as possible, while leaving the String creations, concatenations, and printing (which together take a small but nonzero amount of time) outside the "protected" area. This is both good style (as a guide to the reader of your code) and more efficient, because fewer threads get stuck waiting to get into protected areas.

SafePointPrinter

The astute reader, though, may still be worried by the last example. It seems as if you made sure that no one executes *your* calls to x() and y() out of order, but have you prevented the Point p from changing out from under you? The answer is no, you still have not solved the problem. You really do need the full power of the synchronized statement:

```
public class  SafePointPrinter {
    public void  print(Point p) {
        float  safeX, safeY;

        synchronized(p) {        // no one can change p
            safeX = p.x();       // while these two lines
            safeY = p.y();       // are happening atomically
        }
        System.out.print("The point's x is " + safeX
                               + " y is " + safeY);
    }
}
```

Now you've got it. You actually needed to protect the Point p to protect from changes, so you lock it by giving it as the argument to your synchronized statement. Now when x() and y() happen together, they can be sure to get the current x and y of the Point p, without any other thread being able to call a modifying method between. You're still assuming, however, that the Point p has properly protected *itself.* (You can always assume this about system classes—but *you* wrote this Point class.) You can make sure by writing the only method that can change x and y inside p yourself:

```
public class  Point {
    private float  x, y;

    . . .          // the x() and y() methods

    public synchronized void  setXAndY(float  newX,  float  newY) {
        x = newX;
        y = newY;
    }
}
```

By making the only "set" method in Point synchronized, you guarantee that any other thread trying to grab the Point p and change it out from under you has to wait: you've locked the Point p with your synchronized(p) statement, and any other thread has to try to lock the same Point p via the implicit synchronized(this) statement p now executes when entering setXAndY(). Thus, at last, you are thread-safe.

> **Note:** By the way, if Java had some way of returning more than one value at once, you could write a synchronized getXAndY() method for Points that returns both values safely. In the current Java language, such a method could return a new, unique Point to guarantee to its callers that no one else has a copy that might be changed. This sort of trick can be used to minimize the parts of the system that need to worry about synchronization.

ReallySafePoint

An added benefit of the use of the synchronized modifier on methods (or of synchronized(this) {. . .}) is that only one of these methods (or blocks of code) can run at once. You can use that knowledge to guarantee that only one of several crucial methods in a class will run at once:

```
public class  ReallySafePoint {
    private float  x, y;

    public synchronized Point  getUniquePoint() {
        return new Point(x, y);      // can be a less safe Point
    }                                // because only the caller has it
```

```
public synchronized void    setXAndY(float   newX,   float   newY) {
    x = newX;
    y = newY;
}

public synchronized void    scale(float   scaleX,   float   scaleY) {
    x *= scaleX;
    y *= scaleY;
}

public synchronized void    add(ReallySafePoint   aRSP) {
    Point   p = aRSP.getUniquePoint();

    x += p.x();
    y += p.y();
}   // Point p is soon thrown away by GC; no one else ever saw it
}
```

This example combines several of the ideas mentioned previously. To avoid a caller's having to synchronize(p) whenever getting your x and y, you give them a synchronized way to get a unique Point (like returning multiple values). Each method that modifies the object's instance variables is also synchronized to prevent it from running between the x and y references in getUniquePoint() and from stepping on the others as they each modify the local x and y. Note that add() itself uses getUniquePoint() to avoid having to say synchronized(aRSP).

Classes that are this safe are a little unusual; it is more often your responsibility to protect yourself from other threads' use of commonly held objects (such as Points). Only when you know for certain that you're the only one that knows about an object, can you fully relax. Of course, if you created the object and gave it to no one else, you *can* be that certain.

Protecting a Class Variable

Finally, suppose you want a class variable to collect some information across all a class's instances:

```
public class   StaticCounter {
    private static int   crucialValue;

    public synchronized void   countMe() {
        crucialValue += 1;
    }
}
```

Is this safe? If crucialValue were an instance variable, it would be. Because it's a class variable, however, and there is only one copy of it for all instances, you can still have multiple threads modifying it by using different *instances* of the class. (Remember, the synchronized modifier locks the object this—an instance.) Luckily, you already know the tools you need to solve this:

```
public class   StaticCounter {
    private static int   crucialValue;
```

```
public void  countMe() {
    synchronized(getClass()) {    // can't directly reference StaticCounter
        crucialValue += 1;        // the (shared) class is now locked
    }
}
}
```

The trick is to "lock" on a different object—not on an instance of the class, but on the class itself. Because a class variable is "inside" a class, just as an instance variable is inside an instance, this shouldn't be all that unexpected. In a similar way, classes can provide global resources that any instance (or other class) can access directly by using the class name, and lock by using that same class name. In this example, `crucialValue` is used from within an instance of `StaticCounter`, but if `crucialValue` were declared `public` instead, from anywhere in the program, it would be safe to say the following:

```
synchronized(new StaticCounter().getClass()) {
    StaticCounter.crucialValue += 1;
}
```

Note: The direct use of another object's variable is really bad style—it's used here simply to demonstrate a point quickly. `StaticCounter` normally provides a `countMe()`-like class method of its own to do this sort of dirty work.

You can appreciate how much work the Java team has done for you by thinking all these hard thoughts for each and every class (and method!) in the Java class library.

Creating and Using Threads

Now that you understand the power (and the dangers) of having many threads running at once, how are those threads actually created?

Warning: The system itself always has a few so-called *daemon* threads running, one of which is constantly doing the tedious task of garbage collection for you in the background. There is also a main user thread that listens for events from your mouse and keyboard. If you're not careful, you can sometimes lock out this main thread. If you do, no events are sent to your program and it appears to be dead. A good rule of thumb is that whenever you're doing something that *can* be done in a separate thread, it probably *should* be. Threads in Java are relatively cheap to create, run, and destroy, so don't use them too sparingly.

Because there is a class java.lang.Thread, you might guess that you could create a thread of your own by subclassing it—and you are right:

```
public class  MyFirstThread extends Thread { // a.k.a., java.lang.Thread
    public void  run() {
        . . .                 // do something useful
    }
}
```

You now have a new type of Thread called MyFirstThread, which does something useful (unspecified) when its run() method is called. Of course, no one has created this thread or called its run() method, so it does absolutely nothing at the moment. To actually create and run an instance of your new thread class, you write the following:

```
MyFirstThread  aMFT = new MyFirstThread();

aMFT.start();    // calls our run() method
```

What could be simpler? You create a new instance of your thread class and then ask it to start running. Whenever you want to stop the thread, you use this:

```
aMFT.stop();
```

Besides responding to start() and stop(), a thread can also be temporarily suspended and later resumed:

```
Thread  t = new Thread();

t.suspend();
. . .           // do something special while t isn't running
t.resume();
```

A thread will automatically suspend() and then resume() when it's first blocked at a synchronized point and then later unblocked (when it's that thread's "turn" to run).

The *Runnable* Interface

This is all well and good if every time you want to create a Thread you have the luxury of being able to place it under the Thread class in the single-inheritance class tree. What if it more naturally belongs under some other class, from which it needs to get most of its implementation? The interfaces of Day 16 come to the rescue:

```
public class  MySecondThread extends ImportantClass implements Runnable {
    public void  run() {
        . . .                 // do something useful
    }
}
```

By implementing the interface Runnable, you declare your intention to run in a separate thread. In fact, the class Thread itself implements this interface, as you might expect from the design discussions on Day 16. As you also might guess from the example, the interface Runnable specifies only one method: run(). As in MyFirstThread, you expect someone to create an instance of a thread and somehow call your run() method. Here's how this is accomplished:

```
MySecondThread   aMST = new MySecondThread();
Thread           aThread = new Thread(aMST);

aThread.start();   // calls our run() method, indirectly
```

First, you create an instance of MySecondThread. Then, by passing this instance to the constructor making the new Thread, you make it the target of that Thread. Whenever that new Thread starts up, its run() method calls the run() method of the target it was given (assumed by the Thread to be an object that implements the Runnable interface). When start() is called, aThread (indirectly) calls your run() method. You can stop aThread with stop(). If you don't need to talk to the Thread explicitly or to the instance of MySecondThread, here's a one line shortcut:

```
new Thread(new MySecondThread()).start();
```

Note: As you can see, the class name, MySecondThread, is a bit of a misnomer—it does not descend from Thread, nor is it actually the thread that you start() and stop(). It probably should have been called MySecondThreadedClass or ImportantRunnableClass.

18

ThreadTester

Here's a longer example:

```
public class  SimpleRunnable implements Runnable {
    public void  run() {
        System.out.println("in thread named '"
                            + Thread.currentThread().getName() + "'");
    } // any other methods run() calls are in current thread as well
}

public class  ThreadTester {
    public static void  main(String argv[]) {
        SimpleRunnable  aSR = new SimpleRunnable();

        while (true) {
            Thread  t = new Thread(aSR);

            System.out.println("new Thread() " + (t == null ?
                                             "fail" : "succeed") + "ed.");
            t.start();
            try { t.join(); } catch (InterruptedException ignored) { }
                        // waits for thread to finish its run() method
        }
    }
}
```

> **Note:** You may be worried that only one instance of the class SimpleRunnable is created, but many new Threads are using it. Don't they get confused? Remember to separate in your mind the aSR instance (and the methods it understands) from the various threads of execution that can pass through it. aSR's methods provide a template for execution, and the multiple threads created are sharing that template. Each remembers where it is executing and whatever else it needs to make it distinct from the other running threads. They all share the same instance and the same methods. That's why you need to be so careful, when adding synchronization, to imagine numerous threads running rampant over each of your methods.

The class method currentThread() can be called to get the thread in which a method is currently executing. If the SimpleRunnable class were a subclass of Thread, its methods would know the answer already (*it* is the thread running). Because SimpleRunnable simply implements the interface Runnable, however, and counts on someone else (ThreadTester's main()) to create the thread, its run() method needs another way to get its hands on that thread. Often, you'll be deep inside methods called by your run() method when suddenly you need to get the current thread. The class method shown in the example works, no matter where you are.

> **Warning:** You can do some reasonably disastrous things with your knowledge of threads. For example, if you're running in the main thread of the system and, because you think you are in a different thread, you accidentally say the following:
>
> ```
> Thread.currentThread().stop();
> ```
>
> it has unfortunate consequences for your (soon-to-be-dead) program!

The example then calls on getName(), the current thread to get the thread's name (usually something helpful, such as Thread-23) so it can tell the world in which thread run() is running. The final thing to note is the use of the method join(), which, when sent to a thread, means "I'm planning to wait forever for you to finish your run() method." You don't want to do this lightly: if you have anything else important you need to get done in your thread any time soon, you can't count on how long the join()ed thread may take to finish. In the example, its run() method is short and finishes quickly, so each loop can safely wait for the previous thread to die before creating the next one. (Of course, in this example, you didn't have anything else you wanted to do while waiting for join() anyway.) Here's the output produced:

```
new Thread() succeeded.
```

```
in thread named 'Thread-1'
new Thread() succeeded.
in thread named 'Thread-2'
new Thread() succeeded.
in thread named 'Thread-3'
^C
```

Ctrl+C was pressed to interrupt the program, because it otherwise would continue forever.

NamedThreadTester

If you want your threads to have particular names, you can assign them yourself by using a two-argument form of Thread's constructor:

```
public class  NamedThreadTester {
    public static void  main(String argv[]) {
        SimpleRunnable  aSR = new SimpleRunnable();

        for (int  i = 1;  true;  ++i) {
            Thread  t = new Thread(aSR, "" + (100 - i)
                                        + " threads on the wall...");

            System.out.println("new Thread() " + (t == null ?
                                        "fail" : "succeed") + "ed.");
            t.start();
            try { t.join(); } catch (InterruptedException ignored) { }
        }
    }
}
```

which takes a target object, as before, and a String, which names the new thread. Here's the output:

```
new Thread() succeeded.
in thread named '99 threads on the wall...'
new Thread() succeeded.
in thread named '98 threads on the wall...'
new Thread() succeeded.
in thread named '97 threads on the wall...'
^C
```

Naming a thread is one easy way to pass it some information. This information flows from the parent thread to its new child. It's also useful, for debugging purposes, to give threads meaningful names (such as network input) so that when they appear during an error—in a stack trace, for example—you can easily identify which thread caused the problem. You might also think of using names to help group or organize your threads, but Java actually provides you with a ThreadGroup class to perform this function. A ThreadGroup allows you to group threads, to control them all as a unit, and to keep them from being able to affect other threads (useful for security).

Knowing When a Thread has Stopped

Let's imagine a different version of the last example, one that creates a thread and then hands the thread off to other parts of the program. Suppose it would then like to know when that thread dies so that it can perform some cleanup operation. If SimpleRunnable were a subclass of Thread, you might try to catch stop() whenever it's sent—but look at Thread's declaration of the stop() method:

```
public final void  stop(); { . . . }
```

The final here means that you can't override this method in a subclass. In any case, SimpleRunnable is *not* a subclass of Thread, so how can this imagined example possibly catch the death of its thread? The answer is to use the following magic:

```
public class  SingleThreadTester {
    public static void  main(String argv[]) {
        Thread  t = new Thread(new SimpleRunnable());

        try {
            t.start();
            someMethodThatMightStopTheThread(t);
        } catch (ThreadDeath  aTD) {
            . . .            // do some required cleanup
            throw aTD;       // re-throw the error
        }
    }
}
```

You understand most of this magic from yesterday's lesson. All you need to know is that if the thread created in the example dies, it throws an error of class ThreadDeath. The code catches that error and performs the required cleanup. It then rethrows the error, allowing the thread to die. The cleanup code is not called if the thread exits normally (its run() method completes), but that's fine; you posited that the cleanup was needed only when stop() was used on the thread.

> **Note:** Threads can die in other ways—for example, by throwing exceptions that no one catches. In these cases, stop() is never called, and the previous code is not sufficient. (If the cleanup always has to occur, even at the normal end of a thread's life, you can put it in a finally clause.) Because unexpected exceptions can come out of nowhere to kill a thread, multithreaded programs that carefully catch and handle all their exceptions are more predictable, robust, and easier to debug.

Thread Scheduling

You might wonder exactly what order your threads will be run in, and how you can control that order. Unfortunately, the current implementations of the Java system cannot precisely answer the former, though with a lot of work, you can always do the latter.

NEW☞ TERM The part of the system that decides the real-time ordering of threads is called the *scheduler*.

Preemptive Versus Nonpreemptive

Normally, any scheduler has two fundamentally different ways of looking at its job: non-preemptive scheduling and preemptive time-slicing.

NEW☞ TERM With *non-preemptive scheduling*, the scheduler runs the current thread forever, requiring that thread explicitly to tell it when it is safe to start a different thread. With *preemptive time-slicing*, the scheduler runs the current thread until it has used up a certain tiny fraction of a second, and then "preempts" it, suspend()s it, and resume()s another thread for the next tiny fraction of a second.

Non-preemptive scheduling is very courtly, always asking for permission to schedule, and is quite valuable in extremely time-critical, real-time applications where being interrupted at the wrong moment, or for too long, could mean crashing an airplane.

Most modern schedulers use preemptive time-slicing, because, except for a few time-critical cases, it has turned out to make writing multithreaded programs much easier. For one thing, it does not force each thread to decide exactly when it should "yield" control to another thread. Instead, every thread can just run blindly on, knowing that the scheduler will be fair about giving all the other threads their chance to run.

It turns out that this approach is still not the ideal way to schedule threads. You've given a little too much control to the scheduler. The final touch many modern schedulers add is to allow you to assign each thread a priority. This creates a total ordering of all threads, making some threads more "important" than others. Being higher priority often means that a thread gets run more often (or gets more total running time), but it always means that it can interrupt other, lower-priority threads, even before their "time-slice" has expired.

The current Java release does not precisely specify the behavior of its scheduler. Threads can be assigned priorities, and when a choice is made between several threads that all want to run, the highest-priority thread wins. However, among threads that are all the same priority, the behavior is not well-defined. In fact, the different platforms on which Java currently runs have different behaviors—some behaving more like a preemptive scheduler, and some more like a non-preemptive scheduler.

18

> **Note:** This incomplete specification of the scheduler is terribly annoying and, presumably, will be corrected in later releases. Not knowing the fine details of how scheduling occurs is perfectly all right, but not knowing whether equal priority threads must explicitly yield or face running forever, is not all right. For example, all the threads you have created so far are equal priority threads, so you don't know their basic scheduling behavior!

Testing Your Scheduler

To find out what kind of scheduler you have on your system, try the following:

```
public class  RunnablePotato implements Runnable {
    public void  run() {
        while (true)
            System.out.println(Thread.currentThread().getName());
    }
}

public class  PotatoThreadTester {
    public static void  main(String argv[]) {
        RunnablePotato  aRP = new RunnablePotato();

        new Thread(aRP, "one potato").start();
        new Thread(aRP, "two potato").start();
    }
}
```

For a non-preemptive scheduler, this prints the following:

```
one potato
one potato
one potato
. . .
```

forever, until you interrupt the program. For a preemptive scheduler that time-slices, it repeats the line one potato a few times, followed by the same number of two potato lines, over and over:

```
one potato
one potato
...
one potato
two potato
two potato
...
two potato
. . .
```

until you interrupt the program. What if you want to be sure the two threads will take turns, no matter what the system scheduler wants to do? You rewrite RunnablePotato as follows:

```
public class  RunnablePotato implements Runnable {
    public void  run() {
        while (true) {
            System.out.println(Thread.currentThread().getName());
            Thread.yield();  // let another thread run for a while
        }
    }
}
```

> **Tip:** Normally you have to say Thread.currentThread().yield() to get your hands on the current thread, and then call yield(). Because this pattern is so common, however, the Thread class provides a shortcut.

The yield() method explicitly gives any other threads that want to run a chance to begin running. (If there are no threads waiting to run, the thread that made the yield() simply continues.) In our example, there's another thread that's just *dying* to run, so when you now run the class ThreadTester, it should output the following:

```
one potato
two potato
one potato
two potato
one potato
two potato
. . .
```

even if your system scheduler is non-preemptive, and would never normally run the second thread.

PriorityThreadTester

To see whether priorities are working on your system, try this:

```
public class  PriorityThreadTester {
    public static void  main(String argv[]) {
        RunnablePotato  aRP = new RunnablePotato();
        Thread          t1  = new Thread(aRP, "one potato");
        Thread          t2  = new Thread(aRP, "two potato");

        t2.setPriority(t1.getPriority() + 1);
        t1.start();
        t2.start();   // at priority Thread.NORM_PRIORITY + 1
    }
}
```

18

✓ **Tip:** The values representing the lowest, normal, and highest priorities that threads can be assigned are stored in class variables of the Thread class: Thread.MIN_PRIORITY, Thread.NORM_PRIORITY, and Thread.MAX_PRIORITY. The system assigns new threads, by default, the priority Thread.NORM_PRIORITY. Priorities in Java are currently defined in a range from 1 to 10, with 5 being normal, but you shouldn't depend on these values; use the class variables, or tricks like the one shown in this example.

If one potato is the first line of output, your system does not preempt using priorities.

Why? Imagine that the first thread (t1) has just begun to run. Even before it has a chance to print anything, along comes a higher-priority thread (t2) that wants to run right away. That higher-priority thread should preempt (interrupt) the first, and get a chance to print two potato before t1 finishes printing anything. In fact, if you use the RunnablePotato class that never yield()s, t2 stays in control forever, printing two potato lines, because it's a higher priority than t1 and it never yields control. If you use the latest RunnablePotato class (with yield()), the output is alternating lines of one potato and two potato as before, but starting with two potato.

Here's a good, illustrative example of how complex threads behave:

```
public class  ComplexThread extends Thread {
    private int  delay;

    ComplexThread(String  name,  float  seconds) {
        super(name);
        delay = (int) seconds * 1000;    // delays are in milliseconds
        start();                         // start up ourself!
    }

    public void  run() {
        while (true) {
            System.out.println(Thread.currentThread().getName());
            try {
                Thread.sleep(delay);
            } catch (InterruptedException  ignored) {
                return;
            }
        }
    }

    public static void  main(String argv[]) {
        new ComplexThread("one potato",   1.1F);
        new ComplexThread("two potato",   0.3F);
        new ComplexThread("three potato", 0.5F);
        new ComplexThread("four",         0.7F);
    }
}
```

This example combines the thread and its tester into a single class. Its constructor takes care of naming (itself) and of starting (itself), because it is now a Thread. The main() method creates new instances of its own class, because that class is a subclass of Thread. run() is also more complicated, because it now uses, for the first time, a method that can throw an unexpected exception.

The Thread.sleep() method forces the current thread to yield() and then waits for at least the specified amount of time to elapse before allowing the thread to run again. It might be interrupted, however, while sleeping by another thread. In such a case, it throws an InterruptedException. Now, because run() is not defined as throwing this exception, you must "hide" the fact by catching and handling it yourself. Because interruptions are usually requests to stop, you should exit the thread, which you can do by simply returning from the run() method.

This program should output a repeating but complex pattern of four different lines, where every once in a while you see the following:

```
. . .
one potato
two potato
three potato
four
. . .
```

18

You should study the pattern output to prove to yourself that true parallelism is going on inside Java programs. You may also begin to appreciate that, if even this simple set of four threads can produce such complex behavior, many more threads must be capable of producing near chaos if not carefully controlled. Luckily, Java provides the synchronization and thread-safe libraries you need to control that chaos.

Summary

Today, you learned that parallelism is desirable and powerful, but introduces many new problems—methods and variables now need to be *protected* from thread conflicts—that can lead to chaos if not carefully controlled.

By "thinking multithreaded," you can detect the places in your programs that require synchronized statements (or modifiers) to make them thread-safe. A series of Point examples demonstrated the various levels of safety you can achieve and showed how subclasses of Thread, or classes that implement the Runnable interface, are created and run() to generate multithreaded programs.

You also learned how to yield(), how to start(), stop(), suspend(), and resume() your threads, and how to catch ThreadDeath whenever it happens.

Finally, you learned about preemptive and non-preemptive scheduling, both with and without priorities, and how to test your Java system to see which of them your scheduler is using.

This wraps up the description of threads. You now know enough to write the most complex of programs: multithreaded ones. As you get more comfortable with threads, you may begin to use the ThreadGroup class or to use the enumeration methods of Thread to get your hands on all the threads in the system and manipulate them. Don't be afraid to experiment; you can't permanently break anything, and you learn only by trying.

Q&A

Q **If they're so important to Java, why haven't threads appeared throughout the entire book?**

A Actually, they have. Every stand-alone program written so far has "created" at least one thread, the one in which it is running. (Of course the system created that Thread for it automatically.)

Q **How exactly do these threads get created and run? What about applets?**

A When a simple, stand-alone Java program starts up, the system creates a main thread, and its run() method calls your main() method to start your program—you do nothing to get that Thread. Likewise, when a simple applet loads into a Java-aware browser, a Thread has already been created by the browser, and its run() method calls your init() and start() methods to start your program. In either case, a new Thread() of some kind was done somewhere, by the Java environment itself.

Q **The ThreadTester class had an infinite loop that created Threads and then join()ed with them. Is it really infinite?**

A In theory, yes. In actuality, how far the loop runs determines the resource limits of (and tests the stability of) the threads package and garbage collector in your Java release. Over time, all Java releases will converge on making the loop truly infinite.

Q **I know Java releases are still a little fuzzy about the scheduler's behavior, but what's the current story?**

A Here are the gruesome details for the beta release, relayed by Arthur van Hoff at Sun: the way Java schedules threads "...depends on the platform. It is usually preemptive, but not always time-sliced. Priorities are not always observed, depending on the underlying implementation." This final clause gives you a hint that all this confusion is an implementation problem, and that someday soon, the design and implementation will both be clear about scheduling behavior.

Q Does Java support more complex multithreaded concepts, such as semaphores?

A The class `Object` in Java provides methods that can be used to build up condition variables, semaphores, and any higher-level parallel construct you might need. The method `wait()` (and its two variants with a timeout) causes the current thread to wait until some condition has been satisfied. The method `notify()` (or `notifyAll()`), which must be called from within a `synchronized` method or block, tells the thread (or *all* threads) to wake up and check that condition again, because something has changed. By careful combinations of these two primitive methods, any data structure can be manipulated safely by a set of threads, and all the classical parallel primitives needed to implement published parallel algorithms can be built.

Q My parallel friends tell me I should worry about something called "deadlock." Should I?

A Not for simple multithreaded programs. However, in more complicated programs, one of the biggest worries does become one of avoiding a situation in which one thread has locked an object and is waiting for another thread to finish, while that other thread is waiting for the first thread to release that same object before it can finish. That's a deadlock—both threads will be stuck forever. Mutual dependencies like this involving more than two threads can be quite intricate, convoluted, and difficult to locate, much less rectify. They are one of the main challenges in writing complex multithreaded programs.

18

19

Streams

by Charles L. Perkins

Today, you'll explore Java's streams:

☐ Input streams—and how to create, use, and detect the end of them—and filtered input streams, which can be nested to great effect

☐ Output streams, that are mostly analogous to (but the inverse of) input streams

You'll also learn about two stream interfaces that make the reading and writing of typed streams much easier (as well as about several utility classes used to access the file system). Let's begin with a little history behind the invention of streams.

One of the early inventions of the UNIX operating system was the pipe. By unifying all these disparate ways of communicating into a single metaphor, UNIX paved the way for a whole series of related inventions, culminating in the abstraction known as streams.

NEW☞ A *pipe* is an uninterpreted stream of bytes that can be used for communicating between
TERM programs (or other "forked" copies of your own program) or for reading and writing to peripheral devices and files.

A *stream* is a path of communication between the source of some information and its destination.

That information, an uninterpreted byte stream, can come from any "pipe source," the computer's memory, or even from the Internet. In fact, the source and destination of a stream are completely arbitrary producers and consumers of bytes, respectively. Therein lies the power of the abstraction. You don't need to know about the source of the information when reading from a stream, and you don't need to know about the final destination when writing to one.

General-purpose methods that can read from any source accept a stream argument to specify that source; general methods for writing accept a stream to specify the destination. Arbitrary *processors* (or *filters*) of data have two stream arguments. They read from the first, process the data, and write the results to the second. These processors have no idea of either the source *or* the destination of the data they are processing. Sources and destinations can vary widely: from two memory buffers on the same local computer, to the ELF transmissions to and from a submarine at sea, to the real-time data streams of a NASA probe in deep space.

By decoupling the consuming, processing, or producing of data from the sources and destinations of that data, you can mix and match any combination of them at will as you write your program. In the future, when new, previously nonexistent forms of source or destination (or consumer, processor, or producer) appear, they can be used within the same framework, with no changes to your classes. New stream abstractions, supporting higher levels of interpretation "on top of" the bytes, can be written completely independently of the underlying transport mechanisms for the bytes themselves.

At the pinnacle of this stream framework are the two abstract classes, InputStream and OutputStream. If you turn briefly to the diagram for java.io in Appendix B, you'll see that below these classes is a virtual cornucopia of categorized classes, demonstrating the wide range of streams in the system, but also demonstrating an extremely well-designed hierarchy of relationships between these streams, one well worth learning from. Let's begin with the parents and then work our way down this bushy tree.

Input Streams

All the methods you will explore today are declared to throw IOExceptions. This new subclass of Exception conceptually embodies all the possible I/O errors that might occur while using streams. Several subclasses of it define a few, more specific exceptions that can be thrown as well. For now, it is enough to know that you must either catch an IOException, or be in a method that can "pass it along," to be a well-behaved user of streams.

The *abstract* Class *InputStream*

InputStream is an abstract class that defines the fundamental ways in which a destination consumer reads a stream of bytes from some source. The identity of the source, and the manner of the creation and transport of the bytes, is irrelevant. When using an input stream, you are the destination of those bytes, and that's all you need to know.

read()

The most important method to the consumer of an input stream is the one that reads bytes from the source. This method, read(), comes in many flavors, and each is demonstrated in an example in today's lesson.

Each of these read() methods is defined to "block" (wait) until all the input requested becomes available. Don't worry about this limitation; because of multithreading, you can do as many other things as you like while this one thread is waiting for input. In fact, it is a common idiom to assign a thread to each stream of input (and for each stream of output) that is solely responsible for reading from it (or writing to it). These input threads might then "hand off" the information to other threads for processing. This naturally overlaps the I/O time of your program with its compute time.

Here's the first form of read():

```
InputStream  s      = getAnInputStreamFromSomewhere();
byte[]       buffer = new byte[1024];   // any size will do

if (s.read(buffer) != buffer.length)
    System.out.println("I got less than I expected.");
```

> **Note:** Here, and throughout the rest of today's lesson, assume that either an `import` `java.io` appears before all the examples or that you mentally prefix all references to `java.io` classes with the prefix `java.io`.

This form of `read()` attempts to fill the entire buffer given. If it cannot (usually due to reaching the end of the input stream), it returns the actual number of bytes that were read into the buffer. After that, any further calls to `read()` return `-1`, indicating that you are at the end of the stream. Note that the `if` statement still works even in this case, because `-1 != 1024` (this corresponds to an input stream with no bytes in it all).

> **Note:** Don't forget that, unlike in C, the `-1` case in Java is not used to indicate an error. Any I/O errors `throw` instances of `IOException` (which you're not `catching` yet). You learned on Day 17 that all uses of distinguished values can be replaced by the use of exceptions, and so they should. The `-1` in the last example is a bit of a historical anachronism. You'll soon see a better approach to indicating end of the stream using the class `DataInputStream`.

You can also read into a "slice" of your buffer by specifying the offset into the buffer, and the length desired, as arguments to `read()`:

```
s.read(buffer, 100, 300);
```

This example tries to fill in bytes `100` through `399` and behaves otherwise exactly the same as the previous `read()` method. In fact, in the current release, the default implementation of the former version of `read()` uses the latter:

```
public int  read(byte[]  buffer) throws IOException {
    return  read(buffer, 0, buffer.length);
}
```

Finally, you can read in bytes one at a time:

```
InputStream  s = getAnInputStreamFromSomewhere();
byte         b;
int          byteOrMinus1;

while ((byteOrMinus1 = s.read()) != -1) {
b = (byte) byteOrMinus1;
. . .    // process the byte b
}
. . .    // reached end of stream
```

Note: Because of the nature of integer promotion in Java in general, and because in this case the read() method returns an int, using the byte type in your code may be a little frustrating. You'll find yourself constantly having explicitly to cast the result of arithmetic expressions, or of int return values, back to your size. Because read() really should be returning a byte in this case, I feel justified in declaring and using it as such (despite the pain)—it makes the size of the data being read clearer. In cases wherein you feel the range of a variable is naturally limited to a byte (or a short) rather than an int, please take the time to declare it that way and pay the small price necessary to gain the added clarity. By the way, a lot of the Java class library code simply stores the result of read() in an int. This proves that even the Java team is human—*everyone* makes style mistakes.

skip()

What if you want to skip over some of the bytes in a stream, or start reading a stream from other than its beginning? A method similar to read() does the trick:

```
if (s.skip(1024) != 1024)
    System.out.println("I skipped less than I expected.");
```

This skips over the next 1024 bytes in the input stream. skip() takes and returns a long integer, because streams are not required to be limited to any particular size. The default implementation of skip in this release simply uses read():

```
public long  skip(long n) throws IOException {
    byte[]  buffer = new byte[(int) n];

    return  read(buffer);
}
```

19

Note: This implementation does not support large skips correctly, because its long argument is cast to an int. Subclasses must override this default implementation if they want to handle this more properly. This won't be as easy as you might think, because the current release of the Java system does not allow integer types larger than int to act as array subscripts.

available()

If for some reason you would like to know how many bytes are in the stream right now, you can ask:

```
if (s.available() < 1024)
    System.out.println("Too little is available right now.");
```

This tells you the number of bytes that you can read() without blocking. Because of the abstract nature of the source of these bytes, streams may or may not be able to tell you a reasonable answer to this question. For example, some streams always return 0. Unless you use specific subclasses of InputStream that you know provide a reasonable answer to this question, it's not a good idea to rely upon this method. Remember, multithreading eliminates many of the problems associated with blocking while waiting for a stream to fill again. Thus, one of the strongest rationales for the use of available() goes away.

mark() and *reset()*

Some streams support the notion of marking a position in the stream, and then later resetting the stream to that position to reread the bytes there. Clearly, the stream would have to "remember" all those bytes, so there is a limitation on how far apart in a stream the mark and its subsequent reset can occur. There's also a method that asks whether or not the stream supports the notion of marking at all. Here's an example:

```
InputStream  s = getAnInputStreamFromSomewhere();

if (s.markSupported()) {     // does s support the notion?
    . . .            // read the stream for a while
    s.mark(1024);
    . . .            // read less than 1024 more bytes
    s.reset();
    . . .            // we can now re-read those bytes
} else {
    . . .                    // no, perform some alternative
}
```

When marking a stream, you specify the maximum number of bytes you intend to allow to pass before resetting it. This allows the stream to limit the size of its byte "memory." If this number of bytes goes by and you have not yet reset(), the mark becomes invalid, and attempting to reset() will throw an exception.

Marking and resetting a stream is most valuable when you are attempting to identify the type of the stream (or the next part of the stream), but to do so, you must consume a significant piece of it in the process. Often, this is because you have several black-box parsers that you can hand the stream to, but they will consume some (unknown to you) number of bytes before making up their mind about whether the stream is of their type. Set a large size for the read limit above, and let each parser run until it either throws an error or completes a successful parse. If an error is thrown, reset() and try the next parser.

close()

Because you don't know what resources an open stream represents, nor how to deal with them properly when you're finished reading the stream, you must usually explicitly close down a stream so that it can release these resources. Of course, garbage collection and a finalization method can do this for you, but what if you need to reopen that stream or those resources before they have been freed by this asynchronous process? At best, this is annoying or confusing; at worst, it introduces an unexpected, obscure, and difficult-to-track-down bug. Because you're interacting with the outside world of external resources, it's safer to be explicit about when you're finished using them:

```
InputStream  s = alwaysMakesANewInputStream();

try {
    . . .      // use s to your heart's content
} finally {
    s.close();
}
```

Get used to this idiom (using `finally`); it's a useful way to be sure something (such as closing the stream) always gets done. Of course, you're assuming that the stream is always successfully created. If this is not always the case, and `null` is sometimes returned instead, here's the correct way to be safe:

```
InputStream  s = tryToMakeANewInputStream();

if (s != null) {
    try {
        . . .
    } finally {
        s.close();
    }
}
```

All input streams descend from the `abstract` class `InputStream`. All share in common the few methods described so far. Thus, stream s in the previous examples could have been any of the more complex input streams described in the next few sections.

ByteArrayInputStream

The "inverse" of some of the previous examples would be to create an input stream *from* an array of bytes. This is exactly what `ByteArrayInputStream` does:

```
byte[]  buffer = new byte[1024];

fillWithUsefulData(buffer);

InputStream  s = new ByteArrayInputStream(buffer);
```

Readers of the new stream s see a stream 1024 bytes long, containing the bytes in the array buffer. Just as read() has a form that takes an offset and a length, so does this class's constructor:

```
InputStream  s = new ByteArrayInputStream(buffer, 100, 300);
```

Here, the stream is 300 bytes long and consists of bytes 100-399 from the array buffer.

> **Note:** Finally, you've seen your first examples of the *creation* of a stream. These new streams are attached to the simplest of all possible sources of data, an array of bytes in the memory of the local computer.

ByteArrayInputStreams only implement the standard set of methods that all input streams do. Here, however, the available() method has a particularly simple job—it returns 1024 and 300, respectively, for the two instances of ByteArrayInputStream you created previously, because it knows exactly how many bytes are available. Finally, calling reset() on a ByteArrayInputStream resets it to the beginning of the stream (buffer), no matter where the mark is set.

FileInputStream

One of the most common uses of streams, and historically the earliest, is to attach them to files in the file system. Here, for example, is the creation of such an input stream on a UNIX system:

```
InputStream  s = new FileInputStream("/some/path/and/fileName");
```

> **Caution:** Applets attempting to open, read, or write streams based on files in the file system can cause security violations (depending on the paranoia level set by the user of the browser). Try to create applets that do not depend on files at all, by using servers to hold shared information. If that's impossible, limit your applet's I/O to a single file or directory to which the user can easily assign file access permission. (Stand-alone Java programs have none of these problems, of course.)

You also can create the stream from a previously opened file descriptor:

```
int         fd = openInputFileInTraditionalUNIXWays();
InputStream  s = new FileInputStream(fd);
```

In either case, because it's based on an actual (finite length) file, the input stream created can implement available() precisely and can skip() like a champ (just as ByteArrayInputStream can, by the way). In addition, FileInputStream knows a few more tricks:

```
FileInputStream  aFIS = new FileInputStream("aFileName");

int  myFD = aFIS.getFD();

/* aFIS.finalize(); */  // will call close() when automatically called by GC
```

> ✓ **Tip:** To call the new methods, you must declare the stream variable aFIS to be of
> type FileInputStream, because plain InputStreams don't know about them.

The first is obvious: getFD() returns the file descriptor of the file on which the stream is based.
The second, though, is an interesting shortcut that allows you to create FileInputStreams
without worrying about closing them later. FileInputStream's implementation of finalize(),
a protected method, closes the stream. Unlike in the previous contrived example in comments,
you almost never can nor should call a finalize() method directly. The garbage collector calls
it after noticing that the stream is no longer in use, but before actually destroying the stream.
Thus, you can go merrily along using the stream, never closing it, and all will be well. The system
takes care of closing it (eventually).

You can get away with this because streams based on files tie up very few resources, and these
resources cannot be accidentally reused before garbage collection (these were the things worried
about in the previous discussion of finalization and close()). Of course, if you were also *writing*
to the file, you would have to be more careful. (Reopening the file too soon after writing might
make it appear in an inconsistent state because the finalize()—and thus the close()—
might not have happened yet). Just because you don't *have* to close the stream doesn't mean
you might not want to do so anyway. For clarity, or if you don't know precisely what type of
an InputStream you were handed, you might choose to call close() yourself.

FilterInputStream

This "abstract" class simply provides a "pass-through" for all the standard methods of
InputStream. It holds inside itself another stream, by definition one further "down" the chain
of filters, to which it forwards all method calls. It implements nothing new but allows itself to
be nested:

```
InputStream        s  = getAnInputStreamFromSomewhere();
FilterInputStream  s1 = new FilterInputStream(s);
FilterInputStream  s2 = new FilterInputStream(s1);
FilterInputStream  s3 = new FilterInputStream(s2);

... s3.read() ...
```

Whenever a read is performed on the filtered stream s3, it passes along the request to s2; then s2 does the same to s1, and finally s is asked to provide the bytes. Subclasses of FilterInputStream will, of course, do some nontrivial processing of the bytes as they flow past. The rather verbose form of "chaining" in the previous example can be made more elegant:

```
s3 = new FilterInputStream(new FilterInputStream(new FilterInputStream(s)));
```

You should use this idiom in your code whenever you can. It clearly expresses the nesting of chained filters, and can easily be parsed and "read aloud" by starting at the innermost stream s and reading outward—each filter stream applying to the one within—until you reach the outermost stream s3.

> **Note:** FilterInputStream is called "abstract," rather than abstract, because it is not actually declared to be abstract. This means that, as useless as they are, you can create instances of FilterInputStream directly. The same will hold for its output stream "brother" class, described later today.

Now let's examine each of the subclasses of FilterInputStream in turn.

BufferedInputStream

This is one of the most valuable of all streams. It implements the full complement of InputStream's methods, but it does so by using a buffered array of bytes that acts as a cache for future reading. This decouples the rate and the size of the "chunks" you're reading from the more regular, larger block sizes in which streams are most efficiently read (from, for example, peripheral devices, files in the file system, or the network). It also allows smart streams to read ahead when they expect that you will want more data soon.

Because the buffering of BufferedInputStream is so valuable, and it's also the only class to handle mark() and reset() properly, you might wish that every input stream could somehow share its valuable capabilities. Normally, because those stream classes do not implement them, you would be out of luck. Fortunately, you already saw a way that filter streams can wrap themselves "around" other streams. Suppose that you would like a buffered FileInputStream that can handle marking and resetting correctly. Et voilà:

```
InputStream  s = new BufferedInputStream(new FileInputStream("foo"));
```

You have a buffered input stream based on the file "foo" that can mark() and reset().

Now you can begin to see the power of nesting streams. Any capability provided by a filter input stream (or output stream, as you'll see soon) can be used by any other, basic stream via nesting. Of course, any *combination* of these capabilities, and in any order, can be as easily accomplished by nesting the filter streams themselves.

DataInputStream

All the methods that instances of this class understand are defined in a separate interface, which both `DataInputStream` and `RandomAccessFile` (another class in `java.io`) implement. This interface is general-purpose enough that you might want to use it yourself in the classes you create. It is called `DataInput`.

The *DataInput* Interface

When you begin using streams to any degree, you'll quickly discover that byte streams are not a really helpful format into which to force all data. In particular, the primitive types of the Java language embody a rather nice way of looking at data, but with the streams you've been defining thus far in this book, you could not read data of these types. The DataInput interface specifies a higher-level set of methods that, when used for both reading and writing, can support a more complex, typed stream of data. Here are the set of methods this interface defines:

```
void    readFully(byte[] buffer)                          throws IOException;
void    readFully(byte[] buffer, int offset, int length)  throws IOException;
int     skipBytes(int n)                                   throws IOException;

boolean readBoolean()       throws IOException;
byte    readByte()          throws IOException;
int     readUnsignedByte()  throws IOException;
short   readShort()         throws IOException;
int     readUnsignedShort() throws IOException;
char    readChar()          throws IOException;
int     readInt()           throws IOException;
long    readLong()          throws IOException;
float   readFloat()         throws IOException;
double  readDouble()        throws IOException;

String  readLine()          throws IOException;
String  readUTF()           throws IOException;
```

The first three methods are simply new names for `skip()` and the two forms of `read()` you've seen previously. Each of the next ten methods reads in a primitive type, or its unsigned counterpart (useful for using every bit efficiently in a binary stream). These latter methods must return an integer of a wider size than you might think; because integers are signed in Java, the unsigned value does not fit in anything smaller. The final two methods read a newline (`'\r'`, `'\n'`, or `"\r\n"`) terminated string of characters from the stream—the first in ASCII, and the second in Unicode.

Now that you know what the interface that `DataInputStream` implements looks like, let's see it in action:

```
DataInputStream  s = new DataInputStream(getNumericInputStream());

long  size = s.readLong();    // the number of items in the stream

while (size-- > 0) {
    if (s.readBoolean()) {    // should I process this item?
```

```
int     anInteger     = s.readInt();
int     magicBitFlags = s.readUnsignedShort();
double  aDouble       = s.readDouble();

if ((magicBitFlags & 0100000) != 0) {
    . . .     // high bit set, do something special
}
    . . .     // process anInteger and aDouble
    }
}
```

Because the class implements an interface for all its methods, you can also use the following interface:

```
DataInput  d = new DataInputStream(new FileInputStream("anything"));
String     line;

while ((line = d.readLine()) != null) {
    . . .     // process the line
}
```

The *EOFException*

One final point about most of DataInputStream's methods: when the end of the stream is reached, they throw an EOFException. This is tremendously useful and, in fact, allows you to rewrite all the kludgy uses of -1 you saw earlier today in a much nicer fashion:

```
DataInputStream  s = new DataInputStream(getAnInputStreamFromSomewhere());

try {
    while (true) {
    byte  b = (byte) s.readByte();
    . . .     // process the byte b
    }
} catch (EOFException e) {
    . . .     // reached end of stream
}
```

This works just as well for all but the last two of the read methods of DataInputStream.

> **Caution:** skipBytes() does nothing at all on end of stream, readLine() returns null, and readUTF() might throw a UTFDataFormatException, if it notices the problem at all.

LineNumberInputStream

In an editor or a debugger, line numbering is crucial. To add this valuable capability to your programs, use the filter stream LineNumberInputStream, which keeps track of line numbers as its stream "flows through" it. It's even smart enough to remember a line number and later restore it, during a mark() and reset(). You might use this class as follows:

```
LineNumberInputStream  aLNIS;
aLNIS = new LineNumberInputStream(new FileInputStream("source"));

DataInputStream  s = new DataInputStream(aLNIS);
String           line;

while ((line = s.readLine()) != null) {
    . . .      // process the line
    System.out.println("Did line number: " + aLNIS.getLineNumber());
}
```

Here, two filter streams are nested around the FileInputStream actually providing the data—the first to read lines one at a time and the second to keep track of the line numbers of these lines as they go by. You must explicitly name the intermediate filter stream, aLNIS, because if you did not, you couldn't call getLineNumber() later. Note that if you invert the order of the nested streams, reading from the DataInputStream does not cause the LineNumberInputStream to "see" the lines.

You must put any filter streams acting as "monitors" in the middle of the chain and "pull" the data from the outermost filter stream so that the data will pass through each of the monitors in turn. In the same way, buffering should occur as far inside the chain as possible, because it won't be able to do its job properly unless most of the streams that need buffering come after it in the flow. For example, here's a doubly silly order:

```
new BufferedInputStream(new LineNumberInputStream(
          ➥new DataInputStream(new FileInputStream("foo")));
```

and here's a much better order:

```
new DataInputStream(new LineNumberInputStream(
          ➥new BufferedInputStream(new FileInputStream("foo")));
```

LineNumberInputStreams can also be told to setLineNumber(), for those few times when you know more than they do.

PushbackInputStream

The filter stream class PushbackInputStream is commonly used in parsers, to "push back" a single character in the input (after reading it) while trying to determine what to do next—a simplified version of the mark() and reset() utility you learned about earlier. Its only addition to the standard set of InputStream methods is unread(), which as you might guess, pretends that it never read the byte passed in as its argument, and then gives that byte back as the return value of the next read().

The following is a simple implementation of readLine() using this class:

```
public class  SimpleLineReader {
    private FilterInputStream  s;
```

```
        public  SimpleLineReader(InputStream  anIS) {
            s = new DataInputStream(anIS);
        }

        . . .     // other read() methods using stream s

        public String  readLine() throws IOException {
            char[]  buffer = new char[100];
            int     offset = 0;
            byte    thisByte;

            try {
loop:           while (offset < buffer.length) {
                    switch (thisByte = (byte) s.read()) {
                        case '\n':
                            break loop;
                        case '\r':
                            byte  nextByte = (byte) s.read();

                            if (nextByte != '\n') {
                                if (!(s instanceof PushbackInputStream)) {
                                    s = new PushbackInputStream(s);
                                }
                                ((PushbackInputStream) s).unread(nextByte);
                            }
                            break loop;
                        default:
                            buffer[offset++] = (char) thisByte;
                            break;
                    }
                }
            } catch (EOFException e) {
                if (offset == 0)
                    return null;
            }
            return String.copyValueOf(buffer, 0, offset);
        }
    }
```

This demonstrates numerous things. For the purpose of this example, readLine() is restricted to reading the first 100 characters of the line. In this respect, it demonstrates how *not* to write a general-purpose line processor (you should be able to read any size line). It also reminds you how to break out of an outer loop, and how to produce a String from an array of characters (in this case, from a "slice" of the array of characters). This example also includes standard uses of InputStream's read() for reading bytes one at a time, and of determining the end of the stream by enclosing it in a DataInputStream and catching EOFException.

One of the more unusual aspects of the example is the way PushbackInputStream is used. To be sure that '\n' is ignored following '\r' you have to "look ahead" one character; but if it is not a '\n', you must push back that character. Look at the next two lines as if you didn't know much about the stream s. The general technique used is instructive. First, you see whether s is already an instanceof some kind of PushbackInputStream. If so, you can simply use it. If not, you enclose the current stream (whatever it is) inside a new PushbackInputStream and use this new stream. Now, let's jump back into the context of the example.

The line following wants to call the method unread(). The problem is that s has a "compile-time type" of FilterInputStream, and thus doesn't understand that method. The previous two lines have guaranteed, however, that the *run-time type* of the stream in s is PushbackInputStream, so you can safely cast it to that type and then safely call unread().

> **Note:** This example was done in an unusual way for demonstration purposes. You could have simply declared a PushbackInputStream variable and always enclosed the DataInputStream in it. (Conversely, SimpleLineReader's constructor could have checked whether its argument was already of the right class, the way PushbackInputStream did, before creating a new DataInputStream.) The interesting thing about this approach of "wrapping a class only when needed" is that it works for any InputStream that you hand it, and it does additional work only if it needs to. Both of these are good general design principles.

All the subclasses of FilterInputStream have now been described. It's time to return to the direct subclasses of InputStream.

PipedInputStream

This class, along with its "brother" class PipedOutputStream, are covered later today (they need to be understood and demonstrated together). For now, all you need to know is that together they create a simple, two-way communication conduit between threads.

SequenceInputStream

Suppose you have two separate streams, and you would like to make a composite stream that consists of one stream followed by the other (like appending two Strings together). This is exactly what SequenceInputStream was created for:

```
InputStream  s1 = new FileInputStream("theFirstPart");
InputStream  s2 = new FileInputStream("theRest");

InputStream  s  = new SequenceInputStream(s1, s2);

... s.read() ...    // reads from each stream in turn
```

You could have "faked" this example by reading each file in turn—but what if you had to hand the composite stream s to some other method that was expecting only a single InputStream?

Here's an example (using s) that line-numbers the two previous files with a common numbering scheme:

```
LineNumberInputStream  aLNIS = new LineNumberInputStream(s);

... aLNIS.getLineNumber() ...
```

> **Note:** Stringing together streams this way is especially useful when the streams are of unknown length and origin, and were just handed to you by someone else.

What if you want to string together more than two streams? You could try the following:

```
Vector  v = new Vector();
. . .   // set up all the streams and add each to the Vector
InputStream  s1 = new SequenceInputStream(v.elementAt(0), v.elementAt(1));
InputStream  s2 = new SequenceInputStream(s1, v.elementAt(2));
InputStream  s3 = new SequenceInputStream(s2, v.elementAt(3));
. . .
```

> **Note:** A Vector is a growable array of objects that can be filled, referenced (with elementAt()) and enumerated.

However, it's much easier to use a different constructor that SequenceInputStream provides:

```
InputStream  s  = new SequenceInputStream(v.elements());
```

It takes an enumeration of all the sequences you wish to combine and returns a single stream that reads through the data of each in turn.

StringBufferInputStream

StringBufferInputStream is exactly like ByteArrayInputStream, but instead of being based on a byte array, it's based on an array of characters (a String):

```
String        buffer = "Now is the time for all good men to come...";
InputStream  s       = new StringBufferInputStream(buffer);
```

All comments that were made about ByteArrayInputStream apply here as well. (See the earlier section on that class.)

> **Note:** StringBufferInputStream is a bit of a misnomer, because this input stream is actually based on a String. It should really be called StringInputStream.

Output Streams

Output streams are, in almost every case, paired with a "brother" InputStream that you've already learned. If an InputStream performs a certain operation, the "brother" OutputStream performs the *inverse* operation. You'll see more of what this means soon.

The *abstract* Class *OutputStream*

OutputStream is the abstract class that defines the fundamental ways in which a source (producer) writes a stream of bytes to some destination. The identity of the destination, and the manner of the transport and storage of the bytes, is irrelevant. When using an output stream, *you* are the source of those bytes, and that's all you need to know.

write()

The most important method to the producer of an output stream is the one that writes bytes to the destination. This method, write(), comes in many flavors, each demonstrated in an example below.

19

> **Note:** Every one of these write() methods is defined to "block" (wait) until all the output requested has been written. You don't need to worry about this limitation—see the note under InputStream's read() method if you don't remember why.

```
OutputStream  s      = getAnOutputStreamFromSomewhere();
byte[]        buffer = new byte[1024];    // any size will do

fillInData(buffer);    // the data we want to output
s.write(buffer);
```

You also can write a "slice" of your buffer by specifying the offset into the buffer, and the length desired, as arguments to write():

```
s.write(buffer, 100, 300);
```

This writes out bytes 100 through 399 and behaves otherwise exactly the same as the previous write() method. In fact, in the current release, the default implementation of the former version of write() uses the latter:

```
public void  write(byte[]  buffer) throws IOException {
    write(buffer, 0, buffer.length);
}
```

Finally, you can write out bytes one at a time:

```
while (thereAreMoreBytesToOutput()) {
    byte  b = getNextByteForOutput();

    s.write(b);
}
```

flush()

Because you don't know what an output stream is connected to, you might be required to "flush" your output through some buffered cache to get it to be written (in a timely manner, or at all). OutputStream's version of this method does nothing, but it is expected that subclasses that require flushing (for example, BufferedOutputStream and PrintStream) will override this version to do something nontrivial.

close()

Just like for an InputStream, you should (usually) explicitly close down an OutputStream so that it can release any resources it may have reserved on your behalf. (All the same notes and examples from InputStream's close() method apply here, with the prefix In replaced everywhere by Out.)

All output streams descend from the abstract class OutputStream. All share the previous few methods in common.

ByteArrayOutputStream

The inverse of ByteArrayInputStream, which creates an input stream from an array of bytes, is ByteArrayOutputStream, which directs an output stream *into* an array of bytes:

```
OutputStream  s = new ByteArrayOutputStream();

s.write(123);
. . .
```

The size of the (internal) byte array grows as needed to store a stream of any length. You can provide an initial capacity as an aid to the class, if you like:

```
OutputStream  s = new ByteArrayOutputStream(1024 * 1024);  // 1 Megabyte
```

Note: You've just seen your first examples of the creation of an output stream. These new streams were attached to the simplest of all possible destinations of data, an array of bytes in the memory of the local computer.

Once the `ByteArrayOutputStream`s has been "filled," it can be output to another output stream:

```
OutputStream          anotherOutputStream = getTheOtherOutputStream();
ByteArrayOutputStream  s = new ByteArrayOutputStream();

fillWithUsefulData(s);
s.writeTo(anotherOutputStream);
```

It also can be extracted as a byte array or converted to a `String`:

```
byte[]  buffer            = s.toByteArray();
String  bufferString      = s.toString();
String  bufferUnicodeString = s.toString(upperByteValue);
```

Note: The last method allows you to "fake" Unicode (16-bit) characters by filling in their lower bytes with ASCII and then specifying a common upper byte (usually 0) to create a Unicode `String` result.

`ByteArrayOutputStreams` have two utility methods: one simply returns the current number of bytes stored in the internal byte array, and the other resets the array so that the stream can be rewritten from the beginning:

```
int  sizeOfMyByteArray = s.size();

s.reset();      // s.size() would now return 0
s.write(123);
. . .
```

FileOutputStream

One of the most common uses of streams is to attach them to files in the file system. Here, for example, is the creation of such an output stream on a UNIX system:

```
OutputStream  s = new FileOutputStream("/some/path/and/fileName");
```

Caution: Applets attempting to open, read, or write streams based on files in the file system can cause security violations. See the note under `FileInputStream` for more details.

19

You also can create the stream from a previously opened file descriptor:

```
int          fd = openOutputFileInTraditionalUNIXWays();
OutputStream  s = new FileOutputStream(fd);
```

`FileOutputStream` is the inverse of `FileInputStream`, and it knows the same tricks:

```
FileOutputStream  aFOS = new FileOutputStream("aFileName");

int  myFD = aFOS.getFD();

/* aFOS.finalize(); */  // will call close() when automatically called by GC
```

> **Note:** To call the new methods, you must declare the stream variable `aFOS` to be of type `FileOutputStream`, because plain `OutputStreams` don't know about them.

The first is obvious. `getFD()` simply returns the file descriptor for the file on which the stream is based. The second, commented, contrived call to `finalize()` is there to remind you that you don't have to worry about closing the stream—it is done for you automatically. (See the discussion under `FileInputStream` for more.)

FilterOutputStream

This "abstract" class simply provides a "pass-through" for all the standard methods of `OutputStream`. It holds inside itself another stream, by definition one further "down" the chain of filters, to which it forwards all method calls. It implements nothing new but allows itself to be nested:

```
OutputStream        s = getAnOutputStreamFromSomewhere();
FilterOutputStream  s1 = new FilterOutputStream(s);
FilterOutputStream  s2 = new FilterOutputStream(s1);
FilterOutputStream  s3 = new FilterOutputStream(s2);

... s3.write(123) ...
```

Whenever a write is performed on the filtered stream `s3`, it passes along the request to `s2`. Then `s2` does the same to `s1`, and finally `s` is asked to output the bytes. Subclasses of `FilterOutputStream`, of course, do some nontrivial processing of the bytes as they flow past. This chain can be tightly nested—see its "brother" class, `FilterInputStream` for more.

Now let's examine each of the subclasses of `FilterOutputStream` in turn.

BufferedOutputStream

`BufferedOutputStream` is one of the most valuable of all streams. All it does is implement the full complement of `OutputStream`'s methods, but it does so by using a buffered array of bytes that acts as a cache for writing. This decouples the rate and the size of the "chunks" you're writing from the more regular, larger block sizes in which streams are most efficiently written (to peripheral devices, files in the file system, or the network, for example).

`BufferedOutputStream` is one of two classes in the Java library to implement `flush()`, which pushes the bytes you've written through the buffer and out the other side. Because buffering is so valuable, you might wish that every output stream could somehow be buffered. Fortunately, you can surround any output stream in such a way as to achieve just that:

```
OutputStream  s = new BufferedOutputStream(new FileOutputStream("foo"));
```

You now have a buffered output stream based on the file "foo" that can be `flush()`ed.

Just as for filter input streams, any capability provided by a filter output stream can be used by any other basic stream via nesting and any combination of these capabilities, in any order, can be as easily accomplished by nesting the filter streams themselves.

DataOutputStream

All the methods that instances of this class understand are defined in a separate interface, which both `DataOutputStream` and `RandomAccessFile` implement. This interface is general-purpose enough that you might want use it yourself in the classes you create. It is called `DataOutput`.

The *DataOutput* Interface

In cooperation with its "brother" inverse interface, `DataInput`, `DataOutput` provides a higher-level, typed-stream approach to the reading and writing of data. Rather than dealing with bytes, this interface deals with writing the primitive types of the Java language directly:

```
void   write(int i)                                 throws IOException;
void   write(byte[]  buffer)                         throws IOException;
void   write(byte[]  buffer, int  offset, int  length) throws IOException;

void   writeBoolean(boolean b) throws IOException;
void   writeByte(int i)        throws IOException;
void   writeShort(int i)       throws IOException;
void   writeChar(int i)        throws IOException;
void   writeInt(int i)         throws IOException;
void   writeLong(long l)       throws IOException;
void   writeFloat(float f)     throws IOException;
void   writeDouble(double d)   throws IOException;

void   writeBytes(String s) throws IOException;
void   writeChars(String s) throws IOException;
void   writeUTF(String s)   throws IOException;
```

Most of these methods have counterparts in the interface `DataInput`.

The first three methods mirror the three forms of `write()` you saw previously. Each of the next eight methods write out a primitive type. The final three methods write out a string of bytes or characters to the stream: the first one as 8-bit bytes; the second, as 16-bit Unicode characters; and the last, as a special Unicode stream (readable by DataInput's `readUTF()`).

> **Note:** The unsigned read methods in `DataInput` have no counterparts here. You can write out the data they need via `DataOutput`'s signed methods because they accept `int` arguments and also because they write out the correct number of bits for the unsigned integer of a given size as a side effect of writing out the signed integer of that same size. It is the method that reads this integer that must interpret the sign bit correctly; the writer's job is easy.

Now that you know what the interface that `DataOutputStream` implements looks like, let's see it in action:

```
DataOutputStream  s   = new DataOutputStream(getNumericOutputStream());
long              size = getNumberOfItemsInNumericStream();

s.writeLong(size);

for (int  i = 0;  i < size;  ++i) {
    if (shouldProcessNumber(i)) {
        s.writeBoolean(true);      // should process this item
        s.writeInt(theIntegerForItemNumber(i));
        s.writeShort(theMagicBitFlagsForItemNumber(i));
        s.writeDouble(theDoubleForItemNumber(i));
    } else
        s.writeBoolean(false);
}
```

This is the exact inverse of the example that was given for `DataInput`. Together, they form a pair that can communicate a particular array of structured primitive types across any stream (or "transport layer"). Use this pair as a jumping-off point whenever you need to do something similar.

In addition to the interface above, the class itself implements one (self-explanatory) utility method:

```
int  theNumberOfBytesWrittenSoFar = s.size();
```

Processing a File

One of the most common idioms in file I/O is to open a file, read and process it line-by-line, and output it again to another file. Here's a prototypical example of how that would be done in Java:

```
DataInput   aDI = new DataInputStream(new FileInputStream("source"));
DataOutput  aDO = new DataOutputStream(new FileOutputStream("dest"));
String      line;
```

```
while ((line = aDI.readLine()) != null) {
    StringBuffer  modifiedLine = new StringBuffer(line);

    . . .       // process modifiedLine in place
    aDO.writeBytes(modifiedLine.toString());
}
aDI.close();
aDO.close();
```

If you want to process it byte-by-byte, use this:

```
try {
    while (true) {
        byte  b = (byte) aDI.readByte();

        . . .        // process b in place
        aDO.writeByte(b);
    }
} finally {
    aDI.close();
    aDO.close();
}
```

Here's a cute two-liner that just copies the file:

```
try { while (true) aDO.writeByte(aDI.readByte()); }
finally { aDI.close(); aDO.close(); }
```

Caution: Many of the examples in today's lesson (and the last two) assume that they appear inside a method that has `IOException` in its `throws` clause, so they don't have to "worry" about `catching` those exceptions and handling them more reasonably. Your code should be a little less cavalier.

PrintStream

You may not realize it, but you're already intimately familiar with the use of two methods of the `PrintStream` class. That's because whenever you use these method calls:

```
System.out.print(. . .)
System.out.println(. . .)
```

you are actually using a `PrintStream` instance located in the `System`'s class variable `out` to perform the output. `System.err` is also a `PrintStream`, and `System.in` is an `InputStream`.

Note: On UNIX systems, these three streams will be attached to standard output, standard error, and standard input.

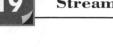

PrintStream is uniquely an output stream class (it has no "brother"). Because it is usually attached to a screen output device of some kind, it provides an implementation of flush(). It also provides the familiar close() and write() methods, as well as a plethora of choices for outputting the primitive types and Strings of Java:

```
public void  write(int b);
public void  write(byte[]  buffer, int  offset, int  length);
public void  flush();
public void  close();

public void  print(Object o);
public void  print(String s);
public void  print(char[]  buffer);
public void  print(char c);
public void  print(int i);
public void  print(long l);
public void  print(float f);
public void  print(double d);
public void  print(boolean b);

public void  println(Object o);
public void  println(String s);
public void  println(char[]  buffer);
public void  println(char c);
public void  println(int i);
public void  println(long l);
public void  println(float f);
public void  println(double d);
public void  println(boolean b);

public void  println();   // output a blank line
```

PrintStream can also be wrapped around any output stream, just like a filter class:

```
PrintStream  s = PrintStream(new FileOutputStream("foo"));

s.println("Here's the first line of text in the file foo.");
```

If you provide a second argument to the constructor for PrintStream, it is a boolean that specifies whether the stream should auto-flush. If true, a flush() is sent after each character is written (or for the three-argument form of write(), after a whole group of characters has been written.)

Here's a simple example program that operates like the UNIX command cat, taking the standard input, line-by-line, and outputting it to the standard output:

```
import java.io.*;   // the one time in the chapter we'll say this

public class  Cat {
    public static void  main(String args[]) {
        DataInput  d = new DataInputStream(System.in);
        String     line;

        try { while ((line = d.readLine()) != null)
            System.out.println(line);
```

```
            } catch (IOException  ignored) { }
    }
}
```

PipedOutputStream

Along with `PipedInputStream`, this pair of classes supports a UNIX-pipe-like connection between two threads, implementing all the careful synchronization that allows this sort of "shared queue" to operate safely. To set up the connection:

```
PipedInputStream    sIn  = PipedInputStream();
PipedOutputStream   sOut = PipedOutputStream(sIn);
```

One thread writes to `sOut`, and the other reads from `sIn`. By setting up two such pairs, the threads can communicate safely in both directions.

Related Classes

The other classes and interfaces in `java.io` supplement the streams to provide a complete I/O system.

The `File` class abstracts "file" in a platform-independent way. Given a filename, it can respond to queries about the type, status, and properties of a file or directory in the file system.

A `RandomAccessFile` is created given a file, a filename, or a file descriptor. It combines in one class implementations of the `DataInput` and `DataOutput` interfaces, both tuned for "random access" to a file in the file system. In addition to these interfaces, `RandomAccessFile` provides certain traditional UNIX-like facilities, such as `seek()`ing to a random point in the file.

Finally, the `StreamTokenizer` class takes an input stream and produces a sequence of tokens. By overriding its various methods in your own subclasses, you can create powerful lexical parsers.

You can learn more about any and all of these classes from the full (online) API descriptions in your Java release.

19

Summary

Today, you learned about the general idea of streams and met input streams based on byte arrays, files, pipes, sequences of other streams, and string buffers, as well as input filters for buffering, typing data, line numbering, and pushing-back characters.

You also met the analogous "brother" output streams for byte arrays, files, and pipes, and output filters for buffering and typing data, and the unique output filter used for printing.

Along the way, you became familiar with the fundamental methods all streams understand (such as read() and write()), as well as the unique methods many streams add to this repertoire. You learned about catching IOExceptions—especially the most useful of them, EOFException.

Finally, the twice-useful DataInput and DataOutput interfaces formed the heart of RandomAccessFile, one of the several utility classes that round out Java's I/O facilities.

Java streams provide a powerful base on which you can build multithreaded, streaming interfaces of the most complex kinds, and the programs (such as HotJava) to interpret them. The higher-level Internet protocols and services of the future that your applets can build upon this base are really limited only by your imagination.

Q&A

Q **In an early read() example, you did something with the variable byteOrMinus1 that seemed a little clumsy. Isn't there a better way? If not, why recommend the cast later?**

A Yes, there is something a little odd about those statements. You might be tempted to try something like this instead:

```
while ((b = (byte) s.read()) != -1) {
. . .    // process the byte b
}
```

The problem with this short-cut occurs when read() returns the value 0xFF (0377). Since this value is signed-extended before the test gets executed, it will appear to be identical to the integer value -1 that indicates end of stream. Only saving that value in a separate integer variable, and then casting it later, will accomplish the desired result. The cast to byte is recommended in the note for orthogonal reasons—storing integer values in correctly sized variables is always good style (and besides, read() really should be returning something of byte size here and throwing an exception for end of stream).

Q **What input streams in java.io actually implement mark(), reset(), and markSupported()?**

A InputStream itself does—and in their default implementations, markSupported() returns false, mark() does nothing, and reset() throws an exception. The only input stream in the current release that correctly supports marking is BufferedInputStream, which overrides these defaults. LineNumberInputStream actually implements mark() and reset(), but in the current release, it doesn't answer markSupported() correctly, so it looks as if it does not.

Q Why is `available()` useful, if it sometimes gives the wrong answer?

A First, for many streams, it gives the right answer. Second, for some network streams, its implementation might be sending a special query to discover some information you couldn't get any other way (for example, the size of a file being transferred by `ftp`). If you were displaying a "progress bar" for network or file transfers, for example, `available()` would often give you the total size of the transfer, and if it did not—usually by returning `0`—it would be obvious to you (and your users).

Q What's a good example use of the `DataInput`/`DataOutput` pair of interfaces?

A One common use of such a pair is when objects want to "pickle" themselves for storage or movement over a network. Each object implements read and write methods using these interfaces, effectively converting itself to a stream that can later be reconstituted "on the other end" into a copy of the original object.

19

Native Methods
and Libraries

by Charles L. Perkins

Today, you'll learn all the reasons you might (or might not) want to write `native` methods in Java, about all of Java's built-in optimizations, and about the tricks you can use to make your programs faster. You'll also learn the procedure for creating, making headers and stubs for, and linking `native` methods into a dynamically loadable library.

Let's begin, however, with the reasons that you might want to implement `native` methods in the first place.

There are only two reasons that you might need to declare some of your methods `native`, that is, implemented by a language other than Java.

The first, and by far the best reason to do so, is because you need to utilize a special capability of your computer or operating system that the Java class library does not already provide for you. Such capabilities include interfacing to new peripheral devices or plug-in cards, accessing a different type of networking, or using a unique, but valuable feature of your particular operating system. Two more concrete examples are acquiring real-time audio input from a microphone or using 3D "accelerator" hardware in a 3D library. Neither of these is provided to you by the current Java environment, so you must implement them outside Java, in some other language (currently C or any language that can link with C).

The second, and often illusory reason to implement `native` methods, is speed—illusory, because you rarely need the raw speeds gained by this approach. It's even more rare to not be able to gain that speed-up in other ways (as you'll see later today). Using `native` methods in this case takes advantage of the fact that, at present, the Java release does not perform as well as, for example, an optimized C program on many tasks. For those tasks, you can write the "needs to be fast" part (critical, inner loops, for example) in C, and still use a larger Java shell of classes to hide this "trick" from your users. In fact, the Java class library uses this approach for certain critical system classes to raise the overall level of efficiency in the system. As a user of the Java environment, you don't even know (or see) any results of this (except, perhaps, a few classes or methods that are `final` that might not be otherwise).

Disadvantages of *native* Methods

Once you decide you'd like to, or must, use `native` methods in your program, this choice costs you dearly. Although you gain the advantages mentioned earlier, you lose the portability of your Java code.

Before, you had a program (or applet) that could travel to any Java environment in the world, now and forever. Any new architectures created—or new operating systems written—were irrelevant to your code. All it required was that the (tiny) Java Virtual Machine (or a browser that had one inside it) be available, and it could run anywhere, anytime—now and in the future.

Now, however, you've created a library of native code that must be linked with your program to make it work properly. The first thing you lose is the ability to "travel" as an applet; you simply can't be one! No Java-aware browser currently in existence allows native code to be loaded with an applet, for security reasons (and these are good reasons). The Java team has struggled to place as much as possible into the java packages because they are the only environment you can *count* on as an applet. (The sun packages, shipped primarily for use with stand-alone Java programs, are not always available to applets.)

> **Note:** Actually, any classes that anyone writes *without* native code should be able to be loaded with an applet, as long as they depend only on the java packages. Unfortunately, many of the sun packages contain classes that *must* use native code to provide crucial, missing functionality from the java packages. All these missing pieces, and some additional multimedia and sound capabilities, will be added to the java packages in the future. (This has been informally promised in discussions I've had with the Java team.)

Losing the ability to travel anywhere across the Net, into any browser written now or in the future, is bad enough. What's worse, now that you can't be an applet, you have further limited yourself to only those machines that have had the Java Virtual Machine ported to their operating system. (Applets automatically benefit from the wide number of machines and operating systems that *any* Java-aware browser is ported to, but now you do not.)

Even worse, you have assumed something about that machine and operating system by the implementation of your native methods. This often means that you have to write different *source* code for some (or all) of the machines and operating systems on which you want to be able to run. You're already forced, by using native methods, to produce a separate binary library for every machine and operating system pair in the world (or at least, wherever you plan to run), and you must continue to do so forever. If changing the source is also necessary, you can see that this is not a pleasant situation for you and your Java program.

20

The Illusion of Required Efficiency

If, even after the previous discussion, you *must* use native methods anyway, there's help for you later in today's lesson—but what if you're still thinking you need to use them for efficiency reasons?

You are in a grand tradition of programmers throughout the (relatively few) ages of computing. It is exciting, and intellectually challenging, to program with constraints. If you believe efficiency is always required, it makes your job a little more interesting—you get to consider all sorts of baroque ways to accomplish tasks, because it is the efficient way to do it. I myself was caught up in this euphoria of creativity when I first began programming, but it is creativity misapplied.

When you design your program, all that energy and creativity should be directed at the design of a tight, concise, minimal set of classes and methods that are maximally general, abstract, and reusable. (If you think that is easy, look around for a few years and see how bad most software is.) If you spend most of your programming time on thinking and rethinking these fundamental goals and how to achieve them, you are preparing for the future. A future where software is assembled as needed from small components swimming in a sea of network facilities, and anyone can write a component seen by millions (and reused in their programs) in minutes. If, instead, you spend your energy worrying about the speed your software will run right now on some computer, you will be irrelevant after the 18 to 36 months it will take hardware to be fast enough to hide that minor inefficiency in your program.

Am I saying that you should ignore efficiency altogether? Of course not! Some of the great algorithms of computer science deal with solving hard or "impossible" problems in reasonable amounts of time—and writing your programs carelessly can lead to remarkably slow results. This, however, can as easily lead to incorrect, fragile, or nonreusable results. If you achieve all those other goals first, the resulting software will be clean, will naturally reflect the structure of the problem you're trying to solve, and thus will be amenable to "speeding up" later.

> **Note:** There are always cases where you *must* be fanatical about efficiency in many parts of a set of classes. The Java class library itself is such a case, as is anything that must run in real-time for some critical real-world application (such as flying a plane). Such applications are rare, however.
>
> When speaking of a new kind of programming that must soon emerge, Bill Joy, a founder at Sun, likes to invoke the four S's of Java: small, simple, safe, and secure. The "feel" of the Java language itself encourages the pursuit of clarity and the reduction of complexity. The intense pursuit of efficiency, which increases complexity and reduces clarity, is antithetical to these goals.

Once you build a solid foundation, debug your classes, and your program (or applet) works as you'd like it to, *then* it's time to begin optimizing it. If it's just a user interface applet, you may need to do nothing at all. The user is very slow compared to modern computers (and getting relatively slower every 18 months). The odds are that your applet is already fast enough—but suppose it isn't.

Built-In Optimizations

Your next job is to see whether your release supports turning on the "just-in-time" compiler, or using the java2c tool.

The first of these is an experimental technology that, while a method's bytecodes are running in the Java Virtual Machine, translates each bytecode into the native binary code equivalent for the local computer, and then keeps this native code around as a cache for the next time that method is run. This trick is completely transparent to the Java code you write. You need know nothing about whether or not it's being done—your code can still "travel" anywhere, anytime. On any system with "just-in-time" technology in place, however, it runs a lot faster. Experience with experimental versions of this technology shows that, after paying a small cost the first time a method is run, this technique can reach the speed of compiled C code.

> **Note:** More details on this technique, and the java2c tool, will be presented tomorrow. As of the beta release, neither of these tools are in the Java environment, but both are expected in the final release.

The java2c translator takes a whole .class file full of the bytecodes for a class and translates them (all at once) into a portable C source code version. This version can then be compiled by a traditional C compiler on your computer to produce a native-method-like cached library of fast code. This large cache of native code will be used whenever the class's methods are called, but only on the local computer. Your original Java code can still travel as bytecodes and run on any other computer system. If the virtual machine automatically takes these steps whenever it makes sense for a given class, this can be as transparent as the "just-in-time" technology. Experience with an experimental version of this tool shows that fully optimized C performance is achievable. (This is the best anyone can hope to do!)

So you see, even without taking any further steps to optimize your program, you may discover that for your release of Java (or for releases elsewhere or coming in the near future), your code is already fast enough. If it is not, remember that the world craves speed. Java will only get faster, the tools will only get better. Your code is the only permanent thing in this new world—it should be the best you can make it, with no compromises.

Simple Optimization Tricks

Suppose that these technologies aren't available or don't optimize your program far enough for your taste. You can profile your applet or program as it runs, to see in which methods it spends the most time. Once you know this crucial information, you can begin to make *targeted* changes to your classes.

> ✓ **Tip:** Use `java -prof ...` to produce this profile information. In an early release (and, presumably, the final release) the `javaprof` tool can "pretty-print" this information in a more readable format. (`javaprof` is not in the beta release—but try the latest Java release's documentation for details.)
>
> Before you begin making optimizations, you also may want to save a copy of your "clean" classes. As soon as computer speeds allow it (or a major rewrite necessitates it), you can revert to these classes, which embody the "best" implementation of your program.

First, identify the crucial few methods that take most of the time (there are almost always just a few, and often just one, that take up the majority of your program's time). If they contain loops, examine the inner loops to see whether they: call methods that can be made `final`, call a group of methods that can be collapsed into a single method, or create objects that can be reused rather than created anew each loop.

If you notice that a long chain of, for example, four or more method calls is needed to reach a destination method's code, *and* this execution path is in one of the critical sections of the program, you can "short-circuit" directly to that destination method in the topmost method. This may require adding a new instance variable to reference the object for that method call directly. This quite often violates layering or encapsulation constraints. This violation, and any added complexity, is the price you pay for efficiency.

If, after all these tricks (and the numerous others you should try that have been collected over the years into various programming books), your Java code is still just too slow, you will have to use `native` methods after all.

Writing *native* Methods

For whatever reasons, you've decided to add `native` methods to your program. You've already decided which methods need to be `native`, and in which classes, and you're rarin' to go.

First, on the Java side, all you do is delete the method bodies (all the code between the brackets { and } and the brackets themselves) of each method you picked and replace them with a single semicolon (;). Then add the modifier `native` to the method's existing modifiers. Finally, add a `static` (class) initializer to each class that now contains `native` methods to load the native code library you're about to build. (You can pick any name you like for this library—details follow.) You're done!

That's all you need to do in Java to specify a `native` method. Subclasses of any class containing your new `native` methods can still override them, and these new methods are called for instances of the new subclasses (just as you'd expect).

Unfortunately, what needs to be done in your native language environment is not so simple.

> **Note:** The following discussion assumes that C and UNIX are your language and environment. This means that some of the steps may differ slightly on your actual system, but such differences will be outlined in the notes surrounding the native method documentation in your release (in the document called Implementing Native Methods in the alpha, but folded into the programmer's tutorial in the beta). The following discussion is purposely parallel to this documentation.

The Example Class

Imagine a version of the Java environment that does not provide file I/O. Any Java program needing to use the file system would first have to write `native` methods to get access to the operating system primitives needed to do file I/O.

This example combines simplified versions of two actual Java library classes, `java.io.File` and `java.io.RandomAccessFile`, into a single new class, `SimpleFile`:

```
public class  SimpleFile {
    public static final char     separatorChar = '>';
    protected           String  path;
    protected           int     fd;

    public  SimpleFile(String s) {
        path = s;
    }

    public String  getFileName() {
        int  index = path.lastIndexOf(separatorChar);

        return (index < 0) ? path : path.substring(index + 1);
    }

    public String  getPath() {
        return path;
    }

    public native boolean  open();
    public native void     close();
    public native int      read(byte[]  buffer, int  length);
    public native int      write(byte[]  buffer, int  length);
```

20

```
    static {
        System.loadLibrary("simple");   // runs when class first loaded
    }
}
```

Note: The unusual separatorChar ('>') is used simply to demonstrate what an implementation might look like on some strange computer whose file system didn't use any of the more common path separator conventions. Early Xerox computers used '>' as a separator, and several existing computer systems still use strange separators today, so this is not all that farfetched.

SimpleFiles can be created and used by other methods in the usual way:

```
SimpleFile  f = new SimpleFile(">some>path>and>fileName");

f.open();
f.read(...);
f.write(...);
f.close();
```

The first thing you notice about SimpleFile's implementation is how unremarkable the first two-thirds of its Java code is! It looks just like any other class, with a class and an instance variable, a constructor, and two normal method implementations. Then there are four native method declarations. You'll recognize these, from previous discussions, as being just a normal method declaration with the code block replaced by a semicolon and the modifier native added. These are the methods you have to implement in C code later.

Finally, there is a somewhat mysterious code fragment at the very end of the class. You should recognize the general construct here as a static initializer. Any code between the brackets { and } is executed exactly once, when the class is first loaded into the system. You take advantage of that fact to run something you want to run only once—the loading of the native code library you'll create later today. This ties together the loading of the class itself with the loading of its native code. If either fails for some reason, the other fails as well, guaranteeing that no "half-set-up" version of the class can ever be created.

Generating Header and Stub Files

In order to get your hands on Java objects and data types, and to be able to manipulate them in your C code, you need to include some special .h files. Most of these will be located in your release directory under the subdirectory called include. (In particular, look at native.h in that directory, and all the headers it points to, if you're a glutton for detail punishment.)

Some of the special forms you need must be tailored to fit your class's methods precisely. That's where the javah tool comes in.

Using *javah*

To generate the headers you need for your native methods, first compile SimpleFile with javac, just as you normally would. This produces a file named SimpleFile.class. This file must be fed to the javah tool, which then generates the header file you need (SimpleFile.h).

> **Tip:** If the class handed to javah is inside a package, it prepends the package name to the header file name (and to the structure names it generates inside that file), after replacing all the dots (.) with underscores (_) in the package's full name. Thus, if SimpleFile is contained in a hypothetical package called acme.widgets.files, javah generates a header file named acme_widgets_files_SimpleFile.h, and the various names within are renamed in a similar manner.
>
> When running javah, you should pass it only the class name itself, and not the filename, which has .class on the end.

The Header File

Here's the output of javah SimpleFile:

```
/* DO NOT EDIT THIS FILE - it is machine generated */
#include <native.h>
/* Header for class SimpleFile */

#ifndef _Included_SimpleFile
#define _Included_SimpleFile
struct Hjava_lang_String;

typedef struct ClassSimpleFile {
#define SimpleFile_separatorChar 62L
struct Hjava_lang_String *path;
long fd;
} ClassSimpleFile;
HandleTo(SimpleFile);

extern /*boolean*/ long SimpleFile_open(struct HSimpleFile *);
extern void SimpleFile_close(struct HSimpleFile *);
extern long SimpleFile_read(struct HSimpleFile *,HArrayOfByte *,long);
extern long SimpleFile_write(struct HSimpleFile *,HArrayOfByte *,long); #endif
```

> **Note:** `HandleTo()` is a "magic" macro that uses the structures created at run-time by the stubs you'll generate later today.

The members of the `struct` generated above are in a one-to-one correspondence with the variables of your class.

In order to "massage" an instance of your class gently into the land of C, use the macro `unhand()` (as in "unhand that Object!"). For example, the `this` pseudo-variable in Java appears as a `struct` `HSimpleFile *` in the land of C, and to use any variables inside this instance (you), you must `unhand()` yourself first. You'll see some examples of this in a later section today.

Using *javah -stubs*

To "run interference" between the Java world of Objects, arrays, and other high-level constructs and the lower-level world of C, you need stubs.

NEW TERM *Stubs* are pieces of "glue" code that automatically translate arguments and return values back and forth between the worlds of Java and C.

Stubs can be automatically generated by `javah`, just like the headers. There isn't much you need to know about the stubs file, just that it has to be compiled and linked with the C code you write to allow it to interface with Java properly. A stubs file (SimpleFile.c) is created by running `javah` on your class by using the option `-stubs`.

> **Note:** One interesting side-effect of stub generation is the creation of *method signatures*, informally called method descriptions elsewhere. These signatures are quite useful—they can be passed to special C functions that allow you to call back into the Java world from C. You can use stub generation to learn what these signatures look like for different method arguments and return values, and then use that knowledge to call arbitrary Java methods from within your C code. (Brief descriptions of these special C functions, along with further details, appear later today.)

The Stubs File

Here's the result of running `javah -stubs SimpleFile`:

```
/* DO NOT EDIT THIS FILE - it is machine generated */
#include <StubPreamble.h>
```

```
/* Stubs for class SimpleFile */
/* SYMBOL: "SimpleFile/open()Z", Java_SimpleFile_open_stub */
stack_item *Java_SimpleFile_open_stub(stack_item *_P_,struct execenv *_EE_) {
    extern long SimpleFile_open(void *);
    _P_[0].i = SimpleFile_open(_P_[0].p);
return _P_ + 1;
}
/* SYMBOL: "SimpleFile/close()V", Java_SimpleFile_close_stub */
stack_item *Java_SimpleFile_close_stub(stack_item *_P_,struct execenv *_EE_) {
    extern void SimpleFile_close(void *);
    (void) SimpleFile_close(_P_[0].p);
    return _P_;
}
/* SYMBOL: "SimpleFile/read([BI)I", Java_SimpleFile_read_stub */
stack_item *Java_SimpleFile_read_stub(stack_item *_P_,struct execenv *_EE_) {
    extern long SimpleFile_read(void *,void *,long);
    _P_[0].i = SimpleFile_read(_P_[0].p,((_P_[1].p)),((_P_[2].i)));
    return _P_ + 1;
}
/* SYMBOL: "SimpleFile/write([BI)I", Java_SimpleFile_write_stub */
stack_item *Java_SimpleFile_write_stub(stack_item *_P_,struct execenv *_EE_) {
    extern long SimpleFile_write(void *,void *,long);
    _P_[0].i = SimpleFile_write(_P_[0].p,((_P_[1].p)),(( P_[2].i)));
    return _P_ + 1;
}
```

Each comment line contains the method signature for one of the four native methods you're implementing. You can use one of these signatures to call into Java and run, for example, a subclass's overriding implementation of one of your native methods. More often, you'd learn and use a signature to call some useful Java method from within C to get something done in the Java world.

You do this by calling a special C function in the Java run-time called `execute_java_dynamic_method()`. Its arguments include the target object of the method call and the method's signature. The general form of a fully qualified method signature is any/package/ name/ClassName/methodName(...)X. (You can see several in the last example, where SimpleFile is the class name and there is no package name.) The X is a letter (or string) that represents the return type, and the ... contains a string that represents each of the argument's types in turn. Here are the letters (and strings) used, and the types they represent, in the example: [T is array of type T, B is byte, I is int, V is void, and Z is boolean.

The method close(), which takes no arguments and returns void, is represented by the string "SimpleFile/close()V" and its inverse, open(), that returns a boolean instead, is represented by "SimpleFile/open()Z." Finally, read(), which takes an array of bytes and an int as its two arguments and returns an int, is "SimpleFile/read([BI)I." (See the "Method Signatures" section in tomorrow's lesson for the full details.)

Creating SimpleFileNative.c

Now you can, at last, write the C code for your Java native methods.

The header file generated by javah, SimpleFile.h, gives you the prototypes of the four C functions you need to implement to make your native code complete. You then write some C code that provides the native facilities that your Java class needs (in this case, some low-level file I/O routines). Finally, you assemble all the C code into a new file, include a bunch of required (or useful) .h files, and name it SimpleFileNative.c. Here's the result:

```c
#include "SimpleFile.h"       /* for unhand(), among other things */

#include <sys/param.h>        /* for MAXPATHLEN */
#include <fcntl.h>            /* for O_RDWR and O_CREAT */

#define LOCAL_PATH_SEPARATOR  '/'    /* UNIX */

static void  fixSeparators(char *p) {
    for (; *p != '\0'; ++p)
            if (*p == SimpleFile_separatorChar)
                    *p = LOCAL_PATH_SEPARATOR;
}

long  SimpleFile_open(struct HSimpleFile  *this) {
    int    fd;
    char  buffer[MAXPATHLEN];

    javaString2CString(unhand(this)->path, buffer, sizeof(buffer));
    fixSeparators(buffer);
    if ((fd = open(buffer, O_RDWR | O_CREAT, 0664)) < 0)     /* UNIX open */
            return(FALSE); /* or, SignalError() could throw an exception */
    unhand(this)->fd = fd;           /* save fd in the Java world */
    return(TRUE);
}

void  SimpleFile_close(struct HSimpleFile  *this) {
    close(unhand(this)->fd);
    unhand(this)->fd = -1;
}

long  SimpleFile_read(struct HSimpleFile  *this, HArrayOfByte  *buffer,
                                                    ➡ long  count) {
    char  *data    = unhand(buffer)->body;  /* get array data   */
    int    len     = obj_length(buffer);    /* get array length */
    int    numBytes = (len < count ? len : count);

    if ((numBytes = read(unhand(this)->fd, data, numBytes)) == 0)
            return(-1);
    return(numBytes);          /* the number of bytes actually read */
}
```

```
long  SimpleFile_write(struct HSimpleFile  *this, HArrayOfByte  *buffer,
                                                  ➥ long   count) {
    char  *data = unhand(buffer)->body;
    int   len  = obj_length(buffer);

    return(write(unhand(this)->fd, data, (len < count ? len : count)));
}
```

Once you finish writing your .c file, compile it by using your local C compiler (usually called cc or gcc). On some systems, you may need to specify special compilation flags that mean "make it relocatable and dynamically linkable."

Note: If you don't have a C compiler on your computer, you can always buy one. You also could get a copy of the GNU C compiler (gcc), one of the best C compilers in the world, which runs on almost every machine and operating system on the planet. The best way to get gcc is to buy the "GNU release" on CD-ROM, the profits of which go to support the Free Software Foundation. You can find both the GNU CD-ROM and the Linux CD-ROM (which includes GNU) in select places that sell software or technical books, or you can contact the F.S.F. directly. The GNU CD-ROM is a bit pricey, and, though the Linux CD-ROM is very inexpensive, if you can't afford either, or want the latest version and already own a CD-ROM, you can download the gzip file ftp://prep.ai.mit.edu/pub/gnu/gcc-2.7.0.tar.gz, which contains all 7M of the latest gcc release. (If you'd like to make a donation to, or buy gcc or its manual from, the F.S.F., you can e-mail them at gnu@prep.ai.mit.edu or call 617.542.5942.)

Some Useful Functions

When writing the C code for native implementations, a whole set of useful (internal) macros and functions are available for accessing Java run-time structures. (Several of them were used in SimpleFileNative.c.)

Let's take a brief digression to understand some of them a little better.

Warning: Don't rely on the exact form given for any of the following macros and functions. Because they're all internal to the Java run-time, they're subject to change at any moment. Check to see what the latest versions of them look like in your Java release before using them.

20

> **Note:** The following brief descriptions are taken from an alpha release of Java, because descriptions of them for the beta release were not available as of this writing. How Java data types map into C types, and vice versa, is detailed in the documentation there. Refer to it for more details on that or on any of the sparsely documented items below. (Many are listed just to give you a taste of the capabilities of the available functions.)

The following example:

```
Object  *unhand(Handle *)
int     obj_length(HArray *)
```

returns a pointer to the data portion of an object and returns the length of an array. The actual pointer type returned is not always `Object *`, but varies, depending on the type of `Handle` (or `HArray`).

This example:

```
ClassClass    *FindClass(struct execenv *e, char *name, bool_t  resolve)
HArrayOfChar  *MakeString(char *string, long  length)
Handle        *ArrayAlloc(int  type, int  length)
```

finds a class (given its `name`), makes an array of characters of length `length` and allocates an array of the given `length` and `type`.

Use the function:

```
long  execute_java_dynamic_method(ExecEnv *e, HObject *obj, char *method_name,
                                             ↪char *signature, ...);
```

to call a Java method from C. `e` is `NULL` to use the current environment. The target of the method call is `obj`. The method `method_name` has the given method `signature`. It can have any number of arguments and returns a 32-bit value (`int`, `Handle *`, or any 32-bit C type).

Use the following:

```
HObject *execute_java_constructor(ExecEnv *e, char *classname, ClassClass *c,
                                             ↪char *signature, ...);

long  execute_java_static_method(ExecEnv *e, ClassClass *c, char *method_name,
                                             ↪char *signature, ...);
```

to call a Java constructor from C and call a class method from C. `c` is the target class; the rest are as in `executemethod()`.

Calling this:

```
SignalError(0, JAVAPKG "ExceptionClassName", "message");
```

posts a Java exception that will be thrown when your native method returns. It is somewhat like the Java code:

```
throw new ExceptionClassName("message");
```

Finally, here are some useful string conversion functions:

```
void  javaStringPrint(Hjava_lang_String *s)
int   javaStringLength(Hjava_lang_String *s)

Hjava_lang_String  *makeJavaString(char  *string, int  length)

char  *makeCString(Hjava_lang_String *s)
char  *allocCString(Hjava_lang_String *s)

unicode *javaString2unicode(Hjava_lang_String *s, unicode *buf, int  len)
char    *javaString2CString(Hjava_lang_String *s, char    *buf, int  len)
```

The first two methods print a Java String (like System.out.print()), and get its length, respectively. The third makes a Java String out of a C string. The fourth and fifth do the reverse, turning a Java String into a C string (allocated from temporary or heap storage, respectively). The final two methods copy Java Strings into preexisting Unicode or ASCII C buffers.

Compiling the Stubs File

The final step you need to take in the C world is to compile the stubs file SimpleFile.c by using the same compilation flags you used for SimpleFileNative.c.

Note: If you have several classes with native methods, you can include all their stubs in the same .c file, if you like. Of course you might want to name it something else, such as Stubs.c, in that case.

20

You're now finished with all the C code that must be written (and compiled) to make your loadable native library.

A Native Library

Now you'll finally be able to tie everything together and create the native library, simple, that was assumed to exist at the beginning of today's lesson.

Linking It All

It's time to link everything you've done into a single library file. This looks a little different on each system that Java runs on, but here's the basic idea, in UNIX syntax:

```
cc -G SimpleFile.o SimpleFileNative.o -o simple
```

The `-G` flag tells the linker that you're creating a dynamically linkable library; the details differ from system to system.

> **Note:** By naming the library `simple`, you're disobeying a UNIX convention that dynamic library names should have the prefix lib and the suffix .so (on your system, these prefixes and suffixes may differ). You can call your library libsimple.so to obey the convention, if you like, but just for the clarity of this example, the simpler name is used.

Using Your Library

Now, when the Java class `SimpleFile` is first loaded into your program, the `System` class attempts to load the library named simple, which (luckily) you just created. Look back at the Java code for `SimpleFile` to remind yourself.

How does it locate it? It calls the dynamic linker, which consults an environment variable named `LD_LIBRARY_PATH` that tells it which sequence of directories to search when loading new libraries of native code. Because the current directory is in Java's load path by default, you can leave "simple" in the current directory, and it will work just fine.

Summary

Today, you learned about the numerous disadvantages of using `native` methods, about the many ways that Java (and you) can make your programs run faster, and also about the often illusory need for efficiency.

Finally, you learned the procedure for creating `native` methods, from both the Java and the C sides, in detail—by generating header files and stubs, and by compiling and linking a full example.

After working your way through today's difficult material, you've mastered one of the most complex parts of the Java language. You now know how the Java run-time environment itself was created, and how to extend that powerful environment yourself, at its lowest levels.

As a reward, tomorrow you look "under the hood" to see some of the hidden power of Java, and you can just sit back and enjoy the ride.

Q&A

Q **What can I use to supplement the "Implementing Native Methods" document you recommended?**

A Looking online is highly recommended. Nearby and within "Implementing Native Methods" is a Makefile, other related build information, and a more detailed version of both the next example in this book and its explanation. This following discussion will be enough to get you started on your first `native` methods.

Q **Does the Java class library need to call System.loadLibrary() to load the built-in classes?**

A No, you won't see any `loadLibrary()` calls in the implementation of any classes in the Java class library. That's because the Java team had the luxury of being able to statically link most of their code into the Java environment, something that really makes sense only when you're in the unique position of providing an entire system, as they are. Your classes must *dynamically* link their libraries into an already-running copy of the Java system. This is, by the way, more flexible than static linking; it allows you to unlink old and relink new versions of your classes at any time, making updating them trivial.

Q **Can I statically link my own classes into Java like the Java team did?**

A Yes. You can, if you like, ask Sun Microsystems for the sources to the Java run-time environment itself, and, as long as you obey the (relatively straightforward) legal restrictions on using that code, you can relink the entire Java system plus your classes. Your classes are then statically linked into the system, but you have to give everyone who wants to use your program this special version of the Java environment. Sometimes, if you have strong enough requirements, this is the only way to go, but most of the time, dynamic linking is not only good enough, but preferable.

Q **My applet needs some key functionality, missing from the Java library. Given their many disadvantages, I'd like to avoid using `native` methods. Do I have any alternatives?**

A Because it's still early in the history of Java, a valid alternative to `native` methods is to try to convince the Java team that your needed capability is of interest to a broad range of future Java programmers; then they may include it directly into the java packages. There are already plans to do this with certain "missing" pieces of functionality, so this may not be as hard a sell as you might think. Start by posting some messages to the `comp.lang.java` newsgroup, to be sure no one else at Sun or elsewhere is already doing it, and then see what happens. This is a young, vibrant community of enthusiasts; you are not alone.

Under the Hood

by Charles L. Perkins

On today, your final day, the inner workings of the Java system will be revealed.

You'll find out all about Java's vision, Java's virtual machine, those bytecodes you've heard so much about, that mysterious garbage collector, and why you might worry about security but don't have to.

Let's begin, however, with the big picture.

The Big Picture

The Java team is very ambitious. Their ultimate goal is nothing less than to revolutionize the way software is written and distributed. They've started with the Internet, where they believe much of the interesting software of the future will live.

To achieve such an ambitious goal, a large fraction of the Internet programming community itself must be marshalled behind a similar goal and given the tools to help achieve it. The Java language, with its four S's (small, simple, safe, secure), and its flexible, net-oriented environment, hopes to become the focal point for the rallying of this new legion of programmers.

To this end, Sun Microsystems has done something rather gutsy. What was originally a secret, tens-of-millions-of-dollars research and development project, and 100 percent proprietary, has become a free, open, and relatively unencumbered technology standard upon which anyone can build. They are literally *giving it away* and reserving only the rights they need to maintain and grow the standard.

> **Note:** Actually, as Sun's lawyers have more and more time to think, the original intentions of the Java team get further obscured by legal details. It is still relatively unencumbered, but its earlier releases were completely unencumbered. Let's hope that this is not a pattern that will continue.

Any truly open standard must be supported by at least one excellent, freely available "demonstration" implementation. Sun has already shipped an alpha, and now a beta, of one to the Internet and plans on a final release soon. In parallel, several universities, companies, and individuals have already expressed their intention to duplicate the Java environment, based on the open API that Sun has created.

Several other languages are even contemplating compiling down to Java bytecodes, to help support them in becoming a more robust and commonplace standard for moving executable content around on the Net.

Why It's a Powerful Vision

One of the reasons this brilliant move on Sun's part has a real chance of success is the pent-up frustration of literally a whole generation of programmers who desperately want to share their code with one another. Right now, the computer science world is balkanized into factions at universities and companies all over the world, with hundreds of languages, dozens of them widely used, dividing and separating us all. It's the worst sort of Tower of Babel. Java hopes to build some bridges and help tear down that tower. Because it is so simple, because it's so useful for programming over the Internet, and because the Internet is so "hot" right now—this confluence of forces should help propel Java onto centerstage.

It deserves to be there. It is the natural outgrowth of ideas that, since the early 1970s inside the Smalltalk group at Xerox PARC, have lain relatively dormant in the mainstream. Smalltalk, in fact, invented the first object-oriented bytecode interpreter and pioneered many of the deep ideas that Java builds on today. Those efforts were not embraced over the intervening decades as a solution to the general problems of software, however. Today, with those problems becoming so much more obvious, and with the Net crying out for a new kind of programming, the soil is fertile to grow something stronger from those old roots, something that just might spread like wildfire. (Is it a coincidence that Java's previous internal names were Green and OAK?)

This new vision of software is one in which the Net becomes an ocean of objects, classes, and the open APIs between them. Traditional applications have vanished, replaced by skeletal frameworks like the Eiffel tower, into which can be fitted any parts from this ocean, on demand, to suit any purpose. User interfaces will be mixed and matched, built in pieces and constructed to taste, whenever the need arises, *by their own users*. Menus of choices will be filled by dynamic lists of *all* the choices available for that function, at that exact moment, across the entire ocean (of the Net).

In such a world, software distribution is no longer an issue. Software will be *everywhere* and will be paid for via a plethora of new micro-accounting models, which charge tiny fractions of cents for the parts as they are assembled and used. Frameworks will come into existence to support entertainment, business, and the social (cyber-)spaces of the near future.

This is a dream that many of us have waited *all our lives* to be a part of. There are tremendous challenges to making it all come true, but the powerful winds of change we all feel must stir us into action, because, at last, there is a base on which to build that dream—Java.

21

The Java Virtual Machine

To make visions like this possible, Java must be ubiquitous. It must be able to run on any computer and any operating system—now, and in the future. In order to achieve this level of portability, Java must be very precise not only about the language itself, but about the environment in which the language lives. You can see, from earlier in the book and Appendix B, that the Java environment includes a generally useful set of packages of classes and a freely available implementation of them. This takes care of a part of what is needed, but it is crucial also to specify exactly how the run-time environment of Java behaves.

This final requirement is what has stymied many attempts at ubiquity in the past. If you base your system on any assumptions about what is "beneath" the run-time system, you lose. If you depend in any way on the computer or operating system below, you lose. Java solves this problem by *inventing* an abstract computer of its own and running on that.

This "virtual" machine runs a special set of "instructions" called bytecodes that are simply a stream of formatted bytes, each of which has a precise specification of exactly what each bytecode does to this virtual machine. The virtual machine is also responsible for certain fundamental capabilities of Java, such as object creation and garbage collection.

Finally, in order to be able to move bytecodes safely across the Internet, you need a bulletproof model of security—and how to maintain it—and a precise format for how this stream of bytecodes can be sent from one virtual machine to another.

Each of these requirements is addressed in today's lesson.

> **Note:** This discussion blurs the distinction between the run-time and the virtual machine of Java. This is intentional but a little unconventional. Think of the virtual machine as providing *all* the capabilities, even those that are conventionally assigned to the run-time. This book uses the words "run-time" and "virtual machine" interchangeably. Equating the two highlights the single *environment* that must be created to support Java.
>
> Much of the following description is based closely on the alpha "Virtual Machine Specifications" documents (and the beta bytecodes), so if you delve more deeply into the details online, you will cover some familiar ground.

An Overview

It is worth quoting the introduction to the Java virtual machine documentation here, because it is so relevant to the vision outlined earlier:

> The Java virtual machine specification has a purpose that is both like and unlike equivalent documents for other languages and abstract machines. It is intended to present an abstract, logical machine design free from the distraction of inconsequential

details of any implementation. It does not anticipate an implementation technology, or an implementation host. At the same time it gives a reader sufficient information to allow implementation of the abstract design in a range of technologies.

However, the intent of the [...] Java project is to create a language [...] that will allow the interchange over the Internet of "executable content," which will be embodied by compiled Java code. The project specifically does not want Java to be a proprietary language and does not want to be the sole purveyor of Java language implementations. Rather, we hope to make documents like this one, and source code for our implementation, freely available for people to use as they choose.

This vision [...] can be achieved only if the executable content can be reliably shared between different Java implementations. These intentions prohibit the definition of the Java virtual machine from being fully abstract. Rather, relevant logical elements of the design have to be made sufficiently concrete to allow the interchange of compiled Java code. This does not collapse the Java virtual machine specification to a description of a Java implementation; elements of the design that do not play a part in the interchange of executable content remain abstract. But it does force us to specify, in addition to the abstract machine design, a concrete interchange format for compiled Java code.

The Java virtual machine specification consists of the following:

☐ The bytecode syntax, including opcode and operand sizes, values, and types, and their alignment and endian-ness

☐ The values of any identifiers (for example, type identifiers) in bytecodes or in supporting structures

☐ The layout of the supporting structures that appear in compiled Java code (for example, the constant pool)

☐ The Java .class file format

Each of these is covered today.

Despite this degree of specificity, there are still several elements of the design that remain (purposely) abstract, including the following:

☐ The layout and management of the run-time data areas

☐ The particular garbage-collection algorithms, strategies, and constraints used

☐ The compiler, development environment, and run-time extensions (apart from the need to generate and read valid Java bytecodes)

☐ Any optimizations performed, once valid bytecodes are received

These places are where the creativity of a virtual machine implementor has full rein.

21

The Fundamental Parts

The Java virtual machine can be deconstructed into five fundamental pieces:

- ☐ A bytecode instruction set
- ☐ A set of registers
- ☐ A stack
- ☐ A garbage-collected heap
- ☐ An area for storing methods

These might be implemented by using an interpreter, a native binary code compiler, or even a hardware chip—but all these logical, abstract components of the virtual machine must be supplied in *some* form in every Java system.

> **Note:** The memory areas used by the Java virtual machine are not required to be at any particular place in memory, to be in any particular order, or even to use contiguous memory. However, all but the method area must be able to represent 32-bit values (for example, the Java stack is 32 bits wide).

The virtual machine, and its supporting code, is often referred to as the run-time environment, and when this book refers to something being done at run-time, the virtual machine is what's doing it.

Java Bytecodes

The Java virtual machine instruction set is optimized to be small and compact. It is designed to travel across the Net, and so has traded off speed-of-interpretation for space. (Given that both Net bandwidth and mass storage speeds increase less rapidly than CPU speed, this seems like an appropriate trade-off.)

As mentioned, Java source code is "compiled" into bytecodes and stored in a .class file. On Sun's Java system, this is performed using the javac tool. It is not exactly a traditional "compiler," because javac translates source code into bytecodes, a lower-level format that cannot be run directly, but must be further interpreted by each computer. Of course, it is exactly this level of "indirection" that buys you the power, flexibility, and extreme portability of Java code.

Note: Quotation marks are used around the word "compiler" when talking about `javac` because later today you will also learn about the "just-in-time" compiler, which acts more like the back end of a traditional compiler. The use of the same word "compiler" for these two different pieces of Java technology is unfortunate, but somewhat reasonable, because each is really one-half (either the front or the back end) of a more traditional compiler.

A bytecode instruction consists of a one-byte opcode that serves to identify the instruction involved and zero or more operands, each of which may be more than one byte long, that encode the parameters the opcode requires.

Note: When operands are more than one byte long, they are stored in big-endian order, high-order byte first. These operands must be assembled from the byte stream at run-time. For example, a 16-bit parameter appears in the stream as two bytes so that its value is `first_byte * 256 + second_byte`. The bytecode instruction stream is only byte-aligned, and alignment of any larger quantities is not guaranteed (except for "within" the special bytecodes `lookupswitch` and `tableswitch`, which have special alignment rules of their own).

Bytecodes interpret data in the run-time's memory areas as belonging to a fixed set of types: the primitive types you've seen several times before, consisting of several signed integer types (8-bit `byte`, 16-bit `short`, 32-bit `int`, 64-bit `long`), one unsigned integer type (16-bit `char`), and two signed floating-point types (32-bit `float`, 64-bit `double`), plus the type "reference to an object" (a 32-bit pointer-like type). Some special bytecodes (for example, the `dup` instructions), treat run-time memory areas as raw data, without regard to type. This is the exception, however, not the rule.

These primitive types are distinguished and managed by the compiler, `javac`, not by the Java run-time environment. These types are not "tagged" in memory, and thus cannot be distinguished at run-time. Different bytecodes are designed to handle each of the various primitive types uniquely, and the compiler carefully chooses from this palette based on its knowledge of the actual types stored in the various memory areas. For example, when adding two integers, the compiler generates an `iadd` bytecode; for adding two floats, `fadd` is generated. (You'll see all this in gruesome detail later.)

21

Registers

The registers of the Java virtual machine are just like the registers inside a "real" computer.

NEW☞ TERM *Registers* hold the machine's state, affect its operation, and are updated after each bytecode is executed.

The following are the Java registers:

- ☐ pc, the program counter, which indicates what bytecode is being executed
- ☐ optop, a pointer to the top of the operand stack, which is used to evaluate all arithmetic expressions
- ☐ frame, a pointer to the execution environment of the current method, which includes an activation record for this method call and any associated debugging information
- ☐ vars, a pointer to the first local variable of the currently executing method

The virtual machine defines these registers to be 32 bits wide.

> **Note:** Because the virtual machine is primarily stack-based, it does not use any registers for passing or receiving arguments. This is a conscious choice skewed toward bytecode simplicity and compactness. It also aids efficient implementation on register-poor architectures, which most of today's computers, unfortunately, are. Perhaps when the majority of CPUs out there are a little more sophisticated, this choice will be reexamined, though simplicity and compactness may still be reason enough!
>
> By the way, the pc register is also used when the run-time handles exceptions; catch clauses are (ultimately) associated with ranges of the pc within a method's bytecodes.

The Stack

The Java virtual machine is stack-based. A Java stack frame is similar to the stack frame of a conventional programming language—it holds the state for a single method call. Frames for nested method calls are stacked on top of this frame.

NEW☞ TERM The *stack* is used to supply parameters to bytecodes and methods, and to receive results back from them.

Each stack frame contains three (possibly empty) sets of data: the local variables for the method call, its execution environment, and its operand stack. The sizes of these first two are fixed at the start of a method call, but the operand stack varies in size as bytecodes are executed in the method.

Local variables are stored in an array of 32-bit slots, indexed by the register vars. Most types take up one slot in the array, but the long and double types each take up two slots.

> **Note:** long and double values, stored or referenced via an index N, take up the (32-bit) slots N and N + 1. These 64-bit values are thus not guaranteed to be 64-bit-aligned. Implementors are free to decide the appropriate way to divide these values among the two slots.

The execution environment in a stack frame helps to maintain the stack itself. It contains a pointer to the previous stack frame, a pointer to the local variables of the method call, and pointers to the stack's current "base" and "top." Additional debugging information can also be placed into the execution environment.

The operand stack, a 32-bit first-in-first-out (FIFO) stack, is used to store the parameters and return values of most bytecode instructions. For example, the iadd bytecode expects two integers to be stored on the top of the stack. It pops them, adds them together, and pushes the resulting sum back onto the stack.

Each primitive data type has unique instructions that know how to extract, operate, and push back operands of that type. For example, long and double operands take two "slots" on the stack, and the special bytecodes that handle these operands take this into account. It is illegal for the types on the stack and the instruction operating on them to be incompatible (javac outputs bytecodes that always obey this rule).

> **Note:** The top of the operand stack and the top of the overall Java stack are almost always the same. Thus, "the stack," refers to both stacks, collectively.

21

The Heap

The heap is that part of memory from which newly created instances (objects) are allocated.

In Java, the heap is often assigned a large, fixed size when the Java run-time system is started, but on systems that support virtual memory, it can grow as needed, in a nearly unbounded fashion.

Because objects are automatically garbage-collected in Java, programmers do not have to (and, in fact, *cannot*) manually free the memory allocated to an object when they are finished using it.

Java objects are referenced indirectly in the run-time, via handles, which are a kind of pointer into the heap.

Because objects are never referenced directly, parallel garbage collectors can be written that operate independently of your program, moving around objects in the heap at will. You'll learn more about garbage collection later.

The Method Area

Like the compiled code areas of conventional programming language environments, or the TEXT segment in a UNIX process, the method area stores the Java bytecodes that implement almost every method in the Java system. (Remember that some methods might be native, and thus implemented, for example, in C.) The method area also stores the symbol tables needed for dynamic linking, and any other additional information debuggers or development environments which might want to associate with each method's implementation.

Because bytecodes are stored as byte streams, the method area is aligned on byte boundaries. (The other areas are all aligned on 32-bit word boundaries.)

The Constant Pool

In the heap, each class has a constant pool "attached" to it. Usually created by `javac`, these constants encode all the names (of variables, methods, and so forth) used by any method in a class. The class contains a count of how many constants there are and an offset that specifies how far into the class description itself the array of constants begins. These constants are typed by using specially coded bytes and have a precisely defined format when they appear in the .class file for a class. Later today, a little of this file format is covered, but everything is fully specified by the virtual machine specifications in your Java release.

Limitations

The virtual machine, as currently defined, places some restrictions on legal Java programs by virtue of the choices it has made (some were previously described, and more will be detailed later today).

These limitations and their implications are

☐ 32-bit pointers, which imply that the virtual machine can address only 4G of memory (this may be relaxed in later releases)

- [ ] Unsigned 16-bit indicies into the exception, line number, and local variable tables, which limit the size of a method's bytecode implementation to 64K (this limitation may be eliminated in the final release)
- [ ] Unsigned 16-bit indices into the constant pool, which limits the number of constants in a class to 64K (a limit on the complexity of a class)

In addition, Sun's implementation of the virtual machine uses so-called _quick bytecodes, which further limit the system. Unsigned 8-bit offsets into objects may limit the number of methods in a class to 256 (this limit may not exist in the final release), and unsigned 8-bit argument counts limit the size of the argument list to 255 32-bit words. (Although this means that you can have up to 255 arguments of most types, you can have only 127 of them if they're all long or double.)

Bytecodes in More Detail

One of the main tasks of the virtual machine is the fast, efficient execution of the Java bytecodes in methods. Unlike in the discussion yesterday about generality in Java programs, this is a case where speed is of the upmost importance. Every Java program suffers from a slow implementation here, so the run-time must use as many "tricks" as possible to make bytecodes run fast. The only other goal (or limitation) is that Java programmers must not be able to see these tricks in the behavior of their programs.

A Java run-time implementer must be extremely clever to satisfy both these goals.

The Bytecode Interpreter

A bytecode interpreter examines each opcode byte (bytecode) in a method's bytecode stream, in turn, and executes a unique action for that bytecode. This might consume further bytes for the operands of the bytecode and might affect which bytecode will be examined next. It operates like the hardware CPU in a computer, which examines memory for instructions to carry out in exactly the same manner. It is the software CPU of the Java virtual machine.

Your first, naive attempt to write such a bytecode interpreter will almost certainly be disastrously slow. The inner loop, which dispatches one bytecode each time through the loop, is notoriously difficult to optimize. In fact, smart people have been thinking about this problem, in one form or another, for more than 20 years. Luckily, they've gotten results, all of which can be applied to Java.

The final result is that the interpreter shipped in the current release of Java has an extremely fast inncr loop. In fact, on even a relatively slow computer, this interpreter can perform more than 330,000 bytecodes per second! This is really quite good, because the CPU in that computer does only about 30 times better using *hardware.*

This interpreter is fast enough for most Java programs (and for those *requiring* more speed, they can always use native methods—see yesterday's discussion)—but what if a smart implementor wants to do better?

The "Just-in-Time" Compiler

About a decade ago, a really clever trick was discovered by Peter Deutsch while trying to make Smalltalk run faster. He called it "dynamic translation" during interpretation. Sun calls it "just-in-time" compiling.

The trick is to notice that the really fast interpreter you've just written—in C, for example—already has a useful sequence of native binary code for each bytecode that it interprets: *the binary code that the interpreter itself is executing.* Because the interpreter has already been compiled from C into native binary code, for each bytecode that it interprets, it passes through a sequence of native code instructions for the hardware CPU on which it is running. By saving a copy of each binary instruction as it "goes by," the interpreter can keep a running log of the binary code it *itself* has run to interpret a bytecode. It can just as easily keep a log of the set of bytecodes that it ran to interpret an entire method.

You take that log of instructions and "peephole-optimize" it, just as a smart compiler does. This eliminates redundant or unnecessary instructions from the log, and makes it look just like the optimized binary code that a good compiler might have produced.

> **Note:** This is where the name compiler comes from, in "just-in-time" compiler, but it's really only the back end of a traditional compiler—the part that does code generation. By the way, the front end here is javac.

Here's where the trick comes in. The next time that method is run (in exactly the same way), the interpreter can now simply execute directly the stored log of binary native code. Because this optimizes out the inner-loop overhead of each bytecode, as well as any other redundancies between the bytecodes in a method, it can gain a factor of 10 or more in speed. In fact, an experimental version of this technology at Sun has shown that Java programs using it can run as fast as compiled C programs.

> **Note:** The parenthetical in the last paragraph is needed because if anything is different about the input to the method, it takes a different path through the interpreter and must be relogged. (There are sophisticated versions of this technology that solve this, and other, difficulties.) The cache of native code for a method must be invalidated whenever the method has changed, and the interpreter must pay a small cost up front each time a method is run for the first time. However, these small bookkeeping costs are far outweighed by the amazing gains in speed possible.

The *java2c* Translator

Another, simpler, trick, which works well whenever you have a good, portable C compiler on each system that runs your program, is to translate the bytecodes into C and then compile the C into binary native code. If you wait until the first use of a method or class, and then perform this as an "invisible" optimization, it gains you an additional speedup over the approach outlined previously, without the Java programmer needing to know about it.

Of course, this does limit you to systems with a C compiler, but as you learned yesterday, there are extremely good, freely available C compilers. In theory, your Java code might be able to travel with its own C compiler, or know where to pull one from the Net as needed, for each new computer and operating system it faced. (Because this violates some of the rules of normal Java code movement over the Net, though, it should be used sparingly.)

If you're using Java, for example, to write a server that lives only on *your* computer, it might be appropriate to use Java for its flexibility in writing and maintaining the server (and for its capability of dynamically linking new Java code on the fly), and then to run java2c by hand to translate the basic server itself entirely into native code. You'd link the Java run-time environment into that code so that your server remains a fully capable Java program, but it's now an extremely fast one.

In fact, an experimental version of the java2c translator inside Sun shows that it can reach the speed of compiled and optimized C code. This is the best that you can hope to do!

> **Note:** Unfortunately, as of the beta release, there is still no publicly available java2c tool, and Sun's virtual machine does not perform "just-in-time" compilation. Both of these have been promised in a later release.

The Bytecodes Themselves

Let's look at a (progressively less and less) detailed description of each class of bytecodes.

For each bytecode, some brief text describes its function, and a textual "picture" of the stack, both before and after the bytecode has been executed, is shown. This text picture will look like the following:

```
..., value1, value2 => ..., value3
```

This means that the bytecode expects two operands—`value1` and `value2`—to be on the top of the stack, pops them both off the stack, operates on them to produce `value3`, and pushes `value3` back onto the top of the stack. You should read each stack from right to left, with the rightmost value being the top of the stack. The . . . is read as "the rest of the stack below," which is irrelevant to the current bytecode. All operands on the stack are 32-bit wide.

Because most bytecodes take their arguments from the stack and place their results back there, the brief text descriptions that follow only say something about the source or destination of values if they are *not* on the stack. For example, the description `Load integer from local variable.` means that the integer is loaded onto the stack, and `Integer add.` intends its integers to be taken from—and the result returned to—the stack.

Bytecodes that don't affect control flow simply move the `pc` onto the next bytecode that follows in sequence. Those that do affect the `pc` say so explicitly. Whenever you see `byte1`, `byte2`, and so forth, it refers to the first byte, second byte, and so on, that follow the opcode byte itself. After such a bytecode is executed, the `pc` automatically advances over these operand bytes to start the next bytecode in sequence.

> **Note:** The next few sections are in "reference manual style," presenting each bytecode separately in all its (often redundant) detail. Later sections begin to collapse and coalesce this verbose style into something shorter, and more readable. The verbose form is shown at first because the online reference manuals will look more like it, and because it drives home the point that each bytecode "function" comes in many, nearly identical bytecodes, one for each primitive type in Java.

Pushing Constants onto the Stack

```
bipush          ... => ..., value
```

Push one-byte signed integer. `byte1` is interpreted as a signed 8-bit value. This `value` is expanded to an `int` and pushed onto the operand stack.

```
sipush          ... => ..., value
```

Push two-byte signed integer. byte1 and byte2 are assembled into a signed 16-bit value. This value is expanded to an int and pushed onto the operand stack.

```
ldc1            ... => ..., item
```

Push item from constant pool. byte1 is used as an unsigned 8-bit index into the constant pool of the current class. The item at that index is resolved and pushed onto the stack.

```
ldc2            ... => ..., item
```

Push item from constant pool. byte1 and byte2 are used to construct an unsigned 16-bit index into the constant pool of the current class. The item at that index is resolved and pushed onto the stack.

```
ldc2w           ... => ..., constant-word1, constant-word2
```

Push long or double from constant pool. byte1 and byte2 are used to construct an unsigned 16-bit index into the constant pool of the current class. The two-word constant at that index is resolved and pushed onto the stack.

```
aconst_null     ... => ..., null
```

Push the null object reference onto the stack.

```
iconst_m1       ... => ..., -1
```

Push the int -1 onto the stack.

```
iconst_<I>      ... => ..., <I>
```

Push the int <I> onto the stack. There are six of these bytecodes, one for each of the integers 0-5: iconst_0, iconst_1, iconst_2, iconst_3, iconst_4, and iconst_5.

```
lconst_<L>      ... => ..., <L>-word1, <L>-word2
```

Push the long <L> onto the stack. There are two of these bytecodes, one for each of the integers 0 and 1: lconst_0, and lconst_1.

```
fconst_<F>      ... => ..., <F>
```

Push the float <F> onto the stack. There are three of these bytecodes, one for each of the integers 0-2: fconst_0, fconst_1, and fconst_2.

```
dconst_<D>      ... => ..., <D>-word1, <D>-word2
```

Push the double <D> onto the stack. There are two of these bytecodes, one for each of the integers 0 and 1: dconst_0, and dconst_1.

21

Loading Local Variables onto the Stack

```
iload          ... => ..., value
```

Load `int` from local variable. Local variable `byte1` in the current Java frame must contain an `int`. The `value` of that variable is pushed onto the operand stack.

```
iload_<I>      ... => ..., value
```

Load `int` from local variable. Local variable `<I>` in the current Java frame must contain an `int`. The `value` of that variable is pushed onto the operand stack. There are four of these bytecodes, one for each of the integers 0-3: `iload_0`, `iload_1`, `iload_2`, and `iload_3`.

```
lload          ... => ..., value-word1, value-word2
```

Load `long` from local variable. Local variables `byte1` and `byte1 + 1` in the current Java frame must together contain a long integer. The values contained in those variables are pushed onto the operand stack.

```
lload_<L>      ... => ..., value-word1, value-word2
```

Load `long` from local variable. Local variables `<L>` and `<L>` + 1 in the current Java frame must together contain a long integer. The value contained in those variables is pushed onto the operand stack. There are four of these bytecodes, one for each of the integers 0-3: `lload_0`, `lload_1`, `lload_2`, and `lload_3`.

```
fload          ... => ..., value
```

Load `float` from local variable. Local variable `byte1` in the current Java frame must contain a single precision floating-point number. The `value` of that variable is pushed onto the operand stack.

```
fload_<F>      ... => ..., value
```

Load `float` from local variable. Local variable `<F>` in the current Java frame must contain a single precision floating-point number. The value of that variable is pushed onto the operand stack. There are four of these bytecodes, one for each of the integers 0-3: `fload_0`, `fload_1`, `fload_2`, and `fload_3`.

```
dload          ... => ..., value-word1, value-word2
```

Load `double` from local variable. Local variables `byte1` and `byte1 + 1` in the current Java frame must together contain a double precision floating-point number. The value contained in those variables is pushed onto the operand stack.

```
dload_<D>      ... => ..., value-word1, value-word2
```

Load `double` from local variable. Local variables `<D>` and `<D>` + 1 in the current Java frame must together contain a double precision floating-point number. The value contained in those variables is pushed onto the operand stack There are four of these bytecodes, one for each of the integers 0-3: `dload_0`, `dload1`, `dload_2`, and `dload_3`.

```
aload          ... => ..., value
```

Load object reference from local variable. Local variable `byte1` in the current Java frame must contain a return address or reference to an object or array. The value of that variable is pushed onto the operand stack.

```
aload_<A>      ... => ..., value
```

Load object reference from local variable. Local variable `<A>` in the current Java frame must contain a return address or reference to an object. The array value of that variable is pushed onto the operand stack. There are four of these bytecodes, one for each of the integers 0-3: `aload_0`, `aload_1`, `aload_2`, and `aload_3`.

Storing Stack Values into Local Variables

```
istore         ..., value => ...
```

Store `int` into local variable. `value` must be an `int`. Local variable `byte1` in the current Java frame is set to `value`.

```
istore_<I>     ..., value => ...
```

Store `int` into local variable. `value` must be an `int`. Local variable `<I>` in the current Java frame is set to `value`. There are four of these bytecodes, one for each of the integers 0-3: `istore_0`, `istore_1`, `istore_2`, and `istore_3`.

```
lstore         ..., value-word1, value-word2 => ...
```

Store `long` into local variable. `value` must be a long integer. Local variables `byte1` and `byte1` + 1 in the current Java frame are set to `value`.

```
lstore_<L>     ..., value-word1, value-word2 => ...
```

Store `long` into local variable. `value` must be a long integer. Local variables `<L>` and `<L>` + 1 in the current Java frame are set to `value`. There are four of these bytecodes, one for each of the integers 0-3: `lstore_0`, `lstore_1`, `lstore_2`, and `lstore_3`.

```
fstore         ..., value                    => ...
```

Store `float` into local variable. `value` must be a single precision floating-point number. Local variables `byte1` and `byte1` + 1 in the current Java frame are set to `value`.

21

```
fstore_<F>      ..., value                 => ...
```

Store `float` into local variable. `value` must be a single precision floating-point number. Local variables `<F>` and `<F>` + 1 in the current Java frame are set to `value`. There are four of these bytecodes, one for each of the integers 0-3: `fstore_0`, `fstore_1`, `fstore_2`, and `fstore_3`.

```
dstore          ..., value-word1, value-word2 => ...
```

Store `double` into local variable. `value` must be a double precision floating-point number. Local variables `byte1` and `byte1` + 1 in the current Java frame are set to `value`.

```
dstore_<D>      ..., value-word1, value-word2 => ...
```

Store `double` into local variable. `value` must be a double precision floating-point number. Local variables `<D>` and `<D>` + 1 in the current Java frame are set to `value`. There are four of these bytecodes, one for each of the integers 0-3: `dstore_0`, `dstore_1`, `dstore_2`, and `dstore_3`.

```
astore          ..., handle => ...
```

Store object reference into local variable. `handle` must be a return address or a reference to an object. Local variable `byte1` in the current Java frame is set to `value`.

```
astore_<A>      ..., handle => ...
```

Store object reference into local variable. `handle` must be a return address or a reference to an object. Local variable `<A>` in the current Java frame is set to `value`. There are four of these bytecodes, one for each of the integers 0-3: `astore_0`, `astore_1`, `astore_2`, and `astore_3`.

```
iinc            -no change-
```

Increment local variable by constant. Local variable `byte1` in the current Java frame must contain an `int`. Its value is incremented by the value `byte2`, where `byte2` is treated as a signed 8-bit quantity.

Managing Arrays

```
newarray        ..., size => result
```

Allocate new array. `size` must be an `int`. It represents the number of elements in the new array. `byte1` is an internal code that indicates the type of array to allocate. Possible values for `byte1` are as follows: `T_BOOLEAN` (4), `T_CHAR` (5), `T_FLOAT` (6), `T_DOUBLE` (7), `T_BYTE` (8), `T_SHORT` (9), `T_INT` (10), and `T_LONG` (11).

An attempt is made to allocate a new array of the indicated type, capable of holding `size` elements. This will be the `result`. If size is less than zero, a `NegativeArraySizeException` is thrown. If there is not enough memory to allocate the array, an `OutOfMemoryError` is thrown. All elements of the array are initialized to their default values.

```
anewarray        ..., size => result
```

Allocate new array of objects. `size` must be an `int`. It represents the number of elements in the new array. `byte1` and `byte2` are used to construct an index into the constant pool of the current class. The item at that index is resolved. The resulting entry must be a class.

An attempt is made to allocate a new array of the indicated class type, capable of holding `size` elements. This will be the `result`. If `size` is less than zero, a `NegativeArraySizeException` is thrown. If there is not enough memory to allocate the array, an `OutOfMemoryError` is thrown. All elements of the array are initialized to `null`.

Note: anewarray is used to create a single dimension of an array of objects. For example, the request new `Thread[7]` generates the following bytecodes:

```
bipush 7
anewarray <Class "java.lang.Thread">
```

anewarray can also be used to create the outermost dimension of a multidimensional array. For example, the array declaration new `int[6][]` generates this:

```
bipush 6
anewarray <Class "[I">
```

(See the section "Method Signatures" for more information on strings such as [I.)

```
multianewarray  ..., size1 size2...sizeN => result
```

Allocate new multidimensional array. Each `size<I>` must be an `int`. Each represents the number of elements in a dimension of the array. `byte1` and `byte2` are used to construct an index into the constant pool of the current class. The item at that index is resolved. The resulting entry must be an array class of one or more dimensions.

`byte3` is a positive integer representing the number of dimensions being created. It must be less than or equal to the number of dimensions of the array class. `byte3` is also the number of elements that are popped off the stack. All must be `int`s greater than or equal to zero. These are used as the sizes of the dimensions. An attempt is made to allocate a new array of the indicated class type, capable of holding `size<1>` * `size<2>` * ... * `<sizeN>` elements. This will be the `result`. If any of the `size<I>` arguments on the stack is less than zero, a `NegativeArraySizeException` is thrown. If there is not enough memory to allocate the array, an `OutOfMemoryError` is thrown.

> **Note:** `new int[6][3][]` generates these bytecodes:
>
> ```
> bipush 6
> bipush 3
> multianewarray <Class "[[[I"> 2
> ```
>
> It's more efficient to use `newarray` or `anewarray` when creating arrays of single dimension.

```
arraylength      ..., array => ..., length
```

Get length of array. `array` must be a reference to an array object. The `length` of the array is determined and replaces array on the top of the stack. If `array` is null, a `NullPointerException` is thrown.

```
iaload           ..., array, index => ..., value
laload           ..., array, index => ..., value-word1, value-word2
faload           ..., array, index => ..., value
daload           ..., array, index => ..., value-word1, value-word2
aaload           ..., array, index => ..., value
baload           ..., array, index => ..., value
caload           ..., array, index => ..., value
saload           ..., array, index => ..., value
```

Load *<type>* from array. `array` must be an array of *<type>*s. `index` must be an int. The *<type>* value at position number `index` in `array` is retrieved and pushed onto the top of the stack. If `array` is null, a `NullPointerException` is thrown. If `index` is not within the bounds of `array`, an `ArrayIndexOutOfBoundsException` is thrown. *<type>* is, in turn, int, long, float, double, object reference, byte, char, and short. *<type>*s long and double have two word values, as you've seen in previous `load` bytecodes.

```
iastore          ..., array, index, value => ...
lastore          ..., array, index, value-word1, value-word2 => ...
fastore          ..., array, index, value => ...
dastore          ..., array, index, value-word1, value-word2 => ...
aastore          ..., array, index, value => ...
bastore          ..., array, index, value => ...
castore          ..., array, index, value => ...
sastore          ..., array, index, value => ...
```

Store into *<type>* array. `array` must be an array of *<type>*s, `index` must be an integer, and `value` a *<type>*. The *<type>* value is stored at position `index` in `array`. If `array` is null, a `NullPointerException` is thrown. If `index` is not within the bounds of `array`, an `ArrayIndexOutOfBoundsException` is thrown. *<type>* is, in turn, int, long, float, double, object reference, byte, char, and short. *<type>*s long and double have two word values, as you've seen in previous `store` bytecodes.

Stack Operations

```
nop         -no change-
```

Do nothing.

```
pop         ..., any => ...
```

Pop the top word from the stack.

```
pop2        ..., any2, any1 => ...
```

Pop the top two words from the stack.

```
dup         ..., any => ..., any, any
```

Duplicate the top word on the stack.

```
dup2        ..., any2, any1 => ..., any2, any1, any2,any1
```

Duplicate the top two words on the stack.

```
dup_x1      ..., any2, any1 => ..., any1, any2,any1
```

Duplicate the top word on the stack and insert the copy two words down in the stack.

```
dup2_x1     ..., any3, any2, any1 => ..., any2, any1, any3,any2,any1
```

Duplicate the top two words on the stack and insert the copies two words down in the stack.

```
dup_x2      ..., any3, any2, any1 => ..., any1, any3,any2,any1
```

Duplicate the top word on the stack and insert the copy three words down in the stack.

```
dup2_x2     ..., any4, any3, any2, any1 => ..., any2, any1, any4,any3,any2,any1
```

Duplicate the top two words on the stack and insert the copies three words down in the stack.

```
swap        ..., any2, any1 => ..., any1, any2
```

Swap the top two elements on the stack.

Arithmetic Operations

```
iadd        ..., v1, v2 => ..., result
ladd        ..., v1-word1, v1-word2, v2-word1, v2-word2 => ..., r-word1, r-word2
fadd        ..., v1, v2 => ..., result
dadd        ..., v1-word1, v1-word2, v2-word1, v2-word2 => ..., r-word1, r-word2
```

v1 and v2 must be *<type>*s. The vs are added and are replaced on the stack by their *<type>* sum. *<type>* is, in turn, int, long, float, and double.

```
isub      ..., v1, v2 => ..., result
lsub      ..., v1-word1, v1-word1, v2-word1, v2-word2 => ..., r-word1, r-word2
fsub      ..., v1, v2 => ..., result
dsub      ..., v1-word1, v1-word2, v2-word1, v2-word2 => ..., r-word1, r-word2
```

v1 and v2 must be <type>s. v2 is subtracted from v1, and both vs are replaced on the stack by their <type> difference. <type> is, in turn, int, long, float, and double.

```
imul      ..., v1, v2 => ..., result
lmul      ..., v1-word1, v1-word2, v2-word1, v2-word2 => ..., r-word1, r-word2
fmul      ..., v1, v2 => ..., result
dmul      ..., v1-word1, v1-word2, v2-word1, v2-word2 => ..., r-word1, r-word2
```

v1 and v2 must be <type>s. Both vs are replaced on the stack by their <type> product. <type> is, in turn, int, long, float, and double.

```
idiv      ..., v1, v2 => ..., result
ldiv      ..., v1-word1, v1-word2, v2-word1, v2-word2 => ..., r-word1, r-word2
fdiv      ..., v1, v2 => ..., result
ddiv      ..., v1-word1, v1-word2, v2-word1, v2-word2 => ..., r-word1, r-word2
```

v1 and v2 must be <type>s. v2 is divided by v1, and both vs are replaced on the stack by their <type> quotient. An attempt to divide by zero results in an ArithmeticException being thrown. <type> is, in turn, int, long, float, and double.

```
irem      ..., v1, v2 => ..., result
lrem      ..., v1-word1, v1-word2, v2-word1, v2-word2 => ..., r-word1, r-word2
frem      ..., v1, v2 => ..., result
drem      ..., v1-word1, v1-word2, v2-word1, v2-word2 => ..., r-word1, r-word2
```

v1 and v2 must be <type>s. v2 is divided by v1, and both vs are replaced on the stack by their <type> remainder. An attempt to divide by zero results in an ArithmeticException being thrown. <type> is, in turn, int, long, float, and double.

```
ineg      ..., value => ..., result
lneg      ..., value-word1, value-word2 => ..., result-word1, result-word2
fneg      ..., value => ..., result
dneg      ..., value-word1, value-word2 => ..., result-word1, result-word2
```

value must be a <type>. It is replaced on the stack by its arithmetic negation. <type> is, in turn, int, long, float, and double.

Note: Now that you're familiar with the look of the bytecodes, the summaries that follow will become shorter and shorter (for space reasons). You can always get any desired level of detail from the full virtual machine specification in the latest Java release.

Logical Operations

```
ishl        ..., v1, v2 => ..., result
lshl        ..., v1-word1, v1-word2, v2 => ..., r-word1, r-word2
ishr        ..., v1, v2 => ..., result
lshr        ..., v1-word1, v1-word2, v2 => ..., r-word1, r-word2
iushr       ..., v1, v2 => ..., result
lushr       ..., v1-word1, v1-word2, v2-word1, v2-word2 => ..., r-word1, r-word2
```

For types int and long: arithmetic shift-left, shift-right, and logical shift-right.

```
iand        ..., v1, v2 => ..., result
land        ..., v1-word1, v1-word2, v2-word1, v2-word2 => ..., r-word1, r-word2
ior         ..., v1, v2 => ..., result
lor         ..., v1-word1, v1-word2, v2-word1, v2-word2 => ..., r-word1, r-word2
ixor        ..., v1, v2 => ..., result
lxor        ..., v1-word1, v1-word2, v2-word1, v2-word2 => ..., r-word1, r-word2
```

For types int and long: bitwise AND, OR, and XOR.

Conversion Operations

```
i2l         ..., value => ..., result-word1, result-word2
i2f         ..., value => ..., result
i2d         ..., value => ..., result-word1, result-word2
l2i         ..., value-word1, value-word2 => ..., result
l2f         ..., value-word1, value-word2 => ..., result
l2d         ..., value-word1, value-word2 => ..., result-word1, result-word2
f2i         ..., value => ..., result
f2l         ..., value => ..., result-word1, result-word2
f2d         ..., value => ..., result-word1, result-word2
d2i         ..., value-word1, value-word2 => ..., result
d2l         ..., value-word1, value-word2 => ..., result-word1, result-word2
d2f         ..., value-word1, value-word2 => ..., result

int2byte    ..., value => ..., result
int2char    ..., value => ..., result
int2short   ..., value => ..., result
```

These bytecodes convert from a value of type <lhs> to a result of type <rhs>. <lhs> and <rhs> can be any of i, l, f, and d, which represent int, long, float, and double, respectively. The final three bytecodes have types that are self-explanatory.

Transfer of Control

```
ifeq        ..., value => ...
ifne        ..., value => ...
iflt        ..., value => ...
ifgt        ..., value => ...
ifle        ..., value => ...
ifge        ..., value => ...

if_icmpeq   ..., value1, value2 => ...
if_icmpne   ..., value1, value2 => ...
if_icmplt   ..., value1, value2 => ...
```

```
if_icmpgt    ..., value1, value2 => ...
if_icmple    ..., value1, value2 => ...
if_icmpge    ..., value1, value2 => ...

ifnull       ..., value => ...
ifnonnull    ..., value => ...
```

When value *<rel>* 0 is true in the first set of bytecodes, value1 *<rel>* value2 is true in the second set, or value is null (or not null) in the third, byte1 and byte2 are used to construct a signed 16-bit offset. Execution proceeds at that offset from the pc. Otherwise, execution proceeds at the bytecode following. *<rel>* is one of eq, ne, lt, gt, le, and ge, which represent equal, not equal, less than, greater than, less than or equal, and greater than or equal, respectively.

```
lcmp     ..., v1-word1, v1-word2, v2-word1, v2-word2 => ..., result

fcmpl    ..., v1, v2 => ..., result
dcmpl    ..., v1-word1, v1-word2, v2-word1, v2-word2 => ..., result

fcmpg    ..., v1, v2 => ..., result
dcmpg    ..., v1-word1, v1-word2, v2-word1, v2-word2 => ..., result
```

v1 and v2 must be long, float, or double. They are both popped from the stack and compared. If v1 is greater than v2, the int value 1 is pushed onto the stack. If v1 is equal to v2, 0 is pushed onto the stack. If v1 is less than v2, -1 is pushed onto the stack. For floating-point, if either v1 or v2 is NaN, -1 is pushed onto the stack for the first pair of bytecodes, +1 for the second pair.

```
if_acmpeq    ..., value1, value2 => ...
if_acmpne    ..., value1, value2 => ...
```

Branch if object references are equal/not equal. value1 and value2 must be references to objects. They are both popped from the stack. If value1 is equal/not equal to value2, byte1 and byte2 are used to construct a signed 16-bit offset. Execution proceeds at that offset from the pc. Otherwise, execution proceeds at the bytecode following.

```
goto     -no change-
goto_w   -no change-
```

Branch always. byte1 and byte2 (plus byte3 and byte4 for goto_w) are used to construct a signed 16-bit (32-bit) offset. Execution proceeds at that offset from the pc.

```
jsr      ... => ..., return-address
jsr-w    ... => ..., return-address
```

Jump subroutine. The address of the bytecode immediately following the jsr is pushed onto the stack. byte1 and byte2 (plus byte3 and byte4 for goto_w) are used to construct a signed 16-bit (32-bit) offset. Execution proceeds at that offset from the pc.

```
ret      -no change-
ret2_w   -no change-
```

Return from subroutine. Local variable byte1 (plus byte2 are assembled into a 16-bit index for ret_w) in the current Java frame must contain a return address. The contents of that local variable are written into the pc.

Note: jsr pushes the address onto the stack, and ret gets it out of a local variable. This asymmetry is intentional. The jsr and ret bytecodes are used in the implementation of Java's `finally` keyword.

Method Return

```
return      ... => [empty]
```

Return (`void`) from method. All values on the operand stack are discarded. The interpreter then returns control to its caller.

```
ireturn      ..., value => [empty]
lreturn      ..., value-word1, value-word2 => [empty]
freturn      ..., value => [empty]
dreturn      ..., value-word1, value-word2 => [empty]
areturn      ..., value => [empty]
```

Return <type> from method. `value` must be a <type>. The `value` is pushed onto the stack of the previous execution environment. Any other values on the operand stack are discarded. The interpreter then returns control to its caller. <type> is, in turn, `int`, `long`, `float`, `double`, and object reference.

Note: The stack behavior of the "return" bytecodes may be confusing to anyone expecting the Java operand stack to be just like the C stack. Java's operand stack actually consists of a number of discontiguous segments, each corresponding to a method call. A return bytecode empties the Java operand stack segment corresponding to the frame of the returning call, but does not affect the segment of any parent calls.

Table Jumping

```
tableswitch   ..., index => ...
```

tableswitch is a variable-length bytecode. Immediately after the tableswitch opcode, zero to three 0 bytes are inserted as padding so that the next byte begins at an address that is a multiple of four. After the padding are a series of signed 4-byte quantities: default-offset, low, high, and then (`high - low + 1`) further signed 4-byte offsets. These offsets are treated as a 0-based jump table.

The `index` must be an `int`. If `index` is less than `low` or `index` is greater than `high`, `default-offset` is added to the `pc`. Otherwise, the (`index - low`)'th element of the jump table is extracted and added to the `pc`.

```
lookupswitch  ..., key => ...
```

`lookupswitch` is a variable-length bytecode. Immediately after the `lookupswitch` opcode, zero to three 0 bytes are inserted as padding so that the next byte begins at an address that is a multiple of four. Immediately after the padding is a series of pairs of signed 4-byte quantities. The first pair is special; it contains the `default-offset` and the number of pairs that follow. Each subsequent pair consists of a `match` and an `offset`.

The `key` on the stack must be an `int`. This `key` is compared to each of the `matches`. If it is equal to one of them, the corresponding `offset` is added to the `pc`. If the `key` does not match any of the `matches`, the `default-offset` is added to the `pc`.

Manipulating Object Fields

```
putfield      ..., handle, value => ...
putfield      ..., handle, value-word1, value-word2 => ...
```

Set field in object. `byte1` and `byte2` are used to construct an index into the constant pool of the current class. The constant pool item is a field reference to a class name and a field name. The item is resolved to a field block pointer containing the field's width and offset (both in bytes).

The field at that offset from the start of the instance pointed to by `handle` will be set to the `value` on the top of the stack. The first stack picture is for 32-bit, and the second for 64-bit wide fields. This bytecode handles both. If `handle` is `null`, a `NullPointerException` is thrown. If the specified field is a `static` field, an `IncompatibleClassChangeError` is thrown.

```
getfield      ..., handle => ..., value
getfield      ..., handle => ..., value-word1, value-word2
```

Fetch field from object. `byte1` and `byte2` are used to construct an index into the constant pool of the current class. The constant pool item will be a field reference to a class name and a field name. The item is resolved to a field block pointer containing the field's width and offset (both in bytes).

`handle` must be a reference to an object. The `value` at offset into the object referenced by `handle` replaces `handle` on the top of the stack. The first stack picture is for 32-bit, and the second for 64-bit wide fields. This bytecode handles both. If the specified field is a `static` field, an `IncompatibleClassChangeError` is thrown.

```
putstatic        ..., value => ...
putstatic        ..., value-word1, value-word2 => ...
```

Set static field in class. byte1 and byte2 are used to construct an index into the constant pool of the current class. The constant pool item will be a field reference to a static field of a class. That field will be set to have the value on the top of the stack. The first stack picture is for 32-bit, and the second for 64-bit wide fields. This bytecode handles both. If the specified field is not a static field, an IncompatibleClassChangeError is thrown.

```
getstatic        ..., => ..., value_
getstatic        ..., => ..., value-word1, value-word2
```

Get static field from class. byte1 and byte2 are used to construct an index into the constant pool of the current class. The constant pool item will be a field reference to a static field of a class. The value of that field is placed on the top of the stack. The first stack picture is for 32-bit, and the second for 64-bit wide fields. This bytecode handles both. If the specified field is not a static field, an IncompatibleClassChangeError is thrown.

Method Invocation

```
invokevirtual    ..., handle, [arg1, arg2, ...]], ... => ...
```

Invoke instance method based on run/time. The operand stack must contain a reference to an object and some number of arguments. byte1 and byte2 are used to construct an index into the constant pool of the current class. The item at that index in the constant pool contains the complete method signature. A pointer to the object's method table is retrieved from the object reference. The method signature is looked up in the method table. The method signature is guaranteed to exactly match one of the method signatures in the table.

The result of the lookup is an index into the method table of the named class that's used to look in the method table of the object's run/time type, where a pointer to the method block for the matched method is found. The method block indicates the type of method (native, synchronized, and so on) and the number of arguments (nargs) expected on the operand stack.

If the method is marked synchronized, the monitor associated with handle is entered.

The base of the local variables array for the new Java stack frame is set to point to handle on the stack, making handle and the supplied arguments (arg1, arg2, ...) the first nargs local variables of the new frame. The total number of local variables used by the method is determined, and the execution environment of the new frame is pushed after leaving sufficient room for the locals. The base of the operand stack for this method invocation is set to the first word after the execution environment. Finally, execution continues with the first bytecode of the matched method.

If handle is null, a NullPointerException is thrown. If during the method invocation a stack overflow is detected, a StackOverflowError is thrown.

21

```
invokenonvirtual   ..., handle, [arg1, arg2, ...]] ... => ...
```

Invoke instance method based on compile-time type. The operand stack must contain a reference (`handle`) to an object and some number of arguments. `byte1` and `byte2` are used to construct an index into the constant pool of the current class. The item at that index in the constant pool contains the complete method signature and class. The method signature is looked up in the method table of the class indicated. The method signature is guaranteed to exactly match one of the method signatures in the table.

The result of the lookup is a method block. The method block indicates the type of method (`native`, `synchronized`, and so on) and the number of arguments (`nargs`) expected on the operand stack. (The last three paragraphs are identical to the previous bytecode.)

```
invokestatic       ..., , [arg1, arg2, ...]] ... => ...
```

Invoke class (`static`) method. The operand stack must contain some number of arguments. `byte1` and `byte2` are used to construct an index into the constant pool of the current class. The item at that index in the constant pool contains the complete method signature and class. The method signature is looked up in the method table of the class indicated. The method signature is guaranteed to match one of the method signatures in the class's method table exactly.

The result of the lookup is a method block. The method block indicates the type of method (`native`, `synchronized`, and so on) and the number of arguments (`nargs`) expected on the operand stack.

If the method is marked `synchronized`, the monitor associated with the class is entered. (The last two paragraphs are identical to those in `invokevirtual`, except that no `NullPointerException` can be thrown.)

```
invokeinterface    ..., handle, [arg1, arg2, ...] => ...
```

Invoke interface method. The operand stack must contain a reference (`handle`) to an object and some number of arguments. `byte1` and `byte2` are used to construct an index into the constant pool of the current class. The item at that index in the constant pool contains the complete method signature. A pointer to the object's method table is retrieved from the object reference. The method signature is looked up in the method table. The method signature is guaranteed to exactly match one of the method signatures in the table.

The result of the lookup is a method block. The method block indicates the type of method (`native`, `synchronized`, and so on) but, unlike the other "invoke" bytecodes, the number of available arguments (`nargs`) is taken from `byte3`; `byte4` is reserved for future use. (The last three paragraphs are identical to those in `invokevirtual`.)

Exception Handling

athrow   ..., handle => [undefined]

Throw exception. handle must be a handle to an exception object. That exception, which must be a subclass of Throwable, is thrown. The current Java stack frame is searched for the most recent catch clause that handles the exception. If a matching "catch-list" entry is found, the pc is reset to the address indicated by the catch-list pointer, and execution continues there.

If no appropriate catch clause is found in the current stack frame, that frame is popped and the exception is rethrown, starting the process all over again in the parent frame. If handle is null, then a NullPointerException is thrown instead.

Miscellaneous Object Operations

new   ... => ..., handle

Create new object. byte1 and byte2 are used to construct an index into the constant pool of the current class. The item at that index should be a class name that can be resolved to a class pointer, class. A new instance of that class is then created and a reference (handle) for the instance is placed on the top of the stack.

checkcast   ..., handle => ..., [handle¦...]

Make sure object is of given type. handle must be a reference to an object. byte1 and byte2 are used to construct an index into the constant pool of the current class. The string at that index of the constant pool is presumed to be a class name that can be resolved to a class pointer, class.

checkcast determines whether handle can be cast to a reference to an object of that class. (A null handle can be cast to any class.) If handle can be legally cast, execution proceeds at the next bytecode, and the handle for handle remains on the stack. If not, a ClassCastException is thrown.

instanceof   ..., handle => ..., result

Determine whether object is of given type. handle must be a reference to an object. byte1 and byte2 are used to construct an index into the constant pool of the current class. The string at that index of the constant pool is presumed to be a class name that can be resolved to a class pointer, class.

If handle is null, the result is (false). Otherwise, instanceof determines whether handle can be cast to a reference to an object of that class. The result is 1 (true) if it can, and 0 (false) otherwise.

Monitors

```
monitorenter        ..., handle => ...
```

Enter monitored region of code. handle must be a reference to an object. The interpreter attempts to obtain exclusive access via a lock mechanism to handle. If another thread already has handle locked, the current thread waits until the handle is unlocked. If the current thread already has handle locked, execution continues normally. If handle has no lock on it, this bytecode obtains an exclusive lock.

```
monitorexit         ..., handle => ...
```

Exit monitored region of code. handle must be a reference to an object. The lock on handle is released. If this is the last lock that this thread has on that handle (one thread is allowed to have multiple locks on a single handle), other threads that are waiting for handle are allowed to proceed. (A null in either bytecode throws NullPointerException.)

Debugging

```
breakpoint          -no change-
```

Call breakpoint handler. The breakpoint bytecode is used to overwrite a bytecode to force control temporarily back to the debugger prior to the effect of the overwritten bytecode. The original bytecode's operands (if any) are not overwritten, and the original bytecode is restored when the breakpoint bytecode is removed.

The _quick Bytecodes

The following discussion, straight out of the Java virtual machine documentation, shows you an example of the cleverness mentioned earlier that's needed to make a bytecode interpreter fast:

> The following set of pseudo-bytecodes, suffixed by _quick, are all variants of standard Java bytecodes. They are used by the run-time to improve the execution speed of the bytecode interpreter. They aren't officially part of the virtual machine specification and are invisible outside a Java virtual machine implementation. However, inside that implementation they have proven to be an effective optimization.
>
> First, you should know that javac still generates only non-_quick bytecodes. Second, all bytecodes that have a _quick variant reference the constant pool. When _quick optimization is turned on, each non-_quick bytecode (that has a _quick variant) resolves the specified item in the constant pool, signals an error if the item in the constant pool could not be resolved for some reason, turns itself into the _quick variant of itself, and then performs its intended operation.

This is identical to the actions of the non-_quick bytecode, except for the step of overwriting itself with its _quick variant. The _quick variant of a bytecode assumes that the item in the constant pool has already been resolved, and that this resolution did not produce any errors. It simply performs the intended operation on the resolved item.

Thus, as your bytecodes are being interpreted, they are automatically getting faster and faster! Here are all the _quick variants in the current Java run-time:

```
ldc1_quick
ldc2_quick
ldc2w_quick

anewarray_quick
multinewarray_quick

putfield_quick
putfield2_quick
getfield_quick
getfield2_quick
putstatic_quick
putstatic2_quick
getstatic_quick
getstatic2_quick

invokevirtual_quick
invokevirtualobject_quick
invokenonvirtual_quick
invokestatic_quick
invokeinterface_quick

new_quick
checkcast_quick
instanceof_quick
```

If you'd like to go back in today's lesson and look at what each of these does, you can find the name of the original bytecode on which a _quick variant is based by simply removing the _quick from its name. The bytecodes putstatic, getstatic, putfield, and getfield have two _quick variants each, one for each stack picture in their original descriptions. invokevirtual has two variants: one for objects and one for arrays to do fast lookups in javala.Object).

> **Note:** One last note on the _quick optimization, regarding the unusual handling of the constant pool (for detail fanatics only):
>
> When a class is read in, an array constant_pool[] of size nconstants is created and assigned to a field in the class. constant_pool[0] is set to point to a dynamically allocated array that indicates which fields in the constant_pool have already been resolved. constant_pool[1] through constant_pool[nconstants - 1] are set to point at the "type" field that corresponds to this constant item.

21

When a bytecode is executed that references the constant pool, an index is generated, and `constant_pool[0]` is checked to see whether the index has already been resolved. If so, the value of `constant_pool[index]` is returned. If not, the value of `constant_pool[index]` is resolved to be the actual pointer or data, and overwrites whatever value was already in `constant_pool[index]`.

The .class File Format

You won't be given the entire .class file format here, only a taste of what it's like. (You can read all about it in the release documentation.) It's mentioned here because it is one of the parts of Java that needs to be specified carefully if all Java implementations are to be compatible with one another, and if Java bytes are expected to travel across arbitrary networks—to and from arbitrary computers and operating systems—and yet arrive safely.

The rest of this section paraphrases, and extensively condenses, the latest (alpha) release of the .class documentation.

.class files are used to hold the compiled versions of both Java classes and Java interfaces. Compliant Java interpreters must be capable of dealing with all .class files that conform to the following specification.

A Java .class file consists of a stream of 8-bit bytes. All 16-bit and 32-bit quantities are constructed by reading in two or four 8-bit bytes, respectively. The bytes are joined together in big-endian order. (Use `java.io.DataInput` and `java.io.DataOutput` to read and write class files.)

The class file format is presented below as a series of C-struct-like structures. However, unlike a C `struct`, there is no padding or alignment between pieces of the structure, each field of the structure may be of variable size, and an array may be of variable size (in this case, some field prior to the array gives the array's dimension). The types `u1`, `u2`, and `u4` represent an unsigned one-, two-, or four-byte quantity, respectively.

Attributes are used at several different places in the .class format. All attributes have the following format:

```
GenericAttribute_info {
    u2 attribute_name;
    u4 attribute_length;
    u1 info[attribute_length];
}
```

The `attribute_name` is a 16-bit index into the class's constant pool; the value of `constant_pool[attribute_name]` is a string giving the name of the attribute. The field `attribute_length` gives the length of the subsequent information in bytes. This length does not include the four bytes needed to store `attribute_name` and `attribute_length`. In the following text, whenever an attribute is required, names of all the attributes that are currently understood are listed. In the future, more attributes will be added. Class file readers are expected to skip over and ignore the information in any attributes that they do not understand.

The following pseudo-structure gives a top-level description of the format of a class file:

```
ClassFile {
    u4  magic;
    u2  minor_version
    u2  major_version
    u2  constant_pool_count;
    cp_info          constant_pool[constant_pool_count - 1];
    u2  access_flags;
    u2  this_class;
    u2  super_class;
    u2  interfaces_count;
    u2  interfaces[interfaces_count];
    u2  fields_count;
    field_info       fields[fields_count];
    u2  methods_count;
    method_info      methods[methods_count];
    u2  attributes_count;
    attribute_info  attributes[attribute_count];
}
```

Here's one of the smaller structures used:

```
method_info {
    u2  access_flags;
    u2  name_index;
    u2  signature_index;
    u2  attributes_count;
    attribute_info  attributes[attribute_count];
}
```

Finally, here's a sample of one of the later structures in the .class file description:

```
Code_attribute {
    u2  attribute_name_index;
    u2  attribute_length;
    u1  max_stack;
    u1  max_locals;
    u2  code_length;
    u1  code[code_length];
    u2  exception_table_length;
    {   u2_    start_pc;
        u2_    end_pc;
        u2_    handler_pc;
        u2_    catch_type;
    }  exception_table[exception_table_length];
    u2  attributes_count;
    attribute_info  attributes[attribute_count];
}
```

21

None of this is meant to be completely comprehensible (though you might be able to guess at what a lot of the structure members are for), but just suggestive of the sort of structures that live inside .class files. Because the compiler and run-time sources are available, you can always begin with them if you actually have to read or write .class files yourself. Thus, you don't need to have a deep understanding of the details, even in that case.

Method Signatures

Because method signatures are used in .class files, now is an appropriate time to explore them in the detail promised on earlier days—but they're probably most useful to you when writing the native methods of yesterday's lesson.

NEW☞
TERM   A *signature* is a string representing the type of a method, field, or array.

A field signature represents the value of an argument to a method or the value of a variable and is a series of bytes in the following grammar:

```
<field signature> := <field_type>
<field type>      := <base_type> ¦ <object_type> ¦ <array_type>
<base_type>       := B ¦ C ¦ D ¦ F ¦ I ¦ J ¦ S ¦ Z
<object_type>     := L <full.ClassName> ;
<array_type>      := [ <optional_size> <field_type>
<optional_size>   := [0-9]*
```

Here are the meanings of the base types: B (byte), C (char), D (double), F (float), I (int), J (long), S (short), and Z (boolean).

A return-type signature represents the return value from a method and is a series of bytes in the following grammar:

```
<return signature>    := <field type> ¦ V
```

The character V (void) indicates that the method returns no value. Otherwise, the signature indicates the type of the return value. An argument signature represents an argument passed to a method:

```
<argument signature>  := <field type>
```

Finally, a method signature represents the arguments that the method expects, and the value that it returns:

```
<method_signature>    := (<arguments signature>) <return signature>
<arguments signature> := <argument signature>*
```

Let's try out the new rules: a method called `complexMethod()` in the class `my.package.name.ComplexClass` takes three arguments—a `long`, a `boolean`, and a two-dimensional array of `shorts`—and returns `this`. Then, `(JZ[[S)Lmy.package.name.ComplexClass;` is its method signature.

A method signature is often prefixed by the name of the method, or by its full package (using an underscore in the place of dots) and its class name followed by a slash `/` and the name of the method, to form a *complete method signature*. (You saw several of these generated in stub comments yesterday.) Now, at last, you have the full story! Thus, the following:

```
my_package_name_ComplexClass/complexMethod(JZ[[S)Lmy.package.name.ComplexClass;
```

is the full, complete method signature of method `complexMethod()`. (Phew!)

The Garbage Collector

Decades ago, programmers in both the Lisp and the Smalltalk community realized how extremely valuable it is to be able to ignore memory deallocation. They realized that, although allocation is fundamental, deallocation is forced on the programmer by the laziness of the system—*it* should be able to figure out what is no longer useful, and get rid of it. In relative obscurity, these pioneering programmers developed a whole series of garbage collectors to perform this job, each getting more sophisticated and efficient as the years went by. Finally, now that the mainstream programming community has begun to recognize the value of this automated technique, Java can become the first really widespread application of the technology those pioneers developed.

The Problem

Imagine that you're a programmer in a C-like language (probably not too difficult for you, because these languages are the dominant ones right now). Each time you create something, anything, *dynamically* in such a language, you are completely responsible for tracking the life of this object throughout your program and mentally deciding when it will be safe to deallocate it. This can be quite a difficult (sometime impossible) task, because any of the other libraries or methods you've called might have "squirreled away" a pointer to the object, unbeknownst to you. When it becomes impossible to know, you simply choose *never* to deallocate the object, or at least to wait until every library and method call involved has completed, which could be nearly as long.

The uneasy feeling you get when writing such code is a natural, healthy response to what is inherently an unsafe and unreliable style of programming. If you have tremendous discipline—and so does everyone who writes every library and method you call—you can, in principle,

21

survive this responsibility without too many mishaps. But aren't you human? Aren't they? There must be some small slips in this perfect discipline due to error. What's worse, such errors are virtually undetectable, as anyone who's tried to hunt down a stray pointer problem in C will tell you. What about the thousands of programmers who don't have that sort of discipline?

Another way to ask this question is: Why should any programmers be forced to have this discipline, when it is entirely possible for the system to remove this heavy burden from their shoulders?

Software engineering estimates have recently shown that for every 55 lines of production C-like code in the world, there is one bug. This means that your electric razor has about 80 bugs, and your TV, 400. Soon they will have even more, because the size of this kind of embedded computer software is growing exponentially. When you begin to think of how much C-like code is in your car's engine, it should give you pause.

Many of these errors are due to the misuse of pointers, by misunderstanding or by accident, and to the early, incorrect freeing of allocated objects in memory. Java addresses both of these—the former, by eliminating explicit pointers from the Java language altogether and the latter, by including, in every Java system, a garbage collector that solves the problem.

The Solution

Imagine a run-time system that tracks each object you create, notices when the last reference to it has vanished, and frees the object for you. How could such a thing actually work?

One brute-force approach, tried early in the days of garbage collecting, is to attach a reference counter to every object. When the object is created, the counter is set to 1. Each time a new reference to the object is made, the counter is incremented, and each time such a reference disappears, the counter is decremented. Because all such references are controlled by the language—as variables and assignments, for example—the compiler can tell whenever an object reference might be created or destroyed, just as it does in handling the scoping of local variables, and thus it can assist with this task. The system itself "holds onto" a set of root objects that are considered too important to be freed. The class `Object` is one example of such a V.I.P. object. (V.I.O.?) Finally, all that's needed is to test, after each decrement, whether the counter has hit 0. If it has, the object is freed.

If you think carefully about this approach, you can soon convince yourself that it is definitely correct when it decides to free anything. It is so simple that you can immediately tell that it will work. The low-level hacker in you might also feel that if it's *that* simple, it's probably not fast enough to run at the lowest level of the system—and you'd be right.

Think about all the stack frames, local variables, method arguments, return values, and local variables created in the course of even a few hundred milliseconds of a program's life. For each of these tiny, nano-steps in the program, an extra increment—at best—or decrement, test, and deallocation—at worst—will be added to the running time of the program. In fact, the first garbage collectors were slow enough that many predicted they could never be used at all!

Luckily, a whole generation of smart programmers has invented a big bag of tricks to solve these overhead problems. One trick is to introduce special "transient object" areas that don't need to be reference counted. The best of these generational scavenging garbage collectors today can take less than 3 percent of the total time of your program—a remarkable feat if you realize that many other language features, such as loop overheads, can be as large or larger!

There are other problems with garbage collection. If you are constantly freeing and reclaiming space in a program, won't the heap of objects soon become fragmented, with small holes everywhere and no room to create new, large objects? Because the programmer is now free from the chains of manual deallocation, won't they create even more objects than usual?

What's worse, there is another way that this simple reference counting scheme is inefficient, in space rather than time. If a long chain of object references eventually comes full circle, back to the starting object, each object's reference count remains at least 1 *forever*. None of these objects will ever be freed!

Together, these problems imply that a good garbage collector must, every once in a while, step back to compact or to clean up wasted memory.

 NEW **TERM** *Compaction* occurs when a garbage collector steps back and reorganizes memory, eliminating the holes created by fragmentation. Compacting memory is simply a matter of repositioning objects one-by-one into a new, compact grouping that places them all in a row, leaving all the free memory in the heap in one big piece.

Cleaning up the circular garbage still lying around after reference counting is called *marking and sweeping*. A mark-and-sweep of memory involves first marking every root object in the system and then following all the object references inside those objects to new objects to mark, and so on, recursively. Then, when you have no more references to follow, you "sweep away" all the unmarked objects, and compact memory as before.

The good news is that this solves the space problems you were having. The bad news is that when the garbage collector "steps back" and does these operations, a nontrivial amount of time passes during which your program is unable to run—all its objects are being marked, swept, rearranged, and so forth, in what seems like an uninterruptible procedure. Your first hint to a solution is the word "seems."

21

Garbage collecting can actually be done a little at a time, between or in parallel with normal program execution, thus dividing up the large time needed to "step back" into numerous so-small-you-don't-notice-them chunks of time that happen between the cracks. (Of course, years of smart thinking went into the abstruse algorithms that make all this possible!)

One final problem that might worry you a little has to do with these object references. Aren't these "pointers" scattered throughout your program and not just buried in objects? Even if they're only in objects, don't they have to be changed whenever the object they point to is moved by these procedures? The answer to both of these questions is a resounding *yes*, and overcoming them is the final hurdle to making an efficient garbage collector.

There are really only two choices. The first, brute force, assumes that all the memory containing object references needs to be searched on a regular basis, and whenever the object references found by this search match objects that have moved, the old reference is changed. This assumes that there are "hard" pointers in the heap's memory—ones that point directly to other objects. By introducing various kinds of "soft" pointers, including pointers that are like forwarding addresses, the algorithm improves greatly. Although these brute-force approaches sound slow, it turns out that modern computers can do them fast enough to be useful.

> **Note:** You might wonder how the brute-force techniques identify object references. In early systems, references were specially tagged with a "pointer bit," so they could be unambiguously located. Now, so-called conservative garbage collectors simply assume that if it looks like an object reference, it is—at least for the purposes of the mark and sweep. Later, when actually trying to update it, they can find out whether it really is an object reference or not.

The final approach to handling object references, and the one Java currently uses, is also one of the very first ones tried. It involves using 100 percent "soft" pointers. An object reference is actually a handle, sometimes call an "OOP," to the real pointer, and a large object table exists to map these handles into the actual object reference. Although this does introduce extra overhead on almost every object reference (some of which can be eliminated by clever tricks, as you might guess), it's not too high a price to pay for this incredibly valuable level of indirection.

This indirection allows the garbage collector, for example, to mark, sweep, move, or examine one object at a time. Each object can be independently moved "out from under" a running Java program by changing only the object table entries. This not only allows the "step back" phase to happen in the tiniest steps, but it makes a garbage collector that runs literally in parallel with your program much easier to write. This is what the Java garbage collector does.

> **Warning:** You need to be very careful about garbage collection when you're doing critical, real-time programs (such as those mentioned yesterday that legitimately require native methods)—but how often will your Java code be flying a commercial airliner in real-time, anyway?

Java's Parallel Garbage Collector

Java applies almost all these advanced techniques to give you a fast, efficient, parallel garbage collector. Running in a separate thread, it cleans up the Java environment of almost all trash (it is conservative), silently and in the background, is efficient in both space and time, and never steps back for more than an unnoticeably small amount of time. You should never need to know it's there.

By the way, if you want to force a full mark-and-sweep garbage collection to happen soon, you can do so simply by calling the System.gc() method. You might want to do this if you just freed up a majority of the heap's memory in circular garbage, and want it all taken away quickly. You might also call this whenever you're idle, as a hint to the system about when it would be best to come and collect the garbage. This "meta knowledge" is rarely needed by the system, however.

Ideally, you'll never notice the garbage collector, and all those decades of programmers beating their brains out on your behalf will simply let you sleep better at night—and what's wrong with that?

The Security Story

Speaking of sleeping well at night, if you haven't stepped back yet and said, "You mean Java programs will be running rampant on the Internet!?!" you better do so now, for it is a legitimate concern. In fact, it is one of the major technical stumbling blocks (the others being mostly social and economic) to achieving the dream of ubiquity and code sharing mentioned earlier in today's lesson.

Why You Should Worry

Any powerful, flexible technology can be abused. As the Net becomes mainstream and widespread, it, too, will be abused. Already, there have been many blips on the security radar screens of those of us who worry about such things, warning that (at least until today), not enough attention has been paid by the computer industry (or the media) to solving some of the

21

problems constructively that this new world brings with it. One of the benefits of solving security once and for all will be a flowering unseen before in the virtual communities of the Net; whole new economies based on people's attention and creativity will spring to life, rapidly transforming our world in new and positive ways.

The downside to all this new technology, is that we (or someone!) must worry long and hard about how to make the playgrounds of the future safe for our children, and for us. Fortunately, Java is a big part of the answer.

Why You Might Not Have To

What gives me any confidence that the Java language and environment will be *safe*, that it will solve the technically daunting and extremely thorny problems inherent in any good form of security, especially for networks?

One simple reason is the history of the people, and the company, that created Java. Many of them are the very smart programmers referred to throughout the book, who helped pioneer many of the ideas that make Java great and who have worked hard over the decades to make techniques such as garbage collection a mainstream reality. They are technically capable of tackling and solving the hard problems that need to be solved. In particular, from discussions with Chuck McManis, one of Java's security gurus, I have confidence that he has thought through these hard problems deeply, and that he knows what needs to be done.

Sun Microsystems, the company, has been pushing networks as the central theme of all its software for more than a decade. Sun has the engineers and the commitment needed to solve these hard problems, because these same problems are at the very center of both its future business and its vision of the future, in which networking is the center of everything—and global networks are nearly useless without good security. Just this year, Sun has advanced the state of the art in easy-to-use Internet security with its new SunScreen products, and it has assigned Whitfield Diffie to oversee them, who is the man who discovered the underlying ideas on which essentially *all* interesting forms of modern encryption are based.

Enough on "deep background." What does the Java environment provide *right now* that helps us feel secure?

Java's Security Model

Java protects you against potential "nasty" Java code via a series of interlocking defenses that, together, form an imposing barrier to any and all such attacks.

Caution: Of course, no one can protect you from your own ignorance or carelessness. If you're the kind of person who blindly downloads binary executables from your Internet browser and runs them, you need read no further! You are already in more danger than Java will ever pose.

As a user of this powerful new medium, the Internet, you should educate yourself to the possible threats this new and exciting world entails. In particular, downloading "auto running macros" or reading e-mail with "executable attachments" is just as much a threat as downloading binaries from the Net and running them.

Java does not introduce any new dangers here, but by being the first mainstream use of executable and mobile code on the Net, it is responsible for making people suddenly aware of the dangers that have always been there. Java is already, as you will soon see, much less dangerous than any of these common activities on the Net, and can be made safer still over time. Most of these other (dangerous) activities can never be made safe. So please, do not do them!

A good rule of thumb on the Net is: Don't download anything that you plan to execute (or that will be automatically executed for you) except from someone (or some company) you know well and with whom you've had positive, personal experience. If you don't care about losing all the data on your hard drive, or about your privacy, you can do anything you like, but for most of us, this rule should be law.

Fortunately, Java allows you to relax that law. You can run Java applets from anyone, anywhere, in complete safety.

Java's powerful security mechanisms act at four different levels of the system architecture. First, the Java language itself was designed to be safe, and the Java compiler ensures that source code doesn't violate these safety rules. Second, all bytecodes executed by the run-time are screened to be sure that they also obey these rules. (This layer guards against having an altered compiler produce code that violates the safety rules.) Third, the class loader ensures that classes don't violate name space or access restrictions when they are loaded into the system. Finally, API-specific security prevents applets from doing destructive things. This final layer depends on the security and integrity guarantees from the other three layers.

Let's now examine each of these layers in turn.

21

The Language and the Compiler

The Java language and its compiler are the first line of defense. Java was designed to be a safe language.

Most other C-like languages have facilities to control access to "objects," but also have ways to "forge" access to objects (or to parts of objects), usually by (mis-)using pointers. This introduces two fatal security flaws to any system built on these languages. One is that no object can protect itself from outside modification, duplication, or "spoofing" (others pretending to be that object). Another is that a language with powerful pointers is more likely to have serious bugs that compromise security. These pointer bugs, where a "runaway pointer" starts modifying some other object's memory, were responsible for most of the public (and not-so-public) security problems on the Internet this past decade.

Java eliminates these threats in one stroke by eliminating pointers from the language altogether. There are still pointers of a kind—object references—but these are carefully controlled to be safe: they are unforgeable, and all casts are checked for legality before being allowed. In addition, powerful new array facilities in Java not only help to offset the loss of pointers, but add additional safety by strictly enforcing array bounds, catching more bugs for the programmer (bugs that, in other languages, might lead to unexpected and, thus, bad-guy-exploitable problems).

The language definition, and the compilers that enforce it, create a powerful barrier to any "nasty" Java programmer.

Because an overwhelming majority of the "net-savvy" software on the Internet may soon be Java, its safe language definition and compilers help to guarantee that most of this software has a solid, secure base. With fewer bugs, Net software will be more predictable—a property that thwarts attacks.

Verifying the Bytecodes

What if that "nasty" programmer gets a little more determined, and rewrites the Java compiler to suit his nefarious purposes? The Java run-time, getting the lion's share of its bytecodes from the Net, can never tell whether those bytecodes were generated by a "trustworthy" compiler. Therefore, it must *verify* that they meet all the safety requirements.

Before running any bytecodes, the run-time subjects them to a rigorous series of tests that vary in complexity from simple format checks all the way to running a theorem prover, to make certain that they are playing by the rules. These tests verify that the bytecodes do not forge pointers, violate access restrictions, access objects as other than what they are (InputStreams are always used as InputStreams, and never as anything else), call methods with inappropriate argument values or types, nor overflow the stack.

Consider the following Java code sample:

```
public class VectorTest {
    public int  array[];

    public int  sum() {
        int[]  localArray = array;
        int    sum        = 0;

        for (int  i = localArray.length;  --i >= 0;  )
            sum += localArray[i];
        return sum;
    }
}
```

The bytecodes generated when this code is compiled look something like the following:

aload_0	Load `this`
getfield #10	Load `this.array`
astore_1	Store in `localArray`
iconst_0	Load `0`
istore_2	Store in `sum`
aload_1	Load `localArray`
arraylength	Gets its length
istore_3	Store in `i`
A: iinc 3 -1	Subtract 1 from `i`
iload_3	Load `i`
iflt B	Exit loop if `< 0`
iload_2	Load `sum`
aload_1	Load `localArray`
iload_3	Load `i`
iaload	Load `localArray[i]`
iadd	Add `sum`
istore_2	Store in `sum`
goto A	Do it again
B: iload_2	Load `sum`
ireturn	Return it

21

Note: The excellent examples and descriptions in this section of the book are paraphrased from the tremendously informative security paper in the (alpha) Java release. I'd encourage you to read whatever the latest version of this document is in newer releases, if you want to follow the ongoing Java security story.

Extra Type Information and Requirements

Java bytecodes encode more type information than is strictly necessary for the interpreter. Even though, for example, the `aload` and `iload` opcodes do exactly the same thing, `aload` is always used to load an object reference and `iload` used to load an integer. Some bytecodes (such as `getfield`) include a symbol table reference—and that symbol table has *even more* type information. This extra type information allows the run-time system to guarantee that Java objects and data aren't illegally manipulated.

Conceptually, before and after each bytecode is executed, every slot in the stack and every local variable has some type. This collection of type information—all the slots and local variables—is called the *type state* of the execution environment. An important requirement of the Java type state is that it must be determinable statically by induction—that is, before any program code is executed. As a result, as the run-time systems reads bytecodes, each is required to have the following inductive property: given only the type state before the execution of the bytecode, the type state afterward must be fully determined.

Given "straight-line" bytecodes (no branches), and starting with a known stack state, the state of each slot in the stack is therefore always known. For example, starting with an empty stack:

`iload_1`	Load integer variable. Stack type state is I.
`iconst 5`	Load integer constant. Stack type state is II.
`iadd`	Add two integers, producing an integer. Stack type state is I.

Note: Smalltalk and PostScript bytecodes do not have this restriction. Their more dynamic type behavior does create additional flexibility in those systems, but Java needs to provide a secure execution environment. It must therefore know all types *at all times*, in order to guarantee a certain level of security.

Another requirement made by the Java run-time is that when a set of bytecodes can take more than one path to arrive at the same point, all such paths must arrive there with exactly the same type state. This is a strict requirement, and implies, for example, that compilers cannot generate bytecodes that load all the elements of an array onto the stack. (Because each time through such a loop the stack's type state changes, the start of the loop—"the same point" in multiple paths— would have more than one type state, which is not allowed).

The Verifier

Bytecodes are checked for compliance with all these requirements, using the extra type information in a .class file, by a part of the run-time called the *verifier*. It examines each bytecode in turn, constructing the full type state as it goes, and verifies that all the types of parameters, arguments, and results are correct. Thus, the verifier acts as a gatekeeper to your run-time environment, letting in only those bytecodes that pass muster.

> **Warning:** The verifier is *the crucial piece* of Java's security, and it depends on your having a correctly implemented (no bugs, intentional or otherwise) run-time system. As of this writing, only Sun is producing Java run-times, and theirs are secure. In the future, however, you should be careful when downloading or buying another company's (or individual's) version of the Java run-time environment. Eventually, Sun will implement validation suites for run-times, compilers, and so forth to be sure that they are safe and correct. In the meantime, *caveat emptor*! Your run-time is the base on which all the rest of Java's security is built, so make sure it is a good, solid, secure base.

When bytecodes have passed the verifier, they are guaranteed not to: cause any operand stack under- or overflows; use parameter, argument, or return types incorrectly; illegally convert data from one type to another (from an integer to a pointer, for example); nor access any object's fields illegally (that is, the verifier checks that the rules for public, private, package, and protected are obeyed).

As an added bonus, because the interpreter can now count on all these facts being true, it can run much faster than before. All the required checks for safety have been done up front, so it can run at full throttle. In addition, object references can now be treated as capabilities, because they are unforgeable—capabilities allow, for example, advanced security models for file I/O and authentication to be safely built on top of Java.

21

> **Note:** Because you can now trust that a `private` variable really is private, and that no bytecode can perform some magic with casts to extract information from it (such as your credit card number), many of the security problems that might arise in other, less safe environments simply vanish! These guarantees also make erecting barriers against destructive applets possible, and easier. Because the Java system doesn't have to worry about "nasty" bytecodes, it can get on with creating the other levels of security it wants to provide to you.

The Class Loader

The class loader is another kind of gatekeeper, albeit a higher-level one. The verifier was the security of last resort. The class loader is the security of first resort.

When a new class is loaded into the system, it must come from one of several different "realms." In the current release, there are three possible realms: your local computer, the firewall-guarded local network on which your computer is located, and the Internet (the global Net). Each of these realms is treated differently by the class loader.

> **Note:** Actually, there can be as many realms as your desired level of security (or paranoia) requires. This is because the class loader is under your control. As a programmer, you can make your own class loader that implements your own peculiar brand of security. (This is a radical step: you may have to give the users of your program a whole bunch of classes—and they give you a whole lot of trust—to accomplish this.)
>
> As a user, you can tell your Java-aware browser, or Java system, what realm of security (of the three) you'd like it to implement for you right now or from now on.
>
> As a system administrator, Java has global security policies that you can set up to help guide your users to not "give away the store" (that is, set all their preferences to be unrestricted, promiscuous, "hurt me please!").

In particular, the class loader never allows a class from a "less protected" realm to replace a class from a more protected realm. The file system's I/O primitives, about which you should be *very* worried (and rightly so), are all defined in a local Java class, which means that they all live in the local-computer realm. Thus, no class from outside your computer (from either the supposedly trustworthy local network or from the Internet) can take the place of these classes and "spoof"

Java code into using "nasty" versions of these primitives. In addition, classes in one realm cannot call upon the methods of classes in other realms, unless those classes have explicitly declared those methods `public`. This implies that classes from other than your local computer cannot even *see* the file system I/O methods, much less call them, unless you or the system wants them to.

In addition, every new applet loaded from the network is placed into a separate package-like namespace. This means that applets are protected even from each other! No applet can access another's methods (or variables) without its cooperation. Applets from inside the firewall can even be treated differently from those outside the firewall, if you like.

> **Note:** Actually, it's all a little more complex than this. In the current release, an applet is in a package "namespace" along with any other applets from that *source*. This source, or origin, is most often a host (domain name) on the Internet. This special "subrealm" is used extensively in the next section. Depending on where the source is located, outside the firewall (or inside), further restrictions may apply (or be removed entirely). This model is likely to be extended in future releases of Java, providing an even finer degree of control over which classes get to do what.

The class loader essentially partitions the world of Java classes into small, protected little groups, about which you can safely make assumptions that will *always* be true. This type of predictability is the key to well-behaved and secure programs.

You've now seen the full lifetime of a method. It starts as source code on some computer, is compiled into bytecodes on some (possibly different) computer, and can then travel (as a .class file) into any file system or network anywhere in the world. When you run an applet in a Java-aware browser (or download a class and run it by hand using `java`), the method's bytecodes are extracted from its .class file and carefully looked over by the verifier. Once they are declared safe, the interpreter can execute them for you (or a code generator can generate native binary code for them using either the "just-in-time" compiler or `java2c`, and then run that native code directly).

At each stage, more and more security is added. The final level of that security is the Java class library itself, which has several carefully designed classes and APIs that add the final touches to the security of the system.

The Security Manager

`SecurityManager` is an `abstract` class that was recently added to the Java system to collect, in one place, all the security policy decisions that the system has to make as bytecodes run. You learned before that you can create your own class loader. In fact, you may not have to, because you can subclass `SecurityManager` to perform most of the same customizations.

An instance of some subclass of `SecurityManager` is always installed as the current security manager. It has complete control over which of a well-defined set of "dangerous" methods are allowed to be called by any given class. It takes the realms from the last section into account, the source (origin) of the class, and the type of the class (stand-alone, or loaded by an applet). Each of these can be separately configured to have the effect you (the programmer) like on your Java system. For nonprogrammers, the system provides several levels of default security policies from which you can choose.

What is this "well-defined set" of methods that are protected?

File I/O is a part of the set, for obvious reasons. Applets, by default, can open, read, or write files only with the express permission of the user—and even then, only in certain restricted directories. (Of course, users can always be stupid about this, but that's what system administrators are for!)

Also in this protected set are the methods that create and use network connections, both incoming and outgoing.

The final members of the set are those methods that allow one thread to access, control, and manipulate other threads. (Of course, additional methods can be protected as well, by creating a new subclass of `SecurityManager` that handles them.)

For both file and network access, the user of a Java-aware browser can choose between three realms (and one subrealm) of protection:

☐ *unrestricted* (allows applets to do anything)

☐ *firewall* (allows applets within the firewall to do anything)

☐ *source* (allows applets to do things only with their origin {Internet} host, or with other applets from there)

☐ *local* (disallows all file and network access)

For file access, the *source* subrealm is not meaningful, so it really has only three realms of protection. (As a programmer, of course, you have full access to the security manager and can set up your own peculiar criteria for granting and revoking privileges to your heart's content.)

For network access, you can imagine wanting many more realms. For example, you might specify different groups of trusted domains (companies), each of which is allowed added privileges when applets from that group are loaded. Some groups can be more trusted than others, and you might even allow groups to grow automatically by allowing existing members to recommend new members for admission. (The Java seal of approval?)

In any case, the possibilities are endless, as long as there is a secure way of recognizing the original creator of an applet.

You might think this problem has already been solved, because classes are tagged with their origin. In fact, the Java run-time goes far out of its way to be sure that that origin information is never lost—any executing method can be dynamically restricted by this information anywhere in the call chain. So why *isn't* this enough?

Because what you'd really like to be able to do is permanently "tag" an applet with its original creator (its true origin), and no matter where it has traveled, a browser could verify the integrity and authenticate the creator of that applet. Just because you don't know the company or individual that operates a particular server machine doesn't mean that you *want* to mistrust every applet stored on that machine. It's just that, currently, to be really safe, you *should* mistrust those applets, however.

If somehow those applets were irrevocably tagged with a digital signature by their creator, and that signature could also guarantee that the applet had not been tampered with, you'd be golden.

> **Note:** Luckily, Sun is planning to do exactly that for Java, as soon as export restrictions can be resolved.
>
> Here's a helpful hint of where the team would like to go, from the security documentation: "...a mechanism exists whereby public keys and cryptographic message digests can be securely attached to code fragments that not only identify who originated the code, but guarantee its integrity as well. This latter mechanism will be implemented in future releases."
>
> Look for these sorts of features in every release of Java; they will be a key part of the future of the Internet!

One final note about security. Despite the best efforts of the Java team, there is always a trade-off between useful functionality and absolute security. For example, Java applets can create windows, an extremely useful capability, but a "nasty" applet could use this to spoof the user into typing private password information, by showing a familiar program (or operating system) window and then asking an expected, legitimate-looking question in it. (The beta release adds a special banner to applet-created windows to solve this problem.)

Flexibility and security can't both be maximized. Thus far on the Net, people have chosen maximum flexibility, and have lived with the minimal security the Net now provides. Let's hope that Java can help tip the scales a bit, enabling much better security, while sacrificing only a minimal amount of the flexibility that has drawn so many to the Net.

21

Summary

Today, you learned about the grand vision that some of us have for Java, and about the exciting future it promises.

Under the hood, the inner workings of the virtual machine, the bytecode interpreter (and all its bytecodes), the garbage collector, the class loader, the verifier, the security manager, and the powerful security features of Java were all revealed.

You now know *almost* enough to write a Java run-time environment of your own—but luckily, you don't have to. You can simply download the latest release of Java—or use a Java-aware browser to enjoy most of the benefits of Java right away.

I hope that Java ends up opening new roads in your mind, as it has in mine.

Q&A

Q I'm still a little unclear about why the Java language and compiler make the Net safer. Can't they just be "side-stepped" by nasty bytecodes?

A Yes, they can—but don't forget that the whole point of using a safe language and compiler was to make the Net *as a whole* safer as more Java code is written. An overwhelming majority of this Java code will be written by "honest" Java programmers, who will produce safe bytecodes. This makes the Net more predictable over time, and thus more secure.

Q I know you said that garbage collection is something I don't have to worry about, but what if I want (or need) to?

A So, you *are* planning to fly a plane with Java. Cool! For just such cases, there is a way to ask the Java run-time, during startup (`java -noasyncgc`), *not* to run garbage collection unless forced to, either by an explicit call (`System.gc()`) or by running out of memory. (This can be quite useful if you have multiple threads that are messing each other up and want to "get the gc thread out of the way" while testing them.) Don't forget that turning garbage collection off means that any object you create will live a *long, long time*. If you're real-time, you never want to "step back" for a full gc—so be sure to reuse objects often, and don't create too many of them!

Q I like the control above; is there anything else I can do to the garbage collector?

A You can also force the `finalize()` methods of any recently freed objects to be called immediately via `System.runFinalization()`. You might want to do this if you're about to ask for some resources that you suspect might still be tied up by objects that are "gone but not forgotten" (waiting for `finalize()`). This is even rarer than starting a gc by hand, but it's mentioned here for completeness.

Q What's the last word on Java?

A Java adds much more than it can ever take away. It has always done so for me, and now, I hope it will for you, as well.

The future of the Net is filled with as-yet-undreamt horizons, and the road is long and hard, but Java is a great traveling companion.

21

Language Summary

by Laura Lemay

This appendix contains a summary or quick reference for the Java language, as described in this book.

> **Technical Note:** This is not a grammar overview, nor is it a technical overview of the language itself. It's a quick reference to be used after you already know the basics of how the language works. If you need a technical description of the language, your best bet is to visit the Java Web Site (`http://java.sun.com`) and download the actual specification, which includes a full BNF grammar.

Language keywords and symbols are shown in a monospace font. Arguments and other parts to be substituted are in italic monospace.

Optional parts are indicated by brackets (except in the array syntax section). If there are several options that are mutually exclusive, they are shown separated by pipes (`[¦]`) like this:

```
[ public ¦ private ¦ protected ] type varname
```

Reserved Words

The following words are reserved for use by the Java language itself (some of them are reserved but not currently used). You cannot use these words to refer to classes, methods, or variable names:

abstract	do	implements	package	throw
boolean	double	import	private	throws
break	else	inner	protected	transient
byte	extends	instanceof	public	try
case	final	int	rest	var
cast	finally	interface	return	void
catch	float	long	short	volatile
char	for	native	static	while
class	future	new	sure	
const	generic	null	switch	
continue	goto	operator	synchronized	
default	if	outer	this	

Comments

```
/* this is a multiline comment */
// this is a single-line comment
/** Javadoc comment */
```

Literals

`number`	Type `int`
`number[l [¦] L]`	Type `long`
`0xhex`	Hex integer
`0Xhex`	Hex integer
`0octal`	Octal integer
`[ number ].number`	Type `double`
`number[ f [¦] f]`	Type `float`
`number[ d [¦] D]`	Type `double`
`[ + [¦] - ] number`	Signed
`numberenumber`	Exponent
`numberEnumber`	Exponent
`'character'`	Single character
`"characters"`	String
`" "`	Empty string
`\b`	Backspace
`\t`	Tab
`\n`	Line feed
`\f`	Form feed
`\r`	Carriage return
`\"`	Double quote
`\'`	Single quote
`\\`	Backslash
`\uNNNN`	Unicode escape (NNNN is hex)
`true`	Boolean
`false`	Boolean

Variable Declaration

`[ byte ¦ short ¦ int ¦ long ] varname`	Integers (pick one type)
`[ float ¦ double ] varname`	Floats (pick one type)
`char varname;`	Characters
`boolean varname`	Boolean
`classname varname;`	Class types
`interfacename varname`	Interface types
`type varname, varname, varname;`	Multiple variables

The following options are available only for class and instance variables. Any of these options can be used with a variable declaration

`[ static ] variableDeclaration`	Class variable
`[ final ] variableDeclaration`	Constants
`[ public ¦ private ¦ protected ] variableDeclaration`	Access control
`[volatile] varname`	Modified asynchronously
`[transient] varname`	Not persistent (not yet implemented)

Variable Assignment

`variable = value`	Assignment
`variable++`	Postfix Increment
`++variable`	Prefix Increment
`variable--`	Postfix Decrement
`--variable`	Prefix Decrement
`variable += value`	Add and assign
`variable -= value`	Subtract and assign
`variable *= value`	Multiply and assign
`variable ÷= value`	Divide and assign
`variable %= value`	Modulus and assign
`variable &= value`	AND and assign
`variable ¦= value`	OR and assign

`variable ^= value`	XOR and assign
`variable <<= value`	Left-shift and assign
`variable >>= value`	Right-shift and assign
`variable >>>= value`	Zero-fill right-shift and assign

Operators

`arg + arg`	Addition
`arg - arg`	Subtraction
`arg * arg`	Multiplication
`arg ÷ arg`	Division
`arg % arg`	Modulus
`arg < arg`	Less than
`arg > arg`	Greater than
`arg    arg`	Less than or equal to
`arg    arg`	Greater than or equal to
`arg == arg`	Equal
`arg    arg`	Not equal
`arg && arg`	Logical AND
`arg ¦¦ arg`	Logical OR
`! arg`	Logical NOT
`arg & arg`	AND
`arg ¦ arg`	OR
`arg ^ arg`	XOR
`arg << arg`	Left-shift
`arg >> arg`	Right-shift
`arg >>> arg`	Zero-fill right-shift
`~ arg`	Complement
`(type)thing`	Casting
`arg instanceof class`	Instance of
`test ? trueOp : falseOp`	Tenary (if) operator

Objects

new *class*()	Create new instance
new *class*(*arg*,*arg*,*arg*...)	New instance with parameters
object.*variable*	Instance variable
object.*classvar*	Class variable
Class.*classvar*	Class variable
object.*method*()	Instance method (no args)
object.*method*(*arg*,*arg*,*arg*...)	Instance method
object.*classmethod*()	Class method (no args)
object.*classmethod*(*arg*,*arg*,*arg*...)	Class method
Class.*classmethod*()	Class method (no args)
Class.*classmethod*(*arg*,*arg*,*arg*...)	Class method

Arrays

Note: The brackets in this section are parts of the array creation or access statements. They do not denote optional parts as they do in other parts of this appendix.

type varname[]	Array variable
type[] *varname*	Array variable
new *type*[*numElements*]	New array object
array[*index*]	Element access
array.length	Length of array

Loops and Conditionals

if (*test*) *block*	Conditional
if (*test*) *block*	

`else` *block*	Conditional with `else`

`switch (test) {`
    `case value : statement`
    `case value : statement`
    `...`
    `default : statement`
`}`
	`switch` (only with integer or char types)

`for (initializer, test, change ) block`	`for` loop
`while ( test ) block`	`while` loop
`do block` `while (test)`	`do` loop
`break [ label ]`	`break` from loop or `switch`
`continue [ label ]`	`continue` loops
`label:`	Labeled loops

Class Definitions

`class classname block`	Simple Class definition

Any of the following optional modifiers can be added to the class definition:

`[ final ] class classname block`	Cannot be subclassed
`[ abstract ] class classname block`	Cannot be instantiated
`[ public ] class classname block`	Accessible outside package
`class classname [ extends Superclass ] block`	Define superclass
`class classname [ implements interfaces ] block`	Implement one or more interfaces

Method and Constructor Definitions

The basic method looks like this, where *returnType* is a type name, a class name, or `void`.

`returnType methodName() block`	Basic method
`returnType methodName(parameter, parameter, ...) block`	Method with parameters

Method parameters look like this:

```
type parameterName
```

Method variations can include any of the following optional keywords:

`[ abstract ] `*`returnType methodName() block`*	Abstract method
`[ static ] `*`returnType methodName() block`*	Class method
`[ native ] `*`returnType methodName() block`*	Native method
`[ final ] `*`returnType methodName() block`*	`final` method
`[ synchronized ] `*`returnType methodName() block`*	Thread lock before executing
`[ public ¦ private ¦ protected ] `*`returnType methodName()`*	Block access control

Constructors look like this:

`classname()` `block`	basic constructor
`classname(parameter, parameter, parameter...)` `block`	constructor with parameters
`[ public ¦ private ¦ protected]` *`classname()`*`block`	Access control

In the method/constructor body you can use these references and methods:

`this`	Refers to current object
`super`	Refers to superclass
`super.`*`methodName()`*	Call a superclass's method
`this(...)`	Calls class's constructor
`super(...)`	Calls superclass's constructor
`return [ `*`value`*` ]`	Returns a value

Packages, Interfaces, and Importing

`import `*`package.className`*	Imports specific class name
`import `*`package`*`.*`	Imports all public classes in package
`package `*`packagename`*	Classes in this file belong to this package

```
interface interfaceName [ extends anotherInterface ] block

[ public ] interface interfaceName block

[ abstract ] interface interfaceName block
```

Exceptions and Guarding

synchronized (*object*) *block*	Waits for lock on *object*
try *block*	Guarded statements
catch (*exception*) *block*	Executed if *exception* is thrown
[finally *block*]	Cleanup code
try block	Same as previous example (can
[catch (*exception*) *block*]	use optional catch or finally,
finally *block*	but not both)

Class Hierarchy Diagrams

by Charles L. Perkins

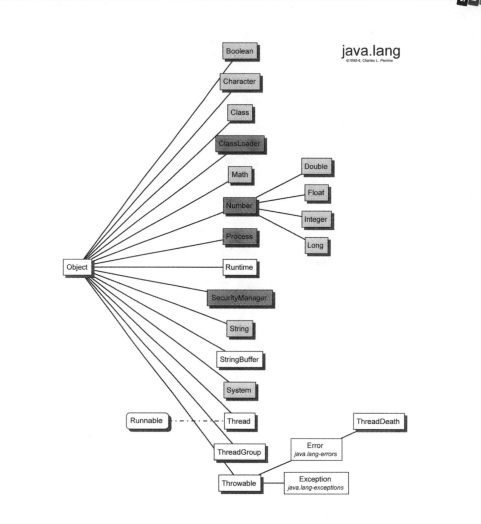

java.lang

©1995-6, Charles L. Perkins

B

java.lang-errors

java.lang-exceptions

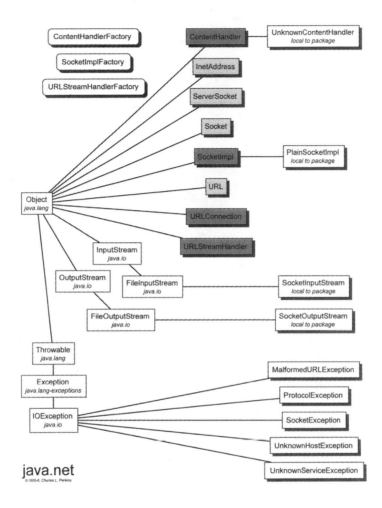

ContentHandlerFactory

SocketImplFactory

URLStreamHandlerFactory

ContentHandler — UnknownContentHandler
local to package

InetAddress

ServerSocket

Socket

SocketImpl — PlainSocketImpl
local to package

URL

URLConnection

URLStreamHandler

Object
java.lang

InputStream
java.io

OutputStream
java.io

FileInputStream
java.io — SocketInputStream
local to package

FileOutputStream
java.io — SocketOutputStream
local to package

Throwable
java.lang

Exception
java.lang-exceptions

IOException
java.io

MalformedURLException

ProtocolException

SocketException

UnknownHostException

UnknownServiceException

java.net
© 1995-6, Charles L. Perkins

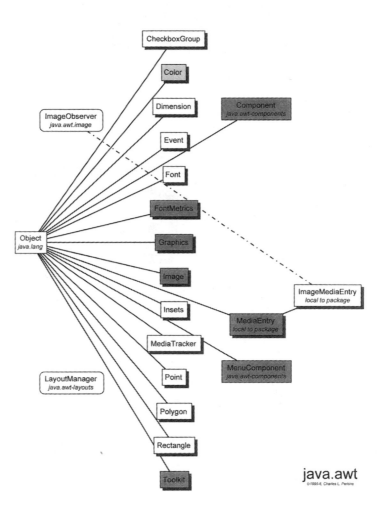

java.awt

© 1995-6, Charles L. Perkins

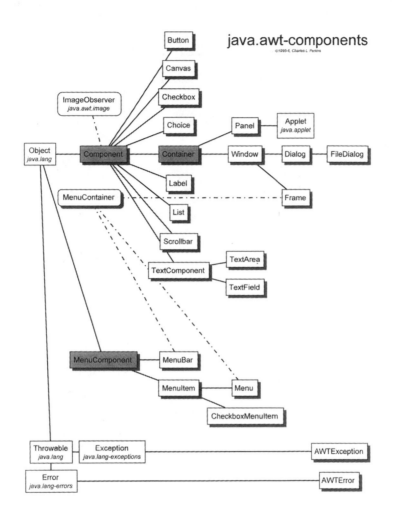

java.awt-components

©1995-6, Charles L. Perkins

java.awt-layouts

java.awt.image

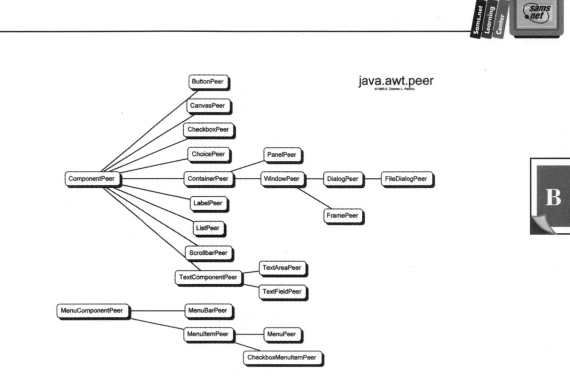

java.awt.peer
©1995-6, Charles L. Perkins

B

493

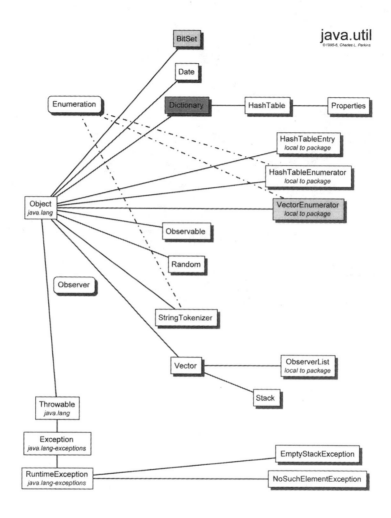

java.util
©1995-6, Charles L. Perkins

About These Diagrams

The diagrams in this appendix are class hierarchy diagrams for the package java and for all the subpackages recursively below it in the Java beta binary release.

Each page contains the class hierarchy for one package (or a subtree of a particularly large package) with all its interfaces included, and each class in this tree is shown attached to its superclasses, even if they are on another page. A detailed key is located on the first page of this appendix.

> **Note:** Win32Process and UNIXProcess appear in their respective distributions of Java, but both implement (essentially) the same protocol as their common abstract superclass—Process—so only it was included. This means that are no platform-dependent classes in the diagrams. (Of course, each release actually has some such classes in its .class directories.) Several abstract classes have no subclasses in the documented library, but any concrete implementation of Java would define subclasses of them.

I supplemented the (incomplete) API documentation by looking through all the source files (below src/java) to find all the (missing) package classes and their relationships.

I've heard there are various programs that auto-layout hierarchies for you, but I did these the old-fashioned way (in other words, I *earned* it, as J.H. used to say). One nice side effect is that these diagrams should be more readable than a computer would produce, though you will have to live with my aesthetic choices (sorry). I chose, for example, to attach lines through the center of each class node, something which I think looks and feels better overall (to me) but which on occasion can be a little confusing. Follow lines through the center of the classes (not at the corners, nor along any line not passing through the center) to connect the dots mentally.

The Java Class Library

by Laura Lemay

This appendix provides a general overview of the classes available in the standard Java packages (that is, the classes that are guaranteed to be available in any Java implementation). This appendix is intended for general reference; for more information about class inheritance and the exceptions defined for each package, see Appendix B. For more specific information about each variable and the methods within each class, see the API documentation from Sun at `http://java.sun.com`.

java.lang

The `java.lang` package contains the classes and interfaces that make up the core Java language.

Interfaces

`Runnable`	Methods for classes that want to run as threads

Classes

`Boolean`	Object wrapper for boolean values
`Character`	Object wrapper for `char` values
`Class`	Run-time representations of classes
`ClassLoader`	Abstract behavior for handling loading of classes
`Double`	Object wrapper for `double` values
`Float`	Object wrapper for `float` values
`Integer`	Object wrapper for `int` values
`Long`	Object wrapper for `long` values
`Math`	Utility class for math operations
`Number`	Abstract superclass of all number classes (`Integer`, `Float`, and so on)
`Object`	Generic `Object` class, at top of inheritance hierarchy
`Process`	Abstract behavior for processes such as those spawned using methods in the `System` class
`Runtime`	Access to the Java run-time
`SecurityManager`	Abstract behavior for implementing security policies
`String`	Character strings
`StringBuffer`	Mutable strings
`System`	Access to Java's system-level behavior, provided in a platform-independent way

Thread	Methods for managing threads and classes that run in threads
ThreadGroup	A group of threads
Throwable	Generic Exception class; all objects thrown must be a Throwable

java.util

The `java.util` package contains various utility classes and interfaces, including random numbers, system properties, and other useful classes.

Interfaces

Enumeration	Methods for enumerating sets of values
Observer	Methods for allowing classes to observe `Observable` objects

Classes

BitSet	A set of bits
Date	The current system date, as well as methods for generating and parsing dates
Dictionary	An abstract class that maps between keys and values (superclass of `HashTable`)
Hashtable	A hash table
Observable	An abstract class for observable objects
Properties	A hashtable that contains behavior for setting and retrieving persistent properties of the system or of a class
Random	Utilities for generating random numbers
Stack	A stack (a last-in-first-out queue)
StringTokenizer	Utilities for splitting strings into a sequence of individual "tokens"
Vector	A growable array of `Objects`

java.io

The java.io package provides input and output classes and interfaces for streams and files.

Interfaces

DataInput	Methods for reading machine-independent typed input streams
DataOutput	Methods for writing machine-independent typed output streams
FilenameFilter	Methods for filtering file names

Classes

BufferedInputStream	A buffered input stream
BufferedOutputStream	A buffered output stream
ByteArrayInputStream	An input stream from a byte array
ByteArrayOutputStream	An output stream to a byte array
DataInputStream	Enables you to read primitive Java types (ints, chars, booleans, and so on) from a stream in a machine-independent way
DataOutputStream	Enables you to write primitive Java data types (ints, chars, booleans, and so on) to a stream in a machine-independent way
File	Represents a file on the host's file system
FileInputStream	An input stream from a file, constructed using a filename or descriptor
FileOutputStream	An output stream to a file, constructed using a filename or descriptor
FilterInputStream	Abstract class which provides a filter for input streams (and for adding stream functionality such as buffering)
FilterOutputStream	Abstract class which provides a filter for output streams (and for adding stream functionality such as buffering)
InputStream	An abstract class representing an input stream of bytes; the parent of all input streams in this package

LineNumberInputStream	An input stream that keeps track of line numbers
OutputStream	An abstract class representing an output stream of bytes; the parent of all output streams in this package
PipedInputStream	A piped input stream, which should be connected to a `PipedOutputStream` to be useful
PipedOutputStream	A piped output stream, which should be connected to a `PipedInputStream` to be useful (together they provide safe communication between threads)
PrintStream	An output stream for printing (used by `System.out.printIn(...)`)
PushbackInputStream	An input stream with a 1-byte push back buffer
RandomAccessFile	Provides random-access to a file, constructed from filenames, descriptors, or objects
SequenceInputStream	Converts a sequence of input streams into a single input steam
StreamTokenizer	Converts an input stream into a sequence of individual tokens
StringBufferInputStream	An input stream from a `StringBuffer` object

java.net

The java.net package contains classes and interfaces for performing network operations, such as sockets and URLs.

Interfaces

ContentHandlerFactory	Methods for creating `ContentHandler` objects
SocketImplFactory	Methods for creating socket implementations (instance of the `SocketImpl` class)
URLStreamHandlerFactory	Methods for creating `URLStreamHandler` objects

Classes

ContentHandler	Abstract behavior for reading data from a URL connection and constructing the appropriate local object, based on MIME types
InetAddress	An object representation of an Internet host (host name, IP address)
ServerSocket	A server-side socket
Socket	A socket
SocketImpl	An abstract class for specific socket implementations
URL	An object representation of a URL
URLConnection	Abstract behavior for a socket that can handle various Web-based protocols (http, ftp, and so on)
URLStreamHandler	Abstract class for managing streams to object referenced by URLs

java.awt

The java.awt package contains the classes and interfaces that make up the Abstract Windowing Toolkit.

Interfaces

LayoutManager	Methods for laying out containers
MenuContainer	Methods for menu-related containers

Classes

BorderLayout	A layout manager for arranging items in border formation
Button	A UI pushbutton
Canvas	A canvas for drawing and performing other graphics operations
CardLayout	A layout manager for HyperCard-like metaphors
Checkbox	A checkbox
CheckboxGroup	A group of exclusive checkboxes (radio buttons)
CheckboxMenuItem	A toggle menu item

Choice	A popup menu of choices
Color	An abstract representation of a color
Component	The abstract generic class for all UI components
Container	Abstract behavior for a component that can hold other components or containers
Dialog	A window for brief interactions with users
Dimension	Width and height
Event	An object representing events caused by the system or based on user input
FileDialog	A dialog for getting file names from the local file system
FlowLayout	A layout manager that lays out objects from left to right in rows
Font	An abstract representation of a font
FontMetrics	Abstract class for holding information about a specific font's character shapes and height and width information
Frame	A top-level window with a title
Graphics	Abstract behavior for representing a graphics context, and for drawing and painting shapes and objects
GridBagConstraints	Constraints for components laid out using GridBagLayout
GridBagLayout	A layout manager that aligns components horizontally and vertically based on their values from GridBagConstraints
GridLayout	A layout manager with rows and columns; elements are added to each cell in the grid
Image	An abstract representation of a bitmap image
Insets	Distances from the outer border of the window; used to lay out components
Label	A text label for UI components
List	A scrolling list
MediaTracker	A way to keep track of the status of media objects being loaded over the net
Menu	A menu, which can contain menu items and is a container on a menubar

MenuBar	A menubar (container for menus)
MenuComponent	The abstract superclass of all menu elements
MenuItem	An individual menu item
Panel	A container that is displayed
Point	x and y coordinates
Polygon	A set of points
Rectangle	x and y coordinates for the top corner, plus width and height
Scrollbar	A UI scrollbar object
TextArea	A multiline, scrollable, editable text field
TextComponent	The superclass of all editable text components
TextField	A fixed-size editable text field
Toolkit	Abstract behavior for binding the abstract AWT classes to a platform-specific toolkit implementation
Window	A top-level window, and the superclass of the Frame and Dialog classes

java.awt.image

The java.awt.image package is a subpackage of the AWT that provides classes for managing bitmap images.

Interfaces

ImageConsumer	Methods for receiving image data created by an ImageProducer
ImageObserver	Methods to track the loading and construction of an image
ImageProducer	Methods to construct or filter image data

Classes

ColorModel	An abstract class for managing color information for images
CropImageFilter	A filter for cropping images to a particular size
DirectColorModel	A specific color model for managing and translating pixel color values

FilteredImageSource	An `ImageProducer` that takes an image and an `ImageFilter` object and produces an image for an `ImageConsumer`
ImageFilter	A filter that takes image data from an `ImageProducer`, modifies it in some way, and hands it off to a `ImageConsumer`
IndexColorModel	A specific color model for managing and translating color values in a fixed-color map
MemoryImageSource	An image producer that gets its image from memory; used to construct an image by hand
RGBImageFilter	Abstract behavior for a filter that modifies the RGB values of pixels in RGB images

java.awt.peer

The `java.awt.peer` package is a subpackage of AWT that provides the (hidden) platform-specific AWT classes (for example, for Motif, Macintosh, or Windows 95) with platform-independent interfaces to implement. Thus, callers using these interfaces need not know which platform's window system these hidden AWT classes are currently implementing.

Each class in the AWT that inherits from either `Component` or `MenuComponent` has a corresponding peer class. Each of those classes is the name of the `Component` with `-Peer` added (for example, `ButtonPeer`, `DialogPeer`, and `WindowPeer`). Because each one provides similar behavior, they are not enumerated here.

java.applet

The `java.applet` package provides applet-specific behavior.

Interfaces

AppletContext	Methods to refer to the applet's context
AppletStub	Methods for nonbrowser applet viewers
AudioClip	Methods for playing audio files

Classes

Applet	The base applet class

How Java Differs
from C and C++

by Laura Lemay

This appendix contains a description of most of the major differences between C, C++ , and the Java language. If you are a programmer familiar with either C or C++, you may want to review this appendix to catch some of the common mistakes and assumptions programmers make when using Java.

Pointers

Java does not have an explicit pointer type. Instead of pointers, all references to objects—including variable assignments, arguments passed into methods, and array elements—are accomplished by using implicit references. References and pointers are essentially the same thing except that you can't do pointer arithmetic on references (nor do you need to).

Reference semantics also enable structures such as linked lists to be created easily in Java without explicit pointers; merely create a linked list node with variables that point to the next and the previous node. Then, to insert items in the list, assign those variables to other node objects.

Arrays

Arrays in Java are first class objects, and references to arrays and their contents are accomplished through explicit references rather than via point arithmetic. Array boundaries are strictly enforced; attempting to read past the ends of an array is a compile or run-time error. As with other objects, passing an array to a method passes a reference to the original array, so changing the contents of that array reference changes the original array object.

Arrays of objects are arrays of references that are not automatically initialized to contain actual objects. Using the following Java code produces an array of type `MyObject` with ten elements, but that array initially contains only nulls:

```
MyObject arrayofobjs[] = new MyObject[10];
```

You must now add actual `MyObject` objects to that array:

```
for (int i; i< arrayofobjs.length. i++) {
    arrayofobjs[i] = new MyObject();
```

Java does not support multidimensional arrays as in C and C++. In Java, you must create arrays that contain other arrays.

Strings

Strings in C and C++ are arrays of characters, terminated by a null character (\0). To operate on and manage strings, you treat them as you would any other array, with all the inherent difficulties of keeping track of pointer arithmetic and being careful not to stray off the end of the array.

Strings in Java are objects, and all methods that operate on strings can treat the string as a complete entity. Strings are not terminated by a null, nor can you accidentally overstep the end of a string (like arrays, string boundaries are strictly enforced).

Memory Management

All memory management in Java is automatic; memory is allocated automatically when an object is created, and a run-time garbage collector (the "GC") frees that memory when the object is no longer in use. C's `malloc` and `free` functions do not exist in Java.

To "force" an object to be freed, remove all references to that object (assign variables holding it to null, remove it from arrays, and so on). The next time the Java GC runs, that object is reclaimed.

Data Types

As mentioned in the early part of this book, all Java primitive data types (`char`, `int`, `long`, and so on) have consistent sizes and behavior across platforms and operating systems. There are no unsigned data types as in C and C++ (except for `char`, which is a 16-bit unsigned integer).

The boolean primitive data type can have two values: `true` or `false`. Boolean is not an integer, nor can it be treated as one, although you cannot cast `0` or `1` (integers) to boolean types in Java.

Composite data types are accomplished in Java exclusively through the use of class definitions. The `struct`, `union`, and `typedef` keywords have all been removed in favor of classes.

Casting between data types is much more controlled in Java; automatic casting occurs only when there will be no loss of information. All other casts must be explicit. The primitive data types (`int`, `float`, `long`, `char`, `boolean`, and so on) cannot be cast to objects or vice versa; there are methods and special "wrapper" classes to convert values between objects and primitive types.

Operators

Operator precedence and association behaves as it does in C. Note, however, that the new keyword (for creating a new object) binds tighter than dot notation (.), which is different behavior from C++. In particular, note the following expression:

```
new foo().bar;
```

This expression operates as if it were written like this:

```
(new foo()).bar;
```

Operator overloading, as in C++, cannot be accomplished in Java. The , operator of C has been deleted.

The >>> operator produces an unsigned logical right shift (remember, there are no unsigned data types).

The + operator can be used to concatenate strings.

Control Flow

Although the if, while, for, and do statements in Java are syntactically the same as they are in C and C++, there is one significant difference. The test expression for each control flow construct must return an actual boolean value (true or false). In C and C++, the expression can return an integer.

Arguments

Java does not support mechanisms for optional arguments or for variable-length argument lists to functions as in C and C++. All method definitions must have a specific number of arguments.

Command-line arguments in Java behave differently from those in C and C++. The first element in the argument vector (argv[0]) in C and C++ is the name of the program itself; in Java, that first argument is the first of the additional arguments. In other words, in Java, argv[0] is argv[1] in C and C++; there is no way to get hold of the actual name of the Java program.

Other Differences

The following other minor differences from C and C++ exist in Java:

- [ ] Java does not have a preprocessor, and as such, does not have #defines or macros. Constants can be created by using the final modifier when declaring class and instance variables.
- [ ] Java does not have template classes as in C++.
- [ ] Java does not include C's const keyword or the ability to pass by const reference explicitly.
- [ ] Java classes are singly inherited, with some multiple-inheritance features provided through interfaces.
- [ ] All functions are implemented as methods. There are no functions that are not tied to classes.
- [ ] The goto keyword does not exist in Java (it's a reserved word, but currently unimplemented). You can, however, use labeled breaks and continues to break out of and continue executing complex switch or loop constructs.

Index

Symbols

FilterOutputStream class

Sams.net
Learning
Center

Sams
net

Notes

Notes

Notes

Notes

Notes

Notes

Notes

Notes

Notes

Notes

Notes

Notes

Notes

Notes

Notes

Notes

Notes

Notes

Notes

Add to Your Sams.net Library Today
with the Best Books for Internet Technologies

ISBN	Quantity	Description of Item	Unit Cost	Total Cost
1-57521-041-X		The Internet Unleashed, 1996	$49.99	
1-57521-039-8		Presenting Java	$25.00	
0-672-30745-6		HTML and CGI Unleashed	$49.99	
0-672-30735-9		Teach Yourself the Internet in a Week, Second Edition	$25.00	
1-57521-004-5		The Internet Business Guide, Second Edition	$25.00	
0-672-30595-X		Education on the Internet	$25.00	
0-672-30718-9		Navigating the Internet, Third Edition	$22.50	
1-57521-040-1		The World Wide Web Unleashed, 1996	$49.99	
1-57521-005-3		Teach Yourself More Web Publishing with HTML in a Week	$29.99	
0-672-30764-2		Teach Yourself Web Publishing with Microsoft Word in a Week	$29.99	
0-672-30669-7		Plug-n-Play Internet	$35.00	
1-57521-010-X		Plug-n-Play Netscape for Windows	$29.99	
0-672-30723-5		Secrets of the MUD Wizards	$25.00	
		Shipping and Handling: See information below.		
		TOTAL		

Shipping and Handling: $4.00 for the first book, and $1.75 for each additional book. If you need to have it NOW, we can ship product to you in 24 hours for an additional charge of approximately $18.00, and you will receive your item overnight or in two days. Overseas shipping and handling adds $2.00. Prices subject to change. Call between 9:00 a.m. and 5:00 p.m. EST for availability and pricing information on latest editions.

201 W. 103rd Street, Indianapolis, Indiana 46290

1-800-428-5331 — Orders   1-800-835-3202 — FAX   1-800-858-7674 — Customer Service

Book ISBN 1-57521-030